A History of
Putnam County, West Virginia
in the Civil War

by Philip Hatfield, PhD

35th Star Publishing
Charleston, West Virginia
www.35thstar.com

Paperback ISBN-13: 979-8-9889020-0-3
Hard cover ISBN-13: 979-8-9889020-1-0
Library of Congress Control Number: 2023944224

35th Star Publishing
Charleston, West Virginia
www.35thstar.com

Cover design by Studio 6 Sense
Interior design by 35th Star Publishing

On the cover:
George C. Bowyer, Courtesy Upper Vandalia Historical Society
Mary Sophia Miller Bowyer, Courtesy Bill Woodrum
Sarah Harris Dickerson, Courtesy Tazewell County Library
8th West Virginia Infantry at Buffalo, Courtesy Steve Cunningham
Battle of Winfield historial marker, photo by the author
Sketch: Surprise of Rebels between Hurricane and Logan by Piatt's Zuoaves (34th Ohio Infantry) , Harper's Weekly,
  January 18, 1862

Dedication

*This book is dedicated
to the loving memory of my parents,
who instilled in me a lifelong passion for history.*

*Calvin Lee Hatfield
Freda Jane Hatfield*

Table of Contents

Illustrations, Photos, Maps

Acknowledgments

There are many people without whom this project would not have been possible, each deserving of my gratitude and thanks. First and foremost, I must thank my parents, Calvin and Freda Hatfield, who are gone now, but whom I will always honor in my heart. They are the reason I developed a passion for Civil War history.

Thanks to retired state archivist, historian and author Joe Geiger, for sharing his expertise and valuable feedback. The excellent staff at the West Virginia State Archives, in particular Chuck Ocheltree, Debra Basham, and Aaron Parsons, were most helpful locating original source materials and photographs. Catherine Rakowski at the West Virginia and Regional History Center supplied valuable assistance locating source materials and photographs. Cassandra Farrell, Senior Map Archivist, Library of Virginia, and Chad Underwood, Special Collections Archivist, Library of Virginia, are owed a debt of gratitude for aid locating maps and manuscripts for this project.

Ron Allen and Betsy Allen at the *Hurricane Breeze* contributed the letters of Dr. Samuel G. Shaw related to the battle at Hurricane Bridge. Larry Frye, Putnam County attorney, provided a great deal of information and access to the James Hoge House at Winfield. Further, my long-time friend, historian and author Terry Lowry, shared his expertise and photos, along with several original source materials from his personal collection. Another lifelong friend, Steve Cunningham of 35th Star Publishing, provided expertise and photos as well as source materials. Richard Wolfe of the Clarksburg Civil War Round Table contributed photographs, and I appreciate his steadfast work preserving West Virginia history. Historian and author Jack Dickinson provided photographs and source materials from the Marshall University Special Collections. Larry Strayer of Ohio is recognized for sharing rare photographs from his amazing collection of Buckeye Civil War soldiers. Amanda Larch helped with transcribing original source materials. Thanks to Matthew Guillen, Reference Coordinator, and Dr. James Brookes, Library Director, along with clerks, Carly Tarne and Kate Weis at the Virginia Historical Society who assisted me in locating original documents related to the Virginia Militia.

The following are also gratefully acknowledged for their contributions of family research and photographs to this work: Debbie Cesta, descendent of Captain John V. Young; Melissa Fizer Conley, descendent of Peter Fizer Conley, 36th Virginia Infantry; Nathan Easter, descendent of Daniel C. Lovett, 8th Virginia Cavalry; Sandy Miller Larch, descendent of John Miller, 8th Virginia Cavalry; Kathy Haskins, descendent of Samuel Gaskins, 13th West Virginia Infantry; Penny Hunt, descendent of William Wolfe, 13th West Virginia; and Keith Sesler, descendent of Mark Hale Sesler, 8th Virginia Cavalry.

Virginia or West Virginia?

Putnam County was part of Virginia until June 20, 1863, when West Virginia was admitted into the Union as the thirty-fifth state. As such, Union regiments formed in western Virginia until statehood was obtained were commonly known as Virginia Volunteers. To avoid confusion herein, those units are referred to as West Virginia Volunteers.

Prelude

The story of Putnam County in the Civil War begins in the Colonial period, when roots of sectional strife became deeply embedded in the fabric of American culture; the following article was published in the *Gallipolis Journal, on* August 8, 1861, and forebodingly set the stage for the terrible events soon to unfold in this otherwise peaceful, rural county in western Virginia:

It is curious to observe how early in our history compromise was introduced as an expedient for settling questions between North and South. When the first Congress under the new Constitution assembled for its second session in 1790, among other perplexing topics brought before it was that of finance. With this was complicated that of the debt that had accumulated during the war. This, which amounted to 42,000,000 dollars at the close for the struggle for independence, had, during the disastrous days of the "Confederacy" swollen to 54,000,000, of which nearly twelve were due of France, Holland and Spain, and the rest at home. Besides this were state debts, Massachusetts owed some 5,000,000, South Carolina about the same, Virginia three and a half, while other states were indebted to a sufficient amount to make the total about 25,000,000 of dollars.

Alexander Hamilton was then secretary of the treasury, and among his plans for restoring the credit of the country was the assumption of these state debts by the Federal government, and the funding of the whole with provisions for the liquidation of the entire amount of national and state indebtedness out of the national resources. A principle object of the measure, although not the avowed one, was thus to make the financial interests of the states so far identical and render it also the interest of the capitalists to sustain the government. The measure was violently opposed. It was thought to look towards a consolidation, the exalting of the influence of the Government at the expense of the several states, and its constitutionality was doubted. It was thought that besides, the measure favored the interests of northern and eastern states more than those of the southern.

The contest was a warm and bitter one. It was the beginning of Congressional gladiatorship and intrigue. True to their favorite idea, some of the southern states threatened to withdraw from the Union. On the 12th of April the final vote was taken and decided in the negative by a vote of two. Hamilton was intensely chagrined. He believed the measure was highly important and was grieved to see it wrecked on the rock of sectionalism. It was determined to introduce it again under a new form. But the opposition of the south must in some way be conciliated. It happened that the final location of the national capital was just then in debate. Congress at that time held its sessions in New York; the president's residence was there and all of the public offices. The places proposed as an ultimate location, were Philadelphia and Georgetown. It was settled that to reconcile the southern states to the assumption of the state debts, a vote should be taken to make Philadelphia the capital for ten years, in the meantime to have public buildings in process of erection at Georgetown, and at the end of that time to remove the capital to that place.

With this understanding two Virginia members agreed to change their vote. The proposition to assume the debts of the states was introduced, modified by naming a specific sum—twenty-one and a half millions. It was carried by a close vote. The other measure was then brought in. A territory ten miles square was ceded by the states of Maryland and Virginia, subsequently designated as the District of Columbia, and it was decided at the end of ten years, during which the seat of government should be at Philadelphia, it should remove to the place selected and prepared on the Potomac. This was done, public buildings having in the interval, been erected and the present city of Washington laid out.

This then, was the first compromise. It was curious to observe how similar the issues raised were to those which have since divided the north and south, and how the same passions and the same angry threats then burst forth which have since made the Congress of the Union a battlefield of sections and parties. Men talked even then of the incompatibility of the northern and southern interests; and threats to dissolve the Union were heard south of the Potomac, just as they ever have since.

Among the most remarkable incidents of the contest we have described, was the wise, dignified and patriotic rebuke which Washington from the Presidential chair administered to the spirit of sectionalism. Writing to Dr. Stuart of Virginia, a tried friend, he says, "I am sorry such jealousies as you speak of should be gaining ground and poisoning the minds of the southern people; but admit the fact, which is alleged as the cause of them, and give it full scope, does it amount to more than was known to every man of information at, and since the adoption of the Constitution? Was it not always believed that there are some points which pecuniarily interest the eastern States? And did anyone who reads human nature, and especially the character of the eastern people, conceive they would not pursue them steadily by a combination of their force? If these states are less than tenacious of their interest, of if, while the eastern move is a solid phalanx to effect their views, the southern are always divided, which of the two is most to be blamed? That there is a diversity of interest in the Union no one has denied.

That is the case also in every state, is equally certain; and that it even extends to the counties of individual states can be as readily proved. Instance the southern and northern parts of Virginia, the upper and lower parts of South Carolina. Have not the interests of these always been at variance? Witness the county of Fairfax, (that in which Washington and his correspondent lived). Have not the interests of the people of that county varied or the inhabitants taught to believe so? These are well known truths, and yet it does not follow that separation was to result from this disagreement. He would have the several districts the Union adjust their differences on these principles and settle their controversies by votes and not by arms, in the Union, not out of it. And he forewarned the southern states that if the eastern and northern states were dangerous in the Union, they would not be less so in the separation. The voice of warning and counsel had been unheeded, and now the question has come to a bloody arbitrament....[1]

Putnam County, Virginia (now West Virginia) is a case study in how the Civil War affected not only the nation, but communities and families. Literally it was a "house divided," with roughly 51.7% of white males serving in the Confederate army and 48.3% in Union regiments, militia, or home guard companies. It was not unusual for soldiers from Putnam County to find themselves facing former friends, family, or coworkers on the battlefields in the region; indeed, the Civil War was a fratricide in Putnam County. Often, the soldiers' families suffered incredible hardships and deprivations at the hands of troops from the opposing side while they were away with the army, as the Kanawha Valley region was a strategic goal for both sides due to the Kanawha River and salt mines. For Putnam citizens, regardless of their political allegiance, the struggle *du jour* was to avoid becoming the victims of raids, theft, arrest, and personal attacks by occupying troops and numerous partisan guerrillas prowling the area. In this context, the soldiers and citizens of Putnam County are not simply a microsample of what transpired in the country during the Civil War, rather they are an archetype of the embittered, violent, and complex struggle society faced from 1861 to 1865, with such divided loyalties and competing ideologies that, ultimately, only the force of arms could settle.

The first explorer to reach Putnam County arrived from France in 1669; Sieur de LaSalle is said to have ventured into the lower Kanawha Valley region that is now Putnam County. His excursions opened the Ohio and Mississippi Rivers to French fur traders and missionaries, and later when the first English settlers arrived in 1742, they found the Natives using French names for the Gauley and Greenbrier rivers. Putnam County was formed on March 11, 1848, from Kanawha, Mason, and Cabell counties by an act of the Virginia General Assembly. Prior to that, the area was at various times, part of six other counties of Virginia, including Orange, Augusta, Botetourt, Fincastle, Montgomery, and Greenbrier. The county was named in honor of Brigadier General Israel Putnam, a Revolutionary War hero who commanded the colonial defense at the battle of Bunker Hill (aka Breed's Hill) in Boston, Massachusetts, on June 17, 1775. Putnam, a veteran of the French and Indian War, became famous for ordering his troops, "Don't fire until you see the whites of their eyes," as the British steadily advanced up the long slope toward the colonial troops.[2]

During the Pre-historic era, Paleo-Indian hunters tracked giant mastodons in Putnam County; archeologists have found those majestic beasts' ribs measuring up to eleven feet in length. Early natives first settled near modern Buffalo along the Kanawha River, most likely due to the shallow water shoals in that area that guaranteed an ongoing source for fishing and freshwater mussels. The first land grants of record for the area now comprising Putnam County were made in 1772 to Dr. James Craik for 4,232 acres near modern Frazier's Bottom. Teays Valley is named after one of the first colonial settlers in the area, Thomas Teays, who was granted 27,000 acres of land in 1780. By 1810, much of the area was settled, with United States Census showing approximately 200 residents in that region.[3]

The geographic area comprising Teays Valley was formed by the course of the Teays River, a tributary of the Mississippi River during the pre-historic period, which began in North Carolina and ran northward through the region that is now Putnam County from a point on the Kanawha River to the mouth of Scary Creek, to the Ohio River near modern Huntington, and emptied into the Gulf of Mexico by St. Louis, Missouri. Modern scientists now believe that the Teays River created much of the land and streams formed as far west as the Mississippi Valley, although its once great gorges and valleys are now buried deeply under massive glacier deposits. The Teays Valley region between modern Nitro and Huntington was abandoned after tributaries of the Teays River became the lower Kanawha River from Nitro to Point Pleasant. Hurricane Creek now carries most of the surface drainage from the eastern half of the abandoned valley, and the Mud and Guyandotte Rivers occupy and drain the western half of the ancestral Teays River.[4]

Travel through Putnam County during Antebellum and the Civil War eras was primarily by boat on the Kanawha River, horseback, stagecoach, or on foot. The main road in the area was the James River and Kanawha Turnpike, a.k.a. James River Turnpike, which ran from Richmond through western Virginia, including Kanawha and Putnam counties, along a route closely following modern U.S. Route 60. This road extended into Cabell and Wayne counties and ended at the Ohio River and was the primary artery connecting eastern and western area commerce in Virginia at that time. As a result, it became a highly coveted strategic objective among military

Putnam Couty historical marker

Area of early Native American settlement

commanders on both sides during the Civil War. By 1832, there were three taverns on the James River Turnpike in Putnam and Cabell counties. Each provided overnight quarters, meals, and barn facilities for the horses. Hiram Ellis owned one tavern seven-and-a-half miles west of the village of Coalsmouth (modern St. Albans), Charles Conner established one at Hurricane Bridge, and John Morris operated another just a few miles west of Conner's Tavern near Mud Bridge.[5]

Accommodations were rough, food was often poorly prepared, and beds were not well kept; however, Morris still charged ninety-five cents for three meals per day. He would also feed the stage horses a half-gallon each of corn and oats for a nickel, and board them with hay overnight for twenty-five cents. Weary travelers in need of liquid refreshment could imbibe a gallon of peach brandy for two dollars, and if that didn't hit the spot, they could consume a half-pint of gin and Cherry Bounce (similar to modern soda) for about eighteen cents. At Conners Tavern, things were not much better; the "Overnight Rules of the Management" stated only five people were allowed in one bed, and boots must be removed beforehand. By the time of the Civil War, there was another tavern at the village of Hurricane Bridge owned by George Duke, which was just above the small ridge where the modern bridge crossing Hurricane Creek is located.[6]

Slavery in Putnam County

Putnam County had a population of about 5,335 in 1850 and saw an 18.1 % increase in the coming decade, with 6,301 cited in the 1860 U.S. Census. At that time, there were 580 slaves (9.2%), and thirteen freed blacks residing in Putnam County. In contrast, the population in Kanawha County was 13,787 whites with 2,184 slaves (13.7%) and 181 freed blacks. Kanawha County was then the second largest slave holding county in western Virginia, and a significant portion of the reported slave population worked in the salt mines within the region. The largest slave holding county in western Virginia was Jefferson County, with 28.2% of the population enslaved. For perspective, Berkeley County had 13.5% enslaved population; Greenbrier County had 12.7% enslaved; Hardy County had 11.2%; and Monroe County was 10.5% enslaved, in contrast to Putnam County, which had 9.2%. The following table provides data for slave population of six counties near Putnam County.[7]

1860 U.S. Census Slave Tables

County	White	Slave	% Slave
Kanawha	13,787	2,184	13.7
Putnam	5,708	580	9.2
Cabell	6,604	143	3.8
Mason	8,762	386	4.2
Wayne	6,604	143	3.8
Logan	4,470	148	3.0

Source: 1860 United States Census, Slave Schedules.
U.S. National Archives, Washington, D.C.

Prior to the Civil War, slavery played a critical role in the economic and agricultural development of Putnam County. When George Washington's land along the Kanawha River was divided among his heirs following his death, his nephew, Lawrence A. Washington, (1774-1824) received 3,110 acres found below the mouth of the Poca River. In 1811, he moved his family with fifteen slaves from Winchester, Virginia, and built a house located along modern U.S. Route 62 near the Winfield locks at Eleanor. During his residency, Washington planted a pair of large boxwoods that survived until 1992. Lawrence Washington described his beliefs about slavery in a letter written on August 27, 1816, to his mother-in-law, Mrs. Comfort Wood:

My Dear Madam,

My Mary [his wife] and myself have lately had many consultations on the situation of our slaves. We both have, upon all the reflection we could give that the very delicate and perplexing subject, come to the conclusion that it is better to free them, with all the real and ideal mischiefs which may follow such a course, than to hold them longer in slavery. We are both decidedly of the opinion that the God of nature made them as free as ourselves, and that they are held in bondage by ruffian force, and savage violence. These are uncouth terms, and I am sincerely sorry they are so applicable to the case. We both believe it is radically wrong for one person to deprive another of the products of his labors, and to impose on him and his posterity forever a state of endless slavery…We have accordingly announced to those hitherto much injured individuals, that as soon as the present crop is secured, all of them will have deeds of emancipation exercised to them.

Washington freed his slaves, and then offered them paid travel to Liberia if they wished to relocate. Unable to afford his large farm without the benefit of slave labor, Washington and his wife moved to Wheeling, Virginia, where they lived until their deaths, "at peace with their conscience.[8]

The 1850 U.S. Census shows the total population in Putnam County was 5,335, with two-thirds of the adults working as farmers or laborers and 632 slaves listed. By 1860, sixty-six-year-old Poca resident Lewis Bowling had become one of the largest land holders in the Kanawha Valley, with 66,600 acres and 125 slaves. Local legend has it that Bowling believed the best way to get the most work out of his slaves was to keep them healthy and content. He was well known for providing them with medical care from local physicians and was in the habit of providing live entertainment for them on Saturday evenings. It was of no effect, however, when the Civil War came, as many of his slaves were among the first to escape into Ohio and gain their freedom, despite his determined efforts to maintain them in slavery.[9]

Dr. Thomas Clarke Atkeson of Buffalo was a nationally recognized leader in early agricultural advances; he and his spouse Mary Meek Atkeson co-authored a popular book entitled *Pioneering in Agriculture* in the 1850s. Atkeson was also a slave owner. His recollection of slavery in Putnam County was recorded as follows:

I remember well the Negroes on our place. My father owned a family of blacks, including the grandmother, Aunt Rose, the mother Aunt Nancy, twin boys about a year older than I was, and a young black man…So far as I know, my father never bought or sold a slave, but came into the ownership of his family as a part of my mother's inheritance. The slaves…were always considerably treated. If they had not been, it would have been very easy for them to run away and cross the river into Ohio…for the most part, they showed a complete loyalty and faithfulness to their masters. My father had been reared in Gallia County, Ohio, and was disposed to dislike slavery, but he accepted it as an established institution of the country. I never knew him to use any physical punishment to enforce discipline, except perhaps the use of a light switch to correct the twin Negro boys when they were children.

Without the use of physical punishment, he was able at all times to secure the most complete obedience and loyal support in the farm operations. They lived a carefree existence. Aunt Nancy's twin boys, about my own age, ran about the farm and played and had a good time generally, just as I did, and my father never pushed his negroes to work harder than he did the members of the family. He believed in everyone working a reasonable amount. And, though my mother and sisters were relieved of much of the cooking and preparing of foods by the work of the Black family, as they called themselves, they were never idle. After the Emancipation Proclamation of President Lincoln, my father notified his Black Family that they were at liberty to leave the farm, but that if they preferred to stay, he would pay them fair wages. They all decided to remain and continued on the farm until several years after the close of the war, when they became so restless that they were unsatisfactory servants. My father advised them to start out for themselves, so they moved to the little town of Buffalo and engaged in various occupations. But our family kept in touch with them as long as they lived. The young Negro who had been sent into Virginia married over there and after the war came back and worked for my father as a farm hand for several years. Those were the days of hard work, long hours, and small pay. And though we look back on them with a remembrance of their good qualities, I am sure we would not return to them even if we could. I think it is a good thing that the "good ole days" will never come again.[10]

During the 1850s, the debate over slavery expanding into western territories emerged as a national focus. In September 1856, the pro-slavery news organ, the *Kanawha Valley Star*, moved to Charleston and was renamed as the *Star of the Kanawha Valley*. By 1860, citizens of the Kanawha Valley were showing signs of strong Sectionalist division. The *Star* published an opinion written by Joseph Lane on May 21, 1860, revealing the depth of conflicted ideologies of the day. Lane, a U.S. Senator from Oregon, ran as Democratic candidate for vice president with John C. Breckinridge, and both were pro-slavery advocates who also proclaimed pro-Union beliefs. Breckinridge and Lane received unanimous support in Putnam County at a public meeting held at the courthouse in July 1860, evidencing the mindset of many voting residents regarding their current crisis. Lane opined:

...Our Union must be preserved! But this can only be done by maintaining the constitution inviolate in all its provisions and guaranties. The judicial authority thus provided by the constitution must be sustained, and its decisions implicitly obeyed, as well as in regard to the rights of property in the Territories and all other matters. Hoping for success and trusting in the truth and principles of justice of the principles of our party, and in that Divine Providence that has watched over us, and made us one of the great nations on earth, and that we may continue to merit Divine protection, I cheerfully accept the nomination so unanimously conferred upon me, and cordially endorse the platform adopted by the convention....[11]

Another editorial similarly emphasizing the growing dissention among southern citizens of the Kanawha Valley appeared in the *Star of the Kanawha Valley* on May 21, 1860:

...We are opposed to any compromise of principles in the selection of candidates for president, nor do we approve of the attempt of the Free State (which in all probability will not give a single Democratic electoral vote for President) to dictate to, and over slaugh, all the Democratic states - the Southern states. Without the support of the South…Illinois and perhaps two other states, Black Republicanism would sweep all the remaining states….[12]

During the Antebellum era, news organs typically only published editorials expressing views consistent with that of the editors on current issues such as slavery, state's rights, etc. Period newspapers are a rich source of information as to what many citizens of the area thought on such matters, and often contradict modern notions that southern residents in western Virginia cared little about the institution of slavery simply because there were much fewer slaves in that region compared to their eastern Virginia counterparts. Many also clearly supported the practice of slavery. While such are indeed offensive to the modern eye, they should be examined in the sociological and political context of the era. An example penned by a Southern resident of Buffalo appeared on October 18, 1856, blaming the British government and Northern shipping business for initiating the practice of slavery in the colonies, seeking to frame the "peculiar institution" as one of paternalized benevolence:

There has always been something extremely nauseating in Yankee and English commiseration of the "poor Negro" and in their denunciation of the atrocious slave holder! The English government and the Yankee ship owners first saddled the institution on us against our consent, and in spite of our earnest remonstrance's. They stole the Negroes in Africa-they were the guilty perpetrators of the horrors of the middle passage. We have Christianized, civilized, and humanized the ones that they foully wronged. We have taught them something of European civilization without demoralizing them.[13]

The subject of emancipation was not new to the Civil War, contrary to many popular narratives. The matter was debated in the Virginia assembly and in Congress for decades prior to the Civil War, and emancipation

Old Market House and Town Hall (on second floor) in Wheeling, West Virginia,
circa 1900, built in 1822. Slaves were sold at the end of the building.
West Virginia and Regional History Center

was becoming an increasingly popular issue in the western region by 1861. Although many Union supporters in western Virginia were also slaveholders, some were beginning to view the institution as an unfair competition with free labor and wanted to end the practice. However, the question of what to do with newly freed slaves became a matter of heavy contention, as Congressional and state officials often disagreed, particularly on the question of colonization. This was the notion that freed slaves could potentially be dangerous to society and should be relocated into their own territory; despite the obvious racial biases to the modern mindset, this was not an unpopular idea in the nineteenth century. The *Gallipolis Journal* published an article on December 26, 1861, summarizing the matter:

> The *National Intelligencer* calls attention to the fact that the colonization of slaves was proposed in Virginia more than sixty years ago, in consequence of the servile revolt, known from the name of its leader, as Gabriel's Insurrection. The House of Delegates instructed James Monroe, then Governor of Virginia, to "open a correspondence with the President of the United States on the subject of purchasing lands without the limits of the state, whither persons obnoxious to the laws or dangerous to the peace of society may be removed." To Gov. Monroe's letter, written in obedience to these instructions, President Jefferson, on November 24, 1801, replied, and suggested the West Indies as possessing great advantages for such purposes, especially St. Domingo, where the blacks had then established an independent sovereignty, and Africa, as a last and undoubted resort, if all others should fail. The General Assembly of Virginia renewed its request on the subject in 1802, and in 1804 passed resolutions instructing their Senators & c., "to use their best efforts for the purpose of obtaining from the general Government a competent portion of territory in the country of Louisiana [then newly acquired] to be appropriated to the residence of such people of color who have been, or shall be emancipated in Virginia or may hereafter to become dangerous to the public safety." The *National Intelligencer* says, 'If the comparatively narrow range of the disturbance created by 'Gabriel's Insurrection' raised the question of colonizing such negroes as could no longer be held in a state of servitude, how much more exigent are the problems likely to be presented for solution by the progress of the pending war?'[14]

Obviously, by 1861, views on slavery in western Virginia—Putnam County in particular—were complex and had divided the citizens. Many Unionists and Southern residents criticized the Federal government, holding it responsible for not taking effective action to end the practice long before the Civil War began. Thus, in April 1861 when the war came to western Virginia, popular opinion among many Union-leaning residents was that years of compromise on the issue of slavery in Congress and state legislatures had resulted in only more division and bitterness. A popular modern belief as to why Union soldiers enlisted to fight in the Civil War asserts that they wanted to free the slaves. However, a large number of Union soldiers made it plain in their private letters that they had not enlisted to end the practice of slavery, but rather to preserve the Union. One resident of Gallipolis, Ohio, stationed in the Kanawha Valley in 1861 quipped: "There are men in this town who are doing their utmost to demoralize the soldiers who have enlisted in defense of the Government. The new recruits are told this is a war to free the negroes; What ought to be done with such secession scoundrels?"[15]

Another example written by a Union soldier on September 12, 1861, indicates that many of his comrades clearly saw it as a war over slavery, albeit also blamed the North for capitalizing on the fugitive slave trade, along with expressing his ire over having to fight a war over the problem of slavery:

> Let it not be supposed for a moment that we have any leaning to the South. We abhor the vicious institutions to which they cling, and which taints and injures everything in the country; and what we

most blame the North for is its readiness to wade through blood to reconnect itself with the slave States, and lend itself again to the capture of poor fugitives claiming their right to their own bodies. If the North had been sincere and honest as regards slavery, it would have rejoiced at the secession of the South delivering it from any part in the abomination. But it was ready to make all concessions to satisfy the Southern States as to slavery, and its sole tenacity has been to protect the tariff. To continue the profit by this wrong to the South, and all commercial interests, it would gladly compound for all wrongs to the blacks.[16]

Several churches in Putnam County were opposed to slavery, however, such as the Methodist Episcopal Church at Buffalo. The General Session met in June 1860 and decreed an "ultra-Anti-Slavery report" by vote of 139 to 74 on the question:

We declare that we are as much as ever convinced of the great evil of Slavery. We believe that the buying, selling, or holding of human beings, as chattels, is inconsistent with the Golden Rule, and with that Rule in our Discipline which requires all who desire to continue among us, to "do no harm, and avoid evil of every kind." We, therefore, affectionately admonish all our preachers and people to keep themselves pure from this great evil, and to seek its extirpation by all lawful and Christian means....[17]

Despite their decree, the Methodist Episcopal church at Buffalo still received criticism from other area religious groups for not forbidding any slave holding members from the Holy Communion. Another common viewpoint in the Civil War era often at odds with certain narratives in modern popular history is the notion that Southern whites were more concerned with "state's rights" than losing their social status to millions of emancipated slaves if that were to occur. To the contrary, many had every intention of preventing emancipation. One Kanawha Valley resident summarized their position in an editorial published in the *Star of the Kanawha Valley* on March 19, 1861:

Lincoln and the Black Republicans are for putting negros and white people on the same footing. The Democrats say our Government is a government *for white people alone.* Chief Justice Taney of the supreme court of the United States decided in the Dred Scott Case, that our government was made by white men and for white men alone; that it was made for neither the Indian nor the negro. Lincoln and the Republicans, however, don't believe in that doctrine. They say the negro is entitled to vote at elections and to be a citizen, and should enjoy the same privileges under our government as a white man. Oh! What disgrace....[18]

Clearly, the inhabitants of western Virginia in 1860 struggled with a diverse range of ideological, ethical, and political conflicts over slavery, but the roots ran even deeper as an economic problem—it was not simply a moral crisis. An example is found in an editorial published in the *Star of the Kanawha Valley* on April 9, 1861; at that time, eight southern states had then seceded, although Virginia yet remained in the Union:

No sooner had the cotton State seceded from the Union, than the Northern States gave a plain indication of their future policy, by the enactment of the Morrill Tariff. This tariff was not enacted for revenue, nor for the mixed purpose of revenue and protection; but for the direct purpose of protecting and encouraging the manufacturers of Pennsylvania and New England, at the expense of the Border States. It imposes a tax from 30 to 70 cents on almost every article that can be manufactured in the north. For every cotton shirt, for every calico dress, for every coat and hat a Kanawha farmer shall hereafter buy, he must pay an enhanced price; the excess over the old price goes in the pocket of the Northern manufacturer....[19]

Another factor showing the role of economics in many western Virginians' decision to support the Confederacy was the impact of taxes on exporting coal. Trans-Allegheny western Virginia advocated for aligning with the South largely because the Confederate government promised to import coal from the region duty free, while in 1861, Northern states charged western Virginia-based coal businesses 24% for shipping coal to Pennsylvania, etc. This would amount to millions of dollars saved and increase the value of western Virginia coal companies. Hence, as a result of polarizing ideologies and economic disparities, by 1861, Virginians tended to define themselves as either Eastern or Western. While this may appear overgeneralized, the origins are found within the State Constitution adopted in 1776.[20]

In this document, voting rights were granted only to white males owning at least twenty-five acres of improved land or fifty acres unimproved land. This inherently favored wealthy planters – most who inhabited the fertile lands of eastern Virginia, owning hundreds of prosperous acres, with dozens of slaves. While there were a few wealthy citizens in western counties, the majority were small farmers, most of whom neither owned their own land nor held slaves. As a result, they were historically underrepresented in the General Assembly and began to voice their discontent early in the nineteenth century. Several attempts were made to modify the State Constitution in favor of western counties from 1825-1849, but each resolution was defeated in the powerful planter dominated legislature. In this context, the discussion of creating a new state emerged among several representatives from the forty-eight western Virginia counties. To help appease growing Sectionalist tensions, however, the General Assembly passed new laws in 1850 enabling white males over age twenty-one who owned any land valued at $25 or higher to vote, and also approved making the office of governor and judges subject to election by the people.[21]

Despite the painfully obvious economic discrepancies between eastern and western Virginia for over a century, many affluent families in the western counties still wanted to maintain social and political ties to the Old Dominion. One historian contends that in doing so, the early frontiersmen who settled those areas created a western version of the eastern colonial oligarchy. Subsequently, they became dependent upon the wealthy and powerful eastern planter culture to provide for its prosperity and protection, and yet also suffered a great deal of economic and sociological inequity as a result. The *Wheeling Intelligencer* newspaper opined on Christmas Day 1860: "The slave population of western Virginia is only nominal, while her white population is some one hundred twenty-five or thirty thousand in excess of eastern Virginia. The consequence is that we suffer all the evils without any benefits of the system..." Thus, while the moral problem of slavery was not a key issue among residents of western Virginia at the beginning of the Civil War, the economic inequities it created clearly played a significant role in sectional divisions.[22]

Another editorial published in the *Grafton Western Virginian* well articulates the sentiment:

We the people of northwestern Virginia...have no objection to slavery existing where it is wanted... and are willing to afford it all necessary protection but will never consent to become the menials of a slave oligarchy...The conflict in Virginia, between the East and West, virtually swallows up the national conflict between North and South, and we are for the West.[23]

In this sense, the Sectionalist division in western Virginia was literally a civil war within a civil war. Recently, two historians well summarized the circumstances facing residents of western Virginia as "...a war of free labor

FREEDOM TO SLAVES!

Whereas, the President of the United States did, on the first day of the present month issue his *Proclamation* declaring "that, *all persons held as Slaves in certain designated States, and parts of States, are, and hencefor- ward shall be free,*" and that the Executive Government of the United States, including the Military and naval authorities thereof, would recognize and mantain the freedom of said persons. *And Whereas,* the County of Fred- rick is included in the teritory designated by the Proclamation of the Presi- dent, in which the *Slaves should become free,* I therefore hereby notify the citizens of the city of Winchester, and of said County, of said Proclamation, and of my intention to maintain and enforce the same,

I expect all citizens to yield a ready compliance with the Proclamation of the Chief Executive, and I admonish all persons disposed to resist its peaceful enforcement, that upon manifesting such disposition by acts, they will be regarded as rebels in arms against the lawful authority of the Federal Government and dealt with accordingly.

All persons liberated by said Proclamation are admonished to abs. n from all violence, and immediatly betake themselves to useful occupations.

The officers of this command are admonished and ordered to act in accord- ance with said proclamation and to yield their ready co-operation in its enforcement.

R. H. Milroy,
Brig. Gen'l Commanding.

Jan. 5th, 1863.

West Virginia State Archives

Slave Auction in the South. Library of Congress

of rough, self-reliant mountain men and slave labor in the East. It clearly was not fought there to free slaves by Union men; rather it was against unfair taxation by wealthy slave holders of the east who dominated the assembly." Summarily, for the inhabitants of western Virginia, sectional loyalty quickly became the paramount issue when South Carolina seceded on December 20, 1860. Then, when the State of Kansas was admitted to the Union as a non-slave state on January 29, 1861, southern Congressional representatives were furious. By February 1861 Alabama, Georgia, Florida, Louisiana, Mississippi and Texas also seceded. On February 4, 1861, delegates from each of the seven states held a convention in Montgomery, Alabama, and formed the Confederate States of America.[24]

Sarah Harris Dickerson
Courtesy Tazewell County Library

Sarah Harris Dickerson Froe

It is rare to find detailed biographical information of slaves during Antebellum and the Civil War eras, although there were a few accounts left for history from Putnam County. One of those persons was Sarah Harris Dickerson Froe, who was born into slavery in Putnam County on October 22, 1843, and lived most of her life in the Buffalo area. She first married Bartley J. Dickerson, a slave born in 1835 from Tazewell County, Virginia. Dickerson was unique in that he was well educated and became a Disciples of Christ minister while still in bondage. Dickerson left a legacy of ministers in his family, which has continued for more than one hundred forty years. Dickerson died in 1873, and Sarah remarried a man named Froe afterward. Sarah died on May 22, 1905.[25]

Melvina (Lavina) Carrington

Melvina Carrington's birth date was likely between 1815-1822, as she was in her eighties when she passed away in 1900. Known to locals as "Aunt Viney" or "Viney," Melvina appears in the 1850 U.S. Census slave schedule as aged twenty-eight years. However, the 1870 US Census listed Melvina as fifty-one years old, and she was listed as sixty-five in the 1880 US Census, so there is obviously some confusion as to her actual age. She is not listed in the 1900 Census, so she likely passed away sometime between January and June 1900 when the census was taken. When Melvina was thirteen years old, she was separated from her mother and sold at a slave auction in Richmond. Dr. William Matthews of Charlotte County, Virginia, purchased her, and relocated his family to Cabell County in the 1830s. Dr. Matthews settled in the area that later became Putnam County along Sycamore Creek, not far from Hurricane Bridge near the modern intersection of U.S. Route 60 and Midland Trail (Route 34). He owned several hundred acres of land there and built a large log frame home in July 1847. Melvina, his only slave, worked in the house, and according to Matthews family tradition, also occasionally worked in the fields with Matthews and his sons. There are no records found indicating how she took the last name Carrington, though family lore speculates she was once married. One of the Matthews sons named Budge left an anecdote about him once finding a dead snake and attaching it to a string on his belt, then running about the house tormenting the other children with it. In this account, Budge recalled that Viney " almost wore me out" with a stick as punishment. Melvina Carrington is buried in the Sycamore Grove Cemetery on modern Sycamore Road in Hurricane, Putnam County.[26]

Fred Conner

A former slave and resident of Buffalo in Putnam County, Fredrick "Fred" Conner was a servant to Colonel William Fife of the 36th Virginia Infantry during the Civil War. Despite laws forbidding slaves to read or write, Conner was quite literate. He left detailed records of wartime events transpiring in Putnam County, as well as activities of the 36th Virginia and other units from the area. In particular, he collected several post-war letters describing battles occurring at Scary Creek, Barboursville, Guyandotte and Hurricane Bridge. Unfortunately, there are also some inaccuracies in Conner's accounts, but such is common with post-war recollections. This is because many were written several years following the war, and with the passing of time, certain details are easily lost or confused. For example, Conner often cites letters written by Colonel Milton J. Ferguson, who had commanded the 16th Virginia Cavalry. Ferguson documented several recollections of the battles of Scary Creek, Barboursville, and Hurricane Bridge; however, he warned the reader to excuse him if some of his recollections did not seem right, noting "…I am now in my 80th year and nervous…" On the other hand, such accounts are still useful, if not always reliable, at least as a starting point in generating hypotheses for researching otherwise relatively unknown early actions of the Civil War in the Kanawha Valley.[27]

Chapter One

1861: Civil War Comes to Putnam County

With years of political tensions reaching a boiling point in western Virginia, soon after Abraham Lincoln was elected president in November 1860, Virginia Governor John Letcher came under pressure to call the Virginia legislature into special session to decide whether Virginia should join the other southern states leaning toward secession. The session was called to order on January 7, 1861, later than those favoring secession had wished, but in keeping with Letcher's desire to allow time for a national compromise that might save the Union. When the Virginia General Assembly convened in Richmond, the House passed a resolution declaring the Union had no power to declare war against the states and opposing any attempt by the federal government to force seceding states back into the Union. The vote was 112 to 5, with Arthur Boreman (Wood), James D. Morris (Marshall), G. McC. Porter (Brooke and Hancock), Nathaniel Richardson (Ohio), and A. S. Watts (Norfolk County) voting against the resolution. The Senate approved this resolution on January 8, 1861. Boreman was later elected as the first governor of the new state of West Virginia in 1863.[1]

Despite Governor Letcher's desire to remain in the Union, the Virginia legislature took its own course, and on January 19, 1861, the Virginia General Assembly passed a joint resolution inviting other states to a peace conference in Washington, D.C., hoping to avert the impending war; however, on January 21, 1861, the legislature adopted a joint resolution stating if differences between the North and South could not be settled, Virginia would join the Confederate States of America. One of the delegates present was a resident of Putnam County who lived on a plantation known as Walnut Grove located just southeast of the village of Winfield: George W. Summers, a successful attorney, who also served as judge in Kanawha County. Summers owned a large amount of land in Putnam County and was strongly opposed to secession; although admittedly skeptical, he hoped that peace was still a possibility when he was appointed to a committee with former president John

George W. Summers.
Public domain.

Tyler, William C. Rives, John W. Brockenbrough, and James A. Seddon as commissioners representing Virginia on February 2, 1861. They met with representatives from various Northern and Southern states for a peace conference, trying to negotiate a last-minute solution to sectional differences. The conference failed to accomplish its objective, and the division grew even more deeply entrenched in western Virginia.[2]

When the Virginia assembly voted on secession on April 17, 1861, Summers voted against it. He was well known as a strong Union supporter and had earlier served as chairman of a committee of "Loyal Virginians" that met at the Kanawha County Courthouse on December 19, 1859; their "Resolves of States Rights" was recorded, with Summers' closing remarks cited as follows:

I have lived all of my days in Virginia and have rarely seen beyond her limits. I love her as one does his mother. My first duty is to her, and where she goes, by the solemn judgment of the people, I go. Her destiny is my destiny. But I desire also, to retain the name and privileges of an American citizen, and am unwilling to give them up, until every possible effort has been fully made for their preservation. God grant that our institutions, both state and national, may come out of this fiery trial unharmed.[3]

Despite his stated Union support and opposition to secession, Summers' loyalty was often questioned during the war, especially by anti-Southern newspaper editors, because of his outspoken efforts as an attorney advocating for due process and fair treatment of Southern citizens who were incarcerated by Union officials. This caused no small amount of ire among Union residents in the Kanawha Valley, to the degree that he was once arrested during October 1862 for his outspoken views. Public opinion became so negative toward Summers that a particularly scathing editorial of him appeared in the *Gallipolis Journal*, a Unionist paper, on January 9, 1862, essentially accusing him of treason:

Concerning Judge Summers, we hear that he stays most of his time out at his farm, some twenty miles from Charleston. Poor man, his locks have been shorn, and he has become as other men - as those who never had a name and fame as he has had. The loyal people who had honored him so long, looked to him for guidance in their dark hour of trial - but they soon found that in him they had no helper. Cold, selfish, timid, he loved his money, his houses and his lands more than he did the cause of the Union. Like the young man of scripture, he turned away, 'for he had great possessions.' He feared confiscation from the rebels. Yet all the while and even now his well wishes are with the Union. But this is all. It must be saved without his voice or his arm. He has no word of cheer for it in its extremity. - Mournful sight, indeed! to see a man whose name was a tower of strength, whose voice was a rallying note for his people, failing them, failing himself, and failing his country, when all eyes were turned to him for leadership.[4]

Virginia Secedes

When Abraham Lincoln was inaugurated as the 16th president of the United States on March 4, 1861, the crisis piqued in western Virginia, although many still hoped for peace. Solomon Minsker, a resident of Charleston, said: "Most people do not like Lincoln's inaugural address. But I hope all will be settled without coming to arms, although the South is preparing for it." On April 4, 1861, the Virginia Secession Convention met in Richmond. Putnam County had another representative there, James William Hoge of Winfield. Hoge was a popular attorney who had six slaves and was known to be sympathetic to the southern cause, though he adamantly opposed secession. The convention voted against secession eighty-nine to forty-five. Briefly, sectional tensions appeared calmer in the western counties, but it did not last long, as southern militia attacked the Union-held Fort Sumter in Charleston, South Carolina, on April 12, 1861. Immediately, President Lincoln called for 75,000 volunteers on April 15, 1861, to "put down the rebellion," and the Virginia Secession Convention reconvened on April 17, 1861, and voted in favor of secession. All of the western county delegates voted against it, many of whom were also slave owners. In protest, they walked out of the assembly, including James W. Hoge. Shortly afterward, Arkansas, Tennessee, and North Carolina also seceded in May 1861, each having earlier voted against it. On the other hand, four slaveholding states including Delaware, Kentucky, Maryland, and Missouri opted not to leave the Union.[5]

Residents of Putnam County were becoming agitated and fearful of what lay ahead. Robert T. Harvey of Buffalo, a well-known and outspoken secessionist, wrote to Virginia Governor John Letcher on April 22, 1861:

Dear Sir,

A gentleman of this county of much credibility, who has just returned from a trip through several counties of Ohio, says he was informed by several of his customers (he being a tobacconist) that efforts were now being made in several of the neighborhoods in Gallia and Jackson Counties, Ohio, to raise a sufficient force to invade this portion of Virginia, and produce an insurrection among the slaves and lay waste to the valley of the Kanawha. Believing this statement to be true, I am induced to write to you, and suggest the propriety of ordering one or more volunteer companies to Point Pleasant, the mouth of the Kanawha River. Buffalo is situated some twenty-two miles up the Kanawha River....

As the Ohio River runs nearly parallel with the Kanawha from Point Pleasant to a point some eighteen or twenty miles below the mouth of the Kanawha, Buffalo would be the most accessible point to the abolitionists of Ohio to enter the valley of the Kanawha. There are more slaves in the neighborhood of Buffalo than there are from Buffalo to Point Pleasant. I would therefore also suggest the necessity of stationing some one or more companies at Buffalo. If we had arms we could soon raise a force to protect ourselves and give to other portions of the State the services of our volunteer companies. The people of this country are heart and soul with you in the defense of the State.[6]

Harvey's forthright views would soon place him in a whirlwind of trouble, as he was later arrested and sent to a Union prison. Following Virginia's secession, Union-minded delegates from the western counties quickly seized the chance to organize and lay plans to form a new state, holding their first convention at Wheeling on May 13, 1861. A second Wheeling convention was held on June 11 and 20, 1861, and representatives unanimously elected Francis Harrison Pierpont as the new governor of the Restored Government of Virginia. The result was a rather confusing and dangerous situation in the western counties: there were now two competing state governments, as well as the Federal government, along with a fourth entity, the Confederate government, each vying for control of western Virginia, including the area comprising Putnam County.[7]

In May 1861, in some areas of western Virginia, law and order were in danger of breaking down completely, and the news media seemed to fan the flames of division. This is evidenced by numerous sectionally biased articles posited in that era, such as an editorial published in the *Kanawha Spectator* summarizing the writer's view on the state of affairs:

When Abraham Lincoln arrived in Washington D.C. in February 1861, he was closely watching the actions of the Old Dominion state, Virginia. He firmly believed that, more than the other four border states, (Missouri, Kentucky, Maryland and Delaware) her decision on secession would have stronger influence on the south than any. In fact, he thought that if Virginia did not "go out," the secession movement could be halted. Virginia was a pivotal state, indeed, and political sentiments were mixed and passionate in the western counties, particularly in the Kanawha Valley. Here, although not an extensive slave-holding section of the country, there was a strongly pro-southern leaning which played a large role influencing political matters. Like eastern Virginia, there were many Whigs in Charleston, but they would not affiliate with the Northern Republican party, which was primarily a Free-Soil party. This is not to imply that all of the pro-southern residents were pro-slavery, or that all of the northern residents were abolitionists. It is impossible to state with certainty what was the preponderant opinion of the people, even in cotton states where non-slave holders were in the majority, but most public offices were dominated by wealthy slaveholders. The 1860 U.S. Census shows 325,000 people owned 3,500,000 slaves in the nation, and the total US population was 9,000,000 with 5,360,000 whites. There were approximately 140,000 free Negroes; the free states had a population of roughly 19,000,000, and the four border states (Missouri, Kentucky, Maryland and Delaware) had a total population of about 3,400,000. By 1860, Northern abolitionists swore they would destroy the institution of slavery "at all hazards" while their southern slaveholding brethren, who controlled the majority of not only public offices, but also much of the press, became convinced that northern politicians only meant to bankrupt them. In the chaotic months prior to the Civil War, southern newspapers largely inflamed public opinion just as Northern emotions became inflamed by books such as Harriet Beecher Stowe's Uncle Tom's Cabin, or H.R. Helper's book, The Impending Crisis during the previous decade. It became impossible to discern who most agitated the subject of secession, southern extremists or northern fanatics, but abolitionists sought to dissolve the Union on the pretense of clearing themselves of the scourge of slavery, while southern slave holders argued states' rights and the slavery question overshadowed all other differences between the two sections.

The northerners accused the slaveholders of inhumane treatment of slaves while the southerners pointed fingers at the intolerable cruelties exercised in northern factories and shops against child laborers, of which then constituted approximately forty percent of the labor force. Such was the agitation, that by 1860 northern arguments were no more logical or accurate than those posited by southern apologists defending the institution with benevolent pictures of affectionate relationships extant between master and slave. While the historic record bears evidence that each in fact existed, generally, the condition of slaves was not a very happy one, evidenced by the thousands who eloped to the north via the Underground Railroad or other means to obtain their freedom.[8]

As the Civil War quickly erupted in western Virginia, Putnam County became a border county within a border state. Residents found themselves distraught and agitated with uncertainties. Men rushed to arms and began enlisting in local volunteer companies. Former friends, family, and neighbors, previously hoping for peace, suddenly had to choose sides. A former slave and resident of Buffalo in Putnam County, Fredrick "Fred" Conner, traveled as a servant to Colonel William Fife of the 36th Virginia Infantry in the war. He astutely observed when the war erupted:

No Sooner did it become evident that the storm of war was about to burst like a might storm over this land, than the mustering of troops began in Putnam County Virginia, now West Virginia. Hundreds of her sons enrolled their names and shouldered arms in defense of their country.[9]

Warfare in western Virginia

The first battle in western Virginia occurred on June 3, 1861. Union troops from Indiana and Ohio, along with the 1st and 2nd West Virginia Infantry regiments, attacked and routed roughly eight hundred Confederates at the town of Philippi in Barbour County. Union newspapers mocked the Confederates for the loss, satirizing the affair as the "Philippi Races" (sung to the tune of the popular tune Camptown Races). War was escalating in

Rebel Guerrillas.
Frank Leslie's Illustrated Newspaper, August 23, 1862.

General George B. McClellan.
Library of Congress.

the Kanawha Valley also at that time, with Brigadier General Henry Wise, a former governor of Virginia, taking command of Confederate volunteers there on June 6, 1861. Wise organized the 2,600-man force into the 1st and 2nd Kanawha Regiments and the Kanawha Battalion, made up of seven independent companies of infantry (later known as the 3rd Kanawha Regiment). He also had three companies of mounted rangers. Reinforcements soon arrived, with Wise then having about 4,000 men with ten pieces of artillery. The Civil War in western Virginia was generally not fought in large engagements; the bulk of combat in the region consisted of small raids, skirmishes, or ambushes, often led by partisan-guerrilla units. The numerous heavily wooded and serpentine mountainous roads allowed bands of insurgents known as "bushwhackers" easy opportunities to ambush Federal soldiers, who quickly learned to dread marching through the mountainous roads in long, heavily encumbered columns. The rough, hilly terrain also made it easy for guerrillas to raid the rural homes of Union citizens, and then quickly vanish into the hills.[10]

Guerrilla warfare had profound psychological effects on both the Union troops and citizens in western Virginia. The use of unconventional, covert tactics was a marked contrast to traditional Napoleonic military tactics of the era, which prescribed large infantry units supported by artillery and cavalry units, engaged in open fields, using linear evolutions of long battle lines. General George McClellan, inspite of being a West Pointer trained in traditional Napoleonic warfare, understood the guerrilla problem in western Virginia, and promised the most severe consequences allowed by military law. Shortly after Union troops under his command captured the town of Grafton without firing a shot in May 1861, a few days later McClellan wrote to Lieutenant General Winfield Scott, who was the overall commander of U.S. forces, stating that he was so pleased that operations there resulted in an increase in "Union feeling," that he decided to also move upon the Kanawha Valley to protect Union citizens there, "I am now organizing a movement upon the valley of the Great Kanawha; I will go there in person, and will endeavor to capture the occupants of the secession camp at Buffalo, then occupy the Gauley Bridge…." McClellan's plan to arrive in person at Buffalo never happened; he was soon removed from command of the Department of the Ohio on July 25, 1861, and sent to Washington, D.C. His later successor, Brigadier General William S. Rosecrans, was president of the Coal River Navigation Company before the war and quite familiar with the people and culture of the Kanawha Valley. Although he was also a West Pointer, Rosecrans similarly discerned that many of the guerrilla bands in the Kanawha Valley were attacking former neighbors, often avenging personal vendettas against Union citizens. He proclaimed an order stating that all citizens must endeavor to take "prompt and vigorous" measures to end such "private wars" and went a step further than McClellan by announcing he would treat those who failed to take proper steps to suppress such violence as "accessories to the crime."[11]

Despite the Union commanders' intentions, the Kanawha Valley became increasingly dangerous for Union citizens during the spring and summer of 1861. Much has been said by historians regarding the general military fratricide occurring in western Virginia during the Civil War, but very little is said of just how bitter, violent, and often brutal the conflict was for citizens. This conflict ran deep, and as men rushed to fill Confederate ranks in the southern part of Virginia, those who opposed secession quickly learned to either refrain from speaking out in their communities in the Kanawha Valley during the early phase of the war or risk severe retaliation. A few Union citizens tried to make speeches but were usually harassed and forced into silence by secessionists. The resentment burned so strongly that some even hired others to conduct public pro-Union speeches for them. Most of the Union-minded citizens had to covertly meet in their homes, while trying to organize and protect their families. Union men were often arrested and taken away from their homes at night by force, and many were often "conscripted," i.e., drafted, into Confederate service against their will.[12]

General McClellan told the U.S. Secretary of War on June 10, 1861, "If we don't muster Virginians into service according to proclamation and arm them, we must quit the territory or prepare to hold it with Federal troops." He also wrote: "I cannot urge too strongly the importance of this matter, on which hinges, I think, the fate of Western Virginia…The anxiety in this regard to this condition arises, I think, not from any unwillingness to fight the battles of the Union on any battlefield, but from the natural solicitude of a simple people for their homes and families. We have it in our power to unite that people firmly to us forever." The Secretary of War agreed and directed McClellan to muster the Union troops from western Virginia into Federal service on June 12, 1861.[13]

One day earlier, the Reformed Government of Virginia (Union) met at Wheeling and passed an order calling out the militia into active state service, although the War Department directed that new regiments be mustered into Federal service but remain styled as state Volunteer Militia. Hence, when it came time to clothe, equip, arm, and feed the regiments, no one knew whether the volunteers were operating under state or Federal authority, including the War Department or Governor Francis Pierpont, because West Virginia was not yet formally admitted into the Union. As such, supply and logistical problems plagued the Union volunteers serving in western Virginia throughout the first two years of the war.[14]

Citizen Patrols

In response to numerous complaints from Union citizens in fear for their safety, the Wheeling Convention passed House Bill Number Five on June 11, 1861, designated as "An Act to Prevent Offences against the Commonwealth, and to provide for the Organization of Patrols during the War." This law enabled the immediate organization of citizen patrol groups, which were armed para-military organizations with a captain, junior officers and privates, with arrest and detainment authority for anyone found opposing the new state or "inciting others to attempt the overthrow of said government." However, many such groups failed to keep muster rolls due to fear of being identified by Confederate forces, which prevented them from receiving pay, although those with documentation who later enlisted in the Federal Army were given time in service credit by the War Department.[15]

A few Union men, including John Valley Young of Putnam County, had already organized a small company of forty men that acted as a Home Guard shortly after Virginia seceded. While details are limited, Young later recalled he recruited and organized this company at Coalsmouth during the early spring of 1861, and they performed scouting patrols throughout the Coalsmouth area during the first and second years of the war. Young, along with his wife Paulina, and their four children, lived on the eastern base of Coal Mountain and were strong Union supporters. Young was the grandson of famed colonial Indian scout and explorer Lewis Tackett, and he worked as a farmer. He was also ordained in 1859 to perform marriages as an Episcopal-Methodist minister. His nineteen-year-old daughter Sarah F. "Sallie" Young kept a detailed wartime diary, and perceived the great conflict looming ahead was imminent on February 6, 1861, when she wrote: "My birthday. And Oh! What may transpire before my next. Our Country seems to be in danger of Civil War and it makes me shudder to think of it. May our blessed Union be preserved in spite of all traitors."[16]

HOUSE BILL.

—

No. 5.

—

An Act to Prevent Offences against the Commonwealth, and to provide for the Organization of Patrols during the War.

1   1. Be it enacted by the General Assembly, that any person who shall oppose by violence, or shall
2   aid or incite others to oppose by violence, the lawful execution of any Ordinance of the Convention
3   which assembled at Wheeling on the 11th day of June, 1861, or any act of this Legislature, or any law-
4   ful act or order of the Governor, or any officer of the re-organized State Government; or shall aid,
5   counsel or incite others to attempt the overthrow of said re-organized Government, or shall raise any
6   riot, or incite others to raise a riot, or shall by violence intimidate, or with the intent or purpose afore-
7   said attempt to intimidate any officer of this Government, in the discharge of his lawful duty, or any of
8   the loyal citizens thereof, be subject to a fine of not less than Fifty nor more than One Thousand Dol-
9   lars, and be imprisoned in the Jail of the County for not less than one month nor more than one year;
10 but if upon the trial for said offence it may appear that the person so charged may be unable or refuses
11 to pay the fine provided for in this section, the Court or Jury trying the case may increase the time of
12 imprisonment at their discretion, not exceeding two years; provided, nevertheless, that any person
13 guilty of treason may be tried, convicted and punished, as if this act had not passed.

14 2. The Governor is hereby authorized to organize one or more patrols, and the officers and privates
15 of said patrols, when commissioned by the Governor and qualified by taking the proper oath, shall, sub-
16 ject to such regulations and instructions as he may prescribe, have throughout the State the police pow-
17 ers which may be lawfully exercised by constables, or the Sergeant of the City of Wheeling and his
18 deputies, in the apprehension of persons suspected of crime. It shall be the duty of said patrols to ap-
19 prehend and cause to be forthwith taken before a Justice, to be dealt with according to law, all persons
20 who are found disturbing the peace, or who there shall be just cause to suspect have been guilty of any
21 offence mentioned in this act. Said patrols shall perform such other duties, in obtaining information
22 and executing the laws, as the Governor may require. They shall be removable from office by the Go-
23 vernor or Legislature, and their office and powers shall terminate when in the opinion of the Executive
24 or Legislature they can be safely dispensed with.

25 3. There shall be a Captain of each patrol; and one Sergeant to every fifteen men. No company
26 to consist of more than one hundred men. There shall also be one Chief of Patrols, who shall rank as
27 Lieutenant Colonel, who shall also be appointed by the Governor. The officers and privates of such
28 patrols when in actual service, shall receive the following compensation: Chief of Patrol $50 per month,
29 Captain $40 per month, Sergeants $30 per month and Privates $15 per month.

30 4. The powers vested in the Governor by this act shall be exercised only upon satisfactory evi-
31 dence, and with the concurrence of a majority of his Council.

32 5. This act shall take effect from its passage.

House Bill No. 5 Broadside.
West Virginia State Archives.

Captain John Valley Young, circa 1865.
West Virginia State Archives.

Governor Francis Pierpont petitioned President Lincoln for help on June 21, 1861, pleading that Confederate military and guerrilla forces were "making war on the loyal people of the State" and were forcing citizens to serve in the Southern Army against their will, and "seizing and appropriating their property to aid in the rebellion." Pierpont contended that he lacked a state military organization large enough to protect the citizens from domestic violence, and begged Lincoln to send a large military force into the region.[17]

In response, Lincoln promised to send a large additional force into western Virginia, but Union citizens in Putnam County would not see relief anytime soon. They often told state authorities that they did not feel safe, even with the 8th West Virginia Infantry organizing at Buffalo, and a few citizen patrol groups roaming the area. The state adjutant general appointed thirty-four-year-old Dr. Edward Naret of Buffalo as adjutant of the 181st Regiment Virginia Militia for the purpose of organizing the seven companies in his area into a full regiment for active service. The 181st Regiment was initially organized February 3, 1849 by order of the Virginia Adjutant General. Naret was quite popular, but he could only organize three companies to serve as citizen patrols in Putnam County, two at Mason County and two in Kanawha County, including John Young's company. Naret was unable to establish contact with several local militia companies, however, as many refused to be part of a formal military unit for fear of exposing their families to retaliation or being sent away from their homes.[18]

Dr. Edward Naret was born August 20, 1780, in Montceaux-les-Provins, Seine-et-Marne, France. The youngest of two siblings, his parents Vincent Augustin and Marie Rose Bureau Naret died in 1815 and 1812, respectively. He relocated to Gallipolis, Ohio, to live with a maternal uncle, Jean-Pierre Romain Bureau. In 1829, he began medical training at the University of Pennsylvania and graduated on March 24, 1831. At that time, medical students had three years of academic training followed by two years under a licensed physician. He returned to Gallipolis and began a medical practice in 1833. By 1841, he was on the board of directors of the Gallipolis Bank and a member of St. Peter's Episcopal Church. In 1843, he married Benoite Henriette Pitrat, the daughter of Antoine Mathieu Pitrat and Gabrielle Henriette Gagniard of Buffalo, Putnam County, Virginia.[19]

Benoite was born on January 22, 1815, at Lyon, France. In 1860, she and Naret had two daughters, aged twelve and fourteen years, and two sons, aged ten and six years according to the US Census. Dr. Naret was not a slave owner and owned a large amount of land valued at $20,000 at that time, which he had bought from another French immigrant, and his personal estate was valued at $4,000. Naret strongly advocated for the advancement of literacy and science, donating the land and tons of clay used to make bricks for the Buffalo Academy. Naret was commissioned as a Captain and appointed as Adjutant of the 181st Regiment Virginia Militia on August 26, 1861, although he struggled to maintain any sense of organization among the local militia companies, and

Dr. Edward (Edouard) Naret.
Peggy Youngs.

never managed to serve with the unit in the field. In fact, he became so frustrated with the avoidant militiamen that he ultimately resigned in 1862. Benoite Naret died before August 1862, and with mounting tensions in Buffalo from partisan divisions and frequent raids by Confederates, Naret relocated to Gallipolis, Ohio, in 1863. In 1869, he re-married Rhoda F. Frazier of Putnam County and raised a second family with her. His brother later moved to Buffalo and is said to have brought one of the first cameras to Putnam County. Naret died on April 20, 1875, at home in Buffalo, West Virginia.[20]

Union militia companies, home guards, and citizen patrols in Putnam County usually lacked firearms or only had their own personal shotguns or outdated hunting rifles; however, at Coalsmouth where John Young's company was based, each night prior to beginning their rounds, they still held a formal guard mount, with his men carrying mainly axes or shotguns. Naret pled his case for firearms to the state adjutant general in Wheeling:

We're being threatened by secessionists who are organizing in large numbers within a very short distance of this place…their purpose is to destroy all of the property of the Union people and to drive them off. The troops in the upper Kanawha Valley are unable to protect us; we shall depend on our own exertions, and we have no arms – our men would fight if placed in a position to do so… Sinister reports are spread about to frighten us away from our homes, and already a number of families from Hurricane and Coal have left rather than be exposed to the attacks of their enemies; among them are many brave men, who would fight if they had arms, but they are powerless and they go away. Much depends in the new state of things on the protection afforded to our valley – if the Secessionists are suffered to gain strength here; our future is uncertain.[21]

Many citizens who fled their homes were unable to return until after the war, becoming refugees. Most relocated with family in Ohio or went into the northern counties of western Virginia, although a few stubbornly remained at home or briefly stayed with family or friends in neighboring towns and villages during times of imminent danger. With so much transience, the process of organizing local militia units was next to impossible, and Naret quickly became frustrated, yet doggedly pursued the militia members throughout the summer and early fall months of 1861.[22]

Putnam County Union Militia and Home Guards

Virginia's secession left Union citizens in a quandary, as rapidly forming Confederate military organizations across the region began recruiting and violence erupted in local areas between factional groups. Nearly all of the extant militia companies in the Kanawha Valley were divided, with many of those men enlisting in Confederate service, leaving Union men and their families to fend for themselves. The sense of urgency and fear among Union citizens, who were a minority in the Kanawha Valley area, was understandable. There were virtually no organized local Union-minded militia units in the area to protect them in the early stages of the war. The State Militia was in disarray from years of neglect during the Antebellum era and was little more than a paper tiger. The Virginia Adjutant General reported having 18, 222 militia members on extant rolls in 1850, and the 27th Brigade, which contained the 181st Regiment Virginia Militia in Putnam County, had 2,743 men on rolls; however, when the Civil War began, officials quickly learned that almost all of the state militia regiments had failed to file annual reports since 1851.[23]

In Putnam County, the 181st Regiment Virginia Militia was ostensibly commanded by attorney and state assemblyman James Hoge of Winfield, who was commissioned as colonel. The 181st Regiment was part of the 22nd Brigade, 5th Division of Virginia Militia, with seven companies with expressed Union sentiment assigned to the regiment in 1861, though none of those units ever drilled or served together in the field as a cohesive battalion under Hoge's immediate command. Union men in the area typically refused to report for musters, because they feared being drafted and sent away from their families and homes, which were in constant danger of raids and harassment from Confederates and guerrillas. Despite this, the 22nd Brigade return filed in the Adjutant General's office on October 10, 1861 indicated the 181st Regiment had 644 men on the rolls, though more than half of those were names likely carried over from the antebellum era.[24]

James William Hoge.
Courtesy Hoge House Historical Site.

James William Hoge was born near Staunton, Virginia, on April 9, 1830, and admitted to the Virginia bar in 1850. Hoge lived in Albemarle County until relocating to Winfield, Putnam County in 1852. In May 1856, he was elected Prosecuting Attorney of his adopted county and a year later married Sarah C. Wright, daughter of John G. Wright, of Charleston. In 1859, he was commissioned as colonel of the 181st Regiment Virginia Militia. In 1860, he was reelected as the Prosecuting Attorney, and resigned his colonelcy without ever having served in the field. Hoge had six slaves, though he strongly opposed secession. He was chosen as Putnam County's delegate to the Virginia Secession Convention convening at Richmond on April 4, 1861, which voted against secession eighty-nine to forty-five. This appeared to temporarily appease conflicted emotions in many western counties, but it did not last long. In the fall of 1866, Daniel Polsley, judge of the Kanawha Valley Circuit, was elected to Congress, and the following February, Hoge was appointed to fill the vacancy upon the bench. At the expiration of the term, he was elected to the same office. He died at Winfield, West Virginia, August 12, 1882.[25]

The village of Winfield was the Putnam County seat during the Civil War. A small but thriving river town in the mid-1800s, it was previously known as Red House Shoals as it was a convenient landing spot for steamboats on the Kanawha River. Initially settled in 1818 on a 400-acre tract owned by Charles Brown, who established a ferry there, it was officially platted in 1847. Located at a bend in the Kanawha River, the bustling village was named for famed Mexican War hero Major General Winfield Scott. The county government was organized shortly after Putnam County was formed in 1848 and first operated at Brown's home located along the bank of the Kanawha River. A brick courthouse was built later that year. The courthouse became dilapidated by the turn of the nineteenth century and partially collapsed during a heavy windstorm on the night of September 6, 1899. A new courthouse was erected in 1900, which still stands in the same location as the original.[26]

As summer faded into fall in 1861, Captain Edward Naret was only able to organize three citizen patrols in Putnam County, two at Mason County and two in Kanawha County, with one at Coalsmouth, which was commanded by John Young. Although Young's men elected him as their captain, his rank was not formally recognized by the State or the U.S. War Department until more than a year later because West Virginia was not yet officially a state. His company was initially intended for assignment in the 3rd West Virginia Cavalry in 1861,

James W. Hoge house, Winfield.
Photo by author.

but in daily operations they worked autonomously without answering to any immediate authority until 1862. However, it is unlikely Young and his men were very visible during the Confederate occupation of the Kanawha Valley from May-July 1861, as Coalsmouth was a very dangerous area for Unionists. Naret was largely unable to establish contact with local militia units; he also found stiff competition with state regiments recruiting in the area, particularly the 8th West Virginia Infantry. Naret groused, "...since we were left to our own resources...The men who helped me in this work & who have since enlisted in the 8th regiment..."[27]

The Reformed Government of Virginia's adjutant general, Henry J. Samuels, acknowledged the militia system in western Virginia was in chaos during early 1861, primarily blaming it on outdated militia regulations. In reality, it was the blatant lack of discipline and enforcement of the military regulations occurring for decades before the war that were responsible for the general state of militia unreadiness when the Civil War came. The primary law governing state militia that Adjutant Samuels referred to was the Federal Militia Act of 1792, which required compulsory military service of all able-bodied men ages eighteen to forty-five years. This law required men to enroll in a company within their district. The aggregate of companies formed in this manner were known as Line Militia, though they were not uniformed and drilled only once annually; many such organizations also lacked weapons beyond outdated personal arms such as old flintlocks or shotguns. Records from that era are sparse, although the annual militia muster days during the Antebellum years were well known for being little more than drunken brawls and a picnic with fancy uniforms.[28]

For example, one officer commanding a militia battalion in western Virginia from 1857-1861 recalled a typical muster day:

> About two years prior to the outbreak of the Great Rebellion of 1861, I was in command of a battalion of militia consisting of about three hundred men...On muster days...the boys after drill would usually indulge in a little horse trading, or swapping, talk of, and appoint logrolling, rail-maulings, house-raisings, apple-cuttings, corn-huskings, and many other kinds of frolics....[29]

Isaac M. Rucker's Company of Independent Scouts

In April 1861, there were seven Union companies in Putnam County assigned to the 181st Regiment Virginia Militia, including Captain Isaac M. Rucker's company of Independent Scouts, comprised of forty men from Buffalo, Winfield, and Hurricane Creek. John J. Ball was 1st Sergeant; Richard S. George 2nd Sergeant; James Reedy 3rd Sergeant; and Richard Lewis was 4th Sergeant. By December 1, 1863, this company had forty-seven enlisted men on the muster roll and was designated as Company A of the 181st Regiment Virginia Militia. However, it should be noted this was essentially no more than a paper trail, as the companies assigned to the 181st Regiment never actually drilled together or served together in the field as a battalion or regiment. Rather, most tended to operate autonomously as small companies during the first months of the war, and as such, the early version of Rucker's Company is best referred to as Home Guards rather than a company of the 181st Regiment. Rucker resided on Hurricane Creek and was one of the first Unionists to organize a company in Putnam County. His company operated mainly in the Hurricane Creek, Buffalo, and Hurricane Bridge areas protecting Union citizens and property.[30]

Captain Isaac Rucker.
Courtesy Steve Cunningham.

Rucker and several of his men enlisted in Company D, 8th West Virginia Volunteer Infantry on September 4, 1861, at Buffalo, for three years. Rucker mustered into state service as a 1st Lieutenant on November 10, 1861, and he was elected as Captain of Company D on January 3, 1862. Rucker resigned on October 27, 1862, due to, "The condition of my family rendered destitute by the Rebels and my inability to tend to their wants and my duties in the service at the same time." Rucker went home and once again organized a new home guard company known as the "Putnam Scouts" who elected him Captain. A December 31, 1863, muster roll indicates Rucker had forty-seven men in this company. The Putnam Scouts' mission was to serve as "state guards" and "aid civil officers and to keep the peace" in the Buffalo, Hurricane Creek and Winfield areas, as well as the southwestern part of Mason County. Rucker later resigned on March 1, 1864, and accepted a commission as 1st Lieutenant of Company D, 7th West Virginia Cavalry. He recommended John J. Ball of Hurricane Creek to replace him, which was unanimously approved by the men and the state adjutant general. Rucker served with the 7th West Virginia Cavalry until mustering out of service on August 1, 1865. The Putnam Scouts were still in service as of February 9, 1867, when Captain Ball wrote to General George Brown inquiring as to whether he should disband the company, and how he could apply for the state service medals West Virginia was offering to Union veterans.[31]

Other companies also assigned to the 181st Regiment from Putnam County in 1861 included Captain David A. Ford's [Foard] Company, identified as Co. No. 5, 181st Regiment Virginia Militia. This company was formed in fall 1861, and Ford was sworn into office as captain on December 25, 1861, at Buffalo. However, similar to the other companies, this outfit functioned primarily as a home guard company. When Isaac Rucker resigned in March 1864, 1st Sergeant John J. Ball took command of the Independent Scouts. His thirty-five men were based at Union Ridge, near the Mason-Cabell County line, and patrolled western Mason County, as well as the Hurricane Creek, Buffalo, and Winfield areas of Putnam County. Captain James W. Bailey also raised a company known as "Bailey's Home Guards on Hurricane Creek," mustering into state service on December 29, 1862. In addition, Benjamin P. Morris, a deputy sheriff of Putnam County, raised a company of Union home guards at Buffalo. However, he told the state Adjutant General A.J. Samuels he "got crippled" and was unable to accept the captaincy when elected on August 21, 1861. He promptly organized another election on August 28, 1861, and his men elected William H. Hudson to be Captain, with Samuel C. Robinson as 1st Lieutenant and James Cass as 2nd Lieutenant. Morris informed Samuels on that date "we have had no mail since Saturday" and to expect delays in his correspondence.[32]

Like many Union militia units in the Kanawha Valley area, Captain Isaac Rucker's company did not receive pay or many supplies in state service during 1861-1862; many did not receive it until several years after the war, if at all. For example, as of February 10, 1868, Captain James W. Bailey had yet to receive pay for his service in 1861-1862. John Bowyer of Winfield wrote to state Adjutant General Isaac Duvall at Wheeling inquiring as to the status of Bailey's company pay and included the muster rolls verifying service. The matter had yet to be resolved on May 8, 1869, when Bowyer again petitioned Duvall to pay Bailey's company for their service in 1861-1863 and noted that several of them had died.[33]

8th West Virginia Volunteer Infantry at Buffalo

The 8th West Virginia Volunteer Infantry was organized in the Kanawha Valley by Major John H. Oley during the fall of 1861. Company D was initially comprised of forty-eight enlisted men recruited primarily from Buffalo and Winfield and was organized by Captain John M. Reynolds in early 1862, while the regiment garrisoned at Buffalo. The enlisted men elected Isaac A. Wade as 1st Lieutenant and Harvey Reynolds as 2nd Lieutenant, and James L. Leadmon was appointed as Orderly Sergeant (First Sergeant). They spent their first months of service patrolling the area and scouting for Confederate guerrillas and cavalry, who frequently raided local farms and harassed Union citizens. However, many of the soldiers lacked adequate firearms, and several had none at all. Colonel Lucien Loeser wrote to Governor Pierpont insisting his regiment receive weapons, stating "'tis' dangerous to send parties out recruiting scouting without arms."

In April 1862, the Regiment was ordered to become part of Major General John C. Fremont's Mountain Department, and along with the 60th Ohio Infantry, were organized into an advance brigade—period military parlance for what amounted to shock troops—under Colonel Gustav P. Cluseret. They were sent to the Shenandoah Valley during Major General John Pope's infamous pursuit of General Thomas "Stonewall" Jackson's army and saw heavy action at Harrisonburg and Cross Keys. On August 29-30, 1862, the 8th West Virginia engaged Jackson again as part of Major General Franz Siegel's First Corps in Brigadier General Henry Bohlen's Brigade, and afterward returned to the Kanawha Valley. On January 26, 1864, the regiment was re-designated as the 7th West Virginia Cavalry and assigned to Brigadier General William Averell's Fourth Separate Brigade, manning various outposts at Charleston, Coalsmouth, Winfield, Point Pleasant, and Hurricane Bridge during 1864-1865.[34]

William A. Whiting's grave at Andersonville, Ga.
Photo by Steve Cunningham.

One of the men who enlisted in Company D was eighteen-year-old William A. Whiting, a resident of Putnam County when the Civil War began. In 1859, he and his mother Nancy Whiting, a widow, and three other children settled on the farm of John Young located on the eastern base of Coal Mountain, and Whiting worked as a farm hand for the Young family until the Civil War began in April 1861. Prior to that time, the Whiting family resided in Monroe County, Virginia and earlier in Albany, Virginia. It is unknown how Whiting's father died. Whiting enlisted in Lieutenant Edgar Blundon's Company F of the 8th West Virginia Infantry on October 3, 1861, at Buffalo. Blundon later became Captain John Young's son-in-law when he married Young's eldest daughter Sallie in September 1863. Whiting was captured on the Salem Raid, on December 19, 1864, at Jackson River near Covington, Virginia, and died of dysentery at Andersonville prison in Georgia on July 25, 1864. He is buried

8th West Virginia Volunteer Infantry at Progress Mills in Buffalo, West Virginia, circa 1862.
Courtesy Steve Cunningham.

Buffalo Flouring Mill

Will exchange 41 pounds of all right flour per bushel for good
No. 2 wheat, or 35 pounds of patent flour.

☞ We pay the highest market price for wheat. Bring your
wheat to us. Good goods and good weight is our motto. Fair
exchange to all.

BUFFALO FLOURING MILLS,

BUFFALO, W. VA.

July 1, '08-1y

Buffalo Flouring Mills was previously Progress Mill.
West Virginia State Archives.

there in the national cemetery. Afterward, his mother Nancy Whiting, aged sixty-five years, who had depended on him for support, filed a pension claim based on her son's service in the Union army on January 21, 1869. After roughly nine years of a legal battle with the government to settle the claim, Ms. Whiting received a pension of $8 per month with backpay retroactive to the date of her son's death.[35]

Buffalo is the oldest established town in Putnam County. Located on the north side of the Kanawha River near the Mason County line, it was originally laid out and incorporated in 1837. During the Antebellum period, Buffalo was a thriving farming community and a busy trade stop along the Kanawha River, which continued to the time of the Civil War. An important business in the village during the 1850s through the 1860s was Progress Mill, located on Front Street. The large water-powered mill was in a four-story building with a basement and with milling stones that ground corn and other grains into flour. During the Civil War, Progress Mill was used as a barracks for soldiers in the 8th West Virginia Infantry, which garrisoned Buffalo during late 1861 and 1862; several men died in the building due to a typhoid outbreak caused by mosquitoes residing in the basement, which often flooded. The mill was later destroyed, but some remnants of the structure can still be found.[36]

Another prominent building in Buffalo was the Presbyterian Church. Built in 1857, the brick Greek Revival style building contained two separate doors for men and women and boxed pews, as genders were typically separated during worship services in the period. There was also an enclosed slave gallery in the balcony. Buffalo was also the home of the Buffalo Academy. Founded in 1848, the academy was chartered as a secondary school in 1849 by the General Assembly of Virginia. Dr. Edward Naret, a prominent local physician, donated the land for the school, as well as several tons of clay used to make the bricks for the building. Students boarded with local residents; room and board cost $2 to $2.50 per week, and tuition for the twenty-week term was $5 for primary grades, $10 for intermediate grades, and $15 for advanced. Courses in art, music, and French and German languages incurred additional fees. At graduation, students were able to begin their junior year of college academics. One of the better-known alumni was Brigadier General John McCausland, who commanded a brigade of Confederate infantry and cavalry during the Civil War. The academy closed during the Civil War, though was often used as a hospital and to house Union and Confederate troops. After the war, the school resumed operations until 1950.[37]

A Buffalo Settlement in Missouri

William and Grace Northrup settled in Buffalo in or about 1823. At that time, they had two daughters, Polly Burch Dana and Emily Burch Lewis. Emily married Howell Lewis, Jr., son of Howell Lewis, Sr., a nephew of George Washington who inherited 1,531 acres at Eleanor. William died in 1826 and is buried at Eleanor. In 1836, Lewis Jr. and Emily moved to Henry County, Missouri, and settled the small village known as Lewis Station. They left a series of letters from various relatives with a minister at Buffalo. These documents revealed previously unknown details of several other families of the Lower Kanawha region that relocated with them to Missouri, including the Bronaughs, Wallaces, Hayes, Menefees, Wears, and Danas. All but the Danas were slave holders and had moved west following the 1820 Missouri Compromise in hope of obtaining land and using slave labor to farm it. The former Putnam County residents were generally happy there until 1856, when border warfare erupted between the Kansas Jayhawkers and the Missouri Bushwhackers over the issue of slavery. Then in 1857, after the U.S. Supreme Court issued the Dred Scott Decision, ruling that slaves would remain as property in the Western Territories, abolitionist John Brown responded by executing his first raid at Pottawatomi Creek, which incinerated passions for war. Polly Burch Dana wrote home to her family at Buffalo on June 14, 1861, from Calhoun, Missouri, describing their plight:

Modern view of Buffalo Academy.
Photo by Steve Cunningham.

Buffalo Academy in the 1850s.
Marshall University Special Collections.

Village of Buffalo, circa 1850s.
West Virginia State Archives.

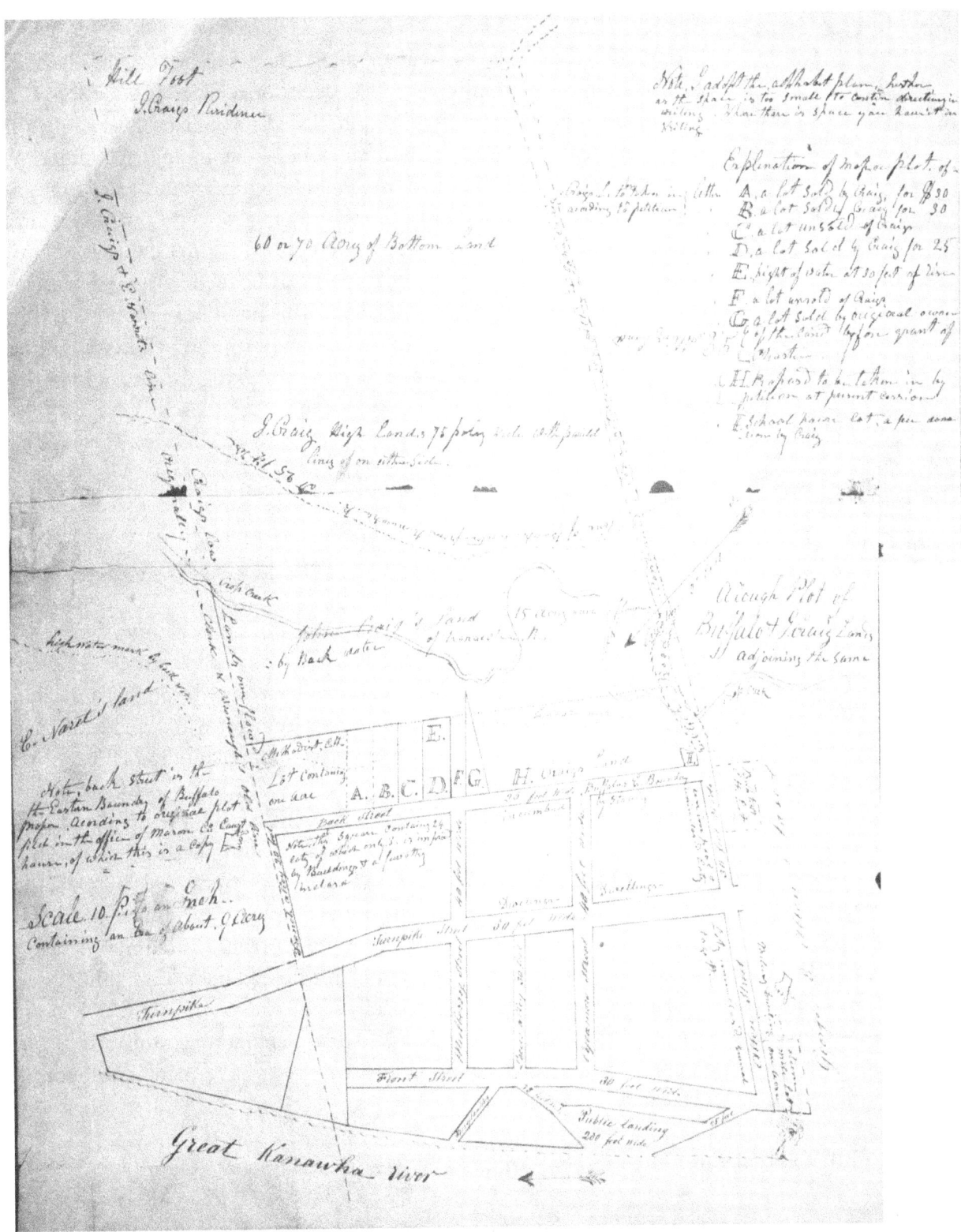

A rough plot map of Buffalo, Virginia circa Jan. 1851. James Craig (b. 1793) of District 4
in Putnam County owned most of the land in Buffalo in the 1850s.
Sources: Map Collection, Ma29-1, West Virginia State Archives; 1860 US Census.

Warren C Bronaugh.
Courtesy Confederate Veteran.

We are all full of cares and war troubles. Our country is again invaded by gorillas [guerrillas] committing their deeds of murder and robbery. Great excitement today, Malitia [Militia] all called to their posts. Twenty-three "Bushwhackers" made their appearance below us killing two Union men and a black man. One hundred of General Blount's men started in pursuit, hope they catch the scoundrels. The same gang robbed Lewis Wallace and Jim Wears' widow. He died in Malitia last fall. Fielding Lewis left home last August to take his negroes south. Reports say he died in Texas, he has left a wife and her little son, poor deluded boy. This Sunday was another troubled day. Early in the morning, Betty Lewis came running and crying for her Uncle, Mr. Dana. The Kansas men were there talking dreadful. He went but could do nothing for them. They had seven wagon loads of Negroes. Took Mr. Lewis' last two Negro women and their three children. They also took two old mares that were fat as seals. The troops did not take Mr. Bronaugh's Negroes, said they would be back in two weeks. I would not give a thousand dollars for no Negro. I should rather use my money otherwise than lay it out for human beings.[38]

Warren Carter "Wall" Bronaugh was born at Buffalo in 1841. His family moved to Henry County, Missouri, shortly after his birth. On July 19, 1862, he enlisted in Company K, 16th Missouri Volunteer Infantry under Colonel P.W.H. Cumming. Bronaugh saw action at Lone Jack and became separated from his unit, along with another soldier. They ran across a young Confederate soldier named Cole Younger who directed them back to their unit, preventing their capture. Bronaugh was also present at Reed's Mountain and Prairie Grove, Missouri. The 16th Missouri was re-designated as the 7th Missouri Infantry on May 6, 1863, and fought at the battle of Helena, Arkansas and also served in the Red River campaign of 1864. Bronaugh surrendered to Federal troops at New Orleans on May 26, 1865. After the war he moved to Texas and became a cattle ranger. He gained national notoriety with his book, *The Younger's Fight for Freedom*, telling of how the young Confederate soldier who prevented his capture at the battle of Lone Jack, Missouri, Cole Younger, and his brother became part of Frank James' outlaw gang after the war; they were later given life sentences in Minnesota for robbery and murder. When Bronaugh realized Cole Younger was the same man who had helped him in the war, he set out on a twenty-year quest to free Younger and his brother, eventually seeing them paroled in 1901. In his later years, Bronaugh was an active member of the United Confederate Veterans and attained the rank of general in that organization, but this was an honorary rank and should not be confused with a regular military rank. He died at home in Kansas City on February 15, 1923.[39]

Confederate General Jubal Anderson Early's ties to Putnam County

Although this story is largely unknown, the infamous Confederate commander, Major General Jubal Anderson Early (b. 1816) had deep roots in Putnam County. His father, Joab Early, owned a large and lucrative plantation from 1845 through the time of the Civil War, located in an area of Mason County that became Putnam County in 1848. Known as West View, the plantation was a popular source for delicious apples. Joab Early also owned a large tobacco plantation in Franklin, Virginia—Jubal Early's boyhood home. Early graduated from West Point in 1837 and served in the 3rd U.S. Artillery Regiment during the Seminole War, though was disappointed he "never even saw a Seminole," only hearing a few bullets whistling through the trees. At his brother Samuel's behest, Early resigned from the army in 1838 to pursue the study of law. He was admitted to the Virginia Bar in 1840. During the Mexican War, Early again volunteered for the army and was commissioned as a major in the 1st Regiment Virginia Volunteers, serving one year without seeing any action. However, while in Mexico, Early contracted rheumatism, which affected him throughout the rest of his life. Sent home, Early recalled the experience in his autobiography.[40]

He begins while stationed at the army post located Buena Vista, Mexico in 1848:

Maj. Gen. Jubal A. Early.
Library of Congress.

> For a short time I was attached, as acting inspector General, to the staff of Brigadier General Caleb Cushing, who commanded the brigade to which my regiment was attached, until he was ordered to the other line. During this period I contracted, in the early part of 1847, a cold and fever, which eventuated in chronic Rheumatism, with which I have ever since been afflicted. My condition became such that I received a leave of absence in the month of November, and returned to the States, on a visit to my friends in the Kanawha Valley. After improving a little I started back to Mexico, and on the way I had the luck to meet with that fate, which is very common to Americans who travel much, that is, I was on a steamboat which was blown up, the 8th of January 1848, on the Ohio River, a few miles below the mouth of the Kanawha. I had a very narrow escape, as half of my state-room was carried off and some pieces of the boiler protruded from the floor, cutting, and burning my feet when I jumped out of the berth. The explosion took place around 1.00 o'clock at night, when it was very dark and extremely cold, and before the passengers, who were not killed, could get ashore and obtain shelter, they were very much exposed; but, after getting over the first effects of the slight injury received, I experienced a decided improvement in my rheumatism, though I would not advise blowing up in a western steamboat as an infallible remedy. I rejoined the regiment about the first of February....[41]

That steamer was the *Blue Ridge,* which exploded on the Ohio River on January 28, 1848—not on the 8th as Early recalled. Fourteen people were killed, including the ship captain, Penn Wright, who is buried at Red House, near where modern Route 34 leaves Route 62. The ship's bell is said to be the same bell hanging over the Putnam County courthouse. Early became famous while serving with General Thomas "Stonewall" Jackson during his Shenandoah Valley Campaign in 1862 and later commanded a division in the Gettysburg Campaign in 1863, as well as in the Shenandoah Valley Campaign of 1864, when his army threatened Washington, D.C. After the war, Early became known as a hardline Confederate apologist, though he was initially a staunch Unionist adamantly opposed to secession during 1860-1861, until President Lincoln called for 75,000 volunteers to put down the rebellion. Early viewed this as the Federal government overreaching its own authority and changed his stance, becoming one of the most dreaded Confederate commanders in the Civil War.[42]

Confederate Volunteers Organize at Buffalo

Possibly the most famous Confederate associated with Putnam County was Brigadier General John McCausland, who played a key role in organizing new volunteers from the area in early 1861. He was born in St. Louis, Missouri, on September 13, 1836, to parents of Scotch-Irish descent. His father was a tax commissioner in St. Louis. One of their neighbors was the Dent family, whose daughter Julia married Ulysses S. Grant in 1848. Both of John's parents died within one month of each other in 1843, and seven-year-old McCausland and his brother Robert went to live with their grandmother Elizabeth McCausland until she passed away in 1849. An uncle, Alexander McCausland, took legal guardianship of both brothers, and send them to live with a widowed aunt, Jane Smith at Henderson, Virginia, not far from Point Pleasant, the place where the Kanawha River intersects with the Ohio River. She had three children of her own, and soon sent young John to study at the Buffalo Academy in Putnam County. McCausland received a classical education there, favoring the Romantic poets. During his tenure at the academy, McCausland is said to have become acquainted with later Confederate icon Jubal Early when he visited neighbors to listen to lectures at the academy as a guest.[43]

As a youth, McCausland was said to be thin, tall and gaunt with a fiery temper, and when angry his eyes supposedly turned black. He graduated from Buffalo Academy in 1853, and was accepted into the Virginia Military Institute, where he matriculated on August 2, 1853. He was an excellent student and served as squad marshal for the Corps of Cadets under instruction of Professor Thomas J. Jackson, who was later known as the famous "Stonewall Jackson." McCausland graduated in 1857, ranked first in his class of fifty-eight. Discipline at VMI was rigid, and cadets were absorbed in military studies with little else to do during that era. James A. Harden of Augusta County, Virginia, who served under McCausland as adjutant of the 36th Virginia Infantry during the Civil War, enrolled as a cadet there in 1861 to learn the intricacies of military drill and tactics, and briefly described the experience to his sister on June 6, 1861:

My Dear Sister

I left for this place on Monday last where I have been ever since. I entered as a regular cadet…I have not had time to do anything…[they] keep a feller running to roll call, drums, drills and lecture every two minutes almost. When a feller comes here he has to give up his liberty in every respect-it is just like you were in jail. Can't leave barracks hardly without permission…in fact I haven't heard any news or seen a newspaper since I have been here."[44]

McCausland next attended the University of Virginia for one year, completing the equivalent of a modern graduate degree; during this period, he also studied law under Judge John H. Brockenbrough, who later became a colonel in the Confederate army. McCausland next joined V.M.I. faculty as a 2nd Lieutenant, professor of mathematics and artillery instructor, and was present with the Corps of Cadets at Harpers Ferry during the execution of abolitionist John Brown on December 2, 1859. When the Civil War began, McCausland quickly organized an artillery battery that became known as the 1st Rockbridge Artillery and was elected as their captain, but declined the post in favor of returning to Putnam County to organize and train Southern volunteers there.[45]

McCausland had a camp servant named Jack Foster who accompanied him during the war. He was previously enslaved by Colonel Christopher Q. Tompkins, who commanded the 1st Kanawha Regiment in 1861, and later the 22nd Virginia Infantry, but somehow ended up with McCausland. Foster was apparently fond of his former master after the war and named his son after him. He wrote a letter to McCausland on December 13, 1883, from his home in Richmond, Virginia:

Dear Sir:

Having met up with Captain Col. [Thomas] Smith and having heard from you through him, no one can tell the felicity and pleasure I felt. I have often times sat down in summer in my humble doorway and wondered what had become of you. Just a few moments before I saw the captain [Colonel] I was thinking of whether you was dead or alive. I often thinks about that bread which I made at the camp. But, I am now married and have a wife and five children, four girls and me boy, my boy is the youngest, his name is Chris McCausland Foster. We are having beautiful weather here indeed. Dear General, I hope you may have the pleasure of enjoying a Merry Christmas and a Happy New Year. You must answer this letter immediately, as I am very anxious to hear from you.

Brigadier General John McCausland.
West Virginia State Archives.

General do you recollect when we were at Camp Narrow? [Giles County, Virginia] There where you took command of Gen Jenkins when he was killed at Floyd's Mountains [Cloyd's Mountain] when I was in the tent and Gen Jenkins rode up from Giles Tavern and came up in the morning at 3 o'clock in the morning You proposed to fight there on the other side of the mountain, but the Gen said no, meet them on the other side. But you during this time was riding on that old gray [horse] up and down the lines.

…old 36th Virginia regiment & western troops commanded by Col Tom Smith with ___ two pieces of Otey [Otey's] Battery we then thought we could beat the whole world. Do you recollect when I made the first light bread at Princeton You said you were going to make me a present of a band ____ gold watch as soon as the war was over? Do you remember the morning when you came out of your tent at Princeton and ordered the whole regiment to stack their arms and put guards around them? That was O.K. Now General do you know who this is writing to you it is Jack Foster who used to belong to Col. Tompkins.

Good night,
Jack Foster[46]

Once he returned to Putnam County, McCausland immediately established camps of instruction (Civil War-era equivalent to basic training) at various strategic points in the Kanawha Valley, including Buffalo and Charleston. He initially found it difficult to recruit, due to the strongly divided population in Putnam and Kanawha counties. Frustrated, he proposed initiating a draft, but the local militia lashed out at him. Interestingly, McCausland was not formally commissioned, until appointed as a Lieutenant Colonel in the

Modern sketch of Gen. John McCausland
by J McQueery.
Courtesy Buffalo Academy Museum.

Provincial Army of Virginia by Governor John Letcher during May 1861. However, McCausland was placed in command of state volunteers in the Kanawha Valley on April 29, 1861, when he received the following order from General Robert E. Lee from Richmond:

Lieut. Col. John McCausland:

You will proceed to the valley of the Kanawha, and muster into the service of the State such volunteer companies (not exceeding ten) as may offer their services, in compliance with the call of the governor; take command of them and direct the military operations for the protection of that section of country. Your policy will be strictly defensive, and you will endeavor to give quiet and assurance to the inhabitants. It has been reported that two companies are already found in Kanawha County, Captain Patten's, and Captain Sevann's, and that there are two in Putnam County, Captain Becket's and Captain Fife's. It is supposed that others will offer their services. The number of enlisted men to a company, fixed by the Convention, is eighty-two. You will report the condition of the arms & c., of each company, and, to enable you to supply deficiencies, five hundred muskets of the old pattern, will be sent. I regret to state that they are the only kind at present for issue. Four field pieces will also be sent you as soon as possible, for the service of which you are desired to organize a company of artillery. The position of the companies at present is left to your judgment, and you are desired to report what points below Charleston will most effectually accomplish the objects in view.

I am, sir, & c.,
R.E. Lee,
Major-General, Commanding.[47]

By May 3, 1861, McCausland had managed to recruit an infantry company of roughly seventy men at Buffalo, nicknamed the "Buffalo Guards", a pre-war volunteer militia outfit formed in 1859, and two newly recruited cavalry companies. During this period McCausland acquired two popular nicknames among the soldiers under his command, one being "Gobbler" due to his rather long and elongated neck and high-pitched voice, and the other "Mack," derived from his surname. On May 3, 1861, forty-seven-year-old Colonel Christopher Q. Tompkins, a successful and popular businessman in the area, was placed over McCausland by Confederate military authorities at Richmond due to such poor response to his recruiting efforts, hoping the colonel's popularity would greatly increase local volunteers. Tompkins was also a West Point alumnus, class of 1836, and had served as an artillery officer in the regular army until he resigned in 1841. Tompkins afterward returned home to the Kanawha Valley and served in the Virginia Militia until 1853. He was not in favor of secession but thought the war would only last a short period; he did not wish to appear disloyal to his state and aligned with the Confederacy when the war began.[48]

McCausland went on to establish himself as a fierce warrior, serving in western Virginia during 1861 with the 36th Virginia Infantry under General Henry Wise, and in 1862 he was present during the disastrous Fort Donaldson campaign, where he managed to save his regiment from capture by eloping against Wise's orders just before Federals captured the fort. He also participated in the Gettysburg campaign during June-July 1863, and in 1864 McCausland was in the Shenandoah Valley campaign. He was promoted to Brigadier General and took command of a brigade on May 18, 1864, following the death of Brigadier General Albert G. Jenkins who was mortally wounded at the battle of Cloyd's Mountain. He gained national notoriety for a raid occurring on June 30, 1864, when his cavalry troopers burned the town of Chambersburg, Pennsylvania, acting under orders of his old acquaintance, Major General Jubal Early. McCausland was later charged with arson for the offense in 1866 but was pardoned by President Ulysses S. Grant. McCausland defended the affair at Chambersburg as a "justified retaliation" for the wanton destruction in the Shenandoah Valley committed by Union troops under Major General David Hunter in 1864.[49]

Later, McCausland went to Petersburg, Virginia, and served in the siege, and he was present during the April 1, 1865 battle of Five Forks where Major General George Pickett's entire division was routed, and was also at Appomattox on April 9, 1865 when the Army of Northern Virginia surrendered. Afterward he returned to Charleston, West Virginia, to visit his brother, Dr. Robert McCausland. Interestingly, he never took the Oath of Allegiance or received a parole; he was unable to peacefully reside in West Virginia due to the area being under control of ardent Unionists familiar with his military activities. As a result, McCausland took exile in Mexico and Europe until President Andrew Johnson granted former Confederates who had not yet received a pardon amnesty on Christmas day in 1867. He then returned to Pliny in Putnam County where he purchased 6,000 acres of land that sprawled into Mason County and moved into a farmhouse located on the Mason County

Grape Hill, post-war home of General John McCausland circa 1970s. Note this home is often attributed to Putnam County but is located just north of the Putnam-Mason County line.
Courtesy Terry Lowry.

TO THE PEOPLE

Of the Department of the KANAWHA VALLEY, embracing the following Counties, viz: Mason, Jackson, Putnam, Cabell, Wayne, Logan, Kanawha, Boone, Wyoming, Raleigh, Fayette, Nicholas and Clay: According to the following order, by the

Governor of Virginia:

Executive Department, April 29, 1861.

LIEUT. COL. McCAUSLAND:

Sir: You will proceed at once to the Kanawha Valley and assume command of the volunteer forces in that section, and organize and muster the same into the service of the State; and as soon as they are formed into Battalions or Regiments, report the fact to me, with the names of the company officers, the number of men in each company, and the kind and quality of arms.

Gen. Lee will give all necessary orders for your government in that command. I am very respectfully,

JOHN LETCHER.

I have arrived here to take command of the Department. I have instructions to call into the field ten companies, and one company of artilery. These troops will be encamped in the Kanawha Valley, near Buffalo, Putnam Co. They are intended for the protection of the Department; and I appeal to the people of the border counties to abstain from anything which will arouse ill feeling on either side of the Ohio river. This Department is organized by the proper authority in the State, and is provided with the credit to sustain itself; but for complete success, I firmly rely on the friendly disposition of the people therein.

The volunteer companies of the counties of Mason, Jackson and Putnam, will rendezvous at BUFFALO, Putnam Co.

The volunteer companies of the counties of Cabell, Wayne, and Logan, will rendezvous at BARBOURSVILLE, Cabell county.

The volunteer companies of the counties of Kanawha, Boone, Wyoming, Raleigh, Fayette, Nicholas and Clay, will rendezvous at CHARLESTON, Kanawha county.

The Captain of the volunteer companies in the above counties will remain at their respective drill grounds, until ordered to their rendezvous by the Commandant of the Department. So soon as preparation to receive them can be made, the companies will be ordered to their respective rendezvous, mustered into the service of the State, and then ordered to the Camp of Instruction. No company will be mustered into service unless it has at least 82 men.

The Captains will see that each man is provided with a uniform, one blanket, one haversack, one extra pair of shoes, two flannel shirts (to be worn in the place of the ordinary shirts), two pairs of drawers, four pairs of woolen socks, four handkerchiefs, towels, one comb and brush and tooth-brush, two pairs white gloves, one pair of rough pantaloons for fatigue duty, needles, thread, wax, buttons, &c., in a small buckskin bag. The whole (excepting the blanket) will be placed in a bag, this bag will be placed on the blanket and rolled up, and be secured to the back of each man by two straps.

Lt. Col. JNO. McCAUSLAND,

Commanding Dep't Ka. Valley.

McCausland's May 1861 Order.
West Virginia State Archives.

side. McCausland married Emmett Charlotte Hannah, whose father was the cashier at the prestigious Kanawha Valley Bank, on October 3, 1878. Ms. Hannah was quite lovely and said to have been quite an accomplished intellectual herself, having attended a female academy in Hillsboro, North Carolina. They had four children: three sons and a daughter.[50]

George S. Patton as a VMI Cadet. Courtesy VMI Museum.

In April 1885, he began building a new home on the Mason County side of his land in Pliny; McCausland paid former slaves, then employed as construction workers, fifty cents per day to haul the large blocks needed to build the stone manor. The home was completed later that year and became known as Grape Hill. Gossip flooded local rumor mills saying that McCausland had kept thousands of dollars from the bank when his troops raided Chambersburg, Pennsylvania, and used that money to build the large stone mansion. This was enhanced by local legend holding that the large octagonal belvedere at the top was meant to allow him a good location to shoot at intruders who were seeking vengeance against him. McCausland was not known for his tact, however, and when President William McKinley was assassinated in September 1901, he loudly exclaimed, "I'm glad of it…He was one of General Hunter's staff!" He later became a successful farmer, developing a unique drainage system using tiles from a nearby factory, and died on January 22, 1927. Meanwhile, McCausland was concerned that the war would begin at Buffalo and published an order on April 29, 1861, for the volunteer companies at Mason, Putnam, and Jackson counties to report there for organization and drill on May 10, 1861. He also ordered companies from Cabell, Wayne, and Logan counties to report at Barboursville, while those in Kanawha, Boone, Wyoming, and Raleigh counties were to muster at Charleston as soon as possible.[51]

In response to McCausland's orders, early in the morning of May 11, 1861, a sharply uniformed and well-drilled volunteer company of ninety-seven men from Charleston, known as the Kanawha Riflemen, boarded the steamer *Julia Moffit* at Charleston and traveled to Buffalo. That company was armed with Harper's Ferry rifles, but had no bayonets according to McCausland, who requested authorization from Governor Letcher to receive the latter on May 28, 1861. There they met another volunteer company, the Buffalo Blues, who were already encamped on grounds behind the Buffalo Academy. The Kanawha Riflemen were led by Captain George S. Patton, grandfather of the modern World War II hero Lieutenant General George S. Patton. Patton was a successful attorney from Richmond who relocated to Charleston in 1855, just days after marrying nineteen-year-old Susan Thornton of Alabama, whom he met while studying law in Richmond two years earlier.[52]

Buffalo Blues/Buffalo Guards

The Buffalo Blues originally formed as a volunteer company in November 1859, just one month after John Brown's raid at Harpers Ferry. Led by twenty-six-year-old Captain William Estill Fife, the company was comprised of young men from Wood and Putnam counties, including several students at the Buffalo Academy. The Buffalo Blues were also known as the Buffalo Guards; this company mustered into Confederate service as Company A, 36th Virginia Infantry on July 15, 1861. William E. Fife was born on February 7, 1834. He was elected as captain of the Buffalo Blues on November 1, 1859, amidst a call to arms due to fear of another uprising sweeping Virginia following the capture of John Brown at Harpers Ferry. Fife attended the Mercer Academy and then matriculated to the Virginia Military Institute in 1851, where he was an above average student, and

Post-war photo of veterans of the Kanawha Riflemen,
with Col. William E.Fife standing in back row, second from right.
Courtesy Terry Lowry.

graduated in July 1855. Fife later studied law and was admitted to the Kanawha County Bar in 1857, although is said to have never actually practiced. Fife was later commissioned as Major on March 31, 1864, and quickly promoted to Lieutenant Colonel of the 36th Virginia Infantry on May 18, 1864. He was later wounded by a bullet in the thigh and captured by Union troops at the battle of Cedar Creek on October 19, 1864. Fife was soon back with the regiment in January 1865, however, and there remained until the end of the war.[53]

One of the founding members of the Buffalo Blues, a.k.a. Buffalo Guards, was Louis Julius Timms. He was born at Buffalo, Putnam County, Virginia, on January 19, 1842. Timms joined the Buffalo Blues in November 1859 and mustered into Company A, 36th Virginia Infantry on May 13, 1861, at Buffalo when he was twenty years old. Timms was present at Fort Donelson in 1862 but escaped capture. He was discharged from service in March 1862 due to an unspecified disability. Timms relocated to Shreveport, Louisiana shortly afterward, and in 1863 enlisted in a cavalry regiment under General Camille de Polignac, a French nobleman, and served until war's end. Timms returned to Buffalo after the war and later served in the State legislature. Known as a quiet, unassuming man, Timms was well respected in his home community. He died at home in Buffalo on January 16, 1918, at age seventy-six and was buried in the Atkeson Cemetery near Buffalo; General John McCausland was one of his pallbearers.[54]

James Democracy Farrar was seventeen when he joined the Buffalo Blues in the spring of 1860, while it was yet a volunteer company. He mustered into Confederate service with Company A, 36th Virginia Infantry on May 13, 1861, at Buffalo, and he was captured at Fort Donelson, Tennessee, on February 16, 1862. Farrar was sent to Camp Chase, where he remained until exchanged at Vicksburg, Mississippi, on August 24, 1862. He returned to the regiment and served until it disbanded at Christiansburg, Virginia, on April 10, 1865. He was paroled May 20, 1865. Farrar and his younger brother started their journey home, some three-hundred-fifty miles west, arriving at Buffalo on May 22, 1865, "after many hardships and trials and finding nothing left to them but the dear, patriotic mother and sister, all stock gone but one faithful dog, who stood sentinel day and night." He moved to Missouri in 1868 and married Eldorado McBain in January 1872, and the couple relocated to Texas, and later to Oklahoma, where he died in April 1921.[55]

Two brothers, William L. and Reece (often appears as Rice) Bryan were also members of the Buffalo Blues. They were born in Campbell County, Virginia, and their family came to Buffalo in 1857. In November 1859, they joined the Buffalo Guards, and William was later elected as Orderly (First) Sergeant. When the Civil War came, they both mustered into Company A, 36th Virginia Infantry on May 13, 1861. William was a carpenter and was often given "extra duties" as a "wagon maker" in service. After the surrender at Fort Donelson, William was detailed as Ordnance Sergeant and declined to re-enlist when his term of service ended on May 13, 1862.

Reece served as a musician in the 36th Virginia until the war's end. The brothers returned to Buffalo and were in the milling business together after the war. William passed away on November 25, 1922, in his ninety-second year, and Reece passed away on July 28, 1928, at Buffalo. Neither of the brothers ever married and were not members of any church. They had the "confidence and respect of all their neighbors for their integrity and their willingness to help others."[56]

Louis J. Timms, Buffalo Blues.
Postwar image.
Courtesy Confederate Veteran.

Border Guards

The other company at Buffalo was the Border Guards, a unit organized in May 1860 by thirty-six-year-old Captain Albert J. Beckett, who had served as postmaster at Hurricane Bridge from 1851 to 1857. This company was initially assigned to the 5th Regiment Virginia Militia, in the 22nd Brigade, 5th Division. Beckett stated the Company was formed at the urging of several influential citizens, "for the express purpose of protecting the border of Virginia and the institutions of Virginia….". This company was mustered into Confederate service at Buffalo on May 16, 1861, by Lieutenant Colonel John McCausland, who reported to Virginia Governor John Letcher on May 28, 1861, that Beckett's Company had fifty men on the roll. Oddly, Captain Beckett was not mustered into service himself until May 23, 1861. The Border Guards were soon re-designated as infantry and became Company A, 36th Virginia Infantry while assigned to the 2nd Kanawha Regiment at Charleston in late July 1861; ultimately, the Company was disbanded by order of Brigadier General John Floyd in September 1861, and several members were absorbed into other companies of the 36th Virginia Infantry. Shortly after the war began, rumors began circulating throughout Hurricane Bridge that Beckett had sought to purchase a replacement for himself to avoid active service during wartime.[57]

This annoyed Beckett, who wrote a rebuttal published in the *Star of the Kanawha Valley* on May 14, 1861:

I find that some unprincipled and worthless individual has thought proper to misrepresent me in regard to my true position relative to the company aforesaid. I find it is currently reported through the country that I had made a proposition to any person that would take my place and rank in the company, that I would give them a good Horse, Saddle and Bridle, and the sum of Three Hundred Dollars – indicating my unwillingness to protect my native state. What I have to say concerning this report is that the same was intentionally done for the purpose of false impressions, and I believe by some meek and cowardly knave who is too cowardly to say his life is his own, and probably thought that I was a coward subjected to misrepresentation, and willing to submit to all reports that might be circulated concerning me. The fact is, I have never thought of such a low thing – as proving false in the confidence of my company in as much as they upon their own responsibility, called me to command them.

I want it emphatically understood that I am for Virginia undivided, for the maintenance of the entire institutions of our glorious old mother State, for well or for woe; and where and when my fellow citizens of whom I have the honor to command, indicate a willingness to go, and in what way they wish to engage in the maintenance of rights and equality of the people of our State, I will be found fighting for and with them until death, and hope that the inoffensive individual who I refer to, will see the error

William Alexander Burdette with his wife.
Courtesy Imogene Burdette and family.

Peter W. Fizer, Jr., Beckett's Border Guards,
with his wife, Margaret Pleasant Roberts
Fizer, and child.
Courtesy Melissa Fizer Conley.

of his way, acknowledge his faults, and engage in defense of the State, and in his own protection, rather than in the base and low calling of misrepresenting others.[58]

Despite Beckett's eloquent appeal, the culprit responsible for the rumor never took public responsibility, at least not in the newspapers. One of Beckett's Border Guards was twenty-three-year-old 2nd Corporal Alexander Burdette, who lived on Trace Fork in Putnam County. He enlisted in Beckett's Company at Hurricane Bridge on May 16, 1861, and was mustered into Confederate service on the same date by Lieutenant Colonel McCausland at Buffalo. Burdette joined the 8th Virginia Cavalry after Beckett's Company was absorbed into the 36th Virginia in August 1861; his name appears on a September 26, 1861 muster roll for Beckett's Company at Camp Arbuckle, and he served throughout the war.[59]

Another of Captain Beckett's Border Guards, thirty-nine-year-old Peter W. Fizer, Jr. and his son, fourteen-year-old William Fizer, of Sycamore near Hurricane Bridge, enlisted together as privates on May 16, 1861, at Hurricane Bridge. They were mustered into Confederate service by McCausland at Buffalo later on the same day. Peter Fizer, Jr. was interviewed by family members about his wartime experiences prior to his death and mentioned that he and his eldest son William rode their own horses, named Pete and Burt, respectively, when they left home that day. Fizer also told of another son, Moses Leander Fizer, who was then aged about twelve years, being robbed of his horse by some Federal soldiers in September 1862 on Coal Mountain. Fizer said he was carrying a load of bread home to his family from Gray's Mill at Coalsmouth and had to go there instead of his usual source near Hamlin because it had been burned out by Federal troops. *En route*, he encountered a soldier belonging to Company G, 13th West Virginia Infantry led by Captain John V. Young, also of Putnam County, who was stationed at Coalsmouth. Fizer described the journey as "very hazardous and dangerous" and recounted how he became entangled with one of the Union soldiers, forty-three-year-old Private James "Jim" Tackett. Fizer stated he pleaded with "Old Jim Tackett" not to take his horse, trying to "reason with him but in vain" and was left with a small bag of bread to continue his journey. Fizer said he never forgave Tackett for robbing him and noted that it was common to see Southern families being robbed of clothing, even bed clothing, horses and food by "Yankee" soldiers during the war. Prior to the war, Peter Fizer, Jr. worked as a cooper, i.e., making barrels in the salt mines located at Malden. He remained with the 36th Virginia Infantry after Beckett's Company dissolved in August 1861.[60]

When Beckett's Company was absorbed into various companies within the 36th Virginia Infantry, his activities are unclear; however, he most likely joined one of the four independent cavalry companies associated with Brigadier General Albert G. Jenkins, as he later appears on muster rolls for Company A, 36th Battalion Virginia Cavalry (Sweeney's Battalion) in August 1862. That regiment was not officially organized until February 5, 1863, under Major James W. Sweeney of Wheeling, Virginia, though it incorporated Jenkins' four independent cavalry companies. Sweeney was formerly in the 60th Virginia Infantry (3rd Kanawha Regiment in 1861). In January 1863, Jenkins relocated to Salem, Virginia, during a harsh winter. Despite this, his men underwent a grueling drill and discipline regimen, and Fizer became ill with rubella. He died in the army hospital at Salem Virginia on March 6, 1863.[61]

William Fizer,
son of Peter W. Fizer, Jr.,
Beckett's Co. Border Guards circa 1861.
Courtesy Melissa Fizer Conley.

Samuel Sterrett and Family

Samuel Alexander Sterrett was born at Buffalo on August 21, 1841. He was twenty years old when the Civil War began. He spent his youth working on his father's farm, known as Fairview, which was located near Red House and was once part of a large land grant George Washington had left to his nephew, Lawrence A. Washington. Known as a kind and hardworking youth, Sterrett attended the Buffalo Presbyterian Church and was well liked in the community. He enlisted in Captain Beckett's Company at Buffalo on May 13, 1861, along with some eighty other area men and was elected 1st Lieutenant. He remained in the company when it was absorbed into Company A, 36th Virginia Infantry in August 1861 after Beckett's Company dissolved. Sterrett was present at the battle of Scary Creek on July 18, 1861, Carnifex Ferry on September 10, 1861, and was captured at Fort Donelson on February 16, 1862, trying to assist the regimental color bearer, Private Tom Harvey, who was wounded, in his escape.[62]

He was sent to Camp Morton, Indianapolis, Indiana, on August 24, 1862, and there remained until exchanged in April 1863 at Vicksburg, Mississippi. While en route, he and other prisoners had to ride atop crowded boxcars on a train ride and were so exhausted, they all fell asleep in the broiling sun. Sterrett returned to the regiment in April 1863 and saw action at the Battle of Fayetteville in May 1863 and at Cloyd's Mountain on May 9, 1864. He was again captured at the battle of Piedmont on June 5, 1864. Sterrett was sent to Camp Morton once more, until exchanged at City Point, Virginia, on March 4, 1865. Once paroled, Sterrett made his way to Lewisburg, West Virginia, in May 1865 and walked from there to Charleston in three days. He took a steamer from there to Buffalo with his friend, John Timms, and hid

Samuel A. Sterrett.
West Virginia State Archives.

Charles E. Shank.
Courtesy Buffalo Academy
Museum.

Homemade cartridge box. Alexander Handley's
name is stamped on the interior flap with the
date Jan. 12, 1878, Buffalo, Putnam County.
Courtesy Buffalo Academy Museum.

at his house until dark because several local Union citizens had threatened his life if he ever returned. The next day, he found someone to ferry him across the river in a small boat to Fairview, where he arrived looking as a "skeleton" wearing only rags. He thought no one would recognize him, but as he approached the house, his mother called out, "That you Sam?" He later married Anne Hutchinson, and they had five children together. Sterrett was said to have looked forward to reading the *Putnam Democrat* newspaper each week after the war, and that he viewed it "as the visit of an old friend." He died on May 11, 1937.[63]

Nineteen-year-old Charles E. Shank was employed as a carpenter when he enlisted in Company A, 36th Virginia Infantry on May 13, 1861, at Buffalo, for one year's service. His service file notes he enlisted "for the bounty $50.00" and left the company at Charleston just after receiving his pay in December 1862. Shank must have experienced a change in his allegiance, as on February 1, 1863, Shank enlisted in Company A, 8th West Virginia Volunteer Infantry at Buffalo. The regiment was re-designated as the 7th West Virginia Cavalry on January 26, 1864, and assigned to General William Averell's Fourth Separate Brigade; Shank was soon promoted to chief bugler on February 1, 1864. He transferred to regimental Field and Staff on December 5, 1864, and served in that capacity until he mustered out of service on August 1, 1865.[64]

Alexander S. Handley and Family

Twenty-five-year-old Alexander G. Handley, born in 1836, was 5'9" with dark hair and dark eyes, and a florid complexion. Employed as a farmer in 1861, he enlisted as a private for one year on May 24, 1861, in the Border Rifles, which became Company A, 22nd Virginia Infantry (Kanawha Riflemen). Handley was elected as 1st Lieutenant of Company A on May 1, 1862, and was commissioned on May 23, 1862. Handley was then formally mustered into service as an officer at White Sulphur Springs in Greenbrier County by Lieutenant Colonel Andrew R. Barbee. He took command of Company A in September 1862 and was present until he was arrested by Captain John Young, Company G, 13th West Virginia Infantry on February 9, 1864, in the Kanawha Valley. Records conflict, however, as some prison documents indicated he was taken at Roane County, and others state Boone County. He was sent to Athenaeum Prison at Wheeling, and then to Camp Chase, Ohio, on March 7, 1864. On March 27, 1864, he transferred to Fort Delaware, where he remained until the end of the war. After the conflict ended, Handley later relocated to

Greenbrier County, West Virginia. Handley had two brothers who also served in the Confederate Army.[65]

Benaniah F. Handley, born in 1843, enlisted as a private in Company A, 22nd Virginia Infantry at Charleston in Kanawha County on September 15, 1862, and was sworn in by his brother, 1st Lieutenant Alexander Handley. He was present until hospitalized with pneumonia at the Union army hospital in Monroe County during January 1863; he died there on February 25, 1863. He is buried in the Handley Cemetery in Teays Valley. Born in 1841, Henry G. Handley had gray eyes, dark hair, and was 6'0" tall, with a fair complexion. He worked as a farmer before

The Alexander W. Handley House is no longer standing, although it survived a tornado in 1976.
Photo Courtesy Angel Lake.

the war, and enlisted as a private in Company D, 8th Virginia Cavalry at the Cabell County Courthouse on September 4, 1862. Henry Handley was on numerous patrols and fought in skirmishes in Putnam County and was present at the battle of Hurricane Bridge on March 28, 1863, which occurred only a few miles from his home. He was arrested by Union troops in Logan County on April 23, 1864, and taken to Athenaeum Prison at Wheeling. From there he transferred to Camp Chase, Ohio, where he died of pneumonia on January 28, 1865. Henry Handley is buried in grave No. 921 at the Confederate Cemetery three miles south of the prison site.[66]

Samuel Handley was the patriarch of most Handley's in Putnam County. He was born in 1770 in Botetourt County, Virginia, and married Sarah Walker Harmon on April 15, 1797, in Greenbrier County. Sarah was born in 1779. In 1815, Samuel acquired a tract of land for 300 acres in Teays Valley where modern Sleepy Hollow Golf course is located. They moved there in 1816 and built a house, which stood until destroyed by developers in 1985. Samuel and Sarah had sixteen children; two of their daughters married into the Bowyer family of Winfield. Victoria E. Handley (b. 1838) married Napoleon B. Bowyer in 1868 and relocated to Red River, Texas. The other, Sarah "Salley" W. Handley, (b. 1846) married Cicero L. Bowyer, a farmer. Samuel died on August 5, 1851, and Sarah died on October 14, 1854. Their fourth son, Alexander Walker, (April 1, 1803-April 3, 1883) was a merchant and married Eliza Sybil Griffin, born in 1810, of Athens, Ohio at Kanawha County in 1830.[67]

In the spring of 1845, Mollie Teays Hansford of Coalsmouth, modern St. Albans, wrote in her diary about visiting the Handley family:

Dr. Maupin's wife of Cabell County invited Cousin Betty Chilton and I to pay her a visit. We left Coalsmouth before sun-up. What a pleasant ride we had going over Coal Mountain. The wild grapes were in bloom and the dew was still on the ground, the perfume was perfectly delicious. We stopped at Mr. Alex Handley's for dinner they were looking for us as Mrs. Maupin had written we were coming. We were very tired, and I shall never forget how cordially we were received, even though we had never met Mrs. Handley before. What a sweet, cool room she gave us, everything was so neat. She also had a nice dinner for us, and they saw that our horses were attended to.[68]

On May 22, 1861, another newly formed company of volunteers arrived at Buffalo: Captain Andrew Russell Barbee's Border Rifles. Barbee described them as "163 bear and deer hunters, most of whom were

Dr. Andrew Barbee.
Courtesy Terry Lowry.

six-footers." Lieutenant Colonel John McCausland described this company as "fine men, accustomed to the rifle," but complained to Governor John Letcher on May 28, 1861, that they were armed with "the old Virginia Musket, many of them in bad condition....These men are experts on the rifle, and consequently dissatisfied with the inferior weapon." Barbee was a physician living in Point Pleasant when the Civil War began, and soon moved to Buffalo in Putnam County. Barbee was born on December 9, 1827, at Hawsburg, Rappahannock County, Virginia, and his father was a tanner by trade. He studied medicine at Petersburg, Virginia, under Dr. John J. Thompson from 1848-1849, attended Richmond Medical College from 1849-1850, and then obtained a medical doctorate from the University of Pennsylvania in April 1851. Afterward, Dr. Barbee moved to Flint Hill, in Rappahannock County, and lived in Criglersvillle in Madison County in 1852. He married Margaret A.G. Thompson, the daughter of his former instructor, Dr. John Thompson, in May 1852. As Sectionalist tensions increased during the 1850s, the two doctors and their families relocated to Poca Bottom in Putnam County, because they were strongly opposed to secession and thought their views would be better tolerated there. Together, they opened a medical practice, but the local population was small, and each also worked as farmers to support themselves. The 1860 U.S. Census shows Barbee having one slave named John Timbles, and he and Margaret had three children.[69]

As war became inevitable, Dr. Barbee chose to remain loyal to Virginia, though he did not support secession. Rather than serve as a physician, Barbee helped organize a company of infantry volunteers at Buffalo nicknamed the Border Rifles. He enlisted on May 12, 1861, at Poca, and was elected Captain on the same day. His company later became Company A, 22nd Virginia Infantry. Although his name is not found on regimental muster rolls or in service records, Dr. Thompson is said to have served briefly with Dr. Barbee in the 22nd Virginia during early 1861. On June 9, 1861, Thompson was caught secretly circulating a petition to John Letcher, governor of Virginia, asking him not to send any more troops into the Kanawha Valley than was already raised, in hopes of shortening the war. Ironically, the principal informant was 1st Sergeant John T. Dudding of Company B, Captain Barbee's son-in-law. According to local tradition, that would not be the only time Thompson's allegiance was questioned. Later that fall, Barbee supposedly learned his father-in-law had arranged for a large shipment of coffee and sugar to land at Winfield, along with three men known to be Unionists, one of which was Arthur I. Boreman, who in 1863 became the first governor of the new state of West Virginia. Rumor had it Boreman was a friend of Thompson and had come to visit as well as see that the coffee and sugar were delivered to Union troops in the area. Thompson's Union leanings often resulted in public scrutiny; one resident editorialized in the Wheeling based *Daily Intelligencer* about him shortly after the battle of Scary Creek later in 1861:

...Dr. Thompson, a very wealthy and influential man, living opposite the mouth of the Pocatalico creek, where the Federal forces were encamped, expressed himself a strong Union man had ever been opposed to Secession yet he stated to our officers that he would suffer his right arm to be paralyzed ere he would take up arms against the State of Virginia. The lens of his Union glasses cannot penetrate beyond the boundaries of that State. I was shown a bill presented to the Quarter Master by this Dr.

Thompson, amounting to $2,300, his assessed damage suffered in the depredations of the Federal troops, while at Pocatalico creek. Now I cannot see wherein he had suffered to any such amount. Four hundred dollars would have been a very high estimate none but myself placed it above two hundred dollars.[70]

Thompson's eighteen-year-old son was a cadet at the Virginia Military Institute and was called home earlier in April to help train new Confederate volunteers at nearby Camp Tompkins; when he arrived, he was met by a slave at the front gate who informed him he would have to sleep in the barn because his father had visitors, including Arthur Boreman. Once he learned of suspicions regarding Thompson's loyalty, Brigadier General Henry Wise, who commanded the Confederate forces in the Kanawha Valley, directed Colonel Charles Q. Tompkins to send Thompson, "whom I wish to deal with, strictly by me, at this place," although the outcome of their meeting is unknown. After the war, it is known that Thompson returned to Poca Bottom and resumed his medical practice until his death.[71]

Governor Arthur I. Boreman.
Library of Congress.

Barbee often found himself in an unusual dual role; he recalled spending days commanding the 36th Regiment in battle and nights tending their wounds as a doctor. Yet he was not immune to injury himself—Barbee was wounded three times during the war. First he received a painful gunshot wound at the battle of Scary Creek on July 17, 1861. The bullet severed the ulnar nerve and broke the bone, though he later recovered and was appointed lieutenant colonel of the 22nd Virginia Infantry on May 1, 1862. Barbee was again wounded at the battle of White Sulphur Springs on August 26, 1863. There, he suffered another gunshot wound to the arm, and a rifle barrel struck him in the hip, penetrating into his groin and causing paralysis of the great muscles of the hip, thigh and right leg. Once recovered from his wounds at White Sulphur Springs, Barbee was transferred to the medical department on the staff of General John C. Breckinridge. He served in the Shenandoah Valley Campaign of 1864 and was assigned to General James Kemper's Division medical staff on May 16, 1864. Although questionable, Barbee claimed in a post-war interview to have briefly succeeded Colonel George S. Patton as commander of the 22nd Virginia Infantry after Patton was mortally wounded at the Third Battle of Winchester on September 19, 1864. Later, Barbee was placed in charge of the reserve forces in southwestern Virginia until the end of the war and was paroled at Charleston on May 9, 1865.[72]

After the war, Barbee and his family moved to Buffalo, where he resided until 1868. At that time, he moved to Point Pleasant and played key roles in passing laws regulating the practice of medicine and surgery in the state, serving on the state medical board. He was close friends with Dr. Samuel G. Shaw of Point Pleasant, who served as regimental surgeon of the 13th West Virginia Volunteer Infantry. After the war, Dr. Shaw was chairman of the Battle of Point Pleasant Centennial Committee in 1874 and worked closely with Barbee in raising funds for the large monument commemorating the October 10, 1774 battle, which still stands at the confluence of the Kanawha and Ohio rivers. Later, Barbee also served as president of the Mason County school board. He became severely ill with pyemic blood poisoning caused by a cut he sustained on his right index finger while performing surgery. He was often found unconscious afterward, although he was elected to the West Virginia State Senate in 1880 and served until 1884. In 1881, Barbee was appointed to the West Virginia Board of Health and was nominated twice to run for Congress but was defeated in each election. Barbee died at Pruntytown, West Virginia, of heart disease in 1903.[73]

1st Lieutenant William S. Morgan,
Co. A, 36th Virginia Infantry.
Courtesy Buffalo Academy Museum.

One of the Border Rifles, 1st Lieutenant John Morgan, similarly reported there were about 160 men in the company, with half of the men being from Putnam County and the other from Kanawha County. Morgan was born on January 30, 1843, the son of John and Elizabeth Morgan. He enlisted at nineteen years old in Company A, 36th Virginia Infantry at Buffalo on May 13, 1861. Morgan had only beaten Barbee in the company election for captain by one vote; he later recalled an incident early in the camp as green volunteers were undergoing their first taste of military discipline. He had recently learned of a family member at home being terminally ill from consumption (tuberculosis) and was decided among his brothers that he should go. Morgan recalled:

…I demanded a pass., which afterwards passed me through any lines in the Confederate States. There were three brothers of us, one of whom was compelled to go home…I told the boys I would come back, that I would be with them when they dug the last ditch…Our company was organized, or made up, before the war began, and numbered one hundred and sixty men…And when I demanded this pass the Board of Examiners, consisting of General John McCausland [(Lieutenant Colonel)], David S. Ruffner, Sam Miller, and Dr. Watkins, objected to giving it. But our captain, A.R. Barbee, told them to give me anything for which I asked, and knowing as he did, that if I became dissatisfied and told my comrades I was going home, half of the company would go with me.[74]

Such was the state of affairs when Colonel Charles Q. Tompkins arrived to take command of the new volunteer companies at Buffalo on May 23, 1861. He found five companies comprised of 350 men present on that date, with all lacking uniforms and ill-equipped with outdated weapons and limited supplies and accoutrements—despite Lieutenant Colonel McCausland's list of required uniforms and effects published in the *Kanawha Valley Star* on May 11, 1861. Former Congressman Albert G. Jenkins of Green Bottom in Cabell County was actively recruiting at Guyandotte for the 8th Virginia Cavalry and had roughly fifteen men from Putnam County in 1861; however, by mid-1862, Colonel Milton J. Ferguson's battalion, which would become the 16th Virginia Cavalry in January 1863, had recruited nearly all of the men in Company D from the Hurricane Bridge and modern Culloden, West Virginia, areas.[75]

Despite their raw appearance, Colonel Tompkins' new volunteers learned quick and soon emerged into a well-disciplined unit. A few days later, on May 29, 1861, Tompkins decided that the division in Putnam County was too strong, and that recruiting would be henceforth impaired, so he ordered the 1st Kanawha Regiment to board two steamers and travel to Charleston, where they began performing guard duties. Captain George Patton objected to the move, because he thought Buffalo would prove to be a critical base for operations in the Kanawha Valley, but Tompkins ignored the warning. The ten companies under McCausland became known as the 1st Kanawha Regiment and mustered into Confederate service on May 23, 1861. The five companies under McCausland were later joined by other volunteer companies at Charleston and Ripley, and the 1st Kanawha Regiment mustered into Confederate service as the 22nd Virginia Infantry on July 1, 1861.[76]

Men of Virginia!
MEN OF KANAWHA!
TO ARMS!

The enemy has invaded your soil and threatens to overrun your country under the pretext of protection.

You cannot serve two masters. You have not the right to repudiate allegiance to your own State. Be not seduced by his sophistry or intimidated by his threats. Rise and strike for your firesides and altars. Repel the aggressors and preserve your honor and your rights. Rally in every neighborhood with or without arms. Organize and unite with the sons of the soil to defend it. Report yourselves without delay to those nearest to you in military position. Come to the aid of your fathers, brothers and comrades in arms at this place who are here for the protection of your mothers, wives and sisters. Let every man who would uphold his rights, turn out with such arms as he may get and drive the invader back.   C. Q. TOMPKINS,
Col. Va., Vol's. Comdg.

Charleston, Kanawha, May 30, 1861.

West Virginia State Archives.

The Kanawha Valley Star of Buffalo

Buffalo was the home to one of the more popular news organs in the area, the *Star of the Kanawha Valley*. The first edition was published on January 1, 1855, by owners John Rundle, William Murrell, and William Kennedy. This paper was decidedly a pro-Southern interest, dedicated to advocating for Southern rights, though initially refusing to support any political party. As further evidence of the strong political tension and division in Putnam County during the last few years of the Antebellum era, the building that housed the press was burned by arsonists, presumably Union supporters, in March 1855. Immediately afterward, Kennedy left the company, and from thence the *Star* began to aggressively promote the interests of the Democratic party, a position it maintained until the paper ceased operation on July 2, 1861.[77]

Twenty-eight-year-old John Rundle was a staunch believer in state sovereignty and limiting the powers of Congress and was strongly pro-slavery. He became the *Star's* sole proprietor on July 23, 1856, and under his control the paper focused on increasing the progress of industry, transportation, and the economy in western Virginia. Rundle stated publicly that "there would be a Constitutional Union or no union" and, beginning with the November 4, 1856 issue, added the motto "State Sovereignty & a Constitutional Union" under the masthead banner. The newspaper was renamed the *Kanawha Valley Star* on September 30, 1856, and the printing office was moved from Buffalo to Charleston "in the first building below the courthouse," presumably due to pressure from local Unionists in the Buffalo area who were displeased with Rundle's aggressive political stance.[78]

Rundle's coverage of regional politics soon gave way to national issues such as the Kansas-Nebraska Act, the Emigrant Aid Society, the American or "Know-Nothing" Party, the emergence of the Republican Party, and, in particular, John Brown's raid on Harpers Ferry. After Abraham Lincoln won the presidential election in November 1860, the *Star* aggressively endorsed the concept of secession and the establishment of the Confederacy, while blatantly denouncing the April 1861 convention held in Wheeling that resulted in a loyal, Unionist government of Virginia. Rundle enlisted in Company D, 36th Virginia Infantry on June 1, 1861, and he was elected as first lieutenant. Union forces occupied the offices of the *Kanawha Valley Star* after they captured Charleston, forcing Rundle to close the newspaper. The final issue was published on July 2, 1861.[79]

Union citizens in the Kanawha Valley received persistent harassment from Confederate guerrillas, although many Union men still refused to take up arms and enlist in the army. Union high command was acutely aware of the problem, and on May 26, 1861, Major General George B. McClellan, commanding the Union forces in western Virginia, issued a proclamation to the to the Union men of western Virginia hoping to motivate them to defend themselves:

VIRGINIANS: The General Government has long enough endured the machinations of a few factious rebels in your midst. Armed traitors have in vain endeavored to deter you from expressing your loyalty at the polls. Having failed in this infamous attempt to deprive you of the exercise of your dearest rights, they now seek to inaugurate a reign of terror, and thus force you to yield to their schemes, and submit to the yoke of the traitorous conspiracy dignified by the name of the Southern Confederacy.

They are destroying the property of the citizens of your State and ruining your magnificent railways. The General Government has heretofore carefully abstained from sending troops across the Ohio, or even from posting them along its banks, although frequently urged by many of your prominent citizens to do so. I determined to await the result of the late election, desirous that no one might be able to say that the slightest effort had been made from this side to influence the free expression of your opinion, although the many agencies brought to bear upon you by the rebels were well known.

You have now shown, under the most adverse circumstances, that the great mass of the people of Western Virginia are true and loyal to that beneficent Government under which we and our fathers have lived so long. As soon as the result of the election was known to the traitors commenced their work of destruction. The General Government cannot close its ears to the demand you have made for assistance. I have ordered troops to cross the river. They come as your friends and brothers-as enemies only to the armed rebels who are preying upon you. Your homes, your families, and your property are safe under our protection. All your rights shall be religiously respected.

Notwithstanding all that has been said by the traitors to induce you to believe that our advent among you will be signalized by interference with your slaves, understand one thing clearly-not only will we abstain from all such interference, but we will, on the contrary, with an iron hand, crush any attempt at insurrection on their part. Now that we are in your midst, I call upon you to fly to arms and support the General Government. Sever the connection that binds you to traitors. Proclaim to the world that the faith and loyalty so long boasted by the Old Dominion are still preserved in Western Virginia, and that you remain true to the Stars and Stripes.[80]

A few days later on May 26, 1861, McClellan wisely issued a proclamation to his troops, who were about to cross the river from Ohio into western Virginia, essentially admonishing them to mind their manners in hopes of building trust for a Union occupation of the region:

SOLDIERS: You are ordered to cross the frontier and enter upon the soil of Virginia. Your mission is to restore peace and confidence, to protect the majesty of the law, and to rescue your brethren from the grasp of armed traitors. You are to act in concert with the Virginia troops, and to support their advance. I place under the safeguard of your honor the persons and property of the Virginians. I know that you will respect their feelings and all their rights. Preserve the strictest discipline; remember that each one of you holds in his keeping the honor of Ohio and of the Union. If you are called upon to overcome armed opposition, I know that your courage is equal to the task; but remember that your only foes are the armed traitors and show mercy even to them when they are in your power, for many of them are misguided. When under your protection the loyal men of Western Virginia have been enabled to organize and arm, they can protect themselves, and you can then return to your homes with the proud satisfaction of having preserved a gallant people from destruction.[81]

Additionally during June 1861, the Virginia Treason Act of 1861 was announced, making it a crime to speak out publicly in support of the Union in Virginia. Some seventy-five Union men were arrested in nearby Cabell County that month for gathering in public to support the Union with a flag raising. On June 6, 1861, Brigadier General Henry Wise was ordered to take command of Confederate provisional forces in the Kanawha Valley and proceeded there at once, as directed by the Adjutant General:

You will, by such means and agencies as may be within your control, rally the people of that valley and the adjoining counties to resist and repel the invading army, which is reported to be on its march towards Lewisburg...You must needs reply upon the arms of the people to supply the requisite armament, and upon their valor and knowledge of the country as a substitute for organization and discipline. If there be any who have arms beyond their power to use, you can take them, with such arrangements as the case may indicate for future settlement. As your transportation will of course be very limited, and the service of such character as will indicate the lightest practicable train, the troops must be taught to rely upon the supplies of the country, but not be permitted to take them except through officers authorized for that purpose, and they should be instructed always to make prompt payment, or to give such receipts as will insure early and adequate renumeration. All officers commanding separate parties should be instructed to unite with the greatest vigilance and closest scrutiny the highest regard for the personal and property rights of all with whom they come in contact, save the common enemy of the State, towards whom the rules of war, as known to civilized nations, will be applied.

The imperfect information possessed of the force and objects of the enemy do not permit specific instructions either as to your line of operations or the movements to be made. You must exercise a sound discretion, so that all your efforts may tend to the result of repelling the enemy if possible, and if not, of checking him as near the border of our territory as may be practicable. If the disparity of numbers should be very great, your defensive positions will for the present necessarily be retired to the mountain passes, and sorties against the enemy should always be made to embarrass and delay his movements without hazarding the loss of detachments from your command, teaching them to wait until you have the means to strike a blow which shall be effective. The several officers of experience who have been directed to report to you will be assigned by you to such duties as the necessities of the case may require....[82]

Union supporters had their hands full in the Kanawha Valley by July 1861, as Lieutenant Colonel John McCausland and Colonel Christopher Q. Tompkins had acquired fifteen companies from the Putnam, Kanawha, Cabell, Logan, and Wayne county areas. The force was divided into two units, the 1st and 2nd Kanawha Regiments. Tompkins took command of the 1st Kanawha Regiment, and McCausland was placed over the 2nd Kanawha Regiment, which included the Buffalo Guards. It was re-designated as the 22nd Virginia Infantry soon afterward. On July 16, 1861, McCausland was commissioned as colonel, the 2nd Kanawha Regiment was re-designated as the 36th Virginia Infantry, and the regiments were under overall command of Brigadier General Henry Wise, in what became known as "Wise's Legion." Confederate forces in the Kanawha Valley during 1861 were also referred to as the "Army of the Kanawha" by General Robert E. Lee.[83]

Brigadier General George McClellan became increasingly concerned about the constant harassment of Union citizens, and the U.S. Secretary of War agreed, telegraphing him on June 10, 1861, "If we don't muster Virginians into service according to proclamation and arm them, we must quit the territory or prepare to hold it with Federal troops." McClellan then telegraphed Assistant Adjutant General Colonel E.D. Townsend in Washington, encouraging the deployment of more Federal troops into western Virginia: "I cannot urge too strongly the importance of this matter, on which hinges, I think, the fate of Western Virginia. I regard the position of Western Virginia as very different from that of Maryland. The anxiety in this regard to this condition arises, I think, not from any unwillingness to fight the battles of the Union on any battle-field, but from the natural solicitude of a simple people for their homes and families. We have it in our power to unite that people firmly to us forever. I hope the opportunity may not be permitted to pass by." The Secretary of War agreed. Major General Winfield Scott, then the overall Union commander, ordered McClellan to muster the Union troops from western Virginia into Federal service on June 12, 1861, with the contingency to McClellan to "proceed in this at your discretion."[84]

On June 11, 1861, the Wheeling Convention passed an order calling out the militia into state service, resulting in utter confusion. The ordnance stated it was intended "to execute the laws of the Union, suppress insurrections and repel invasion." The order prescribed those regiments already in the field, or those enlisted afterward, to be styled "Virginia Volunteer Militia in the service of the United States." The law further indicated said regiments be organized in the usual mode prescribed by Congress for the regular army, while allowing officers to be appointed under existing laws of this Commonwealth. The result was pure chaos when it came time to clothe, equip, arm and feed the regiments, as no one seemed clear whether they were operating under state or Federal authority for several months.[85]

Perplexed, McClellan telegraphed Major General Scott, commanding the Union army, on the same day, June 11, 1861:

…The strong motive of the move here is gone unless their volunteers are received. Such as volunteer for the service will not enter unconditionally, having not State aid. Small force of rebels can control numbers. Have already mustered some informally. When a regiment is ready it will not do to disband. The effect would be disastrous. It is the cheapest way to defend Western Virginia. It is the only way to unite her citizens. Other methods will fail. I fully concur with General Morris and the leading men in Western Virginia and think it would be impolitic to make further movements in Western Virginia at present unless we can follow it up by raising Virginia troops for their own defense. If decision cannot be reversed, shall troops now mustered in be disbanded? I beg and trust not.[86]

Scott responded a day later, advising McClellan: "There has been a misapprehension somewhere. The Secretary of War approves your policy of mustering Western Virginians to defend Western Virginia. Proceed in this at your discretion." Knowing it could take weeks, or even months, before a sufficient number of Federal troops were deployed into western Virginia, and with the militia in disarray, the Wheeling Convention of June 1861 also passed House Bill Number Five, designated as "An Act to Prevent Offences against the Commonwealth, and to provide for the Organization of Patrols during the War, June 1861." This act was in response to the multiple complaints from Union citizens regarding fear for their safety, home intrusions and arrests by Confederate patrols. It enabled Governor Pierpont to legally authorize the immediate organization of citizen patrols across the state, though some were already doing so; by all accounts, these patrols were meant to be an armed para-military organization with a captain, other officers, and privates, who were also given arrest and detainment authority for anyone found opposing the new state government or "inciting others to attempt the overthrow of said government."[87]

House Bill Number Five also stated:

…anyone who shall by violence intimidate, or with the intent or purpose aforesaid attempt to intimidate any officer of this Government, in the discharge of his lawful duty, or any of the loyal citizens thereof, be subject to a fine of not less than Fifty nor more than One Thousand Dollars, and be imprisoned in the Jail of the County for not less than one month nor more than one year; but if upon the trial for said offence it may appear that the person so charged may unable or refuses to pay the fine provided for in this section, the Court or Jury trying the case may increase the time of imprisonment at their discretion; not exceeding two years; provided, nevertheless, that any person guilty of treason may be tried, convicted and punished, as if this act had not passed.[88]

Realizing that the militia was in poor condition, Governor Pierpont knew neither it nor the citizen patrols were sufficient to protect Union citizens from Confederate guerrillas, and he petitioned President Lincoln for help on June 21, 1861:

Reliable information has been received at this department, from various parts of this State, that large numbers of evil-minded persons have banded together in military organizations with intent to overthrow the government of the State, and for that purpose have called to their aid like-minded persons from other States, who, in pursuance of such call, have invaded this commonwealth. They are now making war on the loyal people of the State. They are pressing citizens against their consent into their military organizations and seizing and appropriating their property to aid in the rebellion. I have not at my command sufficient military force to suppress this rebellion and violence. The legislature cannot be convened in time to act in the premises. It therefore becomes my duty, as governor of this commonwealth, to call on the Government of the United States for aid to suppress such rebellion and violence. I therefore earnestly request that you furnish a military force to aid in suppressing the rebellion and to protect the good people of this commonwealth from domestic violence.[89]

Lincoln agreed and promised to soon send "a large additional force" to his relief. In the meantime, Pierpont only had a limited number of Federal troops under General McClellan, the home guards and an uncertain number of militia companies and citizen patrols to protect the Union residents of western Virginia. In attempt to compensate for the inadequate defense network, on July 1, 1861, the new state legislature in Wheeling enacted a law requiring the private volunteer companies not already mustered into United States service to muster into three years' state service, with a company defined as having no less than fifty men, "rank and file." The new law further required them to hold no less than ten musters annually. While this seems reasonable at face value, it also added to the confusion as to not only the identity of Union regiments from western Virginia, but also in terms of jurisdiction. This was because, initially, lawmakers failed to clarify the issue of who would pay and supply those new companies; because they were in state service, but were also considered Federal troops, it was unclear which entity was obligated to pay and provide arms, uniforms, and equipment.[90]

General McClellan issued another proclamation to the inhabitants of western Virginia on June 23, 1861:

The army of this department, headed by Virginia troops, is rapidly occupying all of Western Virginia. This is done in cooperation with, and in support of, such civil authorities of the State as are faithful to the Constitution and laws of the United States. The proclamation issued by me under date of May 26, 1861, will be strictly maintained. Your houses, families, property, and all your rights will be religiously respected; we are enemies to none but the armed rebels and those voluntarily giving them aid. All officers of this army will be held responsible for the most prompt and vigorous action in repressing disorder and punishing aggression by those under their command. To my great regret I find that enemies of the United States continue to carry on a system of hostilities prohibited by the laws of war among belligerent nations, and of course far more wicked and intolerable when directed against loyal citizens engaged in the defense of the common Government of all. Individuals and marauding parties are pursuing a guerrilla warfare, firing upon sentinels and pickets, burning bridges, insulting, injuring, and even killing citizens because of their Union sentiments, and committing many kindred acts.

I do now, therefore, make proclamation, and warn all persons that individuals or parties engaged in this species of warfare – irregular in every view which can be taken of it – thus attacking sentries, pickets, or other soldiers, destroying public or private property, or committing injuries against any of the inhabitants because of Union sentiments or conduct, will be dealt with in their persons and property according to the severest rules of military law. All persons giving information or aid to the public enemies will be arrested and kept in close custody, and all persons found bearing arms, unless of known loyalty, will be arrested and held for examination.[91]

On June 25, 1861, the U.S. War Department authorized the Reformed Government of Virginia to begin raising state regiments for Federal service, as Secretary of War Simon Cameron telegraphed Governor Francis Pierpont:

SIR: In reply to your application of the 21st instant for the aid of the Federal Government to repel from Virginia the lawless invaders now perpetrating every species of outrage upon persons and property throughout a large portion of the State, the President directs me to say that a large additional force will soon be sent to your relief. The full extent of the conspiracy against popular rights which has culminated in the atrocities to which you refer was not known when its first outbreak took place at Charleston. It now appears that it was matured for many years by secret organizations throughout the country, especially in the slave States. By this means, when the President called upon Virginia in April for its quota of troops, then deemed necessary to put it down in the States in which it had shown itself in arms, the call was responded to by an order from the chief confederate in Virginia to his armed followers to seize the navy-yard at Gosport, and the authorities of the State, who had till then shown repugnance to the plot, found themselves stripped of all actual power, and afterwards were manifestly permitted to retain the empty forms of office only because they consented to use them at the bidding of the invaders.

The President, however, never supposed that a brave and free people, though surprised and unarmed, could long be subjugated by a class of political adventurers always adverse to them, and the fact that they have already rallied, reorganized their government, and checked the march of these invaders demonstrates how justly he appreciated them. The failure hitherto of the State authorities, in consequence of the circumstances to which I have adverted, to organize its quota of troops called for by the President, imposed upon him by the necessity of providing himself for their organization, and this has been done to some extent; but instructions have now been given to the agent of the Federal Government to proceed hereafter under your directions, and the company and field officers will be commissioned by you.[92]

As the new state government began mustering militia companies into Union regiments, there was much confusion over their designation as state or Federal volunteer regiments, as well as over whether the citizen patrols were to be considered state militia, home guards or undesignated. As the Reformed Government of Virginia was yet recognized as a Union state, the legal jurisdiction was unclear. As a result, many men serving in citizen patrols, home guards and state regiments were not paid until much later, if at all. In Putnam County, Dr. Edward Naret was frustrated with the state taking men from the same militia companies he was simultaneously trying to organize and assigning them into the new Union regiments. Naret eventually became so annoyed with the process that he resigned in June 1862, although it was not accepted for several months. Despite the militia's disorganization, citizen patrols proved to be rather efficient during 1861 in Putnam and Kanawha counties, including at Coalsmouth where John Young's company was based. For example, Young's group held a formal guard mount each night prior to beginning patrols, which often lasted all night, and served consistently from their inception until they eventually mustered into state service in 1862.[93]

The Confederates, on the other hand, were more successful at organizing their forces in the Kanawha Valley. As of July 8, 1861, Brigadier General Henry Wise, former governor of Virginia, who had command of troops in that region, reported having a total strength of 2,705 troops to General Robert E. Lee. Wise's army was comprised of the 1st and 2nd Kanawha Regiments, 1,483 men; the Kanawha Battalion, 459 men; and seven independent infantry companies, 535 men; along with three companies of mounted rangers: 216 men.[94]

Federal Troops Advance into the Kanawha Valley

Major General George McClellan ordered Brigadier General Jacob Dolson Cox, who commanded Union troops in the Kanawha Valley, to move the 12th Ohio Volunteer Infantry and Companies D and K from the 21st Ohio Volunteer Infantry from Camp Dennison, Ohio, to Point Pleasant on July 9, 1861. From there, Cox's force boarded government steamers and moved down the Kanawha River toward Winfield. Cox planned to remove the Confederate forces occupying the area, under Brigadier General Henry Wise. Jacob Dolson Cox was born on October 27, 1828, in Montreal, Canada, to American parents. An 1851 graduate of Oberlin College in Ohio, Cox was neither a West Pointer nor career soldier, but rather an attorney, similar to his Confederate antagonist, Henry Wise. Cox was also a recognized microbiologist. A strong abolitionist, Cox was elected to the Ohio State Senate in 1859 and served until 1861. In spite of having no prior military experience, his political ties led to an appointment as a Brigadier General of volunteers in April 1861. An insatiable student, Cox immediately absorbed himself in studying military tactics, strategy, and military history.[95]

Cox described the initial Federal movement into Putnam County:

On Thursday the 11th of July the movement from Point Pleasant began. An advance-guard was sent out on each side of the river, marching up the roads to carry messages, and the boats followed, steaming slowly along in rear of the marching men. Most of the two regiments were carried on the steamers, to save fatigue to the men, who were as yet unused to their work. Many of them were footsore from their first long march of twenty-five miles from Gallipolis to Hamden station, where they had been obliged to leave the railway. The arrangement was also a good one in a military point of view, for if an enemy were met on either bank of the stream, the boats could land in a moment and the troops disembark without delay.

Our first days' sail was thirteen miles up the river and it was the very romance of campaigning. I took my position on top of the pilot house of the lead boat, so that I might see over the banks of the stream and across the bottom lands which bounded the valley. The afternoon was a lovely one. Summer clouds lazily drifted across the sky while the boats were dressed in their colors and swarmed with men as a hive of bees. The bands played national tunes, and as we passed the houses of Union citizens, the people would wave their handkerchiefs and were answered by cheers from the troops. The scenery was picturesque, the gently winding river making beautiful reaches that opened new scenes upon us at every turn.

In either side the advance-guard could be seen in the distance, the main body in the road, with skirmishers exploring the way in front, and flankers on the sides. Now and then a horseman would bring some message to the bank from the front, and a small boat would be sent to receive it, giving us the rumors with which the country was rife, and which gave just enough excitement, and the spice of possible danger made this our first day in an enemy's country, key everybody to such a pitch as to double the vividness of every sensation. The landscape seemed more beautiful, the sunshine more bright, and the exhilaration of out-door life more joyous than any we had ever known.[96]

On or about July 13, 1861, as Federal troops were approaching Buffalo, a small scouting party led by 1st Lieutenant Mahon S. Kirtley, of Captain Albert Beckett's Company, encountered Union cavalry from Cox's advance guard near Red House and "paid their respects" by opening fire on the troopers. In this brief exchange, Private William Burdette of Beckett's Company claimed to have fired the first shot of the war in the Kanawha Valley. After the Federals promptly returned fire, Kirtley's squad of five men retreated and crossed the Kanawha River near Vintroux's landing to the southern bank of the river.[97]

Arriving at Buffalo on July 14, 1861, the 12th Ohio Infantry and two companies of the 21st Ohio Infantry disembarked and awaited further orders. Rumors of the Federal advance soon reached nineteen-year-old Sarah Francis Young, who lived on the eastern base of Coal Mountain, approximately two miles from the Confederate Camp Tomkins. About two miles further north, Confederate troops were digging up earthworks at nearby Scary Creek. Her father, 1st Lieutenant John Young, was away from their home with his infantry company searching for Confederate guerrillas prowling the region. On July 13, 1861, Sarah wrote in her diary:

General Jacob D. Cox.
Library of Congress.

> Oh, What a time! The Federal troops are coming up Kanawha. The secessionists are running with their guns to bushwhack them. They are mad because my father doesn't raise arms against our Government. No, we are too glad to see our protectors come. General [Jacob] Cox has landed at Winfield and will move on in a few days.[98]

Sarah also mentioned that a small skirmish occurred near her home the next day, when Federal scouts appeared and encountered some Confederate pickets from nearby Camp Tompkins. The scouts also found artillery near the mouth of Scary Creek. They fired one shot at the Federals, who quickly dispersed, "but hurt no one." Sarah's fears of having two armies in the Kanawha Valley were soon realized, as both Union and Confederate forces were about to clash in the first significant battle in the Kanawha Valley, just a short distance from her home, leaving citizens on each side of the conflict caught betwixt and between.[99]

Skirmish on Hurricane Creek

On July 16, 1861, a small skirmish occurred along Hurricane Creek involving the 120th Regiment Virginia Militia (Cabell County) under Colonel Joseph J. Mansfield and an unidentified company of Union home guards. Mansfield was wounded in the fray by a musket ball to the shoulder but kept on riding his horse to a nearby farmhouse. His regiment was engaged at the battle of Barboursville only three days previous. Realizing his wound was mortal, Mansfield wrote his will on July 19, 1861, and passed away that night. His body was returned to his family by wagon a week later.[100]

Thomas C. Atkeson.
West Virginia Regional and
History Collection.

Thomas Clarke Atkeson of Buffalo, born in 1805, married Virginia Harris Brown in 1836. They settled along the flat lands spanning the Kanawha River along the old Charleston Road, north of Buffalo. They had six children, including Thomas Clarke Atkeson (1852-1935) who was nine years old in July 1861, when he observed Union troops marching toward Buffalo past his home. He later recalled the spectacle:

Soon after the beginning of the war a Union force led by General Cox crossed the Ohio River and marched up the Kanawha Valley. When we heard that Cox's army was coming our way, we children became very much excited. We had sent plenty of Confederate soldiers, but so far, not any Yankees. I remember that my brother, Oscar, and I climbed up in a big poplar tree on the turnpike near the lawn gate, determined to get a good view. Before long we could see far down the road the long lines of blue coats with their bayonets and guns glistening in the sun. We then thought of all we had heard about the Yankees and our nerve failed us and we scuttled down the tree in a hurry and watched the marching army go by, from a safe place behind the lawn fence.[101]

Thomas attended the Buffalo Academy and later West Virginia University, where as a student he established the *West Virginia Agriculturalist* journal and was later known as the father of the agriculture department at the university in 1898. Atkeson next obtained a law degree from the Kentucky Agricultural and Mechanical College and returned to Buffalo to establish a law practice in 1880. He authored numerous scientific articles in academic journals and published four books as president of the West Virginia Board of Agriculture. The Atkeson farm was locally known as Lawndale and was the site of several small skirmishes during the Civil War. Atkeson recalled seeing Federal soldiers for the first time as they passed by his home:

During the entire period of the Civil War there were no regular schools around Buffalo, and in no year during that time did I attend school more than three months. Such schools as we had were private schools, taught usually in private houses. Two winters in an upper room in our home, one of my sisters taught a school, which was attended by children from two or three families on nearby farms. I also attended a three month session of school one fall in a Negro cabin on the farm of Col. Robert T. Harvey about a mile from my home.[102]

Thomas's younger sibling, William Oscar Atkeson, later became a United States congressman. Born August 24, 1854, he also attended the Buffalo Academy and worked on the family farm until he was eighteen in 1873, when he left home to attend the University of Kentucky. He became a schoolteacher after graduation, was a school principal from 1875-1877, and studied law at night. In June 1877, he was admitted to the Putnam County bar at Winfield and also served as editor and part-owner of the *West Virginia Monitor* newspaper in Point Pleasant. By 1915 he had relocated to Bates County, Missouri, and purchased the *Bates County Record*, a local newspaper where he worked as the editor. A tireless scholar, Atkeson authored the *History of Bates and Cass County* published in 1918, and published a novel in 1920. Atkeson was also interested in politics, and unsuccessfully ran for Congress twice before winning the 1921 election as a Republican. Atkeson served in the sixty-seventh U.S. Congress from Missouri's sixth district from 1921-1923. Afterward, he was the state

Modern Red House City Hall. The interior building is the original structure known as Red House.
Photo by author.

warehouse commissioner in Kansas City until he resigned in 1925 and returned to Butler, Missouri, to practice law and follow his literary pursuits. Atkeson died on October 16, 1831, from a cerebral hemorrhage and is buried at Oak Hill Cemetery in Butler, Missouri.[103]

After passing through Buffalo, General Cox's Federals marched through the village of Red House the next day en route to their new camp at the mouth of the Pocatalico River. Red House was originally part of a land grant to George Washington, for serving in the French and Indian War, given to him by King George III. He acquired 7,726 acres sprawling from Little Buffalo Creek to Pocatalico Creek on the north side of the Kanawha River, which later became known as the village of Red House in the 1800s. George Washington's nephew Samuel Washington inherited 2,233 acres of this land in 1805. The land was sold and resold several times until Benjamin F. Ruffner purchased it in 1839; he and his wife Rebecca lived at Red House for forty-four years. The village was named for a house-size red rock that can be seen high on the hill behind the town, although many think it has to do with the red brick building that now contains city hall. It is unclear exactly who built the original structure, but Benjamin Ruffner acquired a hotel license and operated a tavern there in 1842. The current wings on both sides of the building were built after 1900. Ruffner's grandson Joseph Ruffner and his wife inherited the home before 1840. Joseph Ruffner was a co-founder of the city of Charleston and held thirteen slaves, according to the 1840 U.S. Census. Ruffner relocated to Missouri in 1883 and later returned to West Virginia. Although undocumented to date, local tradition claims that the Red House was used as a stop on the Underground Railroad during the Civil War. There is said to have been a tunnel running from under the house to the river, but it has not been located, though it is known that slaves escaping into Ohio from the Kanawha Valley region often traveled along this portion of the Kanawha River toward Point Pleasant.[104]

As the Federal troops passed through the village of Red House, nervous citizens passed rumors throughout the area warning of a large battle coming, though they drastically overestimated the Confederate forces between "7,000 to 10,000 strong" and Cox's force at 5,000 men, according to accounts published in the *Pomeroy Weekly Telegraph* news organ. The same newspaper later erroneously reported that Confederate troop strength in the Kanawha Valley was between 10,000 to 15,000 in July 1861.[105]

Cox arrives at Pocatalico

The Federals continued marching toward Pocatalico on July 14, 1861, where they encamped along the riverbank that evening. General Cox recalled:

The halt for the night had been made at a little village on the northern bank of the stream, which was nestled beneath a ridge and ran down from the hills toward the river. It made an excellent position for defence against any force which might come against us from the upper valley. The sun was getting low behind us in the west as we approached it, and the advance-guard had already halted. Captain Cotter's two bronze guns gleamed bright on the top of the ridge beyond the pretty little town, and before the sun went down, the new white tents had been carried up to the slope and pitched there. The steamers were moored to the shore, and the low slanting rays of the sunset fell upon us as charming a picture as was ever painted.

We moved on the next morning keeping a sharp look out for our troops on either bank. When we caught up, we learned that a party of horsemen had appeared on the southern side of the river and had opened a skirmishing fire but had scampered off as if the Old Nick were after them when a shell from rifled cannon was sent over their heads. The shell, like a good many that were made in those days, did not explode, and the people of the vicinity who had heard its long-continued scream told our men after that they thought it must be going yet. About this time some show of resistance was made by the enemy, and the skirmishing somewhat held up our movement. Still, about ten miles was made each day till the evening of the 16th, when we encamped at the mouth of the Pocatalico. The evening before, we had one of those incidents, not unusual with new troops, which proves that nothing but training can make men cool and confident in their duties.

We had, as usual, moored our boats to the northern bank and made our camp there, placing an outpost on the left bank opposite us supporting a chain of sentinels, to prevent a surprise attack from that direction. A report of some force of the enemy in their front made me order another detachment to their support after nightfall. The detachment had been ferried across in small boats. They were dimly seen marching in the moonlight up the river after landing. Suddenly a shot was heard, and then irregular volley was both seen and heard as the muskets flashed out in the darkness.

A supporting force was quickly sent over; and no further disturbance occurred. A search was made for an enemy, but none was found. A gun had accidentally gone off in the ground, and the rest of the men, surprised and bewildered, had fired, they neither knew why nor at what. Two men were killed, and several others were hurt. This and the chaffing the men got from their comrades was a lesson to the whole command. The soldiers were thoroughly ashamed of themselves, but they were raw; that was all that could be said of it.[106]

On July 15, 1861, members of the 11th Ohio Volunteer Militia were scouting near the village of Poca in Putnam County. Private Thomas Vandyne, Company H, of Troy, Ohio (Miami County) was severely wounded in a brief skirmish with Confederates. He was taken to the U.S. Army hospital at Gallipolis, Ohio, where his wounds were treated; however, Vandyne died at the age of twenty-one a few weeks later. General Cox was soon going to encounter the Confederates, as word soon arrived that a force of some 1,500 troops under Colonel Christopher Tompkins were entrenched with artillery at Scary Creek, a small stream contributory to the Kanawha River some twenty-two miles distant from Pocatalico. During the next few days, not only did both Federal and Confederate troops experience their first combat in the Kanawha Valley, but the civilians found themselves caught in the middle of two armies vying for control, and their lives would be forever altered when a battle occurred at Scary Creek on July 17, 1861.[107]

Colonel George S. Patton.
The Glenwood Estate,
Charleston, West Virginia.

Scary Creek July 17, 1861: "A Hot Little Battle"

On July 17, 1861, along the western bank of the Kanawha River near the point where Scary Creek empties into the river, a small but intense battle was fought between Confederate forces under Captain George S. Patton, including companies of the 1st, 2nd and 3rd Kanawha Infantry, the 8th Virginia Cavalry and militia cavalry companies from Wayne County, as well as Hale's Artillery Battery under 1st Lieutenants James Welch and Charles Quarrier. The 1st and 2nd Kanawha Infantry companies soon afterward became part of the 22nd and 36th Virginia Infantry, respectively; several men from the 3rd Kanawha Infantry Regiment also later enlisted in the 60th Virginia Infantry. The Confederates at Scary Creek were under overall command of former Virginia Governor Brigadier General Henry Wise, who was in control of all Confederate military operations in the Kanawha Valley region. Wise was not well versed in military tactics, being a former attorney and politician. He previously served in the United States Congress from 1833-1844 and was U.S. Minister to Brazil from 1844-1847. In 1856 he was elected as the thirty-third governor of Virginia and served until 1860. Wise was initially opposed to secession, but once Virginia voted to secede, he resigned as governor and accepted a commission as a brigadier general. Wise had recently acquired Captain George S. Patton's command of around 800-1,000 men (sources vary).[108]

General Jacob Cox, who commanded Union troops in the Kanawha Valley, was also a former attorney at law from Marietta, Ohio.[109]

The number of Federal troops under Cox engaged at Scary Creek is estimated at 1,500 men, consisting of the 12th Ohio Volunteer Infantry under Colonel John W. Lowe; Companies B and D of the 21st Ohio Volunteer Militia (90 days volunteers) under Lieutenant Colonel Jesse S. Norton; Captain John S. George's Independent Cavalry Company from Ironton, Ohio; and one company of the Cleveland Light Artillery, Captain Charles S. Cotter's Independent Battery, including Captain William S. Williams' gunners. The Confederate infantry were posted behind a sturdy line earthworks they had constructed in the previous week, and their artillery was located on the heights above them, some two-to-three-hundred foot elevation, with intention of blocking access to the Kanawha River Road and guarding the bridge spanning Scary Creek. General Cox

Colonel John W. Lowe,
12th Ohio Volunteer Infantry.
Dayton, Ohio Metro Library.

ordered Colonel Lowe to take the expedition from the Union camp near the mouth of the Pocatalico River, cross the Kanawha River, and perform reconnaissance and ascertain the Confederate's strength. Cox further admonished Lowe to drive out the Confederates if he could easily do so, but if not to establish and hold a position until reinforcements could arrive. However, as often occurs in war, circumstances would not allow Lowe to do either.[110]

Most local citizens were fully aware of an impending battle. The Henry E. Simms family lived in a small wooden house on the heights above Scary Creek; Simms later claimed to have hosted ranking officers from each army in his home on the night of July 16, 1861, sharing cigars and drinks and discussing plans to refrain from engaging in the impending battle, until the civilians had adequate time to clear the area. While the story is likely apocryphal, the officers present are said to have included Captain George S. Patton and Lieutenant Colonel Jesse N. Norton. Another citizen, twenty-year-old Victoria Teays Hansford, lived in nearby Coalsmouth. Victoria and her family were Southern sympathizers, and she penned the following in her diary on July 16, 1861:

I left home the day before the battle of Scary Creek…We started in the afternoon for Paint Creek… The road was full of refugees going up the valley and from all directions [Confederate] soldiers and armed civilians were going down the valley towards the advancing [Union] foe. Weeping women and sad unhappy children were all along the road…I found many others in the same fix as I was….[111]

Robert Marshall Sims

Born at Culpepper County, Virginia, in 1818, Robert Sims made the three-hundred-mile trip across the Alleghenies with his family as a boy and settled on land near Scary Creek in Putnam County. In 1842 he married Mary Anne Nalle, born in 1822, and they had seven children per the 1850 U.S. Census. Sims owned a great deal of land and acquired eighteen slaves. Their home was large and overlooked the Kanawha River from Sims Hill, located just above the Scary Creek battlefield. Ardent Southern supporters, Sims took his family and slaves, along with fifty-eight other civilians, across the Kanawha River to safety on July 17, 1861, the night before the battle. After the war, Sims became wealthy selling his land to the Chesapeake and Ohio Railroad in 1873. He died in 1891, and his wife Mary Anne passed away in 1897.[112]

Sarah Young, the nineteen-year-old daughter of Union officer John Young, encountered some Confederate soldiers foraging for food at her home near the eastern base of Coal Mountain early in the morning of July 17, 1861:

Two Rebel soldiers came today, begging for something to eat…They had been gone but one hour before the Federals attacked the Rebels at the mouth of Scary Creek. Oh, how our hearts ached while the sound of the booming cannons reached our ears! We could distinctly hear the report of small arms….[113]

Sources often conflict as to when the Federals crossed the Kanawha River. Some indicate it was early on the morning of July 17, 1861, although a post-war account written by Private Cameron L. Thompson, Company H, 1st Kanawha Regiment (later 22nd Virginia Infantry), son of Dr. Robert Thompson, whose family lived near John Morgan on Winfield Road, asserts they crossed on the evening of July 16, 1861, and camped on the two farms, near the modern John Amos Power Plant. Thompson enlisted in Captain J. Ruffner's Company of the 1st Kanawha Regiment on May 8, 1861, at Charleston. Regardless, most accounts agree that while the Union officers ate breakfast in John Morgan's kitchen, a local citizen advised them to use nearby Bill's Creek Road en route to Scary Creek because it was a seldom-used dirt road connecting to Teays Valley Road, which then connected with Winfield Road, a.k.a. River Road, near the mouth of Scary Creek. Colonel Lowe sent the main body of his force along Bill's Creek Road with scouting parties on the flanks and a smaller detachment of infantry along River Road. Private James E.D. Ward of Company H found travel on Bill's Creek Road unpleasant:

> The road (Bill's Creek) being steep, as well as dusty, while a hot sun came down 'the near way' a number of halts were necessary, which rendered the march a slow one. Long before the first shots were exchanged, great fatigue was manifested by the man, and it was evident that some of them would never be able to engage in that day's fight.[114]

1st Sergeant John U. Hiltz, Company C, 12th Ohio Volunteer Infantry, recalled: "At 9 o'clock a.m., the 12th Ohio and two companies of the 21st Ohio, in all about 900 men, crossed the river and instead of taking the river road, which the Rebels no doubt expected, we took what they termed the middle road; a road that leads along the river, through the woods, and joins the river road just at Camp Scary Creek. Three companies were sent ahead as scouts, and as they experienced great difficulty in getting through the thickets, passing over creeks and timber, the column down in the road advanced very slowly." The Federals landed on land owned by John Morgan of Putnam County.[115]

Born in 1807, John Morgan Jr. married Elizabeth Beale Morgan, born in May 1812, and moved to Putnam County from Mount Jackson, in Shenandoah County, Virginia, in 1846. Settling on newly purchased land located near the modern John Amos Power Plant across from Poca on the Kanawha River, they erected a small log house that was later replaced by a large two-story home. Their land was originally owned by Dr. James Craik, George Washington's physician. The 1850 U.S. Census indicated John was 43, Elizabeth's age was incorrectly cited as 36, (she was aged 38 years) and that they had five children. John and Elizabeth had three sons, James, William, and John III. James enlisted in Company A, 22nd Virginia Infantry at Poca on May 22, 1861, and was elected 1st Lieutenant the same

John Morgan plantation circa 1850s.
Courtesy St. Albans Historical Society.

John Morgan house circa 1890.
Courtesy St. Albans Historical Society.

day. He was formally mustered into Confederate service on July 1, 1861, by Captain Andrew R. Barbee. However, he and several other officers lost their commission documents on board the steamer *Julia Moffit* when it burned on July 24, 1861. James resigned in September 1861.[116]

Note that one source indicates James was captain of Company A; however, he was never ranked higher than a 1st Lieutenant. John III enlisted on May 22, 1861, at Poca, and was mustered into service on the same date as James by Andrew Barbee. However, there is conflicting information in service files and muster rolls; compiled service records indicate he enlisted at Charleston on July 3, 1861 and was found away without leave (AWOL) on July 5, 1861. Another Morgan brother, William, is said to have also served in the 22nd Virginia Infantry and was killed at the battle of Fayetteville in May 1863, although neither that unit's service records nor regimental muster rolls bear his name. After the war, John III published a memoir entitled *"The Last Dollar"* telling of his wartime experiences. He worked as a farmer in Putnam County until his death at age fifty-six in 1898 from kidney disease. A letter written by Matthew Morgan, in September 1861 to a cousin in Ohio succinctly evidences the sectional division that had ripped the nation apart. Previously close, Matthew Morgan realized he was no longer on friendly terms with his cousin, "I can conjecture no reason why you do not write to me unless it's because I live in a Southern state, and you think yourself duty bound not to harbor one kindly feeling toward one on Southern soil...."[117]

Once the Federals had crossed the Kanawha River, an unidentified member of the 12th Ohio Volunteer Infantry recalled their movement along the Kanawha River toward the village of Scary Creek:

The expedition embarked on one of three steamers lying in front of our encampment -- our advance thus far having been mainly made by boats -- and was landed at a point a few hundred yards lower down, on the opposite, or Western bank of the river where there is a dirt-road leading to Scary Creek town. They advanced cautiously, a party of skirmishers thoroughly scouring the country on both sides of the road as they progressed. Scary Creek town is a miserable little village of a dozen or twenty log huts, scattered along the right bank of the creek from which it takes its name, and near its mouth. Both banks are precipitous for two or three hundred yards above the Kanawha, where they gradually slope off. The country on the right bank is densely wooded, while that on the left, immediately above the town, is comparatively clear. Directly opposite the village, where the hill runs a bold spin to the Kanawha, there is still considerable timber. This description of the topography of the country is necessary to a proper understanding of the battle.[118]

Another account written by a member of the Cleveland Light Artillery further described the Union advance on that sultry July morning:

The army is encamped near the mouth of Pocatalico Creek, or "Poco" as it is generally called, the advance thus far having been made mainly by steamboats, four of which have been chartered by the Government for the transportation of troops up and down the Kanawha. On one of these (steamboats) the reconnoitering party supplied with forty rounds of ammunition, embarked about nine o'clock in the morning , and were landed on the opposite bank of the river, at a point a few hundred yards lower down, where there is a road [Bill's Creek Road] leading across the country to Scary Creekville [Scary Creek] The column moved cautiously, the scouts thoroughly scouring the country on both sides of the road as they advanced.[119]

Around 10 a.m., Confederate scouts spotted Federal troops moving down Winfield Road toward Scary Creek roughly a mile away. Fighting began when Federal cavalry under Captain John S. George encountered Rebel pickets hiding in buildings along Teays Valley Road:

Private Frank Fornshell,
Co. F, 12th Ohio Volunteer Infantry.
Courtesy Terry Lowry.

...the party reached the vicinity of Scary Creektown, when the fragment of the Ironton Cavalry company, which had somehow fallen to the rear, was ordered to advance. They had no sooner rounded the brow of the hill, which gradually slopes off to the creek, but runs a bolder spur in the direction of the river, when they were met by a discharge from a battery on the opposite shore of the smaller stream, which killed one of their men, and caused the company to retreat in great disorder. Capt. Cotton's company of artillery, which fought like so many tigers, was at once ordered to advance, and took position near the top of the hill, under a clump of trees.[120]

The casualty lost by the Ironton Cavalry was Private Richard Lambert; he was struck in the head and chest by grapeshot, killing him instantly. Sergeant James D. Sedinger of the Border Rangers, Company E, 8th Virginia Cavalry, further recalled skirmishing with the Federals that morning along Teays Road, "The enemy drove in our skirmishers about 11 o'clock in the day, and the fight opened in earnest." An unidentified correspondent of the Cleveland Light Artillery recalled the cavalry's repulse:

Captain Joel H. Abbott,
Co. H, 8th Virginia Cavalry.
Library of Congress.

When the expedition reached the immediate vicinity of the town, the company of cavalry, which had somehow fallen to the rear, was ordered to advance. They had no sooner reached the brow of the hill than two six-pound cannon balls came whistling through their ranks, instantly killing one man, and causing the company to beat a hasty retreat. The disorderly flight of the mounted men had a bad effect on the Twelfth, who were now about to "smell Southern powder" for the first time.[121]

After a brief, but eerie quiet following the Federal cavalry's failed attack on the skirmishers, Colonel Lowe ordered his artillery forward. They rushed ahead at full gallop and unlimbered their guns, and quickly began to shell the Confederate battery on the opposite hillside. One resident later recalled the Federal artillery unit was "splendidly equipped." Although still green recruits, the Federal gunners wreaked havoc on the Confederate battery and skirmishers hiding in the houses below. The Confederate infantry under Captain Patton was posted behind a long line of earthworks along the southern bank of Scary Creek, and their artillery was posted on the hill behind their lines, creating an imposing sight as the Federals crested Simms Hill:

> The principal fortification of the enemy, a huge breastwork of earth, was distinctly visible about halfway up the opposite slope, and seemed to have been prepared with considerable skill. The distance from our battery was about five hundred yards. The rebels had but two pieces of artillery, both rifled 6 pounders, the same as our own. Capt. Cotton had no sooner taken position than two balls whistled over his head, cutting the twigs from the topmost branches of the trees. His men quickly unlimbered their pieces, and went to work, while he posted himself to their right to watch the effect of his shot on the enemy's works.[122]

An unidentified 12th Ohio correspondent waiting to advance along the brow of Simms Hill also saw the Confederate earthworks:

> …the Cleveland Light Artillery, immediately advanced to the brow of the hill, and took a position under a clump of trees, overlooking the town. Before his pieces were unlimbered, two more balls from the enemy's guns whistled high above him, cutting the twigs from the topmost branches of the trees. The rebel intrenchment, a carefully prepared breastwork of earth, about midway of the opposite hill, and not more than four or five hundred yards distant, could be distinctly seen. The Captain's "brass missionaries" now began to preach, while he took a position to the right to watch the effect of his shots. The first few, like those of the rebels, were too high, but the proper elevation was soon attained, when he cried, "Now let them have it, boys!....[123]

1st Sergeant John U. Hiltz, Company C, 12th Ohio Volunteer Infantry, recalled the first few minutes anxiously waiting for the order to advance while under artillery fire:

> About 1 o'clock p.m., our scouts reached the outlet and being observed by the Rebels, they immediately gave the signal. Our column then halted and everything placed in readiness. Our skirmishers with their Enfield rifles [21st Ohio] were ordered to advance, as also our cavalry and artillery. Our field officers soon took a view of the field with their spyglasses, but did not seem to have discovered the exact place of their battery; so we marched down the road, passing a barn, then turning straight forward a few hundred yards when as soon as the rear of the column had reached the turn, the whole column marched in parallel line with the enemy's battery. They opened on us, the report was heard, and to place ourselves in as safe a position as possible, the whole column squatted down, when the next moment, the grape

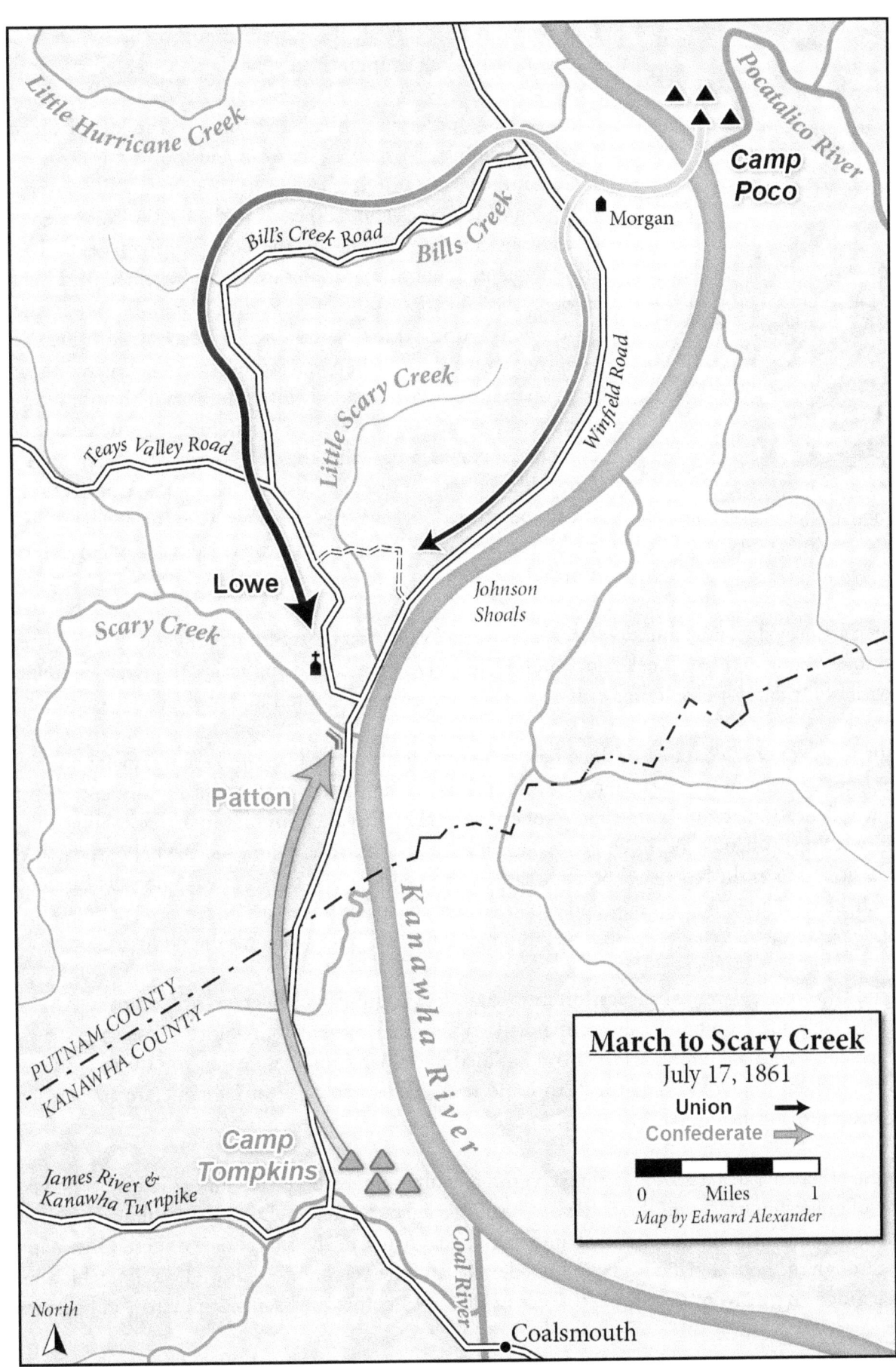

March to Scary Creek

July 17, 1861

Union →

Confederate ⇒

0   Miles   1

Map by Edward Alexander

Private Elijah Beeman,
Co. A., 12th Ohio Volunteer Militia.
Marshall University Special Collections.

flew over our heads like hail; we were about to raise when another one came whistling over our heads; no damage yet.

We were now ordered to break the force to the left of the road, but this seeming too slow a job, we made the best way we could. Here another ball came along, but still too high and another one striking a wheat shock about 30 yards to the rear. At this juncture we reached a steep run, the hills on the side covering us entirely from any danger. For about five minutes everything seemed confused, but through the exertions of the officers, the companies were formed in good order. During this time our artillery, having with the cavalry advanced pretty close to their battery and having observed the exact position besides enjoying the advantage of placing themselves near a church, our gallant cavalry made a splendid charge, while our noble cannoneers played away with the ten-pound rifled cannon. Every shot told, and we could easily distinguish them. A perfect roaring of cannon ensued. Meanwhile our boys were formed, marched up the hill, arrived at the level towards the entrenched enemy. Here the contest began.[124]

A fierce artillery duel now thundered across the small valley between Simms Hill and the opposite heights on the southern bank of Scary Creek between the Union and Confederate batteries, though both units initially aimed too high. It did not take long for them to get their cannons sighted in, however:

The first few rounds, like those of the rebels, were too high, but the Captain kept on crying out "a little lower boys" till the proper elevation was attained, when he played upon them rapidly, and in fifteen minutes silenced their guns, with the loss of only one man, Private John Haven of Scolersville, Putnam County [Ohio] A handsome, intelligent young man, and as brave as a lion, and the pet of the company. Poor fellow! His right hip was shot away as he was passing a ball to his gun. When his captain saw him fall, he ran and picked him up, and conveyed him to a place of safety. "*Never mind me, Captain!*" he cried, "*but don't let that flag go down!*" He still lingers, but can hardly survive the night.[125]

Despite the artillery's ferocity, it was often inaccurate. Private Elijah Beeman of Company A, 12th Ohio, observed his comrades' response to incoming artillery fire after a spent four-ounce grape shot struck one of them in the chest with a loud thud, "The Boys waddled like a parcel of geese when you throw stones amongst them." Private James E.D. Ward of the 12th Ohio recalled his first taste of Confederate artillery fire while awaiting orders to advance:

Suddenly there broke a flash and curling column of white smoke, succeeded immediately by the hissing sound of grapeshot overhead. The battle had been opened by the rebels. Discharges followed each other in rapid succession, with but slightly damaging effect, owing to the inaccuracy of aim. One man was shot through the body and died almost immediately; another was knocked down by a shot which struck his cartridge box, he recovered from the force of the shock before the battle terminated, and performed good service.[126]

The Confederate infantry had a tactical advantage at Scary Creek, being that their earthworks and left flank on the hillside were covered with dense timber growth limiting visibility, but initially they had not only cavalry posted as skirmishers in front of their lines but also infantry, with many of them hiding in several small wooden shacks on the north bank of Scary Creek. In Civil War tactics, the purpose of skirmishers was to confront an advancing enemy force and delay their approach while commanders tried to ascertain the enemy force's strength. Private Levi Welch of the Kanawha Riflemen was one of the skirmishers posted on the left flank, not far from the Federal artillery. He recalled:

The Riflemen were deployed as skirmishers, in advance of the other troops, in front of Hale's Battery extending up the ravine along a brush fence. I was the last file on the left. With considerable interest, not unmixed with anxiety. I saw a glittering line of steel extend through the thin woods and cover our front. I saw, I think, the first puff of powder smoke and a bullet hit the stump on which I sat. A large Beech tree was opportunely near me, and I immediately sought the protection of its trunk. As the puffs of smoke increased the beech tree seemed to wonderfully decrease in size. But for personal reasons I stuck to it.[127]

Captain William S. Williams had one of the cannons present that day, which belonged to his Ohio Independent Artillery company of the Cleveland Light Artillery. He wrote on July 31, 1861, of what he experienced going into the action:

...we drove in one of their pickets, the great body of infantry then flanked our right and left on each side of the road. The artillery was then ordered forward by Colonel Lowe. We went up the road [Teays Road] with our horses under the gallop and the first thing we noticed was a shower of grape and ball falling thick and fast, which apparently for the moment appeared to dumbfound our boys. We were in a narrow lane, and I ordered them to throw down the fence and we took our position over the fence in an open wheat field right in range of their guns, and about 300 yards distant. Their balls at first flew over us, but soon lowering them to bear on us. I came to the conclusion there was rather much buzzing about my ears and took my place by my piece and tried to keep the boys cool, which was unnecessary for they were all right. Charley Myers took my horse and the next thing I saw him doing was leading the horse around hunting some tobacco he had lost in the stubble, cannon balls and grape flying in all directions about his head-characteristic of a Dutchman! About this time Johnny Haven of Ravenna was cut nearly in half by a ball. All of their fire was directed at our guns. The first ball we fired was a little high, passing over their entrenchments and took off a colonel's head while sitting on his horse on the other side of their breastworks. It was diamond cut diamond for a time until we could see through the smoke that their guns were in a bad condition, wheels flying in all directions and in a few minutes one of their guns was knocked about 20 feet and another round dismounted and dismantled their forces entirely, not a soul about them.[128]

The incident Captain Williams mentioned in relation to a Union shell decapitating and killing a colonel was observed by Sergeant James D. Sedinger of the Border Rangers, Company E, 8th Virginia Cavalry. He recalled: "Our company took position with our artillery. Captain [James Clark] Welch was killed while sighting one of his guns." James C. Welch was neither a colonel nor captain, but rather still a 1st Lieutenant at that time and was decapitated while sighting his gun, as a Federal shell from the Ohio Independent Battery exploded on his gun.[129]

Lieutenant Welch's brother, Private Levi Welch, was nearby on the skirmish line when the Federal shell took his brother's life:

Captain Albert G. Jenkins, afterwards a Brigadier General, came up the line of skirmishers, with his hat off, and the blood streaming down his hair and neck, and called for someone to go and get his horse, tied to a stake behind Hale's battery. He did not, like King Richard, promise a kingdom for his horse, but I was thinking of the kingdom to come, and a chance to dodge it. So I left the beech tree, and ran through the brush, over the hill and mounted the horse. I rode up to the battery and saw a dismounted cannon being propped up for service by a lot of determined men. I asked one of them, "where is my brother?" "Who is your brother?" "Lieutenant Welch of this battery." "There he lies. He has done his duty." Then I looked where the soldier pointed, and saw my brother upon the ground lying where he fell with his head almost severed by a flying piece of iron from the cannon that he was aiming when it was struck and dismounted by a cannon ball. As he lay with both arms extended in the shape of a cross, he reminded me of Christ crucified. One died for all mankind, the other for his native state, with the same willingness.[130]

Brigadier General Henry Wise, commanding Confederate forces in the Kanawha Valley, heard of Welch's death later: "The enemy's artillery (rifled cannon) outfired us, doing double our execution. Welch lost his life spiking our disabled gun, thinking, poor fellow, it was to fall into the hands of the enemy, and not surviving to joy in the victory." The gunner who killed Lieutenant James Welch mentioned earlier by Captain Williams was Corporal Jerry Creighton of Gallipolis, Ohio. He wrote a letter to his friend Dr. Kuhn on July 18, 1861, in camp just a few miles from the field of battle:

You will of course, know the result of the recent battle at Scary Creek, three miles from this place before this will reach you. I was in that battle and let me tell you with all candor, it was a hot little battle. We were in range of musketry and rifle shot, and at the same time in range of the enemy's artillery. I must say in due respect to the Rebels, they have done damned good shooting…Your humble servant is gunner of one of the detachments (we had two pieces in action) and, green as he is, being only fifteen days in the service when the battle was fought, he had the good luck of knocking off a Colonel's head by his first shot. Shortly after dismounted one of the enemy's guns sending it a whirling in all directions. I have been highly complimented by my Capt. and Lieut. as being cool and collected. I believe my whole mind was on the enemy's battery, trying my best to knock it to Kingdom Come, and I feel confident having done it to one of them.[131]

After several minutes of heavy artillery fire, Colonel Lowe then gave the order for his infantry to advance; an unidentified soldier from Columbus, Ohio, in the 12th Ohio Infantry reported the following account as they moved out:

When we reached the hill where the battery was planted, the rebels opened fire upon us from two pieces of artillery. We also had two pieces, and tearing down the fences, the guns were placed in position, and our forces wheeled into line on the brow of the hill in such a manner as to bring our fire to bear upon the enemy, while we had partial protection from theirs by a fence on the top of the hill.[132]

Once they stepped off from the brow of the hill, the Federals had to march down the long slope on Simms Hill parallel with Teays Road—some 75-100 yards without cover—and occupy a large open field, with a few small bluffs and several wooden buildings being their only chances for cover. As they moved down the hill, a nearby citizen in one of the houses observed two Confederate cavalrymen trotting by and overheard one say, "There they come." He looked up and: "…saw the hillside black with Yankees. I went in the house to tell mother and the others about it. I thought we would go around the hill and watch the soldiers as they came down. But as I started out the back way, I met them coming in." Private Cameron Thompson, Company H, 1st Kanawha Regiment (later 22nd Virginia Infantry) later recalled: "Soon the lines of Blue Coats could be seen coming down the hill and deploying across the little bottom which lay between us and the Federal Artillery on the Hill. When the infantry came within range of our rifles, we opened with every gun that we had, and the Battle of Scary Creek was on, in earnest."[133]

One of the Federal artillerists observed the infantry marching down the hill and later recalled:

Private Franklin Swank,
Co. B, 21st Ohio Volunteer Infantry.
Library of Congress.

The infantry was now ordered to advance, rapid volleys of musketry followed from each side, which could be distinctly heard at the camp. [near the Pocatalico] The ten or twelve log huts composing the village of Scary Creekville, were filled with rebel infantry, the chinking having been removed so that the cracks could serve as loopholes. From these, every few moments, were seen to issue livid sheets of flame, followed by the rattle of their rifles and whistling of their Minie balls.[134]

A young private from Columbus, Ohio, serving in the 12th Ohio Infantry, recollected seeing Confederate riflemen, still hiding out in the wooden buildings along the creek bank, firing into their ranks, "We were seriously annoyed by a flanking fire from the river, and also from a large log house on the bank of the creek." Private J.H. Collins of Company H, 12th Ohio also described what he saw during the nerve-wracking descent down the hillside along Teays Valley Road into the battle:

No sooner had we emerged from the woods which lined both sides of the road (Teays Valley) than the pop, pop, pop, warned us that we were in the vicinity of the enemy. Companies H and K of the 12th were deployed to the right and passed down the hill in rear of an old church. Companies A and B of the 21st [Ohio] and D of the 12th deployed to the left, passing in rear of the Simms house, over a steep bluff to the river road and were soon engaged. The balance of the 12th Regt. marched down the (Teays Valley) road with arms at shoulder, through a withering fire from the Confederates.[135]

Private Cameron Thompson, Company H, 1st Kanawha Regiment observed:

The loud-mouthed cannon, bursting shells, crashing small arms, and shouting Captains made a royal tumult which tested the nerves of the raw recruits from the field and from the shop; but they stood their ground like veterans, and gave shot for shot. The superiority of the enemy's artillery was quickly shown, for our guns were cut down by their fire. Lieutenant Jim [James Clark] Welch was killed, and our battery silenced. This was a serious loss to us for the full force of the Federal Artillery now concentrated upon our infantry and the shells came in fast and furious....[136]

With Confederates taking potshots at the advancing Union infantry from the several wooden houses near the riverbank, the Federal artillery quickly focused their fire on them; most were soon shattered into splinters during the barrage. A member of the 12th Ohio further described the initial Federal infantry's attack:

"The whole column was then ordered to advance. Quick volleys of musketry followed from both sides, but with little effect. It was now discovered that all the houses of the village were filled with riflemen, the cracks, from which the chinking had been removed, serving as loop-holes. From these livid sheets of flame would issue every few moments, while the woods above seemed all ablaze. Capt. Cotton [Cotter] observing to what use the houses had been put, turned his artillery upon them, hitting one at almost every shot, and knocking it into ruins. As his percussion shells would strike and explode, logs, guns and the mangled bodies of men would be seen flying in all directions."[137]

A soldier in the Cleveland Light Artillery further observed the devastating effect of his battery's work, "The manner in which the logs, guns and limbs of men were scattered about, as his percussion shells would strike, must have been anything but encouraging to the rebels." Despite the Union artillery blasting away at the series of wooden structures, a few stubborn Confederates continued to fire from the remaining buildings. A private in the 12th Ohio described how his regiment eventually rid themselves of their hidden and stubborn tormentors:

Detachments of two companies of the 21st and two companies from the 12th charged the house and routed the rebels at the point of the bayonet. They retreated across the creek, covered by the fire of their own men, - fording it, as they had previously burnt the bridges. In the meantime, our artillery had silenced their battery, entirely destroying the carriage of one piece, and our boys twice silenced the fire of their infantry.[138]

1st Sergeant John Hiltz, Company C, 12th Ohio Volunteer Infantry, witnessed the Confederate skirmish lines faltering about an hour after the fighting started:

A heavy discharge of musketry was at once opened on our boys, but firmly returned; the skirmishers began to play Zouave on the enemy by lying down and firing. The field here had been admirably contested on both sides. All agree that the Virginians fought with desperate courage and resolution, but their artillery proved ineffective. Our noble artillerists (a company from Cleveland) proved to be too good a shot for them, knocking their battery in less than half an hour all to smash, besides, killing most of their cannoneers; those remaining retired hastily with their broken pieces. Their evident purpose was to make a stand there and risk the fortunes of Charleston upon the hazards of the day. We promptly accepted their challenge and though they had occupied all the few buildings, a church, a schoolhouse, cooper shop, and a couple of log houses, a frame building down in the bottoms, besides the many ravines, of which they disputed every inch, and fought here with the utmost desperation, yet a few of our ten-pound balls soon brought them out. The house down in the bottoms served as their magazine and was most desperately defended as they fired from the house through loopholes, but a sure shot from our artillery nearly upset the house, scattering the Rebels like chaff. When they found it impossible to hold their ground any longer, they fell back, until they reached the big hill at the foot of the road which leads to Charleston, and at which place they had their battery planted.[139]

Private James A. Gorsuch, Co. I, 12th Ohio Infantry, also described this phase of the action:

Companies I and Co. G were on the left flank on the bank of the river in the hottest part of the contest. The secessionists had fortified some log houses along the bank of the river from which they were firing, and we were ordered to rout them out. We charged upon them and they ran like sheep. We fired so often that our old muskets got so hot that mine burnt my hands and so dirty that I had to pound down the cartridges with a club.[140]

1st Lieutenant John H. Bolton,
Co. F, 21st Ohio Volunteer Infantry.
Bolton held the rank of Sergeant at Scary Creek.
Courtesy Terry Lowry.

By 1:30 p.m., Federal infantry had managed to push most of the Confederate skirmishers out of the wooden buildings and back into their earthworks, and the Union artillery continued to pound the Confederate lines. From this stalwart position, they decimated the Union infantry attempting to advance on them, marching in linear formations through an open field, unprotected for the most part, other than a few small swales dotting the field.[141]

Despite several attempts to cross the creek, by mid-afternoon the Federal infantry had accomplished little. This was not only because of general inexperienced green troops; it was also partly due to most of the Buckeye troops carrying outdated .69 caliber smoothbore muskets with an effective range of about 100-200 yards, at best, in an open field. While the Confederates carried similar weapons, some even using old squirrel rifles and shotguns, they were also behind earthworks. Not to say their lack of discipline wasn't a factor, though there is at least one instance when it seemed pay off; a private in the 12th Ohio had been particularly obstinate during their training weeks earlier and despised the daily camp ritual of drilling for hours. He devised a clever means to avoid such work, if only for a few minutes, by repeatedly falling on his stomach and blaming his toes for being so clumsy. When his company got their first taste of Confederate fire, the entire unit instinctively fell on their faces, except he somehow remained standing. Gloating, the lazy private looked them over and quipped: "There, that's what comes of all your drilling. Every man's killed deader'n a hammer, and I'm the only one left to tell the tale."[142]

As the battle pitched, Lowe struggled to maneuver his infantry around the field, firing volley after volley, vainly hoping to find a way to cross the creek and breech the Confederate lines. Captain William S. Williams of the Cleveland Light Artillery further recalled this phase of the action:

A number of sharp shooters were stationed under cover of the woods attempting to pick us off at our guns but did not succeed although there was more than one of the boy's caps knocked off. We then moved our pieces over by a house and fired into some old log houses under the hill that were full of Secesh, and who were pouring a destructive fire into Colonel Norton's little band. We bored them and they came out like bees, while the colonel at the head of his men was disputing the ground at the point of bayonet…many a brave fellow was attempting to drag himself away from this point, although men were biting the dust in all directions, yet victory seemed to be ours for the enemy was retreating and where the Secesh battery had been we saw through the smoke the old stars and stripes were waving.

Our artillery boys set up and [gave an] unearthly yell, but before they were through cheering we had a dose of grape from the flag in question. When the smoke cleared away, much to our dismay, we discovered it had but three stripes. I told my gunner Jerry B. Creighton to fetch it down and the next moment the color bearer was seen dangling ten feet in the air…when that flag was replanted on their entrenchments, they had received large reinforcements from Coal Creek [Coal Mountain] along with a field piece which accounted for the grape. We silenced their remaining gun again, but our ammunition was fast giving out and our guns were so hot we could scarcely work them and so with the infantry, those that did not fight had not more ammunition (there was part of the 12th Ohio that had done but little) and our boys were almost exhausted.

When we fired our last ammunition, our boys dipped down by the guns covered black with smoke and powder and lay there panting with fatigue asking for water. All our boys did nobly, not one flinched. We lay there expecting reinforcements from camp; General Cox had about 4,000 men there but none came. The cavalry made one charge, shot off three of their guns, and then stayed behind the church until the battle was over. Thus, out of ammunition and a few men against all of southeastern Virginia, as we have since learned, we had all but one thing to do and that was retreat.[143]

At about 3:00 p.m., Union ammunition was running out. Colonel Lowe ordered Lieutenant Colonel Carr B. White, a former physician and Mexican War veteran, to take Companies D and K of the 12th Ohio and assist Colonel Jesse Norton, whose Companies B and D of the 21st Ohio were still on the Union extreme left fighting in and around the small wooden shacks located along the creek bank, and mount a final bayonet charge on the Confederate position across the creek. At the same time, he had ordered Major Jonathan D. Hines to take four companies of the 12th Ohio across the Teays Road to a point well below the Simms family cemetery on the ridge, crossing the creek and ambushing the Confederates in a surprise attack on their left flank. As usual in warfare, however, things rarely go as planned; an unidentified 12th Ohio correspondent recalled:

The ammunition of our troops was now getting low, and a charge was ordered to be made upon the enemy. The left, composed of the fragment of the Twenty-first, and one or two companies of the Twelfth, under Lieut.-Col. [Carr] White, promptly obeyed, and, dashing down the hill, forded the stream, and in a few minutes were upon the enemy's ground. The right, however, who were exposed to a galling fire from the woods on the opposite hillside, after proceeding a short distance, faltered, and then fell back in great confusion. Had they been as vigorous as the left, the day would have soon been won. But they were badly officered and disciplined and could not stand the sight of their falling comrades. The left, though they had fought like veterans, could not hold their position alone, and were reluctantly compelled to fall back.[144]

Major Hines took his four companies of the 12th Ohio and attempted to flank the Confederate left as ordered, but his movement was hindered by one of the captains in charge of a company who was hiding behind a corn crib with some of his men and refused to move. Adding insult to injury, Hines and his men had trouble locating a suitable place to cross Scary Creek and were said to have become entangled in the dense, heavy underbrush that covered the hillside on the Confederate left. Only Captain Edward M. Carey's Company H managed to cross the creek under the heavy Confederate fire. Carey quickly realized it was useless to continue, however, and fell back across the creek. Meanwhile, Colonel Norton's two companies of the 21st Ohio made several unsuccessful attempts to cross the bridge on the Union left flank, with one in particular having a brutal ending as the Confederates simply held their fire until most of the Federals had crossed the creek—and gotten close to the earthworks—then unleased a furious volley killing and wounded many, forcing Norton back across the bridge. At some point during or after this melee, Confederates also set the bridge on fire.[145]

1st Sergeant John Hiltz, Company C, 12th Ohio Volunteer Infantry, further described Major Hine's assault on the Confederate left:

Lt. Col. Jesse Norton,
21st Ohio Volunteer Infantry.
*History of the 21st Regiment Ohio
Volunteer Infantry.*

"The final attack was then directed upon the hill, which was so steep that persons unencumbered by anything had the greatest difficulty in climbing it, so you may imagine what it was for our boys with their haversacks, canteens, and blankets. Add to this difficulty a rather scorching July sun, and a dense mass of the enemy ahead of them. At this juncture of the game, our boys discovered that they were nearly out of ammunition, besides the approach of the enemy's reinforcements. Having observed that most of our men on the other side of the battlefield had left, the command was given to retreat. Our gallant boys retired slowly and steadily towards the outlet from the woods. The enemy's reinforcement did not pursue them, the same being well covered, as our two rifled cannons had meanwhile been planted on the side of the outlet and in excellent range of the enemy… Of Company C, none were hurt but myself, receiving a shot on the top of my head, knocking me senseless to the ground. The wound is slight."[146]

Once he received Colonel Lowe's orders, Lieutenant Colonel White rapidly moved Companies D and K of the 12th Ohio across a small wheat field and rushed forward; a Buckeye soldier described how they went, "…rushing down the hill forded the stream, which was more than knee deep, and rushed upon the enemy's entrenchments." White's men faced a furious fire as they determinedly waded the creek, and once they mounted the earthworks, several minutes of vicious hand-to-hand combat ensued with men from the 3rd Kanawha Infantry Regiment under Major James F. Sweeney, who was later rebuked by a Charleston resident in the *Daily Intelligencer* for his untoward behavior while garrisoning Charleston before the battle. A resident familiar with Sweeney quipped: "Our fellow-townsman, Mr. James Sweeney, of Nicaraguan notoriety, has been cutting quite a swell in his way about Charleston. He was gloriously drunk most

Lt. Col. Carr B. White,
12th Ohio Volunteer Infantry.
Courtesy Terry Lowry.

Major James F. Sweeney,
3rd Kanawha Infantry.
Courtesy Paul Burig.

Albert Gallatin Jenkins.
Library of Congress.

of the time he was there; and is considered small potatoes. His company has all but left him." The Federals could not gain the advantage, and no reinforcements were on hand to assist them. According to one Ohio soldier, "The left could not hold their position alone, although they did all that could be expected of veterans, and as they only had a few rounds of ammunition, they fell back on the right bank of the stream."[147]

Despite the Federals being unable to gain an advantage, when Patton's men realized Union soldiers had breached their lines, most perceived the battle was turning against them, and panic spread through the ranks. About three-fourths of the Confederates not already engaged abandoned their positions and fled toward Coalsmouth. Patton quickly dashed toward them on horseback trying to rally the skedaddling troops. En route, however, his horse became stubborn and halted, confusing many of the fleeing soldiers who kept running, but Patton was able to stop most of them. At this point, Patton was severely wounded in the left shoulder. Command then fell upon Captain Albert Gallatin Jenkins of the 8th Virginia Cavalry, who later became a brigadier general in command of a large battalion of cavalry in western Virginia. He would be mortally wounded at the battle of Cloyd's Mountain on May 9, 1864. Patton soon recovered and later commanded the 22nd Virginia Infantry until the third battle of Winchester on September 19, 1864, when he also fell mortally wounded.[148]

Earlier in April 1861, Sergeant J.D. Sedinger had written in his diary that the Border Rangers had went into camp at Coalsmouth with 101 men in April 1861 and had to cook their own meals for the first time. Having not yet been issued muskets, he and several other men cut large pieces of pipe to carry as weapons. Poor weapons did not hinder the troopers' confidence, though, as Sedinger wrote, "We drilled cavalry drill and thought we could whip the world." Despite their self-confidence, he neglected to mention the reason Patton had to rally his men for a charge was because many Confederates had panicked thinking the "Yankees" had gained the tactical advantage.[149]

The Confederate retreat did not last long, however, as reinforcements soon appeared from Coal Mountain. Private Cameron Thompson, Company H, 1st Kanawha Regiment witnessed the events next transpiring:

The fight was kept up without much change in the lines until late in the afternoon, when the Federals could be seen forming for a charge to carry the bridge which spanned the creek near its mouth. While the Federal Commander was pressing this assault for the capture of the bridge, Captain Corns, [James M.] with his Sandy Rangers – dressed in red shirts – and Captain Thompson, with the militia, reached the field from Coal Mountain, and brought with them a piece of artillery. The Sandy Rangers went into action, singing a ballad called "Bullets and Steel"; and their song could be heard above the roar of the battle. Our new gun opened with telling effect.[150]

Sergeant James Sedinger of the Border Rangers, Company E, 8th Virginia Cavalry, similarly recalled the Sandy Rangers' arrival:

About this time the right flank was turned, and the Yanks were firing at us from front, flank and rear. Captain Patton ordered the Kanawha Rifles to follow him in a charge and he fell badly wounded. We now received some fresh troops from Coal Mountain who charged the flanking party and drove them back. The charge was successful in turning the flank of the enemy who now broke leaving their Lieut. Col. Neff [Norton] on the field and 18 men killed who we buried the next day.[151]

The reinforcements Sedinger mentioned was a cavalry company known as the Sandy Rangers from Wayne County. Led by Captain James M. Corns, they also brought along Captain B.S. Thompson's Kanawha Militia company and Lieutenant Thomas E. Jackson's artillery piece locally known as "The Peacemaker." They were earlier posted on Coal Mountain guarding the James River and Kanawha Turnpike to prevent a rear attack on the Confederates, and when Patton sent word to Captain Corns to come to Scary Creek at once, they arrived just in time to avert the Federal flanking attempt led by Colonel Norton's Companies B and F of the 21st Ohio and the companies under Lieutenant Colonel Carr White of the 12th Ohio.[152]

The Sandy Rangers rushed onto the field wearing bright red flannel hunting shirts that had earned them the nickname "Blood Tubs." At least one Federal narrative contradicts the accounts of the Sandy Rangers singing "Bullets and Steel," as a Union artillerist thought the reinforcements "…came up with three cheers for Jeff Davis and went to work with a fresh piece of artillery and Minié Muskets." On the other hand, the same source also noted one of the captured prisoners told him the balladeers were from Georgia, and there were no such units present at Scary Creek. 1st Lieutenant J.M. Ferguson of the Sandy Rangers recalled their infamous charge:

…we reached Scary Creek in time to save the day, as the enemy had silenced our artillery, killing Lieutenant Welch. But by our arrival with another gun it took the enemy by surprise, and they retreated by the Hill Road and not by the River Road over which they had come…We then set fire to a cooper shop, which gave quite a light; and the Federals at Poca, seeing the light, supposed they had gained the day, (this signal had been agreed upon if they were victorious)….[153]

A private in the 12th Ohio further described the final Federal assault when Confederate reinforcements arrived:

At this juncture they received reinforcements (their force was nearer 1,500 than 700 at the outset), and our boys had completely exhausted their ammunition. They therefore commenced a retreat, in good order, so soon as they had got beyond the range of the rebels single re-mounted piece, reserving their last single shot in the cannon for any emergency, should the enemy attempt a pursuit…the boys were then so exhausted, having fought for three hours, and exhausted every round in their cartridge boxes, that the attempt was given over.[154]

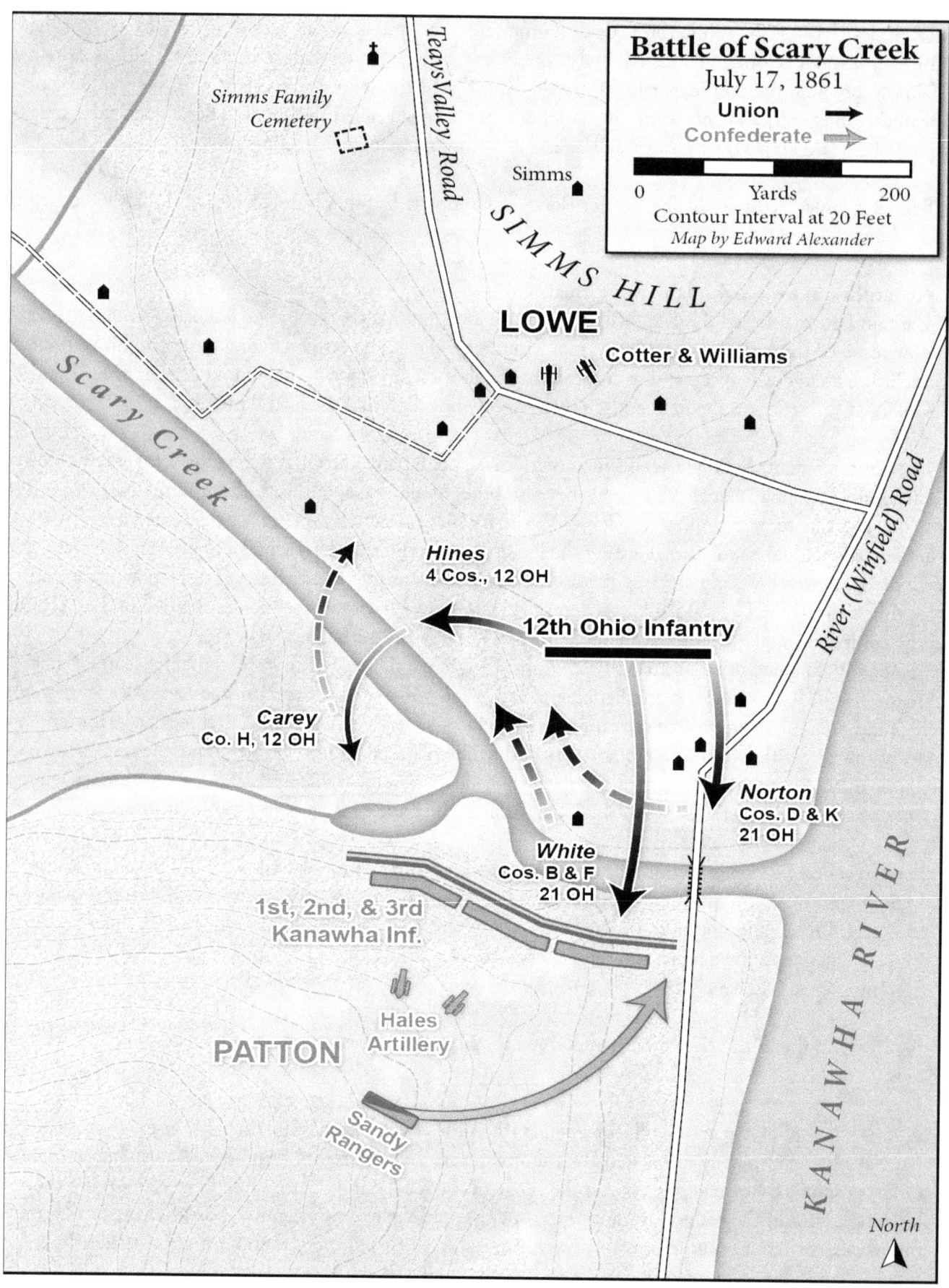

Simms Family
Cemetery

Teays Valley Road

Battle of Scary Creek
July 17, 1861
Union
Confederate

0   Yards   200
Contour Interval at 20 Feet
Map by Edward Alexander

Simms

SIMMS HILL

LOWE

Cotter & Williams

Scary Creek

Hines
4 Cos., 12 OH

12th Ohio Infantry

River (Winfield) Road

Carey
Co. H, 12 OH

Norton
**Cos. D & K
21 OH**

White
**Cos. B & F
21 OH**

**1st, 2nd, & 3rd
Kanawha Inf.**

KANAWHA RIVER

Hales
Artillery

PATTON

Sandy
Rangers

North

Sketch of Scary Creek Battlefield by an unidentified resident.
West Virginia State Archives.

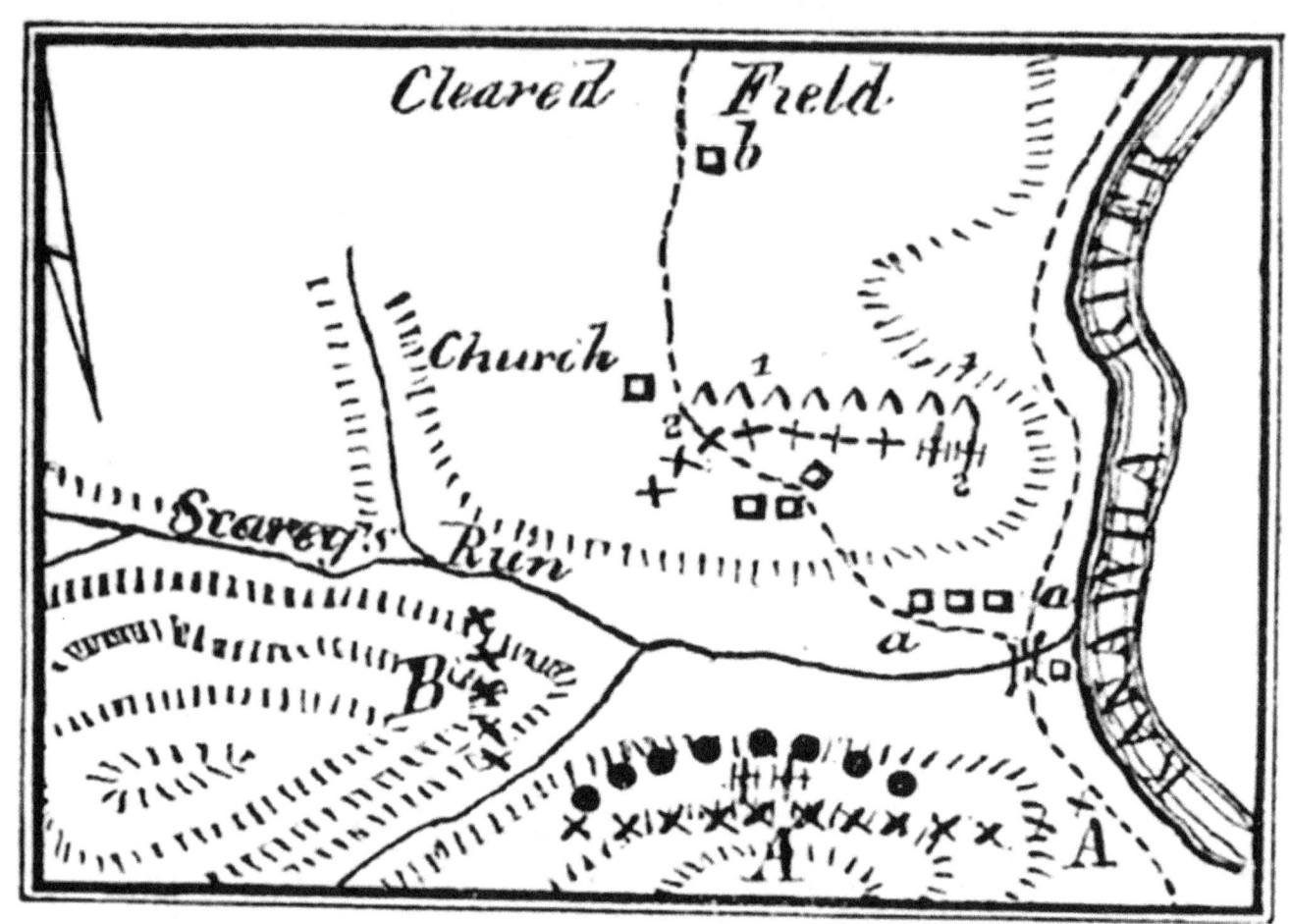

A A.—Rebel line of infantry, two guns and rifle pits.

1 1.—Col. Lowe's first position with the guns.

2 2.—Col. Lowe's second position with the guns.

a a.—Houses, mill and bridge captured by Col. Norton.

b.—Barn where the Rebel pickets were met.

B.—Major Hinds' position.

Map of Scary Creek battlefield by Brigadier General Charles Whittlesey.
Courtesy Terry Lowry.
Scale: 200 yards per inch.

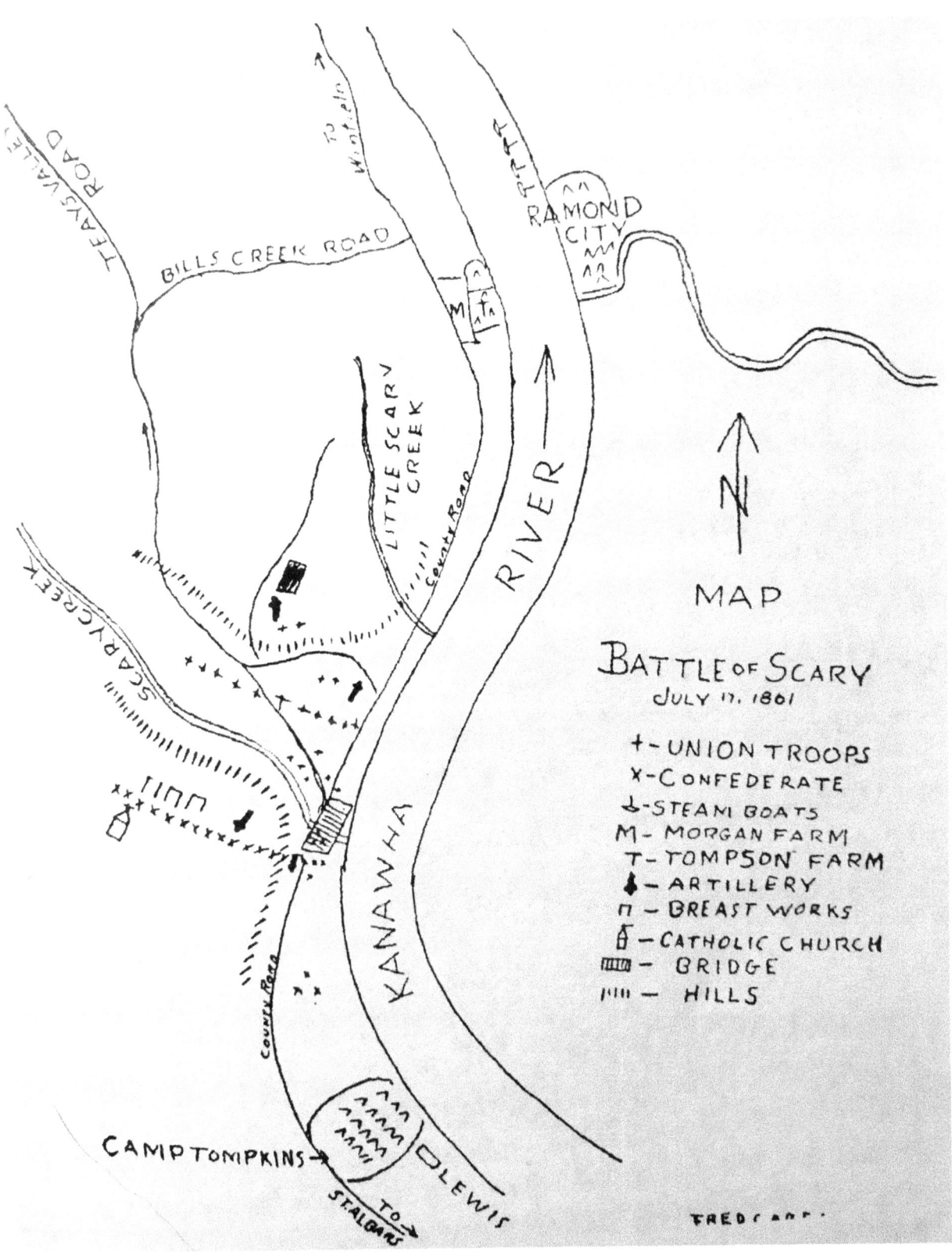

Post war sketch map of Scary Creek battlefield by Fred Conner.
Courtesy St. Albans Historical Society.

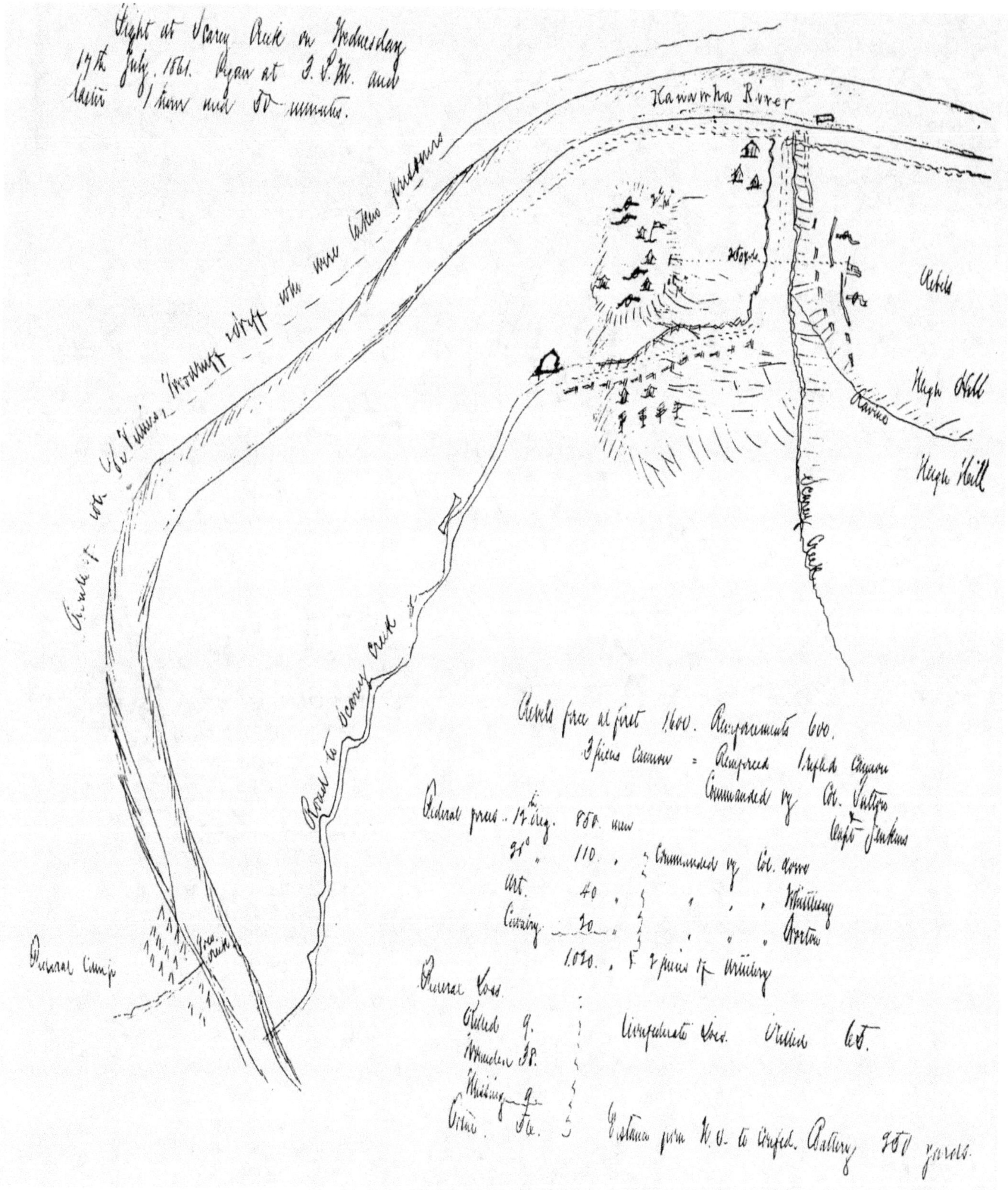

Map of Scary Creek by Thomas Lowe, son of Colonel John W. Lowe.
West Virginia State Archives.

Edward Settle Godfrey. Enlisted in Co. D, 21st Ohio Volunteer Militia on April 12, 1861, and was present at Scary Creek. Godfrey entered West Point in 1863. He served under Major General George C. Custer at the Battle of Little Big Horn on June 25, 1876, and later received the Medal of Honor for leading Company K, Frederick's Battalion, 7th U.S. Cavalry while wounded at the Battle of Snake Creek in Montana on September 30, 1877. Godfrey also served in the Spanish-American War in Cuba and fought during the Philippines Insurrection 1901-1903. He obtained the rank of Brigadier General in 1907 and retired later that year.
Public Domain.

Bridge at Scary Creek, circa 1960s, said to have been roughly in the same location as the one during the battle.
Courtesy Terry Lowry.

Another Buckeye soldier also observed Colonel Norton's bayonet charge near the bridge at the moment when Confederates reinforcements arrived:

About this time, the fight having lasted nearly two hours, the rebels were reinforced by a regiment, armed with Minie rifles, and accompanied by one piece of artillery, which immediately opened upon our battery. Capt. [Williams], who had but seven rounds of ammunition left, returned the fire to that extent, and then drew off his command.[155]

One of the main problems faced by troops on both sides during the early months of the Civil War was a lack of consistent supplies and uniforms. While a detailed study of quartermaster logistics is beyond the scope of this work, suffice it to say that very few units on either side wore matching uniforms early in the war. Ohio faced a cloth shortage early in the war, causing a great deal of variance in their troops deployed to western Virginia. The Confederates had not yet established a supply depot system in July 1861, and Confederate companies at Scary Creek wore a mix of military coats and civilian garb. A good example, aside from the Sandy Rangers wearing red flannel hunting shirts, is the 12th Ohio were wearing the "Undress Uniform" consisting of a regulation black felt "Hardee" hat, regulation dark blue wool blouses or gray hunting shirts, with gray satinet trousers that tended to wear out very quickly.[156]

This caused significant problems discerning the enemy on the battlefield, as evident in the following account, written by a private in the 1st Kanawha Rifles:

About this time a lot of our men rushed in on our left with blue trimmings on their uniforms, one of them fired at me and I yelled to my next file on the right, that we were being outflanked by the Yankees. My gun, at this time, was unloaded. He turned and taking the same view of the situation that I did, with a sudden aim, he shot [one] of the supposed Yankees through and through. I do not remember how the mistake was rectified, but it was before the poor boy died. The artillery of the enemy for some time had been making the most noise, but suddenly we heard a new sound. It came from the "Peacemaker" (a gun cast by Mr. Job Thayer at his foundry in Maiden) the new sound was caused by the miscellaneous missiles it blew at the houses across the creek, behind which the enemy were fighting. Trace chains, mashed horse shoes and other kinds of scrap iron made the boards and shingles fly - - and the Yankees also.[157]

Another Confederate wounded in Norton's flank attack was Captain Andrew Barbee of the Border Rifles. He received a gunshot wound severing the ulnar nerve and breaking the bone.[158]

When Colonel Norton ultimately removed his men to a point up the creek in front of Simms Hill near the Federal artillery, he was severely wounded in the hip and chose to remain on the field, thinking that more Federal troops would arrive to carry the battle. He was captured along with one of his lieutenants. Reinforcements did not arrive, and the day was lost for the Union; Captain Silas S. Canfield of the 21st Ohio later succinctly described the failed final assault, "In the charge which ensued the Union troops were repulsed."[159]

Once Norton's Federals had retreated to a position atop the hill beside Teays [Valley] Road under cover of fire provided by the 12th Ohio, Colonel Lowe reformed their ranks into an orderly column and once more marched over Bill's Creek Road toward the farm of John Morgan, located next to the landing where they originally crossed the Kanawha River. The battle thus ended around 6 p.m., with the Confederates claiming their first victory in the Kanawha Valley. Federals later sent a flag of truce afterward requesting the privilege to gather their dead and recover wounded. A small wooden church on the battlefield was hastily converted into a field hospital, and many Federal wounded were taken inside. Private James H. Mays of the 1st Kanawha Infantry, later Company F, 22nd Virginia Infantry, was out on burial detail that evening and counted fourteen dead Federals. They "dragged" them together and dug a pit six-by-twenty feet, put straw in the bottom, laid the bodies side by side and buried them, noting it was "the best we could do under the circumstances." Mays recalled finding one of the officer's caps with the name "Capt Allen" written inside and left it with the body of Captain Charles W. Allen of Company D, 21st Ohio, who was killed instantly during the final Federal assault when struck by "a ball in the forehead, right between the eyes."[160]

Private William F. Bower,
Co. D, 21st Ohio Volunteer Militia.
Library of Congress.

Federal Officers Captured

Around dusk that evening, a small group of Federal officers, all green volunteers, foolishly decided to leave their camp at Pocatalico without permission, hoping to view the battlefield in the aftermath of the fighting. Moving along the north riverbank, they encountered a local slave who told them the Confederates had retreated and then persuaded him to ferry them across the Kanawha River in a small boat. They landed at a spot near where the Federal infantry position had been earlier that day. This lofty band, Colonel William Woodruff and Lieutenant Colonel Neff of the 2nd Kentucky Infantry, and Colonel De Villiers of the 11th Ohio Volunteer Militia, soon encountered what they thought were Union pickets; it turned out they were Confederates, who quickly took them prisoner. They were taken to Libby Prison in Richmond, Virginia. Private Levi Welch of the Kanawha Riflemen was one of the Confederates detailed that evening with burning several local buildings to prevent the Federals from using them, when the small band of Federal officers approached his squad. Welch recalled:

Colonel William Woodruff,
2nd Kentucky Infantry.
Courtesy Emma Vickers-Byrd.

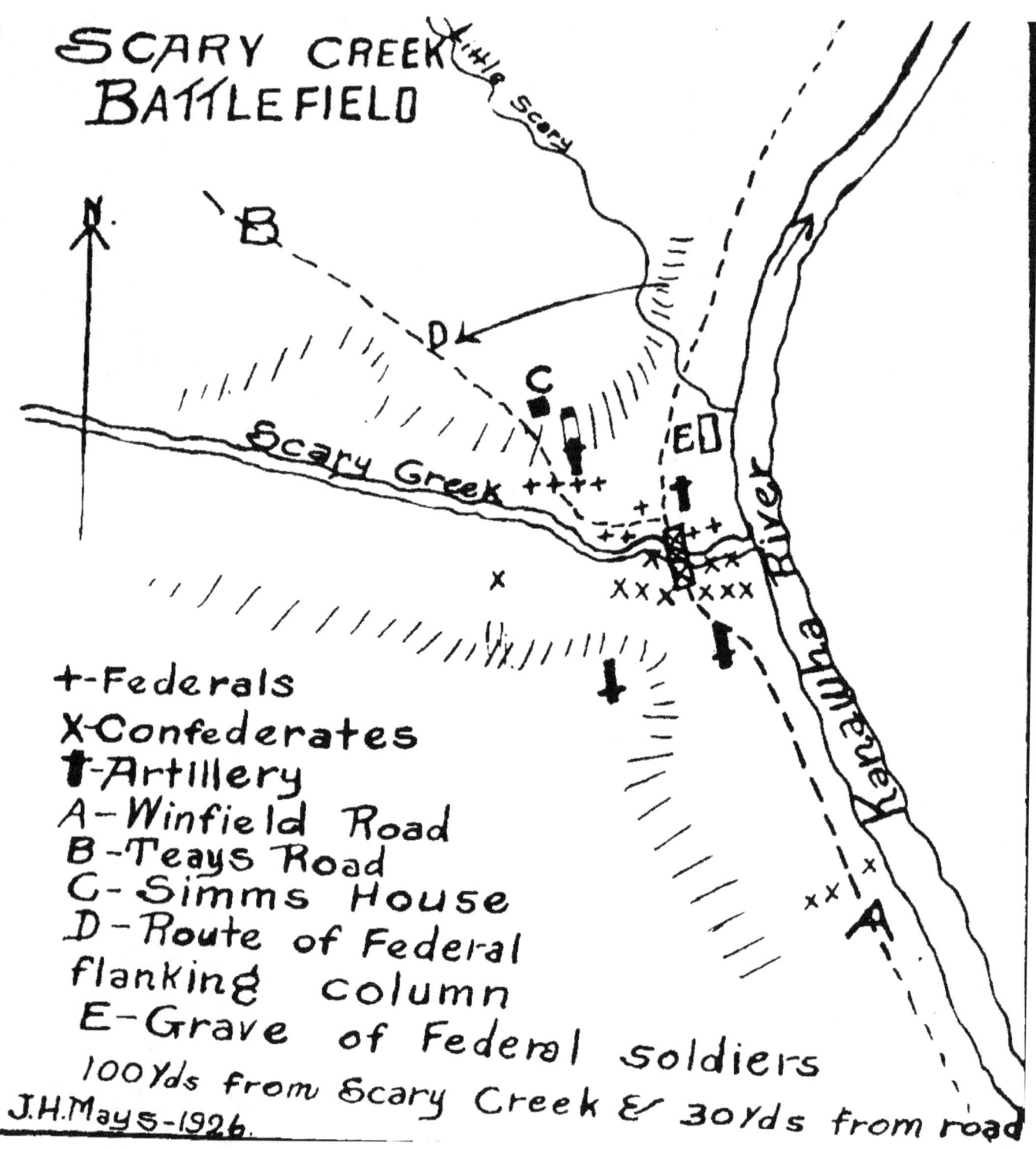

Map of Scary Creek battlefield showing location of Union graves by Confederate veteran James H. Mays in 1926.
Mays was a private in Company F, 1st Kanawha Infantry (22nd Virginia Infantry) during the battle.
Courtesy Terry Lowry.

The order passed to the skirmishers to rally on the center which we did, and Lieutenant Nicholas Fitzhugh led us across the creek, and while we were burning some buildings to prevent their giving shelter again to the enemy, in case they should return, a lot of Federal officers rode up, supposing that we belonged to their army, on account of our incendiary occupation. One of them asked us where the damned rebels were. We closed in around the lot and gave them the information they sought. They were Cols. De Villiers. Col. Neff and others. They consented after some parley to visit Richmond. I then got permission from Lieutenant Fitzhugh to go across the hills to the Upper Falls of Coal River, where my mother was at that time, and tell her the sad tidings of the death of her son. Here ended my first lesson in the catechism that followed.[161]

Aftermath of Scary Creek

As the old maxim of war goes, it was all over but the blame; newspapers created superfluous casualty counts and blew the matter out of proportion. General Cox was later accused of incompetence by several officers for failing to send reinforcements, but it was determined he had been prematurely misinformed by an aide of a Federal victory, causing him not to send more troops. Despite this, he admitted that he still should have sent reinforcements. As such, the 21st Ohio had arrived near the field around the time Colonel Norton was wounded, but because Colonel Lowe had ordered a general retreat, nothing more could be done.[162]

The enlisted men and company officers were furious with the loss of their first engagement, and one frustrated Ohioan who witnessed Lieutenant Colonel Lowe's and Colonel Norton's final assaults attributed the failure on poor leadership and lack of discipline among their comrades on the right wing, who were supposed to have made a simultaneous assault, but failed to do so. He opined the following:

Had the movement on the right been equally prompt, the rebels would have been utterly routed, but owing partly to the incompetency of their officers, and partly to the fact that they were badly disciplined, they faltered. The left could not hold their position alone, although they did all that could have been expected of veterans, and as they only had a few rounds of ammunition, they fell back on the right bank of the stream.[163]

Captain William S. Williams, Independent Battery, Ohio Volunteer Artillery, was thoroughly groused as well, also placing blame on General Cox for not sending reinforcements:

Colonel Lowe was in the rear behind the hill. There we went into things under Lowe's directions, pell-mell, and our retreat of course was about the same thing. Lieutenant Colonel Neibling of the 21st Ohio and several others sent to General Cox and pleaded and begged him to let them take men to our rescue, as they knew well from our firing that we were fighting a much superior force…Well, we retreated, the artillery leaving the field last…The fight lasted about two hours and forty minutes. After we got to camp, we found another regiment coming to our relief, but it was too late. The amount killed on the enemy's side is unknown, nor never will be. Our dead were all left on the field, but a great many of our wounded we brought away with us…The amount of wounded I can't tell, suffice to say the cabins of three steamboats are laying full. We'll give them another turn there in a few days again.[164]

Captain Williams' subordinate, Corporal Jeroboam "Jerry" B. Creighton, a gunner in the Independent Ohio Artillery Battery, was similarly disgruntled, but he blamed the Union loss on General Cox, as well as what he deemed incompetent infantry officers:

We stood a good two hours fighting, and had our ammunition not given out, we would have driven the devils off the field. We are under obligations to Mother Cox, our general, for this inhuman defeat. We were about 1,000 strong with two six-pounder rifle cannon…Had Cox given all the available force under his command, instead of keeping the greater part of it within three miles of the battlefield for his protection, we would have gained a glorious victory. I believe every man in his command is down on him for mismanagement, cowardice, & c. We had 13 killed and 36 wounded, and as far as we can ascertain the enemy has buried 65 of their dead, and the number of their wounded we cannot ascertain at this time…We were only four hundred yards from the enemy's battery, from the commencement of the fight, and closed on them several times during the engagement. Had the infantry officers done their duty after we had silenced the enemy's battery, we would have routed them from the field.[165]

When word got back to Major General George B. McClellan, the overall Union commander in western Virginia, of the Union loss at Scary Creek and the several high-ranking officers who were captured, he was furious with the bumbling, inexperienced officers. He complained to the War Department, refusing to admit the loss:

Cox checked on the Kanawha. Has fought something between a victory and a defeat. A wounded colonel of ours taken prisoner, and a possibility of having lost two colonels and a lieutenant-colonel, who amused themselves by a reconnaissance beyond the pickets…In Heaven's name give me some general officers who understand their profession. I give orders and find some who cannot execute them unless I stand by them. Unless I command every picket and lead every column I cannot be sure of success… Had my orders been executed from beginning, our success would have been brief and final.[166]

Union civilians nearby were also uneasy regarding the loss and captured officers. Sarah Young had earlier indicated in her diary that she "felt afraid the Federals would be whipped," and when news came of the battle results, she noted rumor had it that: "three Rebels were killed and eight Federals. Colonel Norton, with several others, was captured by the Rebels. May they escape soon and join their regiments." Her casualty statistics are significantly different than those reported in the official records, as General Cox stated his losses were fourteen killed, thirty wounded, and several missing. Confederate Commander Brigadier General Henry Wise reported his losses as between one to five killed and six wounded. On the other hand, both Cox and Wise were prone to underrepresent their battle casualties to bring a more favorable reflection upon themselves. The Confederates later withdrew about a mile and a half south toward the area of Camp Tomkins near Coalsmouth, ending the immediate action at Scary Creek. The citizens could now begin the arduous task of trying to piece their lives back together and sorting out what was left of their homes.[167]

The Devil at Scary Creek

There is also another legend associated with the battle of Scary Creek; local lore later emerged claiming that William Anderson "Devil Anse" Hatfield, the famous feudist, was present with the Sandy Rangers in their charge that ended the battle. This is likely apocryphal, as military records from the Sandy Rangers failed to show he was part of that unit; rather, other evidence strongly indicates he was with the 129th Regiment Virginia Militia of Logan County at that time, who were not present. It is noted, however, that prior to mustering into the 8th Virginia Cavalry, the Sandy Rangers were briefly attached to the 36th Virginia Infantry; this connection may also be the basis of various accounts claiming Devil Anse was in the Logan Wildcats, who were Company

D of that regiment. William S. "Rebel Bill" Smith was the antebellum neighbor of Colonel Milton J. Ferguson of Wayne County and was also present at Scary Creek—Hatfield was friends with each. However, these relationships are insufficient to corroborate Devil Anse's presence there.[168]

Even though the battle had ended, civilians in the Scary Creek vicinity were in shock, and many were still terrified of troops on both sides. The Civil War would leave indelible scars in Putnam County, and a deep sense of mistrust and suspicion existed among residents. Rumors were rampant following the first battle in the area, and both sides seemed to accuse the other of untold atrocities, whether factual or not, as shown in a later account of a Union picket's interaction with some locals on July 22, 1861:

Devil Anse Hatfield.
Associated Press.
(Original in author's collection)

Last Saturday a Sergeant of our picket guard, while going his rounds, discovered smoke issuing from a clump of woods at some distance. A nearer approach to it revealed a house, which had previously escaped the observation of our men, and which the Sergeant entered. Here he found two men, three or four women, and a number of children. They all seemed badly frightened at his approach, the men saying they had sought shelter in the house, because it was secluded, to escape impressment into the rebel ranks, and also to avoid molestation from the Union troops, of whom they had heard the most terrible stories. The Secessionists they said had told them that the National troops were all cut-throats and marauders, and would pillage their country and dishonor their women wherever they went. How industriously the rebel leaders have circulated this story! The Sergeant assured them that they had nothing to fear from the Northern troops, who came to protect and not to destroy. At this they seemed greatly relieved, and offered him anything in the premises; but he thanked them kindly, telling them that our men were well taken care of by the Government, and wanted for nothing.[169]

Confederates Retreat from the Kanawha Valley

General Wise ordered a general withdrawal of Confederate forces from the Kanawha Valley on July 20, 1861. Before leaving, he ordered the covered bridge spanning the Coal River at Coalsmouth burned. The bridge was located near modern Main Street in St. Albans, West Virginia, near the Chilton House. Wise intended to impede the Federals' advance into the area, but it made little difference because there were shallow shoals near the bridge and the river's water level was quite low. It did have an adverse effect on the inhabitants of Coalsmouth, however, who had been using the bridge to transport livestock and farm goods back and forth for decades. The Confederates also sank several coal barges that were in the lock near the bridge, which caused the river channel to remain blocked throughout the war.[170]

Approximately seven hundred Confederate soldiers stationed at Camp Coalsmouth boarded the Confederate steamer *Julia Moffat* late the next day, which was waiting on them on the Kanawha River, and evacuated the area. Shortly after they left, the U.S steamer *Economy* was following them up the river, and as they reached the Cross Lanes area near Tyler Shoals, they began to receive cannon fire from the *Economy*, which had a gun posted on the forward deck, and from Federal artillery posted on the hillside above the river. The *Julia Moffat* tried to evade the Federals but was run aground near the mouth of Davis Creek on the Spring Hill side of the Kanawha River. The Confederates abandoned ship, leaving large quantities of their equipage and stores; as they left, the crew set the *Julia Moffat* on fire, and they continued their retreat toward Charleston.[171]

As Confederates left the Kanawha Valley, General Wise also ordered several bridges burned above Poca, and citizens complained about his troops plundering their farms, stealing "everything that was loose." Wise also burnt the steamer *Kanawha Valley*, then later burned the Gauley Bridge after crossing the Gauley River. One Union soldier observed:

The *Silver Lake* has just arrived from the Kanawha, having been some twenty miles above Charleston. She reports entire abandonment by Wise's troops. He was pursued so close by Gen. Cox that he was compelled to leave a great deal of baggage on the way....He has destroyed over $200,000 worth of property In that valley. He became entirely disgusted with Western Virginia when be found he was not able to rally the people to his call; and concluded it was best to do all the damage be could and leave for home. He is represented in Charleston as being nothing but an old tyrant; has no control over his passions, and all his men have a great hatred for him. I think if Gen Cox or Rosecrans do not get him before he gets out of the mountains, we will never be troubled with him again west of the Bine [Blue] Ridge.

Another correspondent told the *Gallipolis Journal* they observed Wise's men were: "completely demoralized and disorderly. All the Western men deserted near the falls and are scattered through the mountains, except a few who have returned to their homes in small squads." In contrast, when General Jacob Cox's Union troops entered Charleston a few days after the battle of Scary Creek, one Ohio solider recalled:

The main army proceeded on I directly through the town of Charleston, with colors flying, and all stepping to martial music. Great cheering and excitement was manifested by the citizens while the column was passing. And all being done without the slaughtering of its women and children (who, by the way, did not appear to be in much bodily fear of these "Northern vandals," the name with which they have been branded,) or with the spitting and roasting of any of the babies, or eating them raw; and still more, without their even appropriating to their own use a single chicken, dock, goose, or anything whatever belonging to an individual of the town, which is much more than can be credited to the rebels flying through it, as they scoured through the town without order, bagging everything of the feathered race, or squealing pig, that dared to show its head. The citizens of Charleston were very indignant-at their treatment by Gov. Wise....The Federal column, after passing Charleston, moved rapidly on the road in pursuit of the fugitives....All along the road for the distance of ten miles, numbers of muskets, knapsacks, blankets, swords and other accoutrements were found lying....[172]

Following his retreat from the Kanawha Valley, General Wise encamped some four miles west of Bunger's Mill, Virginia, on August 1, 1861. His report to General Robert E. Lee on that date is somewhat superfluous, bolstered by overestimated enemy troop strength statistics, typical of commanders during that era attempting to present themselves in a more favorable light following a defeat. Wise wrote:

SIR: I am here, falling back to Covington, under orders left to my discretion by General Cooper. My situation in the Kanawha Valley was critical in the extreme. After the Scarey affair the enemy fell back and were re-enforced strongly. They increased to five thousand. At Gauley I had one thousand;

at Coal, one thousand; and at Elk, and within two miles thereof, about two thousand. Thus divided, necessarily the enemy could attack, when he chose, double or quadruple my numbers, with far better arms and supplies. I found they were collecting some fifteen thousand troops at Weston and moving to Summersville, at the same time moving up the Kanawha Valley and jamming me at any point I might select to occupy. I determined upon a prompt retreat, where my forces could cooperate with Generals Loring or Floyd. In thirty minutes after we fell back from Tyler's Mountain the enemy took possession, and nearly succeeded in cutting off seven hundred of Colonel Tompkins' command at Coal. They escaped, and burned the steamer on which they were moving up the river. Save an accident from the defiant disobedience of orders by the lieutenant of the McCullough Rangers, losing some baggage and causing the death of one of my sick and the wounding of several of my men, the retreat has been, upon the whole, creditably in order.

We left Charleston last Wednesday week [July 24] and Gauley last Saturday, destroying the bridges there behind us. This I was obliged to do by the great deficiency of transportation, owing to gross inefficiency of the quartermaster's department of my brigade. I have come on slowly. The men had marched and countermarched very much, and were sore and sadly worn-out in shoes and clothing and suffered for want of tents. We arrived here yesterday, leaving a strong rear guard of four infantry companies, attached to two hundred and fifty cavalry. They are scouting the enemy to their teeth. Last night my scouts reported that they are moving on in three divisions, converging from Fayetteville, Gauley, and Summersville to a point on this turnpike a few miles back....

The Kanawha Valley is wholly disaffected and traitorous. It was gone from Charleston down to Point Pleasant before I got there. Boone and Cabell are nearly as bad, and the state of things in Braxton, Nicholas and part of Greenbrier is awful. The militia are nothing for war like uses here. They are worthless who are true, and there is no telling who is true. You cannot persuade these people that Virginia can, or will reconquer the northwest, and they are submitting, subdued and debased. I have fallen back not a minute too soon. And here let me say, we have worked and scouted far and wide and fought well, and marched all the shoes and clothes off our bodies, and find our old arms do not stand service. I implore for some (one thousand) stand of good arms, percussion muskets, sabers, pistols, tents, blankets, shoes, rifles, and powder.[173]

While General Wise was begging the Confederate authorities to send him more firearms and equipage, the Reformed Government of Virginia's Adjutant General James S. Wheat wrote to U.S. Secretary of War Simon Cameron, on July 29, 1861, imploring him to allow the fledgling state's volunteer regiments to use the weapons and equipment recently captured from the Confederates:

I write under the instructions of the governor. During the recent operations of the U.S. troops in Western Virginia quantities of arms, ammunition, and other munitions of war have been captured from the rebels, the greater part of which is the property of this State. Our people, who are loyal and true to the Government of the Union, are clamorous for the means of defending themselves and vindicating their loyalty. We are unable to comply with their requests, and the governor directs me to ask that the captured arms, ammunition, and camp equipment to which I have referred, if consistent with the paramount interests of the National Government, may be delivered to the authorities of this State.[174]

An August 19, 1861 letter from Governor Francis Pierpont written to Secretary of War Cameron further reveals the arms supply for Union militia and home guards in western Virginia was quite poor:

> The enrolled uniformed militia or home guards do not exceed 1,500 men, and they are scattered in single companies throughout North-western Virginia, and most of them are watching organized bands of secessionists in their respective neighborhoods. The number that could be spared even for temporary service would be inconsiderable, and from their scattered positions, and the want of improved means of communication could not be got to move for several days. I dont think you can rely on this force for immediate service, and under the circumstances a requisition such as you propose would retard the enrollment of U.S. volunteers. Home guards are without improved arms and other equipment, never having received any from the General Government. The arms they have are smooth-bore muskets loaned us by Massachusetts.[175]

With General Wise's Confederate forces now withdrawn from the Kanawha Valley, the local Confederate volunteer and militia companies were suddenly emboldened. In August 1861, Captain Lewis Ruffner, adjutant of the Kanawha Rifles, posited a call to action for Southern men in the area, whom he scolded for not previously stepping forth:

> The following call to Virginians to take up arms in their own defense is made in the right spirit, and we hope it will be answered by thousands of the brave sons of the Old Dominion. Now is the time to strike, and let your blows fall with all the vengeance of an outraged people. MEN OF KANAWHA. That Government of Virginia, which was destroyed at Richmond, has been reconstructed at Wheeling, and so acknowledged by the Government and People of the United States. At the call of Governor Pierpont the President has sent armies of our friends from Kentucky, Ohio, and Indiana and expelled our 'invaders from the East beaded by a lawless ruffian who in his retreat has left everywhere bloodshed, fire, violence, and pillage, carrying with him several unoffending citizens as captives.
>
> You contributed nothing to his expulsion. You are called upon now by every consideration of defence, loyalty, and patriotism, to rally. Our Civil and Military Departments must be I have been commissioned by the Governor to muster volunteer companies into the service of the State. You must also form yourselves into companies for service under the United States. Turn out, turn out, and range yourselves under one or the other banner, and never let it be said we were made free and cannot keep ourselves so. As fast as companies are formed they will be armed, and presently we shall be able to say to our liberators, go, with our blessing, to serve your country elsewhere, we can defend ourselves.[176]

By late August 1861, nearly all the local Union militia companies were being routed into the state regiments for three years' service, limiting the number of men Captain Edward Naret could organize into the 181st Regiment Virginia Militia in Putnam County. He also found that many of the men who were willing to serve in patrol units were too old to enlist in the state regiments and limited in their capacities, but he did the best he could with what he had. Naret continued to maintain as many citizen patrol units as he could through September 1861. He wrote to Adjutant General James Wheat from Buffalo on September 2, 1861:

> ...By Wednesday next, I hope to have a company of 50 men organized, possibly two. When they are armed and equipped there will be no difficulty in organizing the others. You require the number of our

regiment; I cannot give it to you. If we are to be attached to the Kanawha and Mason companies, we will belong to the same regiment. If we are to have a regiment in this county, the numbering of it belongs to you – in that case the information must come from you. We are anticipating our duties by watching and mounting guard every night; we have a number of Secessionists here who are determined to give all the trouble they can contrive. As soon as we receive our guns, then right away [we can] effect a change.[177]

Naret found the task of organizing the seven Union militia companies in the area daunting, if not impossible. He managed to acquire one new company of infantry volunteers from the Buffalo area under Captain Isaac Rucker, whom he designated the "2nd Volunteer Company of Infantry for Putnam," and administered their oaths for three years' service by September 4, 1861. As rumors of a large Confederate cavalry force of some 800 men lurking at Hurricane Bridge circulated across Putnam County, Naret wrote to the state adjutant general in Wheeling on September 4, 1861, indicating that Rucker's company was ready to be transferred into one of the new volunteer regiments forming in western Virginia. However, he also indicated several of them were unable to be mustered in "owing to their occupations," which required them to be home at that time:

We are very anxious to be organized as soon as possible....We are threatened by the Secessionists who are organizing in large numbers within a very short distance of this place. I had a report made to me by Capt. [Isaac] Rucker that some 800 being at Hurricane Bridge; their purpose is to destroy the property of the Union people and to drive them off. The troops in the Upper Kanawha are unable to protect us; we must defer to our own exertions, and we have no arms. Our men would fight if placed in a position to do so; help me if you can. Sinister reports are spread around to frighten us away from our homes, and already a number of families from Hurricane [Bridge] and Coal [Coalsmouth] have left rather than to be exposed to the attacks of their enemies; among them are many brave men, who would fight if they had arms, but they are powerless and they go away. Much depends in the new state of things on the protection afforded to our valley – if the Secessionists are suffered to gain strength here, the county is lost, I am certain....[178]

Naret again wrote the adjutant general on September 6, 1861: "I can assure you that if the arms are sent immediately each of the companies would have a compliment of 75 to 100 men. Many are afraid to come in as they are afraid of their neighbors the Secessionists who are armed while they themselves have nothing to defend them. There are companies of Secessionists arming all around us....let the governor give orders what is to be done...." Naret attended a meeting of the members of the "Second Volunteer Company of Infantry for the County of Putnam" held at the Buffalo Academy on September 5, 1861, for the stated purpose of electing one captain, two lieutenants, four sergeants, and four corporals. The following men were elected: Captain Isaac M. Rucker, who had already organized his own home guard company, along with 1st Lieutenant Isaac A. Wade and 2nd Lieutenant Zachariah Scott. Enlisted men appointed into the order of rank were 1st Sergeant Thomas E. Ball, 2nd Sergeant John A. Chapman, 3rd Sergeant Wm. F. Lunsford, and 4th Sergeant Andrew W. Ballingee. Corporals were listed as A.M. Ballingee, James Doss, John J. Ball, and Jackson Forth.[179]

Across the Kanawha Valley, even the presence of occupying Union troops did not stop Confederates from harassing Union citizens and forcing military aged males into service when they could find them. Sarah Young diarized on September 3, 1861: "Several Union men from Nicholas, Kanawha and Clay counties are here. The Rebels were going to press them into service or take them to Richmond. They made their escape, and will stay until they think all the Rebels have left." Union forces were not long in settling up with the Confederates, however, as on September 10, 1861, 6,000 Union troops moved on Carnifex Ferry and attacked a force of about 2,000 Confederates at Camp Gauley under Brigadier General John B. Floyd, former U.S. Secretary of War and governor of Virginia.[180]

As Union troops established a stronger foothold in the Kanawha Valley and Gauley region, Sarah Young was elated. On September 23, 1861, she reflected: "Good news! Capt. [John] Vance, 4th Va. Vol. Infty. Has arrested all of the leading Rebels in the Valley. They are very angry. He has taken them to Charleston. I hope the worst ones will be sent off. Pa is almost well." The next day, however, there was pushback from Confederates in the region. Sarah wrote:

> Great excitement! We have heard that the Rebels are marching toward Buffalo….A dispatch came to Winfield that they were near Buffalo. The Union men have all run to the woods. The steamboats have stopped running. Pa was at Coalsmouth with only his Company, but he has been reinforced with Cavalry and Infantry. Oh, may they be successful in holding the post and driving the detestable traitors off![181]

As the fall of 1861 began, Captain John Young and his company continued regular patrols throughout Putnam County, and Kanawha County near Coalsmouth, and arrested several Confederate guerrillas and Southern sympathizers, though this led to retaliation. A guerrilla party led by Dick Herndon came to his house looking for him on October 5, 1861. According to Sarah, it was: "All confusion. A party of Guerrillas, commanded by the notorious Herndon. Two came for Pa, but he had gone to Winfield. Ma sent Ben to meet him and tell him not to come home." They did not give up, though, as Sarah stated on October 6, 1861: "The Rebels went to Winfield. Eleven came by and searched the house for Pa, but he had gone to Charleston. They robbed Mr. Cox's store of some clothing and took Mr. Cash prisoner, but released him. A Government boat was coming up. They fired on it, but the boat turned around and sent back. Then they took Mr. Frederick prisoner and went back to Hurricane Bridge." Sarah also indicated a regiment of Zouaves arrived on October 8, 1861, most likely the 34th Ohio Infantry who were in the area, along with part of the 4th West Virginia regiment, intending to "drive the Rebel Herndon off." But by the time the Federals arrived at Hurricane Bridge, the Confederates had left the area.[182]

Despite Sarah Young's excitement to learn that Captain John Vance's company of the 4th West Virginia Infantry was nearby, Captain Edward Naret was not as pleased with his presence. He wrote to Adjutant General James Wheat from Buffalo, on September 11, 1861:

> Since our companies have been formed and organized, I met with a complication that to me was wholly unexpected. Men who are recruiting for the volunteer service, come and coax our men away, stating to them that under our organization they are not to be armed or equipped paid; This statemen, although proved to be false, has had some influence on two or three of our men who although sworn, have gone to Mason City for the purpose of enlisting under a Mr. [Capt. John] Vance of Gallipolis, Ohio an incomprehensible man, and one not worthy of confidence. He had sent here to recruit a young man by the name of Shepard also from Gallipolis, whom I could only get rid of after proving him guilty of false representations –

> Other men from Mason City have been here for the same purpose, and what mischief they may do it is impossible for me to foretell. We are likewise threatened with the coming of a Mr. Gregg a Preacher, Geologist Topographical Engineer and who in conjunction with two ex-preachers is endeavoring to break up our organization for the purpose of organizing a brigade. All those gentlemen seem to dislike the Home Guards, or patrols, for some cause which I have not yet ascertained. I would be amused at

their efforts if the importance of the reports they may bring about here were not before me. Why are irresponsible men permitted to meddle with us? The patrols, which are established by a law of this state, and the organization under which they were formed, should be fully protected. If what they say is true, that our state militia is inferior in its organization and I must give way to U.S. Volunteer organization, we never can succeed in having enough to protect our homes and families.

Within a few miles of us the Secessionists are organizing companies to disturb us and when on the eve of being able to put down all their efforts against us, men without authority come and take away from us them whom we had enlisted – this ought to be seen to and we claim protection against them. A gentleman by the name of Waterson is receiving a company of riflemen for this county – I encouraged him to go on, his choice of the rifle owing to the fact that his men are used to that arm and can be more efficient with it than with the Musquet [Musket]. They live in a mountainous district, and are fully organized and will be useful on patrols.[183]

The Great Flood of 1861

On the days of September 25-29, 1861, residents of the Kanawha Valley living near the Kanawha and Coal rivers found themselves immersed in a great flood. Mrs. Emma Simms Maginnis (1883-1984) lived in the same house that her great-grandfather Henry Simms built in 1822, near the mouth of Armours Creek in Putnam County. Mrs. Simms told a story passed down from her family about a mysterious white line painted near the top of her chimney: "…it was in 1861 during the Civil War when the great flood covered the valley. The rest of the family had already gone to the hills when my two uncles rowed a skiff back to the house. It was completely under water except for about two feet of the chimney. They rowed up close and marked a high-water line on the brick chimney. Ever since then someone in the family has managed to keep that mark painted white."[184]

The Great Flood of 1861 was said to have risen at a rapid rate of four feet per hour, according to another eyewitness, creating a current so strong that the Ohio River: "seemed to reverse its course and appeared to run upstream from Point Pleasant to Letart Falls. Floating buildings raced out of the mouth of the Kanawha and smashed into the north bank of the Ohio, leaving the wreckage to be carried upstream with other debris to form a drift pile that completely closed the river channel for a time…" John Morgan, who lived on a farm adjacent to the Kanawha River not far from Scary Creek, recalled: "The unprecedented flood of '61, which was over ten feet higher than anything ever before known, swept nearly everything off the farm. The fences, the Negroes, horses, cows, hogs, and everything were gone; never will I forget how bleak, dreary and desolate it looked." General Jacob Cox also described the event: "The flood crested at 16.0 feet above flood stage and the water rose above the banks of the river. It was about four or five feet deep in most of the houses in town, in neighborhoods considered safe from floods. There was an enormous waste of supplies and loss of property."[185]

At Coalsmouth, Confederate supporter Victoria Hansford, her family, and friends anxiously awaited the return of the Confederate army as the great flood hit the Kanawha Valley. Victoria's home was located along the western bank of the Coal River, close to the mouth into the Kanawha River. She recalled:

During the months of August and September we ladies were all busy putting up fruit, jellies, wines and saving everything we could, thinking the Rebs would be back here to winter, as some of them had promised their sweethearts and wives. But we looked in vain. September drew near its close and on the 25th it commenced raining. It rained three days and nights, and on the 28th of September 1861, was the flood. I was aroused about three o'clock in the morning by voices in boats yelling, etc. etc. I got up and went to my window upstairs. I saw what I supposed to be a thick fog, but after listening and peering through the darkness I was afraid it was water. I threw a shawl around me and went down the stairs to my father's room, who was then sleeping soundly. After gently awakening him I told him I believed the water was very high even up in the road. He said I was foolish to think so and had better go to bed. I sat a few minutes and concluded to put on my shoes and another shawl and go and see for myself.

Lo and behold I found it some ten or fifteen feet inside our yard, the road completely submerged long ago. I made haste back into the house, as it was very cold and chilly, and told Father that it was inside of our yard." She noted also that some neighbors were trying to get out but had been "cut off from us by the creek, which was out of its banks. Father could not believe it, citizens had never heard of its being out of its banks (the river I mean). He made haste to get into his pants and boots and took his cane and went to see for himself. He was amazed; stuck his cane at the edge of the water and said it would come no further up the yard, but the next time he went to see about it his cane was beyond his reach. And so it came up, up, up, and daylight revealed a fearful sight. The morning was cloudy and foggy, there was so much water it was hard for us to get anywhere.[186]

Victoria also indicated an uncle came with a small boat and paddled over into Coalsmouth. She and her family had to move out of their home for a season: "Such a sight I never saw before. The water rose steadily all day, but not quite so rapidly as it did in the morning."[187]

While the exact date is unknown, Captain Isaac Rucker, who commanded the Putnam Independent Scouts, held a public auction at Winfield sometime in the fall of 1861. He sold off a cache of "old shotguns, rifles and revolvers captured from bushwhackers and men found bearing arms against the government." Thirteen men, the majority from his company, purchased the arms for about $3 each, and Rucker reported a total of $90.65 sold for the government. Later that month, on September 26, 1861, Captain Edward Naret reported that Captain Rucker's scouts and Captain Elias H. Ferguson's home guard company each had about fifty men and were planning to align with other Union militia at Charleston, though he noted "A few men of each of those companies having enlisted for patrols, and too old to leave home, of course will not form the new organization..." Naret also asserted, "if they could get their equipments, will have no difficulty making up the numbers, say from 90 to 100 men." State Adjutant General James Wheat had recently admonished Naret, suggesting he had impaired the recruiting process for the newly forming state regiments by insisting the companies of the 181st Regiment remain status quo because of the persistent threat to Union residents from guerrillas and Confederate cavalry raids in Putnam County.[188]

Naret denied Wheat's accusation that he had caused problems for recruiting, contending:

I wish to state to you that I never interfered with the recruiting of volunteers, and stated to you what I had done, and thought that I was right. If the patrol companies had been kept up, it was the only means by which I could keep up their organization. On the receipt of your letter, I wrote to the Governor to explain to him the condition of our county, and the necessity for protection. If the companies are authorized to organize here and to drill, and they receive their arms & equipment, we will obviate all the difficulties that surround us for the present: If we are not permitted to have them here, we will be at the mercy of the Secessionists, who sworn as many of them have been, are still bent on mischief.

I am not wishing to bring forward my own case, as I am determined, as any can, to protect myself, but there is not a day I am not advised of threats against me – it may be that the active part which I took in their trouble is the cause of it; but it may be of interest that others who have shown themselves attached to the Union and to the present government are likewise enforced. I forgot to mention that Capt Ferguson, whose influence with the men is great, and whose tact is recruiting is unsurpassed, had a desire to decline the new service, on account of age; I then prevailed upon him to retain his commission until we know whether the companies will be permitted or ordered to remain here for the present. If this were obtained he would devote himself to recruiting and organizing the company to its full complement; and when the company be ordered for active service, he will hand in his resignation. He is 60 years old.[189]

Confederate Partisan-Guerrillas attack Government Steamers at Red House

Another persistent problem Union authorities faced in Putnam County was Confederate guerrillas not only raiding local farms, but also sniping at Union steamers operating on the Kanawha River, particularly in the Red House area. This occurred despite the increased presence of Federal troops in the Kanawha Valley during October 1861, causing many residents to question Union authorities' ability to protect them, which was precisely one of the intended psychological effects the Confederates intended with such activities. One citizen skeptical that Union authorities could provide adequate protection to loyal residents of the Kanawha Valley opined:

A few days since, we noticed in the Eastern papers, that Kanawha Valley was "cleaned out" and secession is that region a "dead dog." From the same source we learn that "Washington is safe." If they are as widely mistaken in the last as the first, troops should hurry on to the Federal city with all speed. Kanawha Valley cleaned out indeed. We think it much easier to clean out the Union men than the Seceshers. We doubt much if a score of effective Union men can be found along the banks of that river. Only last Friday a Government boat was fired into at Red House by a gang of marauding Secessionists who made their appearance suddenly, from behind the houses in that traitorous village. They attempted to shoot the pilot, and from the appearance of the pilot house being riddled with balls, it is miraculous bow he escaped. He left the wheel, ran down over the desk amid a shower of balls, leaving the vessel to her own course. The engineer however by working one engine and wheel, managed to turn her round and she came back to Gallipolis, Two hundred and forty horses were on board of her.

The Silver Lake, also a Government boat, coming down from Gauley, was in sight at the lime of the firing, and although 'she had a cannon loaded with grape, immediately turned back, instead of firing upon the town as she ought to have done. It is high time our Government would open their yes to the fact that war exists yet, on the Kanawha. General Cox's mild system of swearing these gentry and allowing them to go free is only child's play. Capt. Bags' snake hunters take the proper course with them, and that is, leave them where they find them. The story of the Irishman swearing the rattlesnake and setting it free, aptly illustrates the first the terror the traitors have, of the snake hunters prove the second war ended forsooth! They have not begun to fight such demons as Wise, and Jenkins will only cease their hellish acts when they cease to exist not before. They well know that for them there is no hope of pardon.

Death is their fate, and rendered desperate by the thought, they are resolved to fit themselves for high officials in the bottomless pit, by inflicting as much misery and bloodshed as possible on their fellow creatures. They well know, that amongst the citizens of Kanawha they incur no danger. Their love for the Union is of that weak, negative kind, which neither benefits the Union, nor injures Secession. So that they can remain in undisturbed possession of their property, it matters little to them which party prevails as it now stands our troops have to pay the highest prices for anything they need, whilst the traitors either steal it, or pay in Confederate bonds. We are of opinion, that the Union men about Red House are not the bravest men in the world, or they would certainly have given the traitors a warm reception, or at least notified the officers of the boat, what they might expect. General Pope's plan of quartering a body of troops on such delinquents, might have a beneficial effect. General Rosecrans would be justified in doing so at Red House and thus teach those people that to them. Secession is, to say the least of it, "costive."[190]

Winfield Expedition

In response to the frequent attacks on government boats and other steamers, General Jacob Cox ordered Lieutenant Colonel John Toland, 34th Ohio Volunteer Infantry, (Piatt's Zouaves) to march from Camp Piatt at Charleston toward Hurricane Bridge on October 10, 1861. He also ordered Companies G and H, 4th West Virginia Infantry, to march from Point Pleasant to Hurricane Bridge on the same day, a distance of nearly fifty miles. Known as the "Winfield Expedition," Cox intended to capture Confederates who had recently fired upon the steamer *Izetta*. An unidentified member of the 34th Ohio Infantry recalled that the two companies of the 4th West Virginia "deported themselves through out with great bravery and skill." After the skirmish, Companies G and H afterward joined the Zouaves at Camp Red House on October 13, 1861, where the same Buckeye soldier noted: "…is in the center of the village. Our church is given up to the 4th [West] Virginia." Companies G and H returned to Point Pleasant on October 14, 1861, marching some thirty miles. The 34th Ohio remained at Camp Red House operating daily patrols to Hurricane Bridge until October 30, 1861, when they marched to Mud Bridge in Cabell County.[191]

News of the Federal garrison at Red House did not stop the Confederate cavalry from their attacks, as on October 11, 1861, they discovered the steamer *Izetta* as it traversed the Kanawha River from Gallipolis, Ohio, loaded with forty government horses, wagons, and other equipment, destined for Camp Enyart above Charleston. When near Red House, a force of 100 Confederate cavalry attacked the steamer and ordered the pilot to land at Red House Shoals near Winfield. The captain refused and turned the boat back toward Point Pleasant, and although it sustained damages to the pilot house, cabin, engine room and a steam pipe, there were no casualties.[192]

Upon hearing of the attack on the steamer, some 500 soldiers of the 34th Ohio Infantry crossed the Kanawha River at Red House in search of the Confederates but were unsuccessful. While on the north side of the river, they "captured" goods in a store belonging to a southern sympathizer, also deciding to take his chickens for their supper. One witness recalled: "The poor feathered tribe was doomed to a fearful end. More than a thousand of them were sacrificed to appease the stomachs made hungry by a fatiguing march. In less than an hour after our arrival soldiers might have been seen in every part of our company, munching chickens and brandishing chicken legs." The Ohio Zouaves were so successful in capturing and confiscating "Secesh" property, they elected to continue their mission of taking property that might be useful to the government, and in taking advantage of the "remarkable productiveness" of the countryside, collected seventy-five head of cattle, fifty horses, fifteen oxen, one hundred fifty sheep, thirty barrels of flour, two thousand hams, and a load of "fine Virginia tobacco," along with several hundred pounds of dry goods from local southern store keepers. They also captured five prominent local southern men, whom they forced to march alongside their companies. One Buckeye soldier identified only as "Kappa" recalled their proud return to Red House to enjoy the upcoming feast:

Unidentified members of the 34th Ohio Volunteer Infantry, 1861.
Library of Congress.

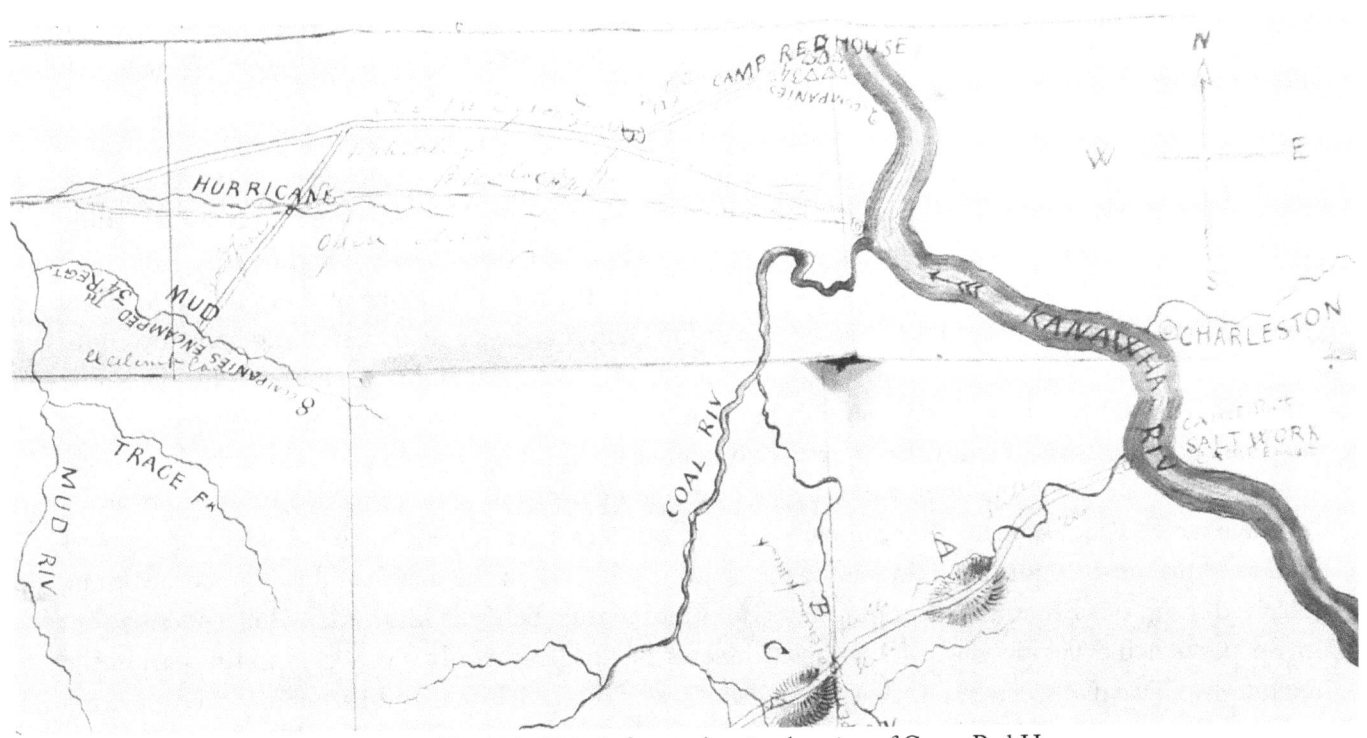

1861 Map used by 34th Ohio Infantry, showing location of Camp Red House.
National Archives. Courtesy Terry Lowry.

Unidentified soldier and officer
of 34th Ohio Volunteer Infantry
with the regimental flag.
Library of Congress.

The appearance of the regiment on the march in return, was novel and amusing in the extreme – men, cattle, sheep, Zouaves mounted on mules and horses; wagons loaded with every variety of secesh valuables; the prisoners marching under guard, the whole forming a cavalcade not unlike the old Roman triumphal entries which attended Pompey and the Caesars in the days of regal pomp and pride. Our regiment came into camp in perfect order, though I imagine our Cincinnati friends would have hardly recognized us as the same body of men who passed through the city a few weeks ago on our departure from the field.[193]

The soldier further confided that his regiment fully appreciated the: "principle that those who seek to destroy our government should not enjoy its protection. We are now stationed at Red House on the left bank of the river. We are drilling while detachments are searching the country for rebels. We promise you that the 34th (regiment) will not be behind in fighting or any other duty called on to perform."[194]

Private William Ludwig, Company G, 34th Ohio Volunteer Infantry, was also stationed at Red House in Putnam County during this period. Ludwig was a resident of Cincinnati, Ohio, and enlisted at nineteen years old in Columbus on July 22, 1861. He was later promoted to corporal and eventually to sergeant in 1864. Ludwig described several incidents occurring on patrols in the Red House vicinity in a letter written to his brother George, on October 22, 1861, from Camp Red House:

I have just returned from a scout in which we had a good time living in chickens and ducks for four days. We returned in good health, killing but one man who was killed by John Welsh. He was standing picket on a hill when he saw two men crawling towards him he halted them when they raised and fired one of the balls taking skin off John's back. John returned the fire, killing one of them dead, the other making his escape. The next night I had charge of the guard on the same post, nothing happened until daylight the next morning when we were fired on from the next hill and returned fire when they fled into the woods. We returned with seventy head of Secesh cattle, one hundred head of sheep, twelve wagon loads of plunder, eight yoke of oxen, and many little things as each man could carry. I took one woolen scarf one pair of kidd gloves one pair of woolen gloves one watch guard, a quilt patch, and a thimble which I sent home....The company are now out on a scout, I went three miles with them but I had to return on account of a tight pair of shoes. John Welsh is on the march and is in good health he received the goods his mother sent him there is nothing wrong between him and me he has been using my paper pencil envelopes and post stamps whenever he needed them It is very cold in this part of the country we have just received our coats of blue cloth read this to Mother and Father and give them my love to all my friends. I have also a splendid gold lead pencil which I will send on the first opportunity
Your brother,
William[195]

Ludwig again wrote to his brother George noting the austere weather and camp conditions at Red House on October 27, 1861:

Private John A. Miller,
Co. G, 8th Virginia Cavalry.
Courtesy Sandy Miller Larch.

Brother George,

We are still in the Kanawha Valley. We expect our company back tomorrow and then we shall make a move for somewhere but I cannot tell where. It is very cold here at night in our tents. I sleep with all of my clothes on three woolen blankets and am then cold we have very heavy frost and expect snow soon. Tell Mother I can stand it a little better than she thought I could. I have gained twenty-two pounds since I left home when I left I weighed 120 lbs and now I weigh 142 lbs. We are living high out here, we had for dinner today (Sunday) fresh beef hash stewed pumpkin fried mutton and fried crackers. We have given them a new dodge on them hard crackers, we boil them until they become soft then we fry them in grease. That makes them taste like fried oysters. We also had some corn bread today which was very nice. Some of our own baking we have plenty of fresh meat. We can hardly get bacon enough to use for fat, yesterday we killed forty-two sheep for three hundred fifty men, they are some we captured on our last scout. John Welsh is out with the company on that scout [and] was well when left I have not heard from him since. John Brunson & Conrad were well when they left. Tell father to send a pair of buck skin gloves & a pocket knife as soon as he can find some responsible person to send them by. Give my love to father and mother & write to me how the little ones are getting along. Write as soon as you can. Give my love to all my friends.
Your brother,
William[196]

A significant by-product of the persistent raids in Putnam County was that by November 1861, southern men from Hurricane Bridge, Buffalo, and Winfield were flocking to enlist. Company G, 8th Virginia Cavalry was comprised mainly of men from Putnam and Monroe counties and organized near Hurricane Bridge on November 4, 1861, for twelve months' service. The company reorganized and mustered into Confederate service on May 29, 1862, for three years. One hundred twenty-one men from Putnam County served in Company G throughout the war, and the unit disbanded on April 9, 1865, when General Robert E. Lee surrendered at Appomattox. One of those recruits was John A. Miller of Hurricane Bridge. As rumors of a civil war circulated in 1860, Albert Beckett formed a cavalry company at Hurricane Bridge, and nineteen-year-old John Miller joined the outfit and began drilling with that unit in his spare time. Beckett's company was one of the first in Putnam County to offer their services to the Confederacy in May 1861, and were known as the Border Rangers. Miller was employed rolling tobacco at a large barn located in the village when he mustered into Confederate service in Company G, 8th Virginia Cavalry, on May 13, 1861. A sturdy youth, Miller was five feet, six inches tall with blue eyes and had "many whiskers" by the end of the war. Miller took the Oath of Allegiance at Charleston, West Virginia on May 8, 1865.[197]

Meanwhile, the frequency of raids along the Kanawha River led one of Winfield's prominent citizens, John Bowyer, a wealthy landowner, to petition Governor Francis Pierpont for protection. Bowyer's significant wealth

John Bowyer.
Courtesy Bill Woodrum.

afforded him considerable political influence. Bowyer was also a member of the state legislature. He wrote on November 4, 1861:

Sir: Some three weeks since a rebel cavalry Captain came into this place with about 60 men – fired upon a Government steamer and arrested several Union men – all of whom have since been released except Mr. Siders Frederick – I was at Charleston at the time in attendance of the Federal Court and came there Col. Piatt's Ohio regiment V.M. and conducted them to the headquarters of the Rebels. They horses fled upon our approach. Col. Piatt's regiment is still here. I have been insisting after he arrested some half dozen prominent Secessionists to hold as hostages for Mr. Frederick – but have not succeeded in doing so – It does seem to me they are allowed to come in here and arrest Union men and we do not retaliate, that as soon as the forces are drawn from here, they will come back and arrest more of us. But if we arrest five or six for everyone they arrest, I think they would desist.

The prominent Secessionists themselves would do all they could to prevent Union men from being arrested – and their own safety would depend on having those things stopped. I will still continue to exert what influence I may have with Col. Piatt to get him to arrest some of the prominent Secessionists but for fear I should fail, I would be glad if you will write to him admonishing or ordering him as the case may be, to attend to it. It is my opinion that the safety of the Union men in this section depends upon this course. Dudley Montague, Esq., the member of the Convention elect from this county, John Bowyer the U.S. Commissioner for this county or your humble servant can give the Col the names of the proper ones to arrest – PS I am a member of the Legislature for this county and was at the last Convention.[198]

Bowyer was born on April 26, 1794, at Lewisburg, Greenbrier County, Virginia, as the eldest of twelve children born to Peter and Catherine Bowyer. At age eighteen, he enlisted in Captain John McClung's Greenbrier Company of the Virginia Militia and was soon commissioned as the regimental ensign, ranked as a lieutenant. When Captain McClung was mortally wounded, Bowyer was promoted to captain after his death, and after the war was often referred to as Captain Bowyer throughout his life. In 1827, he married a widow, Permelia Brown Crawford (1806-1857), in Blue Sulphur Springs, Greenbrier County. They had eight children together, with George Crawford being the eldest son, who later served as assistant adjutant general and a brigadier general of the militia during the Civil War. At one time, Bowyer owned 40,000 acres of land in Putnam County, extending from the Kanawha River to Scott Depot. He originally owned the house occupied by Judge James Hoge during the Civil War and sold it to him in 1852. Bowyer also had an estate in Fayette County comprised of 12,000 acres, as well as large tracts of land in Ohio and other areas.[199]

Bowyer became Justice of the Peace in Putnam County in 1848, and when the new state entered the Union on June 20, 1863, he was elected as a member of the state legislature during the second session in 1864. At the close of the Civil War Bowyer was appointed United States Marshal for the western district of Virginia, a position which he held for twelve years. Afterward he held the position of Commissioner of Revenue and United States Commissioner. Bowyer's first wife died in 1857, and he eventually remarried Elizabeth A. Smith, widow of William Smith of Putnam County, on January 17, 1871. He died at his Winfield home seven years later on December 18, 1878, at age eighty-four and is buried in the Winfield Cemetery beside his first wife Permelia.[200]

John Bowyer's son, George Crawford Bowyer, was elected to the Virginia Assembly in May 1861 as a pro-slavery Union candidate; he was instrumental in establishing the Reformed Government of Virginia. Born in 1829 at White Sulphur Springs, George married Mary Sophia Miller (1835-1882), and they had ten children together. In 1850, he built and operated the first hotel at the village of Winfield. During the Civil War, he was appointed as assistant adjutant general for the newly organized Reformed Government of Virginia at Wheeling 1862-1863. George Bowyer later received a commission as colonel in the 181st Regiment Virginia Militia, replacing Colonel James Hoge of Winfield. He was often

Bowyer family home in Winfield. Built around 1841, John Bowyer named it Shady Dell. Courtesy Bill Woodrum.

taunted by Confederate guerrillas to call up his regiment and fight but was said to have "put them off by one device or another" instead and never commanded the regiment in actual field service. Yet, with his political connections, he eventually obtained an appointment as a brigadier general of militia in his district in 1863 and is often remembered as "General Bowyer" despite having no combat experience. After the war, George served as a member of the West Virginia House of Delegates.[201]

The youngest and fifth child of his parents, Jerome T. Bowyer (1841-1910) was a third-year law student at Ohio University when the Civil War began, forcing him to return home to continue his studies under Judge James Hoge and Captain H. Parsons of Winfield. Jerome was admitted to the bar in 1868 and elected to the House of Delegates in 1869. Later, he was appointed as prosecuting attorney for Putnam County, and in 1889 served on the staff of Governor A.B. Flemming with the rank of colonel. Jerome never married, and after the Civil War, he owned coal mines near Winfield that were active from 1882 through 1889. Jerome Bowyer died on January 30, 1910, and is buried in the Winfield Town Cemetery on Rocky Step Road with two of his siblings, Victoria Dudding and George Bowyer.[202]

On November 10, 1861, John Young's forty-five men elected him captain of his company at Coalsmouth. On the same day, 700 Confederate cavalry under Colonel John Clarkson attacked

George C. Bowyer. Courtesy Upper Vandalia Historical Society.

Mary Sophia Miller Bowyer.
Courtesy Bill Woodrum.

the newly forming 9th West Virginia Volunteer Infantry at the village of Guyandotte in Cabell County, resulting in ten Union soldiers killed, ten wounded, and more than 100 captured. Captain Edward Naret had recently received a reprimand from state Adjutant General James Wheat for assigning himself to the 8th West Virginia Volunteer Infantry, which was then recruiting at Charleston and Buffalo. Naret wrote to Wheat on November 11, 1861, and mentioned that two of his militia companies had already enlisted in the 8th regiment and that both he and the other officers thought that was what he wanted. It was not the case, however, as Naret responded:

…I exhibited your order, and as to the persons to whom I showed it, knew that I had attached myself to the 8th Regiment, they all thought that your order mentioned the 8th Regiment, (8) being between two brackets. I therefore went to Charleston, exhibited my order and commission, to Col. Tyler who was astonished that anyone should have orders to organize the regiment while he himself had orders to that effect from General Rosecrans, however he agreed to communicate the case to the Gen; agreed to on my part to abide by the decision….Major [John] Oley who set me right….By the bye I believe the error was productive of some good – Major Oley came there a stranger unacquainted with the officers many of whom I knew. The information I gave him will enable him to engage the conflicting claims of general officers.

Since my return home I have applied myself to the duty of ascertaining how many men can be mustered; how many officers can be kept in office; but thus far, with little success – The rolls of the regiment have been promised me by the lieutenant colonel, who by the bye is far from being sanguine about the task. When they are obtained, I shall at once proceed to form the companies – some of whom I know to be entirely disorganized. For instance, the company belonging to our district, as many of the members are either in the Secession ranks, or are Secessionists, or have joined the army of the U.S. It must be the case more or less in other districts, and as our county has furnished to both services very nearly 500 men, and after that our militia will be very weak.

Please do give me such discretions as will enable me to go through with this work without any further delays, although know that I am 'right' as to the regiment – I apprehend very little doubt about the duty to be performed. If I were with you for an hour I could give you such facts as to the condition of our county here, that you could at once decide whether the occasion of organizing the militia is opportune….[203]

Despite being elected captain by his company, John Young found that neither the state adjutant general nor the U.S. War Department would recognize his rank due to only having forty-five men. Extant army regulations at the time required no less than eighty-four men to obtain a captaincy; as such, Young was ranked as 1st Lieutenant on his official commission documents. This also meant less pay. A friend of Young's, Greenbury (Greenly) Slack was a prominent Kanawha County resident. He wrote to the U.S. Adjutant General Henry J. Samuels on Young's behalf on November 12, 1861:

...there is a Capt John V. Young in Putnam County, who at considerable expense of time and means, raised a company in his neighborhood near Winfield, of some 40 more or less, who have been advantageously employed for some time in scouting and capturing dangerous persons, who wishes to organize (with the company he has now) a company of cavalry for the purpose of contradicting the raids that are made from time to time in that section, by the rebels from the southern army who dash into unprotected neighborhoods and plunder and murder the inhabitants and dash off again and defy pursuit in consequence of our lack of that necessary arm of our defence, (cavalry). Mr. Young is a man of unflinching courage and would doubtless render good service in that capacity if encouraged. I hope you will exert yourself to secure to Capt Young a commission for the purpose indicate above forthwith; the circumstances with which we are surrounded require prompt action See the affair at your county on Sunday last....[204]

John Morgan's Faithful Guard Dog

During the late fall of 1861, John Morgan III lived on a farm located along the Kanawha River between Winfield and Scary Creek, near modern Bill's Creek in Putnam County. Morgan heard that Peter M. Carpenter, a notorious Confederate guerrilla prowling the area, was coming with his men to steal horses from his farm one night. Ironically, Morgan had earlier enlisted in the 36th Virginia Infantry and was an ardent Confederate supporter. Carpenter was thirty-three-years-old and had a fierce reputation for horse theft and accosting Unionists. He was also known as Peter Slick, or Captain Slick. Carpenter was a resident of Putnam County, although most of his men were from Logan and Wayne counties. His partisan company operated throughout the Kanawha Valley and into the Sandy River Valley area during 1861 and early 1862.[205]

Morgan was standing guard at the stable alone that night, waiting. Morgan had a friend identified only as George who had stolen a large red dog from Federal soldiers in the area that had become a sort of local guard dog. The pooch often went to Morgan's home or his father-in-law, Dr. John Thompson's, house, when his wife was there alone. That evening, the dog was with Morgan; he recalled:

I was standing in the stable alone, and presently I heard soft footsteps come up to the door, then a light tap on it. I had my guns cocked, waiting for the door to be opened. Then the soft steps moved along each side of the stable, as if quietly reconnoitering. This soft moving something proved to be the red dog. It was too dark to see him, but, after going around the table several times, he gave a low whine. I opened the door, the dog came in and dropped down at my feet, and seemed to plainly say: "I wish to stay with you." Well, two men came there before morning, and that dog proved himself as brave as he was wise and benevolent. I have always believed that dog understood the situation and concluded to stay and take a hand on my side of the trouble when he found me, gun in hand, alone in the dark stable.

But not long after this his affection and bravery cost him his life. The Yankee soldiers had come to Dr. Thompson's to arrest his daughter, as they had caught a Rebel mail-carrier, and found a letter she had written to her husband, Captain [Andrew R.] Barbee, in Dixie. The soldiers got off a steamboat and went up through the yard. There was no man at home-no one but Mrs. Thompson and her daughter. The dog, no doubt, saw that the ladies were very much frightened, and ran out to meet the soldiers in the middle of the yard, and did not retreat one inch until they shot him down.[206]

After spending 1861 and part of 1862 operating as a partisan-guerrilla, Carpenter was commissioned as a captain in the 4th Regiment Virginia State Line on August 10, 1862. He later enlisted as a private in Company C, 36th Battalion Virginia Cavalry (Witcher's Battalion) on April 1, 1862. By August 1, 1863, it appears Carpenter was promoted to captain, as Lieutenant Colonel James Witcher petitioned Major General J.E.B. Stuart on that date to allow him to return to western Virginia to recruit a new company, noting "Captain Carpenter commanded a company in the late Virginia State Line and can furnish any reference in regard to capacity to train recruits." Carpenter deserted in Highland County, Virginia, on September 10, 1863, and in fact returned to the Kanawha Valley but instead of recruiting, appears to have returned to partisan activities in February 1864 and joined Colonel Thomas Swann's Battalion Virginia Cavalry on November 1, 1864.[207]

As fall faded into winter, Governor Pierpont wrote to President Lincoln on December 3, 1861, complaining of the constant harassment from Confederate guerrillas. Pierpont stated: "...That part of the territory of Virginia watered by the Guyandotte and the Sandy Rivers is in a perfect state of Anarchy, no one claiming to hold a civil office, and a perfect terrorism paralyzes every effort to restore law and order in that region; and such will be the state of the country as long as the rebel chiefs (Jenkins and Clarkson) are permitted to remain in that region and make their periodic raids through the same at pleasure. The people are divided in sentiment but would flock to that power that would inspire confidence that they would be protected."[208]

Captain Naret soon had more success organizing his militia companies. On December 7, 1861, at Hall's Store in Buffalo, he superintended the elections of Company A, 181st Regiment Virginia Militia, and reported to the adjutant general that the following were unanimously elected: David A. Ford was elected captain, Anderson Bias 1st Lieutenant, and John Ball as 2nd Lieutenant. On December 28, 1861, David Ford of Winfield was elected captain of the 5th Company, 181st Regiment Virginia Militia, and took the oath of office. The 181st was in the 22nd Brigade, 5th Division of Virginia Militia. For the Confederates, on the other hand, the fall of 1861 had proven to be a difficult period for troops in western Virginia, as there were marked shortages of supplies, clothing, and, at times, sustenance. A resident of Richmond, Virginia had recently traveled to the area and posited their observations of the state of affairs in the Kanawha Valley as well as the southern troops encamped at Cotton Mountain in December 1861, in particular the men of the 22nd Virginia Infantry, many of whom were from Putnam County:

I wish to draw public attention to the situation of the Twenty-Second (late Tompkins's) Regiment Virginia Volunteers. This force is composed of the troops that were raised in the Kanawha Valley at the commencement of hostilities, who have been in active service ever since, and now, after a campaign of unsurpassed hardship, suffering, and gallantry, were recently stationed with the command of Gen. Floyd on Cotton Mountain. From that bleak summit they looked down on the encampment of the invaders who have seized on their country, and still hold the fairest region of the Confederation in bondage. Let us remember that the men of this regiment are Virginians, who have gained victories, endured privations, and braved the worst difficulties of a soldier's life for the common cause; and yet are as much strangers now on the soil of the State as the poor exiles of Maryland and Alexandria.

It is generally known that the Kanawha Valley is cut off in a manner from Virginia by reason of geographical position, and lies distant from it by the whole breadth of all its mountain ranges. On this account the trade of all its business interests were with the people of the Ohio Valley, now turned deadly enemies. This trade was once carried on by the Ohio and Kanawha rivers, but when the war broke out, the navigation of these streams gave easy access to their invaders, while the state could lend but little assistance to the brave and unfortunate Virginians of the Kanawha Valley. Yet, soon as hostilities began, they were the first to fly to arms, and expose themselves to the vengeance of the Lincoln government. It was late in the month of June before the authorities at Richmond sent Gen. Wise to their assistance. The results of his expedition are well known…

It has been about four months since these things happened, though the country has passed through so many trials, it seems to us as many years. But the events of that time can never be forgotten by the Kanawhans. They had just triumphed over their enemies at Scarey Creek. Constituting the advance of Gen. Wise's forces, about six hundred Kanawha men met fifteen hundred Lincoln troops, defeated, and utterly routed them. A large number of the invaders had been killed, wounded, and made prisoners; and more superior officers taken, I believe, than anywhere except Manassas; and not even *that*, when all things are considered, was a more intrepid defence, or more decided victory. True, this was one of the minor combats of the war, but nowhere has there been a more gallant fight than on the Scarey.

Just then, news of the Rich Mountain disaster reached Kanawha. At a few hours' notice, its brave defenders were summoned to commence a retreat, and forced to leave home, family and all they had, to the enemy, who have held possession of their country ever since. It will also be remembered that, soon as the government could rally from the discouragement of Garnett's defeat, General Floyd [John B.] was sent to the relief of the Kanawha counties; and the troops of the valley, placed under his command, marched back to meet their invaders again; but new disappointments awaited them. They fought again at Cross Lanes and Carnifex Ferry on the Gauley; shared in the triumphs of those well contested fields, but again gathered nothing but barren laurels. They have now advanced a third time against their enemies. We have heard something of their autumnal storms on Sewell Mountain, the privations and sufferings of troops there, the crossing by Floyd's men across the New River, and their terrible march over the mountains of Fayette.

The last news is that at least half the command are in the hospitals. But I ask particular consideration for the Kanawha regiment. Its present condition is better known to others than myself; but we may imagine their state of destitution and suffering, when we remember that they have been constantly marching and fighting for four months past: that they are cut off from friends and kindred; that driven from their homes, they know not the cares of sister, or wife, or mother, and that even now, it is said, the property they left for the support of their families, lies under decrees of confiscation to the Pierpont Government at Wheeling. The Department does all it can no doubt; but it is very difficult to succor from that quarter, to meet privation such as theirs. The aid of our generous people have lavished on their brave defenders, has heretofore been bestowed on objects nearer home and better known: and not even the acknowledgement due their courage and constancy has yet reached the remote and obscure quarters of the Virginians from Kanawha.[209]

At the close of 1861, as many citizens of Virginia were acutely aware of the tactical, logistical, and strategic importance of that region, it remained a conundrum that Confederate authorities in Richmond still seemed not to take the matter seriously—at least not beyond trying to obtain the salt works in Kanawha County:

There can be no Virginia unless it includes both Eastern and Western Virginia….
We may therefore say, that if we cannot hold Western Virginia we cannot hold Eastern Virginia, and if we cannot hold Virginia we can hardly defend the South. A shrewd Northwestern man, who is true to

the South, declared to us a few days since that if the Southern Confederacy did not maintain its power over Western Virginia, Western Virginia would conquer Eastern Virginia. We consider the remark at least striking. The importance of taking and holding Northwestern Virginia cannot be overestimated. As it is needless to stop to inquire now how it has been lost, it is only practical to inquire how we are to redeem the State authority in that part of Virginia....

This subject is one that deserves the most serious attention of Congress and our State Legislature. We hope they will take it up promptly and act decidedly and harmoniously. Western Virginia is indispensable to Eastern Virginia and the Confederacy. Apart from political considerations, upon the score of the mineral wealth of that part of the State, it is of the vastest importance to the South. The coal and iron deposits are of illimitable extent, and if we had not lost the salt mines: most ridiculously lost them: we would not feel the want of this article of prime necessity now....[210]

Chapter Two

1862: Fighting for the Kanawha Valley

In January 1862, three companies of the 34th Ohio Volunteer Infantry were stationed at Winfield. Another detachment of the 34th Ohio was posted at Hurricane Bridge. Residents of the Kanawha Valley found themselves in the midst of a bitter cold winter encampment, with snow and ice that seemed to last for weeks. A citizen recalled, "We have had one of the most disagreeable winters I ever experienced." Despite freezing weather, Winfield residents were agitated over the arrest of a Union citizen who recently displayed the U.S. flag from his window. 1st Lieutenant Edgar Blundon, Company F, 8th West Virginia Infantry, quickly learned to distrust southern locals, many of whom pretended to be Unionists—"turncoats" who were attempting to appease troops on both sides to avoid harassment. He described a recent encounter: "I am informed that the Rebels came into town and observing the Federal Flag displayed from the window arrested him and took him forty or fifty miles on the road to Richmond. Perhaps he can appreciate the blessedness of making long marches, as he told me he had to march all the way. I hope he may be compelled to take a sufficient number of trips of the same kind to change his traitorous heart that he may learn to appreciate a good and beneficent government...." On January 11, 1862, U.S. Secretary of War Simon Cameron resigned and was replaced by Edwin M. Stanton, who was sworn in on January 20, 1862. Stanton had a reputation for corrupt dealings, though would prove to be an excellent administrator. He was also one of Lincoln's strongest critics, but Lincoln felt obliged to add him to his cabinet for his assistance in the 1860 election.[1]

Major John Oley, 8th West Virginia Infantry, was equally frustrated with locals at Buffalo when his men took a horse from a local southern man, who attempted to take the Oath of Allegiance in order to recover his property. Oley telegraphed Union headquarters afterward on February 1, 1862, stating: "George Miller's horse is in the possession of our Quartermaster. From the testimony of my men Miller has always been a Secessionist

Piatt's Zouaves, 34th Ohio, in pursuit of Confederates on the road from Hurricane to Hamlin in Lincoln County.
Harpers Illustrated, January 18, 1862.
West Virginia State Archives.

in active & following But has taken the oath since his horse was taken-shall I deliver the horse up?" Captain Isaac Rucker's company, the Putnam County Scouts, had recently mustered into the 8th West Virginia Infantry as Company D on November 10, 1861, at Buffalo.[2]

Captain Edward Naret wrote to Adjutant General Henry J. Samuels on February 17, 1862, stating he had repeatedly tried to organize the 181st Regiment in Putnam County to no avail. Naret noted one officer had simply refused to call his men to muster, despite three separate muster dates, and that only one company turned out on those days, but there were never more than twenty-five men present, with 119 on the muster roll. Naret additionally reported the only company that had elected officers was Captain David Ford's unit. He also pointed out that Union citizens of Buffalo were "left to their own resources" since the time that the 8th West Virginia Infantry arrived there and that he had previously formed "two patrols....employed in protecting the people against the attack & depredations of marauding bands...." which often suffered "...many fatigues, and sometimes hard service, in scouting and watching whole nights for fear of an attack...." Naret summarized that in Putnam County, "the situation is a strange one," with most of the Union men who refused to muster suspecting "a plan to force them by drafting into the service," and "the balance is made of secessionists, who although willing to take the oath, would be of little value if called upon...." A few days later on February 28, 1862, Naret again wrote to Samuels, indicating that the June 1861 act of the legislature, House Bill No. 5, enabling Union citizens to form patrols, had resulted in formation of two new companies in Putnam County, one in neighboring Mason County, and four in Kanawha County. Naret mused these companies were "...

probably destined to form a regiment [181st Regiment], which bye the bye, never had any existence....what authority would the commander of the 181st Regiment have to certify my claim, since the regiment has no existence, & had none during the time of service."[3]

On March 11, 1862, the U.S. War Department redesignated the Department of West Virginia as the Mountain Department under Brigadier General William S. Rosecrans, and all Federal troops west of the Alleghenies then fell under overall command of Brigadier General Robert H. Milroy. The District of the Kanawha remained under Brigadier General Jacob D. Cox, who had approximately 12,071 troops scattered across the region, including a newly forming company of the 13th West Virginia Infantry at Point Pleasant; eight companies of the 8th West Virginia throughout the valley; and ten companies of the 12th Ohio Infantry and one company of Ohio Cavalry at Charleston. Also, at Camp Piatt, some twelve miles above Charleston, was the 44th Ohio Infantry and one company of 1st West Virginia Cavalry. To the west at Guyandotte, Cox had eleven companies of the 2nd West Virginia Cavalry with six companies of the 9th West Virginia Infantry, and at Barboursville was the 34th Ohio Infantry, while at Ceredo was 4th West Virginia. In late March 1862, Major General John C. Fremont was given command of the Mountain Department and immediately began planning for a spring campaign.[4]

Robert Trigg Harvey Arrested

Union troops in Putnam County continued to struggle with who to trust; as noted earlier, Confederate supporters were routinely arrested but would take the Oath of Allegiance in order to gain their release, only to return home and renew their anti-Union activities. Another such a case arose in Putnam County on March 27, 1862, involving Robert Trigg Harvey, a former member of the Virginia Legislature, known locally as an "infamous" and outspoken Secessionist. Harvey was a lifelong resident of Buffalo, where he was born June 24, 1814. His father, Henry Harvey, settled there in 1808. Harvey was twice married, initially to Annie Marie Hope, who died in 1889, and then to Charlotte Elizabeth Mitchell, whom he married in 1890. He had five children, one who became a successful businessman—William H. "Coin" Harvey, who was nominated for president of the United States in 1932 by the Liberty Party. Robert T. Harvey was also suspected of participating in partisan-guerrilla activities against Federal troops and Union citizens. Harvey was previously arrested in 1861, and his attorney, James Hoge of Winfield, managed to persuade Judge George Summers, who lived near Winfield in Putnam County, to drop the charges for want of evidence. Harvey was again arrested on April 6, 1862, then being accused of "exciting our people to rebel against the Government" using "every means in his power." Locals were doubtful he would face any serious consequences, as one skeptical resident of Mason County who lived not far from Buffalo opined: "We suppose, however, that Harvey, like all such Secessionist who return, will manifest any amount of penitence for his past misdeeds, and the people, without any fixed or settled policy as to the manner of treatment towards such creatures, will forget all the outrages he has done them, and again receive him into their confidence and society."[5]

This time, however, Harvey was arrested "by authorities at Buffalo," ostensibly to prevent the Union men, who had grown weary of his pro-southern activities, from killing him. Harvey again took the Oath of Allegiance and was about to be released when a contingent of leading local Union men met at the courthouse in Winfield on March 24, 1862, with the objective of discussing his potential release. Rumors buzzed across the community, as he was viewed by local Unionists as an "arch traitor" and said to be "the most loud mouthed and the meanest of all of the infamous pack of Secessionists who have disgraced the Kanawha Valley, from the rebel army." The majority of residents opposed his release. After his arrest, Harvey was escorted by 1st Lieutenant John J. Polsley, adjutant of the 8th West Virginia Infantry, on board the government steamer *Leona* to Atheneum Prison in

Wheeling. Polsley wrote *en route* that he had "Col. Robert T. Harvey" in his custody, and while Harvey was said to have served in the Virginia militia, that name does not appear on muster rolls from any Confederate regiments nor war time militia from Cabell, Kanawha, Mason, Putnam, or Wayne counties.[6]

One of the men present at the March 24, 1862 meeting at the Putnam County Courthouse was Dudley Street Montague. He served as Putnam County Commissioner for Revenue during the 1850s and early part of the Civil War, and later as County Notary and Escheator and Mason County Clerk of Court. Born August 26, 1800, in Cumberland, Virginia, he was the descendent of one of the first English settlers at Jamestown, Virginia in 1603, Peter Montague, and owned a small hotel and tavern located near Red House Shoals on the Kanawha River. During 1861, Montague served as a delegate to the Reformed Government of Virginia Constitutional Convention in November and played an active role in passing the Willey Amendment. This law stated that children of slaves born in the state of West Virginia after July 4, 1863, were to be free; others between age ten and twenty-one years old would be free when they reached age twenty-five; and no slave would be allowed to come into the new state for permanent residence. During the Vicksburg Campaign, Montague traveled to Mississippi and visited the soldiers from West Virginia serving under Brigadier General Joseph A.J. Lightburn in the trenches, conducting personal polls. Montague later served in the second West Virginia Legislature representing Putnam County during 1864.[7]

Montague stated that the object of the March 24, 1862 meeting of local Union leaders at Winfield was to "get some expression of the people in relation to the return of the rebel Robert T. Harvey." Among those present were George C. Bowyer, his father John Bowyer, Joseph Swayne, A.W. Curry, and Alexander S. Young, brother of Captain John Young. The leaders unanimously agreed on the following resolutions, which they sent to Governor Francis Pierpont:

Whereas, The arch traitor, Robert T. Harvey, regardless of the *oath* he had taken to support the Constitution of the United States, has used every means in his power to overthrow the same, by exciting our people to rebel against the Government under which they have lived peaceably and happily for over seventy years; and by inviting the *rebel hordes* to our peaceful valley, to murder our people and destroy our property, has returned to his home in this county, with a view of remaining, and only asks «to be let alone,» Therefore, be it

Resolved, That we have no faith in any professions of repentance said Harvey may make, and believe our people would be better off, were he from amongst them.

Resolved, That the said Harvey be requested to take himself beyond the lines of the Federal army, instanter.

Resolved, That when we need his presence and council we will send for him.

Ordered that these proceedings be published in the Kanawha Republican, and The Weekly Register, and that a copy be furnished to the traitor Robert T. Harvey.[8]

One of the other prisoners they discussed belonged to Colonel Albert G. Jenkins' 8th Virginia Cavalry regiment. That man had earlier returned to the area and attempted to don a disguise; he was "...dressed in female attire...distributing letters to the friends of Jenkins men – he passed through the neighborhood as a strange lady..." Despite his publicly stated Union support, Judge George Summers was viewed by many as a Southern sympathizer because he had presided on several cases of charges against Southern men that resulted in two being dismissed for want of evidence. Summers also received much ire in the regional media for his efforts to assist Southern sympathizers who were imprisoned, including Robert T. Harvey. Despite this, Summers continued to serve as a prominent local attorney until his death in 1868. A bitter editorial posited in the *Wheeling Daily Intelligencer* on April 15, 1862 offers a glimpse of the antagonism toward him for assisting Southerners:

We understand, from reliable authority, that Judge Summers, of Kanawha, is about to present himself before the U. S. Court, and ask leave to plead the cases of those who have been indicted for treason in that county. As the Judge narrowly escaped an indictment himself, contrary, as everybody admits, to his deserts, it is not surprising that he has a strong inclination to make an argument on that side of the question. Before he obtains that privilege, however, we hope that the Court will put him to his purgation's. We trust that Judge Jackson will see narrowly to it, that such a questionable loyalist goes through the last formula necessary to satisfy the standard of practice in his Court. Judge Summers has much to answer for.[9]

A soldier in the 8th West Virginia Infantry identified only as "Dixie" was also present at the March 24, 1862 meeting of leading Union men held at the Putnam County Courthouse and wrote to the editor of the *Pomeroy Weekly Telegraph* summarizing the outcome:

Many who were with the rebels have had time to think and reflect. Ample opportunity was given to view the subject agitating the country in all its bearing. Who will not say that thousands who, in the hurry and excitement of the campaign last summer and fall, were called rebels, and were, perhaps, disaffected, are today true, staunch Union men? The question, as to what is to be done with the leaders of the rebellion when they return to their homes, and, by mock professions of loyalty, escape the clutches of the military officers, receives a very appropriate answer. The people have taken the case of these leading rebels in their own hands. Col. [Robert Trigg] Harvey was chief among those who preached and labored for secession last spring. He urged enlistment in the rebel army. Hundreds who are today disloyal would have been true but for this traitor.

When Gen. Cox crossed the Ohio at Point Pleasant, this rebel hastened to the Southern army for protection, and has been with them until within a few days. His own son, a member of a rebel company, was wounded at Fort Donelson. His father, who, it seems, was present during the engagement, returned to his home with his wounded boy, claiming protection, and making hypocritical pretensions of loyalty. Thus stands his case, the leading man of this county, now hated, and despised by those whom he tried to injure only a year ago. The feeling is so strong against him that he will have to leave, and that soon, else the traitor's death will be meted to him. Is it right to treat returned rebels thus? Is it fair? Let the hunted, abused, cursed, imprisoned Union men of this county and Western Virginia answer.

According to the treatment many returned rebels have received from some of our Generals, it is an honor rather than a disgrace to belong to the enemies of our country. Let them be made to feel the weight of their crime. Let the vengeance of an insulted, loyal people hurl upon the heads of these guilty leaders in sin, all the fury of their just wrath and indignation. Property nor the life of a hated traitor should be sacred in the eyes of the Government. Let the future generation tell of the terrible vengeance meted to those who dared raise the arm of rebellion against a mighty and just Government....[10]

Robert Trig Harvey.
Marshall University Special Collections.

Another Putnam resident succinctly summarized Harvey's plight in *The Weekly Register* on April 17, 1862:

The traitor Robt. T. Harvey was shipped to Wheeling last Monday, by the authorities at Buffalo, where is to be hoped he will be kept as our prisoners are treated in the Southern prisons, or sent to the land of Dixie, there to remain and tuff it until the war is over.... Some say, "he was taken from Buffalo, to get him out of the reach of the Union men, near there, who had threatened to kill him--what a pity he was taken away! Wonder if he thinks Virginia can whip the world, and that the Yankees won't fight? Poor Bob! better hads't thou never been born.

PUTNAM[11]

When soldiers in the 8th West Virginia Infantry, who were still in winter quarters at Buffalo, learned that General John C. Fremont was recently placed in command of the Mountain Department (formerly Department of West Virginia), they were elated. One soldier wrote: "The joy of the army on this river at the appointment of John C. Fremont to its command, is unbounded...All hail Maj. Gen. John C. Fremont! We will gladly do your bidding, for we know triumph and glory are sure wherever you lead the way...The day is dawning, and now, with the Path Finder at our head, we hope to move on over the mountains and into the valley of Virginia, driving the traitors and rebels before us."[12]

The winter of 1862 was both harsh and boring for men in the 8th West Virginia Infantry, with many of them quite ill. As the weather began to improve, a soldier there recalled their plight on March 26, 1862:

The fact of my continued silence, since the early part of last fall, is explained on the ground that nothing new or important has occurred in this section. Now, however, things are beginning to stir and change. The mud, which has so long annoyed us and the whole Federal army, is beginning to dry up. The roads are getting good, the river is rising, and everything indicates an onward move. Long and patiently had the army of the Kanawha waited through the dreary winter months for the coming of spring, sunshine, and dry roads, in the hope that we, too, may be favored with the opportunity of showing our loyalty to the Government, and hatred to rebellion, by earnest, active and telling blows on the foe...The past winter has had an effect upon our army. Many have died. On the mountain back of Charleston there is many a hillock marking the last resting place of the soldier. Sad, indeed, are our thoughts amid this village of dead patriots. Out of their graves they speak to the living in tones of thunder. Their deaths must be avenged. They have fallen far from home and those they loved so dearly. No dear mother, wife or sister sits beside the gloomy grave of the dead to moisten the sod with tears of love. No loved hand pressed the brow as the fingers of death began to paint the victim for the tomb. Strangers only stood near to watch for the last gasping utterances of the dying hero. In heaven above these have their reward. Nor are they forgotten here, a grateful country sheds tears for her loyal sons, and emblems their names in the records of undying love.[13]

Putnam County residents continued to deal with the constant threat of guerrilla attacks and horse theft, especially along Hurricane Creek. One irate Union citizen there had enough, and informed General Cox, "Guerrilla warfare appears to be the determination of the Rebels…I am at liberty to act guerrilla to guerrillas and their aiders of rebellion…I have no wish to become a horse thief or midnight assassin." A resident of Buffalo further groused on the matter: "It is amazing that during the winter the loyal men of Western Virginia have not taken measures to organize themselves for home protection. Their experience last summer must certainly have suggested its value. They knew with what sort of enemy they had to deal, and that nothing but organization and equipment on a war footing would secure immunity from incursions and outrages of the most fearful character…."[14]

Cox responded on April 29, 1862, by ordering 1st Lieutenant John Young to take his company of forty-five Union men from Coalsmouth and detain two local Secessionists at Winfield who were arrested for "bushwhacking;" both were captured the previous day during a skirmish with Federal troops near Garrett's Mill along Mud Creek in Cabell County. John Bowyer of Winfield was a friend of Young's and also knew both men taken prisoner. He petitioned Young requesting their release, advocating for their good character despite the present circumstances. However, Young was acutely aware of the many Southern citizens pretending to have Union sympathies at Winfield and suspected both men of horse thievery and refused to let either go. He afterward had little trust in Bowyer, expressing doubts as to his loyalty.[15]

Young also faced another problem with his immediate subordinate, 2nd Lieutenant Robert Brooks. Brooks had recently managed to manipulate Governor Francis Pierpont into placing him in command, by making false claims of Young's incompetence and dissatisfaction among the men. This was to his own detriment, however, as Young was friends with all of the men whom he had recruited into his company before the war, and when they learned of Brooks' scheming behavior, the non-commissioned officers were furious over Young being removed from command. Brooks, too self-absorbed to realize that he could not effectively lead a group of men who had no allegiance to him and ultimately resented him, gloated over his short-lived victory. The men collectively wrote to Governor Pierpont offering their side of the story, vouching for not only Young's leadership but also clarifying it was he who organized the company, not Brookes, and demanded to have Young reinstated as commander. Pierpont promptly re-instated Young as the rightful commander of Company G on June 5, 1862, which was also his forty-ninth birthday. Needless to say, Young was pleased with his gift. Brooks refused to surrender, however, and continued to usurp authority from Young, who was formerly a close friend. He even wrote to Secretary of War Edwin Stanton again accusing Young of incompetence, only to be deferred to Governor Pierpont, who refused to listen. Brooks eventually resigned in June 1863.[16]

As spring began to blossom, the 8th West Virginia Infantry, still headquartered at Buffalo, had yet to be receive any pay, until April 3, 1861. On that date the Army paymaster delivered $65,000 to the regiment for their "military services." An observer noted: "We are not aware of how much of this immense sum reached Gallipolis, but quite a large amount was sent into this county, whence came a great many men. The regiment has had no opportunity as yet of proving itself as valiant as we know them to be, but when the hour comes we predict they will be all right." This proved prophetic, as the 8th West Virginia was soon ordered to join Major General John Pope's campaign against General Thomas J. "Stonewall" Jackson in the Shenandoah Valley.[17]

Southern residents in the Kanawha Valley found that as the weather improved, Union troops increased the frequency and intensity of patrols around them. This often resulted in troops stealing livestock or other property. Brigadier General Jacob D. Cox had issued clear orders for his men not to engage in plundering, although the malfeasance continued, often with little or no consequences. Cox wrote to Lieutenant Colonel Augustus H. Coleman, 11th Ohio Volunteer Infantry, on April 22, 1862, complaining of such, admonishing him to tighten up discipline on the troops in his regiment, some of whom he had learned were recently guilty of robbing a citizen's farm near Winfield:

Sir: I regret to be under the necessity of calling your attention to a matter of a kind I hoped would never occur again with troops of my command in this valley. On Friday last a party of your regiment went to Mrs. Ann M. Millan's farm, a little above Winfield, and took her yoke of work oxen, which were taken to camp and killed. Mrs. Millan is an ardent Unionist and sister of Judge [George W.] Summers of this place. As I have heard the account I regard it no better than robbery. Indiscriminate seizure of cattle and property in this valley has long since been peremptorily forbidden. No cattle can be taken but by fair purchase, by which the quartermaster must give such voucher as will show the entire legitimacy of the transaction and insure the payment of the agreed price. To work cattle without the owner's consent is simply a crime, and should be treated as such. Officers of detachments who take the responsibility of such acts must be held strictly responsible for them. Western Virginia is not to be regarded as an enemy's country, where foraging is to be permitted, but the same strictness of conduct is to be observed as if we were in Ohio.

There are civil and judicial authorities to take cognizance of civil affairs, and the military are to be kept from any improper interference. These things have been repeated so often that it ought not be necessary to call attention to them again. I desire that you will personally call upon Mrs. Millan and learn her story; that you will strictly investigate the case and report the full facts to these headquarters, and if the officer in charge of the detachment has acted improperly and without authority that you will put him under arrest until further orders. If it has not already been done, Mrs. Millan should be fully indemnified for her loss, and if that loss is more than the ration price of the beef, let the balance be charged to the companies using it, to be deducted from their company savings.

In like manner, wherever unauthorized seizure or stealing of food, animals or forage occurs, let double the value be charged to the company in which it occurs as a punishment for the offense. The quartermaster can, by proper exercise of his authority, buy whatever ought to be taken, and no one else has any right to meddle in the matter. Please see this rule carried out so thoroughly that this sort of demoralizing pillage may be thoroughly stopped.[18]

In May 1862, some of the leading Union citizens of Hurricane Bridge wrote to Governor Pierpont insisting he send troops to their village to protect them from Confederate raids, which were increasing in the area, with several homes recently burned, forcing some residents to relocate. Pierpont directed General Cox to send more troops into the area. Cox responded to Pierpont on May 11, 1862 by telegraph informing him that he would, "…have a Company at Hurricane bridge & Posts at Coalsmouth Charleston Chapmansville & here with orders to officers to be extremely vigilant & I think the people of the Lower Guyandotte are more Scared than hurt but will Spare no pains to protect them thoroughly."[19]

By mid-May 1862, the Reformed Government of Virginia at Wheeling had recruited and organized twelve full regiments into Federal service, although some residents believed Union men in western Virginia had not received due recognition for finally stepping up, likely because so many had earlier refused to enlist from fear of leaving their families vulnerable to Confederate raiders. Despite the surge in enlistments, Unionists in some areas in western Virginia were still holding out, as one resident observed, "...some neighborhoods cannot be canvassed for that object at all except with an armed force, on account of the presence of the sneaking 'Bush-whacker' and 'Moccasin Ranger.'" According to the editor of *The Weekly Register*:

> Western Virginia has not obtained, perhaps, as much credit as she deserves for her patriotism, in furnishing volunteers for the Union army. It is said that her people have been anxious to obtain the protection of the United States forces but have been unwilling to contribute their proportion of men.... There are now twelve complete regiments of Virginia volunteers....Some of these regiments have received a large number of their recruits from Pennsylvania and Ohio, but it is believed by those best informed, that two-thirds of the men composing those regiments are Virginians, and that Virginia's contribution to the army amounts to fully eight thousand men....in none of the late elections held in that state was there more than 35,000 Union votes cast, it must be conceded that the Union men of Western Virginia are not behind their brethren of other States in devotion to their country.[20]

1862 Gubernatorial Elections

On May 23, 1862, the first public election for state offices in the Restored Government of Virginia occurred. A Buffalo resident described the day as uneventful: "The day passed very quietly. It seemed the people did not care about voting, and seemed to want something like a party feeling to stimulate them." Statewide election returns revealed 14,824 voters turned out from thirty-one counties and one independent city—twenty-eight of those counties from what would soon become West Virginia and the city of Alexandria, along with three counties east of the Allegheny Mountains. Results indicated Governor Francis Pierpont defeated incumbent Virginia governor John Letcher 173 to 1, and Daniel Polsley defeated Andrew Parks for Lieutenant Governor 166 to 1. James S. Wheat was re-elected as adjutant general, and Dudley S. Montague was elected as the county revenue commissioner, barely defeating Charles S. Meeks by seven votes. William H. Shaw was elected as Putnam County sheriff. However, it is important to grasp that Southern citizens, as well as a few Unionists, believed the Reformed Government of Virginia was illegitimate and refused to acknowledge the election results.[21]

Afterward, Sectionalist tensions continued, causing a correspondent identified only as "PEG" from Buffalo to write a scathing warning to Secessionists in their midst on June 12, 1862:

> You secessionists of Buffalo and vicinity, you who have persuaded ignorant and unsuspecting men into the traitors trap, who have promised to be a friend to the wife, mother, and children, left here among you. How can you escape the wife and children's curse, which will surely fall upon your guilty heads. Ye doctors, lawyers, magistrates, collectors of customs, tillers of the soil, merchants, and professors of religion, how can you escape the terrible curse now surely coming upon you! Your laughter will be turned into mourning, your sweet shall be turned into gall. Rebel leaders

Governor Francis H. Pierpont.
Library of Virginia.

in our town and country, how very humble you seem; how like lambs you appear in company; you who have caused innocent blood to be spilled – who have sacrificed your sons to this Malloch of secession! You have caused our friends to be killed in battle against the country they have sworn to defend. You have made many a hearth stone vacant!

You have aided villains in the dead hour of night, to surround the home of the poor loyal man, and in the presence of his wife and little ones, drag him forth and in the light of his burning home, hang him until dead, and then maltreat the body after death! Dark and horrid crimes rest against your souls. How can you bearing this blood guiltiness upon your souls, escape the damnation of Hell? Rebels, as sure as vengeance overtakes its victim, so sure the vengeance of an enraged and abused people will come upon you….Think of your doom, traitors, when you see some lie which is pleasing to a traitor's heart, and let your gatherings be few and far between. Look to the conscience as well as the fingers and see blood upon. The fearful – the man standing and hearing these idle tattlings of rebels in our midst, and does not rebuke them, is guilty of not knowing his whole duty. Will hit 'em again."[22]

Also on June 12, 1862, Captain Edward Naret, adjutant of the 181st Regiment Virginia Militia, had finally become so frustrated with being unable to persuade enough Union men to muster into his regiment that he tendered his resignation to the state adjutant general:

Sir: Above is my resignation as adjutant of the 181st Regiment of Va. Militia. I have not the means to give my time to an occupation which I deem unlikely to profit or benefit to the country. The men forming the different companies are in a majority Secessionists, I conceive that militia formed of such materials is dangerous to the state; I was appointed for the purpose of raising patrols at a time when our young men (the well affected) were willing to do duty and protect us; this was a peculiar institution. I raised two companies, and when organized I was ordered to transfer them to the volunteer service; I did so, I was then transferred without any desire on my part to the 181st Regiment. I organized one company and endeavored to organize others (three I believe) and found the material such as to discourage one and did not act any more as [at] that time Mrs. Naret was sick, and I was employed at the hospital as Surgeon; when the 8th Reg't left here, Mrs. Naret was much worse, and her disease terminated fatally. Now I cannot attend to any public duty which is not compensated by sufficient renumeration, as my losses during the last year force me to attend to my own interest….[23]

On June 18, 1862, Mary Sproul Higginbotham of Buffalo received sad news from her sister-in-law Mary Higginbotham, who lived in Grayson, Kentucky, that her sixteen-year-old nephew was murdered by "the Lincolnites" (Federal soldiers) while carrying a load of supplies to the family from the mercantile. She wrote that the boy was confronted by a Federal soldier, and one said he was going to shoot him, so he "threw up his arm." Another man on a horse nearby yelled out, "for Lord's sake don't shoot him," but the soldier fired and struck the boy in the arm, glancing onto his head. He died seven days later. Mary Sproul's nineteen-year-old son, Jonathan E. Higginbotham, appearing as E.J. Higginbotham in some records, was a private in Company D, 8th West Virginia Volunteer Infantry at that time. Jonathan served throughout the war. It is unknown whether Mary ever told her sister-in-law about her son serving in the Union army.[24]

Tensions between Union and Southern residents at Buffalo were anything but resolved by the summer of 1862. The resident identified only as "PEG" was frequently editorializing in local news organs, usually venting their ire toward "secessionists" whom they held responsible for all of the county's current plights, as did the

Southerners toward the Unionists. This time, PEG ominously opined a veiled threat toward an unnamed Confederate leader, on June 19, 1862:

What can be said in favor of, or two screen the rebel leaders, now in our midst? None now should have a heart so full of love akin to treason, as to offer one word in their behalf, so long as they oppose in secret, and openly the government of the United States. Not long since a noted rebel leader came home bringing with him his son, a young man, who was severely wounded. He came among us claiming the protection of that Government he had tried with other arch-rebels like himself, to over-throw. He lives now protected by the government, and in return for it, is carrying on underground, secret communication with rebels, and it is not for our good, nor for the good of the country, although the special interest of farmers seem to be consulted by him, in the construction of a "ditching plow," made I suppose to plow the last ditch into which rebels and rebellion is fast falling.

Mr. Rebel the people can see through your flimsy pretext; you have ruled these people long enough, your power over them is now at end. Your whole purpose is to reorganize that great political humbug- *Breckinridge Democracy*, which is sinking into the depths of obscurity where it and its framers are following with swift pace. The day they saw your hand lifted against your country, saw you robbed of what little honor you retained. You will wander about among men with the murderous guilt upon your soul; till Death shall come, and you go to your dreadful doom. The people know you, and knowing you despise you for persuading their children and husbands into the "Buffalo Guards," causing them to be slain to uphold your hellish schemes. We will remember you.[25]

Captain John Young's company was still technically assigned to the 11th West Virginia Infantry as Company G, though they were functioning autonomously without any immediate command oversight beyond Union headquarters in Charleston in June 1862. Young was a staunchly religious man and had been ordained as a Methodist-Episcopalian minister prior to the war. The correspondent known only as "PEG" recorded an incident involving Young's company enforcing the ban on alcohol:

On the morning of the 23d, Buffalo was taken completely by surprise. Capt. J.V. Young and his little company of Regulators come in town at quite an early hour taking us by storm. It was soon discovered that the Captain and his party were not enemies - were not men apt to "skedaddle"--but were friends to peace and lovers of good order and obedient to military law. Finding some contraband whiskey in town, kept by a Secesh Dutchman, and after some altercation with Mr. Secesh, Capt. Young ordered his men to empty the whiskey out, giving Mr. Secesh a rap on his pate, to teach him to be more civil, and that our military laws cannot be broken with impunity. Some of the Secesh living near their rebel friend, went in haste to see *if the whiskey was spilled*, but they did not seem to care for the [Dutchman's] story, although he declared positively, while running around in fright and madness, "I am kilt!" Mine Got I am kilt!" The boys thought he could halloo and run pretty well for a rebel that was 'kilt' or might 'go dead.' We are under military law now, the civil law cannot stand alone; and when men in violation of the law and order overstep both, they may expect and ought to receive rough handling. Our laws must be obeyed.

Being at the steamboat landing not long after the above occurrence, the boys saw a barrel of "red-eye" about to be put off from the steamer Freestone, -- marked "Apple Vinegar." Capt. Young immediately put a guard over it until he could get orders from Colonel Lightburn by telegraph from Charleston, what to do with the contraband article, received just off the steamer. He soon had his orders, and in obedience to *law* and his superiors, the whiskey was poured out. After this, in obedience, to the same officer and the same law, he poured out more of the contraband article found in town. In all of the above actions, the order and peace loving citizens; and I may say the *true Union* loving citizens heartily concurred. They sincerely thank him and his little band for their timely aid, and wish them great success in all their undertakings of like character.[26]

The summer of 1862 was a time of increased political and social uncertainty in Putnam County; not only were there growing rumors of becoming a new state, but the possibility of emancipation also began circulating. One western Virginia resident articulated, "While convinced of the necessity of abrogating slavery, the Western Virginians are wise enough to recognize the policy of making the change very slowly and with every possible security to the interests of both blacks and whites, and they are not at all indisposed to accept that splendid douceur which Congress promised to any slave initiating a system of gradual emancipation." Earlier on March 3, 1863, Congress approved the Conscription Act, establishing a military draft in Northern states. This piqued the fears of many Union men in the Kanawha Valley, who already dreaded it; although, as western Virginia was not yet a state, the region seemed to be in limbo. When news of heavy Union losses in the bloody Seven Days Campaign around Richmond, Virginia, reached the Kanawha Valley in July 1862, many believed a draft would soon be inevitable, and many began pondering the possibility of leaving the area to avoid conscription. A few had already gone as far to feign or malinger various medical conditions to avoid the shame of not enlisting for military service. According to one Putnam County resident:

...men of Putnam are getting badly scared about being drafted and many are reflecting on their options to enlist or wait it out, or 'skedaddle' altogether....it is astonishing to see how the list of lame, blind, deaf, & c. is increasing-Why sir, if the militia should be called out, or drafting commenced, there would not be a sound secession sympathizer in the county in ten days; those that could not limp, be blind or deaf, would leave for Dixie, we would then have peace and plenty. It is to be hoped that Governor Pierpont will have an eye to these things, and not expect Union men to do all the fighting and leave rebel sympathizers at their homes, attending to their various pursuits, and to circulate Secesh lies, to frighten the wives and children of the Union men who are battling for their liberties. No, let's have them all out in the ranks of the Union army or out of the country. This is the desire of the loyal men and women of Putnam County.[27]

Discussion of West Virginia statehood was also circulating in the Northern states, as the editor of the *Utica Herald* in New York had recently discussed:

The loyal people west of the Alleghenies who wish to inaugurate a government of their own, may be sure that whatever opposition arises to their scheme does not spring from a desire to chain them longer to the chariot wheels of the old Tidewater dynasty. They have suffered injustice and oppression at the hands of that aristocracy amply sufficient to account for their desire to set up for themselves... The taxation of the State has been mainly diverted from negro property in which the wealth of Eastern Virginia largely consists, thus throwing a disproportionate burden upon the small farmers of the west... Politically, the West has been outlawed. The East has had Executives and Judicial officers in profusion, the west none. This state of affairs has made the people of Western Virginia anxious to separate from the Old Dominion, and set up a State in which they might enjoy some of the benefits and powers, as well as all the burdens of sovereignty. But the slaveholders of the East recognized the advantage at which they held the free laborers of the West, and refused to relinquish it.[28]

On July 23, 1861, Major General John Pope, commanding the Department of Western Virginia, issued General Order No. 11, ordering military commanders to: "proceed immediately to arrest all disloyal male citizens within their lines or within their reach, within their respective stations. Such as are willing to take the oath of allegiance to the United States and will furnish security for its observance, shall be permitted to remain at their homes and pursue in good faith their accustomed avocations." Pope also asserted that those refusing to take the oath would be sent southward beyond Union lines, and, if they returned, would be considered spies. He also directed, "If any person having taken the oath of allegiance specified shall be found to have violated it, he shall be shot and his property seized and applied to public use."[29]

Despite Pope's order, such a stern response from Union troops did not immediately occur in Putnam County. The Unionist correspondent to the *Weekly Register*, "PEG," wrote again on July 24, 1863 indicating that recently students of the Buffalo Academy were seen defiantly wearing Secession cockades on their clothing, at the behest of their schoolmaster who was a known Southern supporter, following news of the Union defeat at Richmond in the Seven Days Campaign. PEG declared:

The city famous for mud, dog-fennel, and contraband whiskey, has again been disturbed by rebel sympathizers, who thinking that our army before Richmond had really gone up the spout, commenced to rejoice greatly and be very glad. The scholars of a certain school were rejoiced beyond measure, and the master of the school, who had at one time taken up arms against his country, was also greatly lifted up, and boasted that he wanted to hear no more of Richmond now, that the Yankees were so soundly beaten. His scholars were seen by several persons wearing badges of secession publicly, and from many other demonstrations, we thought a stop had better be put to the rebel school and the instructor removed as a dangerous nuisance.

The Union men here have been very kindly disposed toward the rebels in our town, but to be insulted by them for no other cause than we are in favor of a true Republican form of Government, is more than we can bear. Forbearance has ceased to be a virtue with us-and if we do not lift our hands in defense, what will become of us? We must show the revels that we are in earnest when we say the Constitution and laws, military and civil, must and shall be respected. When will the Union men of Buffalo, learn that they are contending against a blind, vindictive and dishonorable people-these rebels? Never perhaps until they have us foot and hand in their power.

Union men cry peace, peace, and do not lift a finger in trying to get that peace which the Government is battling for. Anything for peace, is the doctrine preached by some of our Union men, which means this; let the rebels alone, if they do us no harm we will not say nay, though they may spit in our faces. Rebels in our midst tray be secretly working our destruction, and these peace men would willingly excuse it. Buffalo rebels must be taught this very important truth, that they cannot live in enjoyment of the rights and privileges of our Government restored, and lift their hands to smite the power which governs and protects them. Union men must know that the duty of each is sternly required of him, and to performed to the letter. We must keep the rebel wolf from our door or basely surrender to his attack.

Shall Union men surrender to any who may violate the law, whether it be civil or military, or relating to contrabands brought among us by selfish and evil men. No, fight hard against all things, which would give the enemy any room to boast, and come out conquerors over Secesh and unlawful traffic at once. Union men should never put self in opposition to the laws of our country, in every case where this is done, the selfish one gives aid and comfort to the enemy. We should not let *false pride* turn us aside from our duty, but should and must show a firm front to the rebels here, if we want peace in honor, and in deed. Union men must stand to their colors, and not show the white feather. Success will surely follow if we but work with a will to do. I will in my next, look at the "greasy rat" Union men, I have only been given a little advice in a modest way, and telling what the Secesh are doing. Let us be up and doing, even if we lose a *peg*.[30]

The Union militia in Putnam County was still largely unorganized, and the few companies in the field were home guards essentially operating as independent commands. Despite Dr. Edward Naret's recent resignation as adjutant of the 181st Regiment Virginia Militia in June 1862, he wrote to General Jacob Cox on July 27, 1862, advising that "secessionists are much excited…. jubilant" at Buffalo, having learned that General Jenkins was nearby at his home, Green Bottom Plantation, in Cabell County. Naret informed Cox that local Southerners were threatening a young man from the area who recently received a commission as a 2nd Lieutenant in the Union army, challenging that "the Yankees must go up." He requested Cox send a company of cavalry to the area to protect Union citizens and that the leading "Rebels" be arrested and have their property confiscated. Cox did not initially believe Naret, however. Benjamin P. Morris of Winfield was commissioned as a 1st Lieutenant and appointed as Naret's replacement. He fared no better than Naret in motivating militia members to attend musters and wrote to state Adjutant General Henry J. Samuels complaining that he had tried to organize elections for officers in the Putnam County companies, but no one had attended the meetings. He noted that Lieutenant George W. Leadman's company included only ten men. Benjamin Morris was the father of Van B. Morris, who became a Sergeant in Company G, 11th West Virginia Infantry, under Captain John Young.[31]

George C. Bowyer of Winfield had recently been appointed as a state assistant adjutant general and was tasked to oversee 1st Lieutenant Benjamin Morris while organizing the militia in Putnam County. Equally annoyed with the lack of cooperation among Union men in the county, Bowyer reported to Henry Samuels on August 15, 1862: "As there is no commanders of companies in this county I do not see how I can comply with the orders…would it not be well to require every person liable to military duty to come forward and enroll themselves in a specified time or take the consequences?…The commissioners of the Revenue have taken no list of those liable to military duty since 1857…" Bowyer also informed Samuels he wanted to see more troops placed at Coalsmouth, as well as a garrison placed at Hurricane Bridge. He warned, "If something is not done immediately, we will have warm work in Putnam…" Bowyer did not care for General Cox's plan for protecting Union citizens in the Kanawha Valley either, as he opined that Federal troops: "…could be stationed at various places in the Kanawha Valley in sufficient strength to defend themselves against the rebel cavalry prowling through the country This plan of putting a few companies in dangerous places - where reinforcements can't get to them in time and where they are liable to be pounced upon and bagged by roving bands of guerrillas… and keeping a heavy force at Flat Top or any other Top when they are doing no good, in perfect inactivity is not my idea of good Generalship."[32]

Union troops leave the Kanawha Valley

Elsewhere, events in the Eastern Theater of war were about to bring significant changes to the Kanawha Valley once again. Brigadier General Jacob Cox was ordered to join Major General John Pope in northern Virginia on August 11, 1862, taking 5,000 troops—half of the Union forces in the Kanawha Valley—with him. Cox turned over command of the district to Colonel Joseph A. J. Lightburn when they met at Gauley Bridge on August 17. Cox, who had commanded Union forces in the Kanawha Valley from mid-1861 until that point, was given command of two brigades: the 1st Kanawha Brigade under command of Colonel Eliakim P. Scammon, comprised of the 12th, 23rd, 30th Ohio Volunteer Infantry regiments, and the 2nd Kanawha Brigade, commanded by Colonel Augustus Moor consisting of the 11th, 28th, and 36th Ohio Volunteer Infantry regiments. Cox also had two artillery batteries, along with Company I of the 1st West Virginia Cavalry and Company L of the 2nd West Virginia Cavalry in the Kanawha Division. On August 27-30, Cox's 1st Brigade participated in the Second Battle of Manassas.[33]

General Cox and the Kanawha Division were next sent to Washington, D.C., where Cox's two brigades briefly served on the outer defenses, until ordered to join the 9th Corps of the Army of the Potomac. Cox's division next participated in the Maryland Campaign, as General Robert E. Lee's Army of Northern Virginia hoped to destroy the Army of the Potomac under Major General George B. McClellan, clearing the path to Washington. The Kanawha Division fought at both the battles of South Mountain on September 14 and the battle of Antietam on September 17, 1862. During the fighting that morning, Major General Jesse Reno, who commanded the 9th Corps, was mortally wounded, and General Cox was given temporary command of the corps. He resisted this idea, pleading with General McClellan that he was too inexperienced at such level of command, but was placed under direct supervision of Major General Ambrose Burnside. Late in the day at Antietam, Cox advanced the 9th Corps on Lee's right and nearly overwhelmed the Confederates, until General A.P. Hill's 3rd Corps arrived to reinforce them, forcing Cox to withdraw. Antietam was afterward known as America's Bloodiest Day, with more than 23,000 men killed, wounded, or missing in action. President Abraham Lincoln was so impressed with Cox's aggressive demeanor that he recommended him to Congress for promotion to Major General, which was approved on October 6, 1862.[34]

Shortly after Cox left the Kanawha Valley, the state adjutant general ordered Colonel William Brown, commanding the 13th West Virginia Infantry, to direct Lieutenant Colonel James R. Hall to remove his three companies, A, B, and D, along with Captain John Young's Company G, from Winfield to Point Pleasant on August 29, 1862. Young's company was temporarily assigned to the 13th West Virginia Infantry as Company G by Governor Francis Pierpont on August 10, 1862. The effect of losing more than half of Cox's Union forces in the Kanawha Valley would prove significant, as it left the area blatantly vulnerable to attack, and the Confederates planned to take immediate advantage of the situation. Earlier on August 22, 1862, a dispatch book belonging to Major General John Pope was captured at Catlett's Station, Virginia, containing valuable intelligence related to Union troop strength, movements, and plans, including Cox's withdrawal of 5,000 troops. The Confederates quickly utilized the information, and on August 29, 1862, the Confederate authorities in Richmond directed Major General William W. Loring to clear the Kanawha Valley, and then to move northwardly to meet General Lee's army; after, Brigadier General John Floyd's Virginia State Line, comprised of four regiments, would hold the Kanawha Valley. Major General Loring's 6,000 Confederates were then gathering near Pearisburg, Virginia, and would soon advance on the Kanawha Valley. Loring, a native of Wilmington, North Carolina, was a career soldier. Known as a hard-edged fighter, he lost his left arm in the Seminole Wars and yet continued to lead troops in combat.[35]

Tea with General Jenkins

Colonel Albert G. Jenkins had seven companies of the 8th Virginia Cavalry, along with five independent companies of cavalry under Captain John P. Sheffey, in August 1862. They were ordered on an expedition throughout the northwestern counties and into the Kanawha Valley, and during this mission, Jenkins entered Ohio via Ravenswood. There, he encountered numerous civilians and later reported on the state of affairs across the river:

It was a subject of the very greatest interest with me to observe the state of feeling in Ohio and the impression our presence would produce. I may say in brief the latter was characterized by the wildest terror – so much so but for the pity of the subjects, of it one could only view it as an absurdity. Women inquired for officers wherever our troops appeared, and having found them, begged them not to permit them to murder them. Others came out of their dwellings and urged as a reason for not burning them that they contained invalids too much afflicted to be removed. To these requests we replied that, though that mode of warfare had been practiced upon ourselves, though many of the soldiers of our command were homeless and their families now exiles on account of the ruthless warfare that had been waged against us, we were not barbarians, but a civilized people struggling for their liberties, and that we would afford them that exemption from the horrors of a savage warfare that had not been extended to us.[36]

Jenkins crossed the Ohio River west of Point Pleasant, and briefly stopped at his home in Green Bottom in Cabell County. He next made his way toward Buffalo, arriving there on September 6, 1862. He had only recently resigned his former seat in the Confederate Congress and had a promotion to the rank of brigadier general pending at Richmond. Immediately upon arrival at Buffalo, he went to the home of Dr. Edward Naret, the former adjutant of the 181st Virginia Militia Regiment, who was not at home. Jenkins indulged himself in an afternoon tea taken from Naret's pantry, and took a horse and sixteen tons of hay for his troopers. Naret, who was already annoyed from his experience with the militia, was enraged when he learned of Jenkins plundering his property. He was later overheard laughing and gloating aloud when he learned that one of Jenkins' men afterward drowned while crossing the Kanawha River and that another died from a broken neck when his horse fell down an embankment.[37]

Lieutenant Colonel Daniel Frost, 11th West Virginia Infantry, telegraphed Governor Pierpont on September 8, 1862, "Jenkins is reported at his farm did not call at Pt Pleasant or here; I will start for Winfield this evening." When Governor Pierpont learned that Jenkins had returned to the Kanawha Valley, he telegraphed Colonel Joseph A.J. Lightburn at Point Pleasant encouraging him to send a large force out to find Jenkins. Lightburn knew that Loring was heading toward Charleston, however, and that doing so would require dividing his 5,000-man force, leaving the region even more dangerously exposed. As a result, he wisely declined Pierpont's request. On the other hand, Lightburn knew he could not ignore Jenkins either and ordered six companies of the 2nd West Virginia Cavalry under Colonel John C. Paxton, along with three companies of the 4th West Virginia Volunteer Infantry, to search for the Confederates.[38]

Paxton scouted the Hurricane Bridge area and heard from locals there that Jenkins was near Mud Bridge in Cabell County. Paxton moved toward Barboursville on September 8, 1862 and there found Jenkins. Paxton attacked, and, following a brief skirmish, Jenkins went into the lower Guyan Valley, while the Federals went to Guyandotte and camped for the night. The next day, Paxton took the James River Turnpike to Hurricane Bridge and from there returned to Coalsmouth. Twenty-two-year-old Joseph F. Sutton, a private in the 2nd West Virginia Cavalry, later recalled that they, "...returned by the same route viz Teays Valley to the mouth

Naret Mansion at Buffalo.
Photo by author.

of Coal River – now St. Albans, W.Va." Paxton crossed Coal Mountain and arrived at Coalsmouth at about 11 p.m. There, he soon learned Jenkins had tricked him, ridden south through Lincoln County, and was once more in the vicinity of Hurricane Bridge, some twelve miles west, with plans to attack the Federal rear, while a larger Confederate force attacked the Union garrison at Charleston under Major General Loring.[39]

While enroute to Coalsmouth on Midland Trail, Colonel Paxton's Federal detachment passed the home of John and Matilda "Tillie" McCallister not far from Hurricane Bridge. McCallister was a wealthy landholder and farmer, and he operated a brickyard and tannery located near the modern City of Hurricane reservoir on State Route 34. His father, Richard McCallister, settled in Teays Valley in the late 1700s and acquired a large tract of land along Midland Trail, modern Route 34. His son John inherited a large plot of the land near modern Cow Creek Road adjacent to Route 34, and using slave labor, built a large brick home there in 1847 that was known as the McCallister mansion in the Civil War period. Said to be the first brick home in the area, the large structure was considered the showpiece of the family's wealth. John McCallister died in 1865 at the age of seventy, survived by his wife Matilda who passed away in 1871 at age seventy-six. They had no children, and Matilda died without a will; the home was sold by the county to Dr. George L. Nye in 1872.[40]

The 1870 U.S. Census indicates Dr. Nye and his wife were living in the home with Matilda at that time as boarders. Nye and his wife had relocated to Teays Valley from Wytheville, Virginia, in the 1860s, where he established a medical practice. Matilda was rumored to be independently wealthy herself, with two large chests full of valuable gold coins. When she died, Nye disappeared from the Teays Valley area for unknown reasons,

McCallister Mansion.
Author's collection.

but he returned to purchase her house in 1872. Local lore speculated that Nye had stolen Matilda's money and returned only to spend it on her house, though there is no known documentation of it. After Nye's death, the home became a popular treasure hunting spot based on the legend of Matilda's gold. William Umberger, a local businessman who owned a popular gas station, inherited the home in the 1940s. His family occupied the property until his death; the house was destroyed by developers when housing subdivisions were constructed on the land during the 1980s.[41]

Confederates at the Door

As rumors of a general Confederate advance continued to flow across the Kanawha Valley, Sarah Young, like most other Unionists in the area, was in a state of hypervigilance and anxiousness. Her fears were justified, as she and her family received a visit from not only her father and some of his soldiers on September 12, 1862, but also a party of Confederates led by Captain James Nounnan, a former resident of Buffalo, who were looking for him. Nounnan and his company joined Colonel Milton J. Ferguson's battalion in August 1862, later becoming Company K, 16th Virginia Cavalry, and a month later were then on Young's doorstep. Sarah Young recalled:

Yesterday evening we heard of some Rebel soldiers in the neighborhood. Ma sent Ben [Benjamin Young, her fourteen-year-old brother] to Coalsmouth immediately to tell Pa, if he had not heard it; but others informed him and after dark Pa and three of his men pressed some "secesh" horses and borrowed one of Mr. Mynes, who is hiding from the Rebels, to come down in this neighborhood. They had been there but a short time before the men became sleepy, and Pa told them he would watch if they wished to sleep a little while. They all laid on the floor and I thought Pa looked tired. Emilie and myself told him we would watch if he wanted to rest. He laid down and in the course of an hour we heard horses coming. We wakened Pa directly, and he and the men ran out though the back door, passed around the corner of the house, but seeing too many Rebels to attack they slipped down the hill back of the house into a ravine thickly set with alders. Two of the men ran on. One concealed himself along the fence to get a shot at them. Pa hid in a large bunch of alders. When the rogues stopped they found the horses tied, and asked us, very authoritatively, what those horses were doing here. Ma told them, as they answered her when she spoke to them, that it was an unfair question, and she would not tell them. I never in my life experienced such a time.

They stayed around the house about two hours, scouting through the yard and listening; no doubt expecting Pa to come after their horses. I never felt so much like abusing men in my life. One rough, ill-bred fellow would not tell me his name. I suppose he was ashamed of it. Burns, one of the set, told Ma his name was Dotson from Guyandotte. All the time they were here they would not move the horses. They were fastened in the back yard, and I reckon they thought Pa would come after them. While Pa was in the alder bush, a large, over-grown horse-thief came sneaking around him, and would stand listening within about ten steps of Pa.

Pa said he fixed to shoot him, but he heard some more talking, and he thought he had better not. They came to the house and we talked with them some. Indeed, my heart ached so I could scarcely talk. Old Dotson said he thought he could get married somewhere on this road. I told him Rebel beaux could not shine with the Union girl, but Yankees went like hot cakes. He said, 'I think I could make a Secesh out of you.' I gave him to understand quite different. He said something about 'homespun Yankees.' I told him they were home-spun Rebels. He said, 'I would like to stay about a week and quarrel with you.' After a while, the notorious horse thief, and blood-thirsty Rebel, Jim Nounnan, came along and called for a candle to search the house.

Emilie carried the candle and helped to search, laughing all the time at them. I told Nounnan I would not tell him who came here, and if I knew where they were I would not tell him. He said it was immaterial to him that he only asked for information here. I think he was mad, but I did not care. Dotson told us we would have to go to the North with our sweethearts of submit to Jeff Davis. I hope he may never live to see the time. Well, I suppose they got tired of searching and waiting,. They bade us goodnight, wishing us good luck. Em [Emily] told them when gentlemen called on us we wanted them to come at a fashionable hour and not scare us half to death in the night. I told them I was not glad to see them, and did not wish them good luck at all. And I don't. After they had left the house, one of the soldiers fired at them. It scared them so that they went double quick down the road.

The soldier declares that he wounded one of them. Pa then came close to the house. I declare he looked so strange it frightened me to look at him. He had left his hat in the house. Ma took it to him and he said he would hide and wait for the boys but he started back to Camp. Ben was at Coalsmouth when he came, and said Pa had to crawl through the Rebel pickets. I suppose they were posted along to catch him. He went most of the way through the woods, and waded Coal river. After a while two of the others came in. They were very uneasy about the other one but before noon he came in. He was the one who fired at the Rebel."[42]

Sarah also mentioned in her diary that evening that she learned the Union cavalry captured a few Confederates as the passed through Hurricane Bridge:

The same evening the evening the Rebels were here, the Federal Cavalry came through Hurricane Bridge and captured six of their men. Good. They had no business here…Some of the Cavalry went to Winfield but made no discoveries.[43]

Skirmish on Coal Mountain

As rumors persisted in the area of a pending Confederate advance, Sarah Young remained at home near Coal Mountain. She again wrote in her diary: "Great excitement! We have heard that the Rebels are marching toward Buffalo…A dispatch came to Winfield that they were near Buffalo. The Union men have all run to the woods. The steamboats have stopped running. Pa was at Coalsmouth with only his company, but he has been reinforced by Cavalry and Infantry. Oh, may they be successful in holding the post and driving the detestable traitors off!" At about 9 p.m. on September 12, 1862, Colonel John Paxton, 2nd West Virginia Cavalry, sent Captain John Young's company, along with Company K, 2nd West Virginia Cavalry, to reconnoiter Hurricane Bridge, looking for Jenkins. They moved west along the James River Turnpike and encountered Jenkins' pickets a few miles from Hurricane Bridge. Jenkins was said to be familiar with Captain Young and had sent word to him that he would "eat supper in Coalsmouth or in Hell" that night, according to Sarah Young.[44]

Around 11 p.m., Company G and the cavalry had driven Jenkins' pickets in, and after a brief skirmish, Paxton's troops withdrew toward Coal Mountain and took up a defensive position on the western face of the summit. Jenkins gave pursuit, and an intense skirmish ensued along the upper ridgeline of the mountain. The fight resulted in two minor casualties in Company G and two of Jenkins' men killed. One Union soldier reported they were "fighting like the devil" but were heavily outnumbered and had to fall back toward Coalsmouth after waiting for nearly three hours on expected reinforcements that never arrived. Colonel Joseph A.J. Lightburn, commanding Union troops in the Kanawha Valley at that time, reported on Paxton's recent expedition to Barboursville and the fight on Coal Mountain: "The Second Virginia Cavalry, under Colonel Paxton, did good service in keeping Jenkin's force at bay, thereby preventing an attack in our rear. I wish also to state, that Colonel Paxton, with 300 men, attacked Jenkins whole force (1,200 to 1,500) and drove them from Barboursville, which, no doubt, kept them from an attempt to harass our retreat." Note that Private James F. Sutton, Company H, 2nd West Virginia Cavalry, later reported that Jenkins had approximately 1,000 to 1,2000 men.[45]

Sarah Young later learned more from her father about the skirmish:

…Pa went to meet him [Jenkins] with horsemen and footmen. They had a skirmish on Coal Mountain last night. The Rebels retreated. We heard that two of Pa's men were wounded, but don't know how true it is. They are pursuing them yet. Oh, when will we enjoy the blessings of sweet peace? When will we be clear of annoying Guerrillas? When will our once happy land boast of its prosperity? Ah, I fear not until many brave and gallant soldiers fall on the battlefield. Our dead soldiers who have offered their lives on the altar of victory; crown their efforts with success; aid them in every trial, and oh, be their hope in distress. May our leaders and Generals call upon Thee for divine wisdom; and, as the immortal

Washington did in the old Revolution, humble themselves before Thee, and ask Thee for Thy assistance. God, give them all they require. The 2nd, Va. Cavalry are pursuing the Rebels yet. We heard that the beautiful flag which we presented to Co. F, 8th Va. Vol. is the only one in the regiment. Oh, may the gallant officers and brave soldiers of that company rally around it, and vow that traitors shall never trail it in the dust so long as they have strength to sustain it!"[46]

Sarah Young also mentioned her father had earlier sent six men from Company G to their home to see if the "...Rebels had disturbed us last night. He was uneasy about us. Oh, I wish the detestable Rebels would stay away from West Virginia! They have come in and caused the Federals to burn up some of the most influential rebel's property..." She also quipped that the Federals had not even given one Secessionist "...time to get his hat out of his house" before burning it.[47]

Battle of Charleston – Lightburn's Retreat

On September 13, 1862, Major General William W. Loring's force of 5,000 Confederates, including the 22nd Virginia Infantry and 36th Virginia Infantry, was marching toward Charleston, with orders to create a diversion from General Robert E. Lee's upcoming Maryland Campaign and capture the salt mines near there. After several hours of heavy fighting, the Federals withdrew toward the Elk River and crossed a large suspension bridge to the western bank, where Lightburn had posted two regiments to cover them. Confederate artillery quickly zeroed in on their position and bombarded them until about 5 p.m., while the Federal artillery provided heavy counter- battery fire. Once all the Federals had crossed, they cut the bridge's cables on the west bank and let it fall into the river to prevent Confederates from pursuing them further. Realizing the town was lost, Colonel Lightburn ordered a general withdrawal toward Point Pleasant, and thousands of dollars in government stores were burned to prevent capture. As Lightburn's troops made their way along the Ohio River toward Point Pleasant by way of Ravenswood with Confederates rapidly pursing, one Ohio soldier described it as "a continual skirmish for fifty miles" under rapid, forced-march conditions.[48]

Once the Confederates had regained control of Charleston, Loring established his headquarters at Coalsmouth. Southern-leaning residents quickly informed Loring that the Union troops garrisoning Coalsmouth had abused them, including Captain John Young and his company, though not all their stories were truthful. Nonetheless, the Confederates retaliated by tormenting and arresting many local Union soldiers' family members in particular, as well as other Unionists. One of Loring's first actions was also to seize control of the *Kanawha Valley Star*, a popular local newspaper that had only recently relocated to Charleston from Buffalo. Another newspaper soon emerged, known as *The Guerilla*. This organ made clear its intent to persuade Union men to side with the Confederacy. The first issue appeared on September 29, 1862, addressing Union citizens then under Confederate martial law:

During the past few days the Kanawha and Ohio rivers have been full of flatboats...laden with the families of Unionists, who find themselves compelled to flee...fearing the rebel General will carry into execution his recently made threat to hang every citizen "Yankee" he found in the Kanawha Valley... they are obliged to leave behind them what they depended on to subsistence during the coming winter...most of them have to seek a charitable home among strangers...It is a pitiful sight to see families adrift... to find a home they knew not where-and all because their father or husband would not renounce his allegiance to the Government of his Fathers. The rebels in Western Virginia have declared themselves unsatisfied with anything less than armed resistance to the Federal power on the part of citizens whom they meet in their raids. It will not do to say you have not taken sides with either way, or that your sympathies only are with one side or the other. They demand active participation in their cause, and "confiscation" robbery and outrage are the punishments for Federalism.[49]

At this point, Union citizens were afraid to leave their homes, though many others had evacuated the area completely, leaving those they left behind isolated and feeling very alone. At Buffalo, Union citizens were anxiously awaiting the return of General Albert G. Jenkins' cavalry, expecting the full measure of his wrath now that Federal troops were gone to Point Pleasant. *The Weekly Register* correspondent "PEG" wrote on September 14, 1862:

Our little town was again thrown into a state of dread by hearing from a reliable source that Jenkins the Moses of the Secesh, whom they are daily expecting to come with a mighty rod, and turn all men into secesh serpents, and the women into garter snakes. This was Sunday evening the 27th ult. Now rebels what will Jenkins do for the cause if he does come? He may take some prisoners, and kill some of our Union men, steal some horses, and burn the town, but will all this cause the government to recognize the rebellious states as an independent government. I think not. I ben [have been wondering] what would bring him in to see us upon your invitation? If this infernal rebel should attack the little towns on the Kanawha, it will only end in your own destruction. As sure as God is in Heaven, and governs the universe at will, so sure will you rebels and rebel sympathizers have to pay the penalty, and that fivefold. You understand the law, profit by your understanding. Quite an amount of chicken fixens and other nice things were prepared by the rebels for somebody, and their actions for the past two weeks has been rather suspicious; and we know that everything is not going on as it should do. Let the consequences seen in other places where secesh guerrillas have been invited in to burn, steal and kill, be a warning to you. It will be a bitter and short lived triumph for your Secesh horse-thieves.

Putnam County has provided quiet liberally for the Volunteers, who obeying the great call of their country, in her present distress, may come forward to the rescue. Having a prospect of aid from the county, our able-bodied men should no longer hesitate. It is your country now dishonored and shamefully abused that calls upon you for help. The Government of the United States has been more than parental toward us, has defended and protected our lives and property, and given us the proud name of citizens of the United States. This government has given you all the blessings which man can enjoy. Freedom of Speech, thought, and religion you have enjoyed, with none to say thou shalt not, or what doest thou! A gigantic and bloody rebellion, is now shaking the nation to its center, laying waste the fruitful fields and valleys, cities, and villages, and robbing many hearthstones of the doated ones, causing sorrow and desolation to fall like lead upon the heart.

This might rebellion the offspring of passion, envy, hatred, ambition, and pride; now seeks with more than a devils' zeal to destroy, waste and consume the blessings of the farmer, where the protection of the government arms made it safe for him to follow the good old plow, and look forward to a harvest of plenty. The rebels are now working their will like the rebellious angels when inspired by a blind ambition, they would willingly have destroyed Heaven, rather than have served the Great Ruler of Heaven and earth. Pretended friends of our country are insinuating themselves into favor, only to act wolf in sheep's clothing, and carry off the fleece; not caring for the sheep of the fold. To crush this wicked rebellion, our government has called for 300,000 additional volunteers, to restore order and obedience to the

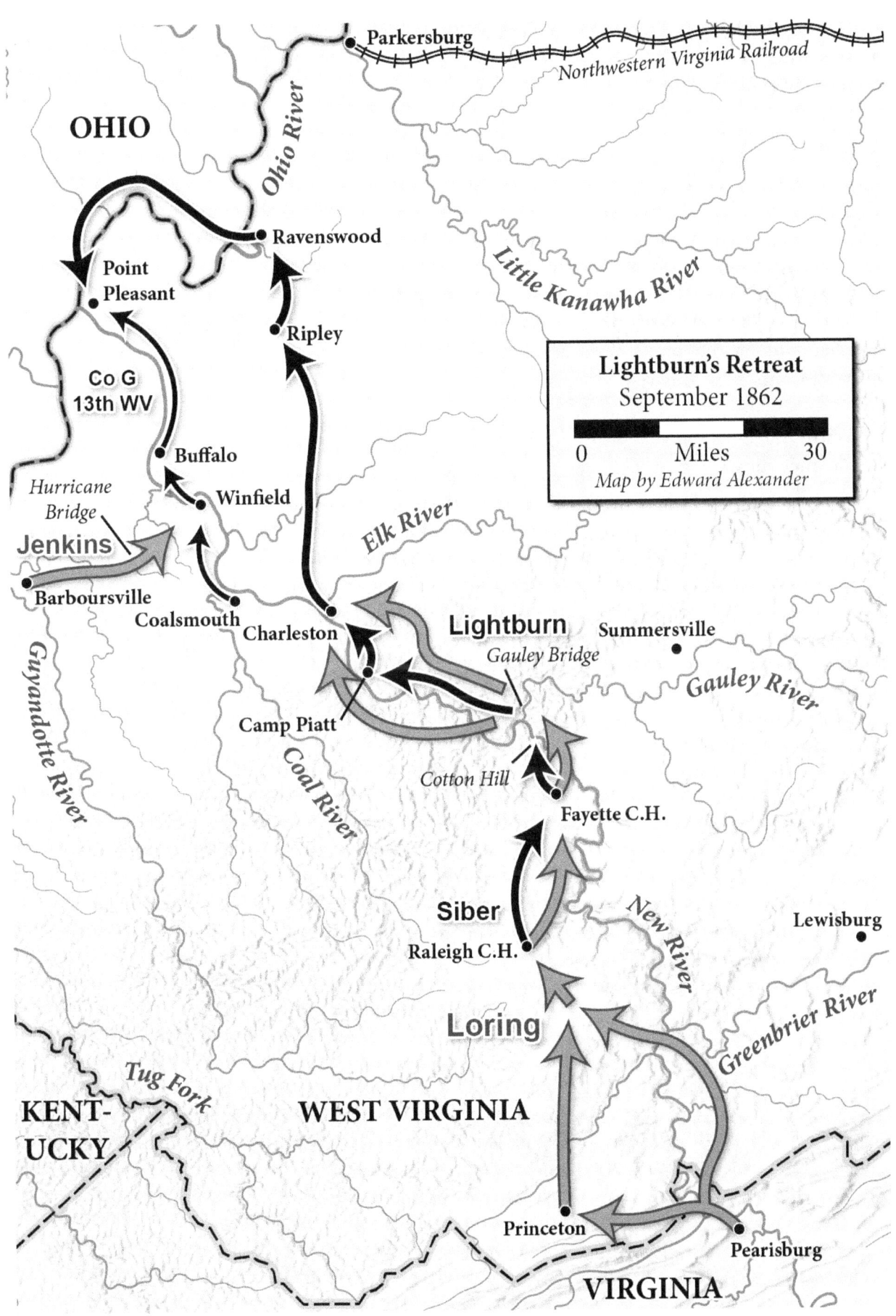

Lightburn's Retreat
September 1862

0   Miles   30

Map by Edward Alexander

Constitution and laws, and to vindicate our honor as a nation, which has been insulted with impunity since our bright banner was desecrated by a rebel's touch, and the Devils in human form spread forth the banner of civil fratricidal war.

Seeing that these things are so, and our bleeding country calling like an outraged maiden to her brothers strong and brave to deliver her from the brute that would ---- let my strong arm help to give the tyrant, "pride and love of power" the fatal blow. You whose circumstances will permit need no thoughts of mine to prompt you to duty, when you see your country calls you. Look at your brothers everywhere, see them hastening away to the tented field, to share the wild excitement of battle and the hardships of a soldier's life, and enjoy the proud satisfaction of being patriots. The day is almost here when our friends will return from the war. Rebellion will be crushed in the land forever, and our brave volunteers will be welcomed home by thousands of warm hearts. Come volunteer and enjoy those proud blessings, with your brave brothers, who have gone to the field before you....[50]

Union citizens had virtually no protection now, though there were still a few home guard companies posted near Buffalo, including Captain E.H. Ferguson's company. Twenty-nine-year-old George Rucker of Putnam County traveled to Point Pleasant to enlist in Company E, 13th West Virginia, on September 15, 1862, under the promise that the company would be trained and armed specifically as sharpshooters. This was a particularly strong incentive for men who had otherwise hesitated to enlist due to fears of being sent away from their homes, or those who dreaded dealing with harsh military discipline, because generally, sharpshooters were excused from boring and mundane camp duties and excessive drill—and they were otherwise required to spend their time in target practice. When it never materialized, the men recruited for that purpose elected to enlist in Captain John Carter's Company E, 13th West Virginia Infantry at Point Pleasant on October 9, 1862.[51]

Rucker later recalled his early soldiering experiences in Putnam County: "...We marched enough to make a trail around the world, and often had to dispossess rebels of territory we desired to occupy, penetrate or traverse. They were a stubborn lot too, and often resisted in a vigorous manner; often too, they were very threatening in their attitude and proximity when we would have preferred their absence from sight and mind. We would indeed, have been very pleased had they gone home and forgotten all about us. But they were seldom disposed to yield to our wishes, and their stubbornness in that respect often made trouble for us and themselves...."[52]

The Union home guards continued to pressure Confederate troops during nocturnal patrols, but the general state of the Union militia in the Kanawha Valley had improved little, if any, since 1861 and citizen patrols stopped functioning with the area under Confederate control. On September 18, 1862, Brigadier General George C. Bowyer, commanding a brigade of Union militia in Kanawha, Putnam, and Mason counties, acting on orders from Governor Pierpont called up the militia to respond to the imminent threat of a large group of Confederate partisans recently spotted raiding in the area. A Union resident of Buffalo observed:

We are informed that the citizens of that portion of the country through which the d----d villains passed, were robbed of about one hundred and twenty-five of their most valuable horses, besides destroying large quantities of their corn and hay. From 13 Mile Creek, the half-starved hounds passed up to the town of Buffalo, where they crossed the Kanawha River, a portion of them dividing into squads, and the balance going in the direction of Hurricane Bridge – or hell, we hope the latter place.[53]

The 106th Regiment Virginia Militia in Mason County immediately responded to Bowyer's orders and turned out *en masse* at the county courthouse; in Putnam County, only a handful of militiamen turned out, however, as many were still fearful doing so would cause them to be drafted into the national army. The order stated:

> Rally, every man who is worthy of the name. Let mean dastards and white-livered cowards skulk from their share of the danger if they will, but do your duty to yourselves and your government, and if necessary, die in its defence. Fight them any way you can. Fire from behind trees, rocks, and logs, and from houses, but be sure and take deliberate aim, and save a secessionist every fire.[54]

On September 22, 1862, President Lincoln announced the Emancipation Proclamation, which would not take effect until January 1, 1863, and included only the Southern slave states in rebellion "and does not apply to those slave states or parts of slave states that have not rebelled...." Some Union citizens in western Virginia reacted with mixed emotions, as one resident opined: "...It is put forth solely as a *war measure* by the President as Commander in Chief...The slaves of rebels being employed to make arms, ammunition, forts, ships, clothing, military roads, & earthworks, etc., and especially in furnishing commissary supplies, common sense, as well as the laws of war, demand that these slave auxiliaries be forcibly taken from our enemy, and used as far as practicable, in support of, instead of against, the Union, and let those we can't employ be speedily colonized by themselves. Let the Union live though slavery die."[55]

A Putnam Farmer meets General Jenkins

An interesting, but otherwise unverified, anecdote from local tradition claims that one day in late September 1862, General Albert G. Jenkins was at Buffalo. He was thirsty, and rode up to the farm of Joseph Martin Butler, who had only recently been commissioned as a 2nd Lieutenant in the 13th West Virginia Infantry as a recruiter on July 8, 1862. Butler was home on a brief furlough, visiting his family. Jenkins rode up to him and requested a drink of water, unaware that Butler was a Union officer. Butler obliged and brought him a pitcher of water. According to Butler's son, Joseph Junior: "He asked if Father knew General Jenkins, Father told him yes. Well, he says, I'm General Jenkins. Father told him he would not have recognized him in uniform...Jenkins lived just below Little Guyan, and he wouldn't allow his men to bother anyone in that neighborhood. They took two horses from Wash Holly, and as soon as he found it out he made them take the horses back. Father didn't hang around very long, he skipped back to Point Pleasant to his regiment."[56]

Battle of Atkeson's Gate: "A continual skirmish"

At 6 p.m. on September 26, 1862, the 91st Ohio Infantry under Colonel John A. Turley left Point Pleasant and marched down the Kanawha River toward Buffalo. The 91st Ohio was yet untested in battle, having mustered into Federal service on September 7, 1862, with roughly 700 to 800 men. Turley was under orders to keep an eye on the Confederate cavalry moving about the area under Brigadier General Jenkins. At that time, Jenkins' force was about 500 to 600, comprised of seven companies of the 8th Virginia Cavalry; four companies of cavalry under Captain Waller R. Preston; and Colonel Milton J. Ferguson's Battalion (five companies), which was then under command of Captain John Preston Sheffey, as Ferguson was severely wounded at French Creek a few days earlier. Those units under Captain Preston were formerly of Major George Jackson's Squadron Virginia Cavalry and were recently assigned to the 14th Virginia Cavalry. Jenkins recently completed an extensive raid through the central and northwestern counties of Virginia from August 11, 1862, through September 19, 1862, covering the towns of Weston, Glenville, Spencer, Ripley, Ravenswood, and Buckhannon and crossed the Ohio

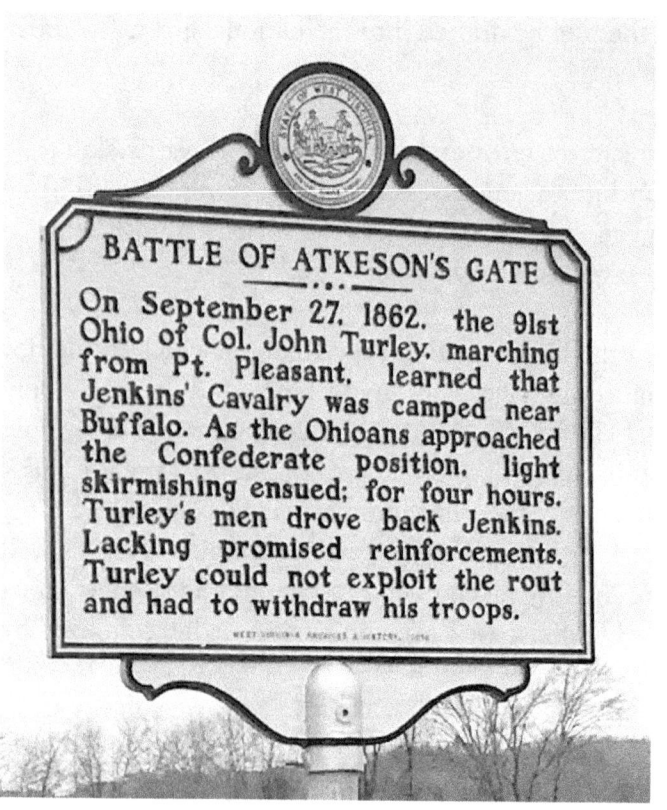

BATTLE OF ATKESON'S GATE

On September 27, 1862, the 91st Ohio of Col. John Turley, marching from Pt. Pleasant, learned that Jenkins' Cavalry was camped near Buffalo. As the Ohioans approached the Confederate position, light skirmishing ensued; for four hours, Turley's men drove back Jenkins. Lacking promised reinforcements, Turley could not exploit the rout and had to withdraw his troops.

Photo by author.

River into the Buckeye state. On September 19, 1862, Jenkins reported capturing 5,000 stands of arms at Buchannan during the expedition, which were used to rearm the 8th Virginia Cavalry regiment. Jenkins stated, "Many of my command were poorly armed, and all were at once supplied with Enfield and Harpers Ferry rifles, except a single company, which I permitted to keep its shotguns for the purpose of heading a charge."[57]

Jenkins also mentioned capturing a "beautiful brass 6-pounder" but had to disable and abandon the gun, as they "could not conveniently take [it] with us.... having found the brass 6-pounder too heavy for transportation over the roads and having sent back the small mountain piece with which I started...." Jenkins had started the mission with a six-pound mountain Howitzer and found it too cumbersome to move over the small bridle paths in the mountainous terrain, and he returned it to the point where the expedition started near Rich Mountain. After Jenkins left Ohio, he returned to Virginia soil about six miles north of Point Pleasant and considered attacking the larger Union garrison there—but decided against it because he lacked artillery. When Confederates regained control of the Kanawha Valley, Jenkins returned to Buffalo and established a camp on the farm of Southern supporter Benjamin F. Sterrett (1813-1892), locally known as Fairview, about 1.25 miles north of the village, near the Thomas Atkeson Farm. Benjamin Sterrett's eighteen-year-old son, Samuel Alexander, was a private on Company A, 36th Virginia Infantry, and his twenty-eight-year-old son Boyd B. was a second lieutenant, also serving in Company A. The Federals soon found Jenkins' videttes (sentries) from the 8th Virginia Cavalry under Major James Nounnan about one mile north of Eighteen Mile Creek, approximately two miles from the Sterrett farm, surprising them in a brief skirmish and driving them southward. The ensuing action is best construed as a series of three brief skirmishes that consecutively occurred along the Charleston Road, modern U.S. Route 62, adjacent to the Kanawha River.[58]

Private James C. Allen, Company F, 91st Ohio Infantry, described the march from Point Pleasant toward Buffalo on September 26, 1862:

We was ordered to prepare 3 days rations and start up to Buffalo, 25 miles from here and we started just before dark. Well we went on all night without stopping only to examine Bridges and just after sunrise we reached the rebel pickets. We fired on them and they fled as fast as their horses could carry them all but one his horse threw him and we got man horse and all. They was all of Jenkins Cavalry well we followed them *at the double quick* for two miles where we found their camp and they were all in confusion and fixing to run as usual but we fired on them so *duently* they hadn't time to run so they passed a few hundred shots before they went. The fight continued about three minutes. I think Company C and F and D only being close enough to fire and the fog was so thick we could not see them till after they took to the hills. They fled like sheep scattered by dogs up the lane toward the little town a mile and a half off.

Benjamin F. Sterrett house (Fairview).
WV State Archives.

Well, we followed them as close as we could leaving enough of our men to catch the horses they had left and attend to stragglers that was left. Being on entering the little town we found the rebels making across the river as fast as they could....they opened cannons on us and we fired at them as long as we could see one of them to shoot at but we could not fall [follow] them across the river so we came back to camp taking 17 head of fine beef cattle 18 horses and 3 men besides clothes and all we could carry and burned what we could not carry having no way to hall [haul] anything....we saw the Elephant, [their first battle] the best we know about them and killed 9 wounded several all the bad luck we had one of our boys got his gun broke into in his hand and they say a ball hit the flag staff....

When we got to the little town the Colonel stormed out where is them cannons tell us or we will burn you up and the women began to throw _____ out white flags and point in the direction the Rebels fled to a thick grove of timber on the opposite side of the river but the cannon soon ceased and the horseman fled so fast we fired after the horse thieves and started back to our camp not being able to overtake them we are now at Point Pleasant safe and sound but wore out with a march of fifty miles without halt or eat or sleep but once for hour that is what I call a scout....I captured....a secesh knapsack blanket shirt one pair of drawers a mans shawl and a woman's shoe. I sold the shawl for one dollar on my way to camp I had more than I could carry it was worth 5 dollars that is all the money I have now I am wearing the shirt and drawers....[59]

Colonel John A. Turley, 91st Ohio Infantry, described the Federal advance and the fighting around the Sterrett and Atkeson farms in his official report; note that it is 1.8 miles from Eighteen Mile Creek to the Thomas Atkeson farm, to the vicinity where the Federals encountered "a warm reception" from the Confederates. Colonel Turley reported:

My regiment…proceeded up the Kanawha River to within 1 mile of Eighteen-Mile Creek without any interruption, at which point we encountered the rebel videttes of Jenkins' cavalry, one of whom my advance captured, and from whom we learned the strength and situation of the enemy's forces in front, and, not yet hearing from either the Second [West] Virginia Cavalry or from the Fortieth Ohio Infantry, both of which were to have co-operated with us, I pushed forward my regiment as rapidly as possible on Buffalo.

…after crossing the creek, I deployed on the right and left of the road and kept up a continual skirmish with rebel cavalry, driving them before us to within 1 mile of Buffalo, when the rebels opened upon us with two pieces of artillery, throwing small shells, which chiefly passed over our heads; and, not yet hearing from the Second Virginia or Fortieth Ohio, *I ordered my regiment to unsling blankets and haversacks and move on, double-quick,* and try to capture the enemy's guns, which were placed near the bridge, at the lower end of the town; but, the enemy being mostly mounted and my force having to cross a marshy ravine, our progress was so impeded that we were unable to overtake them.
We pursued them into the town and to the river, where they separated, panic-stricken, a portion of them retreating up the river and the rest crossing over the river, upon whom we opened a brisk fire, driving them from the opposite bank. We remained one hour in Buffalo, hoping to hear from our forces on my right and left, which were expected to co-operate with me; but, not hearing from them, and ascertaining the strength of the enemy in front, I followed your order to fall back, bringing away all the property my regiment could carry, and destroying all commissary stores below Buffalo belonging to the enemy. Had the bridge along the Kanawha been standing, I should have brought the commissary stores to headquarters. We captured 2 of Jenkins' cavalry, killed 5, and wounded at least as many more, and took a number of horses and 8 or 10 Enfield rifles….[60]

The two cannons employed by the Confederates were M1841 six-pound brass Howitzers; however, it is unknown to which battery they belonged. These guns had a maximum range of approximately 1,500 yards and were generally effective within 1,000 yards, the latter distance being equivalent to nine-tenths of a mile. Note the Atkeson farm gate along the Charleston Road was approximately 1.7 miles from the bridge on the outskirts of Buffalo. Hence, shortly after engaging the Confederates at the Atkeson farm, the 91st Ohio drove the cavalrymen toward Buffalo, and when they were within a mile of the bridge on the outskirts of the village, the regiment came under artillery fire, while loading and firing at the double quick. Chaplain Anthony W. Windsor, 91st Ohio, also described the action at Atkeson's Gate with a somewhat superfluous description suggesting a rout, although contemporaneous accounts indicate the Confederates offered a stubborn resistance, forcing the Federals to contest every step. Windsor observed:

The object of the expedition was to surprise and if possible capture a rebel camp at Buffalo on the Kanawha River. The surprise was most complete. The rebels, astonished at the suddenness of the attack, fled with the utmost precipitation. They seemed to think the whole Yankee nation was upon them, with guns in their hands and vengeance in their hearts....the rebels beat a hasty retreat that has scarcely, if ever, been equaled for rapidity.[61]

Captain John P. Sheffey, Company A, 8th Virginia Cavalry, offered a somewhat different version of the action, and he stated the battle had occurred on September 28, 1862—not September 26, as confirmed by several other accounts. Sheffey, a native of Marion, Virginia, was an attorney prior to the war. He enlisted in Captain John H. Thompson's company in the 50th Virginia Infantry on May 27, 1861, and was promoted to 1st Lieutenant on the same day. He had earlier served as assistant adjutant general in 1861 and was promoted to captain on May 13, 1862. Sheffey wrote about the fighting from his camp a few days later, on October 5, 1862:

Colonel John A. Turley.
New York State Library.

We are encamped at Sterrett's [farm] one and a half miles below Buffalo, from which camp I wrote to you last…On the 20th, ult., our picket at the mouth of Eighteen, [Mile Creek] about five miles below camp, was surprised. One was killed, one wounded and one taken prisoner. Last Saturday morning, Sept. 28th about daybreak, I was standing at Sterrett's gate listening to distant firing in the direction of our lower picket. After a while, a fellow appeared down the road jogging along at a snail's pace. In course of time he came to where I was standing. He was about to pass me when a sudden notion struck him and checking up his *rosinate* [Rosinante] he said with slow, measured tones, "Yer would be better siftin. The pickets is gone up, all but me, and the Yankees is comin."

There was fortunately a heavy fog. The Yankees opened up almost immediately upon [Maj. George] Jackson's squadron, now the 14th Cavalry. They came in on one side of the field in which we were encamped as we went out upon the other. I was thrown in the rear, and we then, as we had only about 300 men, retreated 2 1/2 miles up the valley to a point one mile above Buffalo. I was then sent back with my company and a piece of artillery under command of Major [James W.] Sweeney to check the advance. We went back through Buffalo and crossing a bridge over a creek found ourselves within 75 yards of their advance. We could not see further than that on account of the fog.

We immediately opened upon them with the howitzer, and they upon us with their rifles. A couple of shells thrown amongst them, however, made them as silent as the grave. But they were busily engaged in flanking, and we fell back to about 50 yards to this side of the bridge. From this point we shelled them again. Throwing out our scouts into the fog to give us notice of their flank movements, we fell back slowly to the upper end of the town, about 300 yards from the bridge.

Here I was standing upon the bank of the river when a skiff with two rangers in it shot out from the opposite bank. They had nearly crossed to where I was, when the Yankees saw them & poured in a terrific fire upon them. The two soldiers immediately pulled for the bank from which they had started and reached it through a tempest of balls without injury. By this time the Yankees were within one hundred yards of me, though they did not see me. For the next half mile, we "skedaddled" at a gallop, and at length came up to our main body, which was by this time in good fighting humor. We now

Thomas Atkeson house,
view from Charleston Road, (Rt. 62), circa 1980s.
WV State Archives.

prepared for the fighting in good earnest, planting our two pieces of artillery, and throwing up some rail breastworks. We awaited the onset.

But the Yankees were now schooled to caution, and the onset did not come. After we had lain in wait about an hour, the 36th & 60th Virginia Regts. came from Winfield, 9 miles, double-quick to our assistance. We now assumed the offensive and advanced with thundering artillery and such hostile demonstrations that the Yankees fled in the utmost consternation. Unfortunately, the cavalry had been dismounted to fight on foot, and we consequently could not pursue them more than two or three miles….But we gave them such a fright that we have not been troubled since by them.[62]

Sheffey exaggerated the Federal numbers in his account, stating there were two Federal regiments, one with 600 men and the other with 800, although there was only one Federal regiment involved, the 91st Ohio with around 500. Sheffey often wrote to his sweetheart, Ms. Josephine Spiller of Wytheville, Virginia. While posted at Buffalo the next day, Sheffey indicated the Confederates went on a scouting mission within eight miles of Point Pleasant the next day. He was quite frustrated with lack of access to Southern newspapers and had earlier quipped to Josephine: "Please write as soon as you can. We are very anxious to hear from our armies in the East. We get no papers here but Yankee papers and they are so one-sided." Sheffey was later captured at Moorefield, West Virginia, on August 7, 1864.[63]

Although it is unclear when they arrived, Fred Conner, the camp servant of Colonel William E. Fife, 36th Virginia Infantry, later wrote that the 36th Virginia Infantry marched from Red House Shoals to Buffalo and engaged the Federals as they retreated from Buffalo toward Point Pleasant. Conner's account appears somewhat exaggerated in contrast to other descriptions of this phase of the fighting, as the 91st Ohio was clearly not routed. Conner wrote:

> …they reached a point near the farm of L.L. Bronaugh the hill – known as the Allen Hill – leading into Buffalo – the 36th opened fire completely routing the enemy, some taking to the hills while others went on down the valley towards Pt. Pleasant never having fired a shot.[64]

Two members of the Atkeson family present during the battle, Thomas and Mary, later described the fighting on their farm on that foggy October morning when the Federals:

Captain John Preston Sheffey.
Courtesy Terry Compton.

> …came up the Valley at daylight and began firing on the pickets at the lower camp. The Rebels moved up the Valley in wild confusion to the camp above, where they rallied somewhat and sent a small company of cavalry down the road to check the Federals. About this time my father, growing curious about the situation, walked out to the turnpike [a.k.a. the old Buffalo Road] which is a hundred yard or so from the house. All the rest of us were content to watch the proceedings out of the windows. Just then the rebel cavalrymen were fired upon by the Federals, and back they came with bullets flying about them, and we saw my father start for the house as fast as he could travel. The bullets cut some small branches from the trees on our lawn, but the battle lasted only a few minutes, and, as far as I know, no casualties occurred.[65]

Samantha Atkeson, who was then about sixteen or seventeen years old, later produced a painting of what she witnessed during the battle. The figure on horseback in the center is believed to be Major James H. Nounnan of the 8th Virginia Cavalry. Other residents of the Buffalo area were reportedly "terrified" by the fighting, and afterward many Unionists left to take refuge in Point Pleasant for fear the fighting would resume.[66]

An unidentified Union soldier present that morning also added divergent details of the Confederate retreat:

> …our gallant boys chased the thieves though the town, and to the river, when they separated, part continuing up the river and the rest crossing it, but finding the opposite bank too warm for safety, they unchivalrously retired beyond our range of fire. It is said the blinding dust "kicked up" by the skedaddling cavalry, prevented our boys from aiming with precision, or they doubtless, would have been much more severely handled, and if the 40th reg's O.V.I. which had gone up the river on the other side, and the 2nd [West] Va. Cavalry which had by a circuitous route, obtained their rear, been in cooperating distance, the whole rebel crew might have been bagged; but the expedition was not bootless, notwithstanding this unfortunate failure to "come to time," as we captured three of Jenkins' cavalry killed five and wounded

Cannonball

Believed to have been from the Battle of Atkinson's Gate

Found and Donated By: Jimmy Reedy

Courtesy Buffalo Academy Museum.

Atkeson house, circa 1900. (Lawnvale).
Courtesy Buffalo Academy Museum.

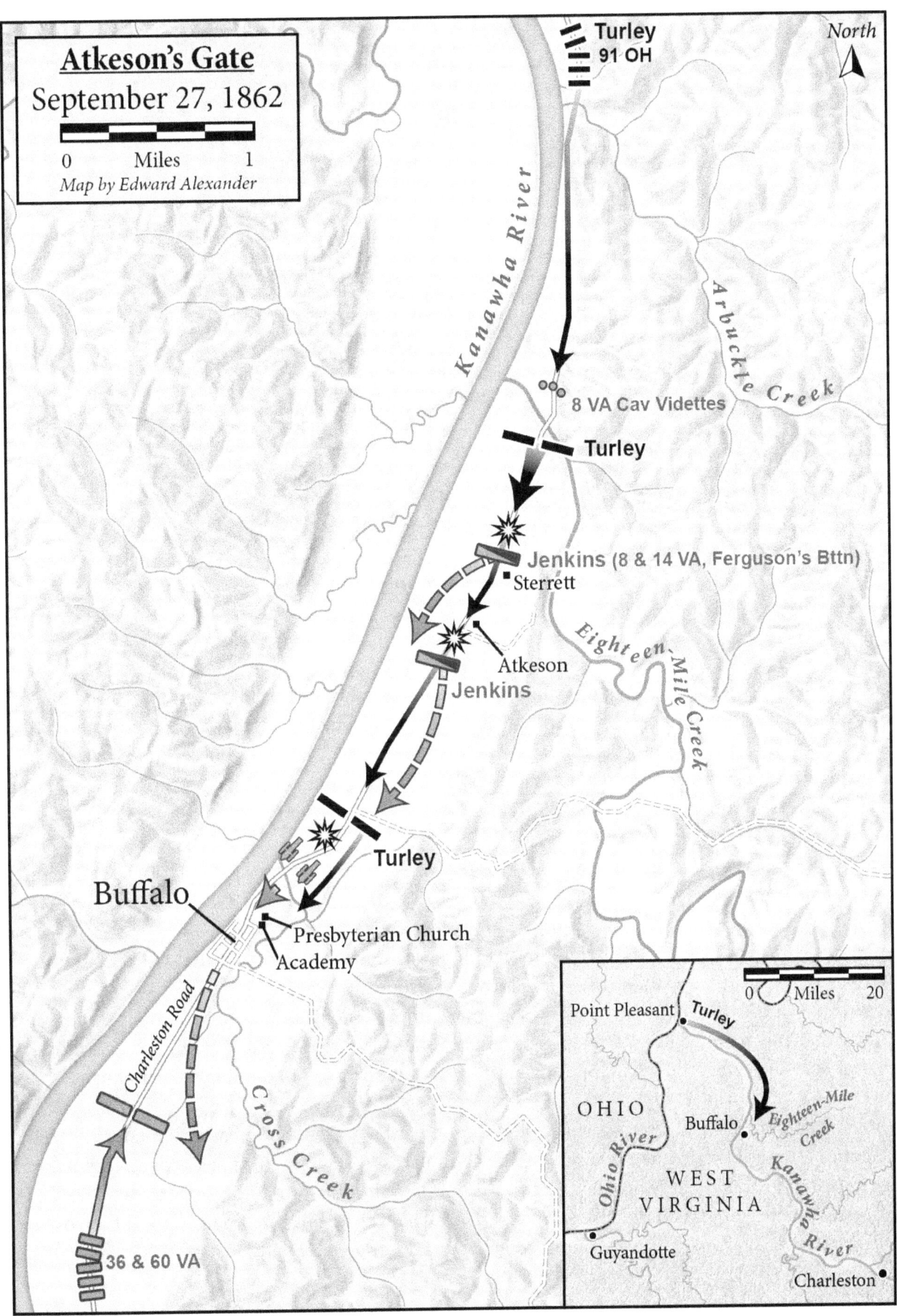

Atkeson's Gate
September 27, 1862

0   Miles   1
Map by Edward Alexander

Turley
91 OH

North

Kanawha River

Arbuckle Creek

8 VA Cav Videttes

Turley

Jenkins (8 & 14 VA, Ferguson's Bttn)
Sterrett

Atkeson

Jenkins

Eighteen-Mile Creek

Turley

Buffalo

Presbyterian Church
Academy

Charleston Road

Cross Creek

36 & 60 VA

0   Miles   20

Point Pleasant   Turley

OHIO

Ohio River

Buffalo

Eighteen-Mile Creek

WEST
VIRGINIA

Kanawha River

Guyandotte

Charleston

Battle of Atkeson's Gate by Samantha Atkeson.
Courtesy Pioneering in Agriculture.
Public Domain.

five, captured all their tents and camp equipage, &c., brought away 13 head of horses, 17 head of cattle, and a number of Enfield rifles. Considering this was the first time the 91st was under fire, after a night march of 22 miles, their conduct deserves the highest praise. A march of 45 miles in thirty hours, and the surprise of the wily foe, with an hours successful skirmishing and without a casualty, may well receive our unqualified commendation.[67]

As might be expected, Southern newspapers portrayed the battle at Atkeson's Gate much differently than the pro-Union organs:

The Yankees made a dash on Gen. Jenkins's command, a few days ago at Buffalo, supposing he was happing. The attack was made early in the morning by some 500 cavalry and infantry, while the valley was covered with fog. They approached close enough to be seen, when Gen J. [Jenkins] let loose upon them with a howitzer, which scattered them like chaff. Our forces pursued them about 9 miles, but owing to the dense fog, thought it prudent to stop pursuit, for fear of falling into an ambush.[68]

Following the affair at Atkeson's farm, Colonel John Turley, 91st Ohio, boasted he could have defeated Jenkins' entire force at Buffalo if the two supporting columns of Federal infantry had arrived earlier from Point Pleasant as planned. He primarily blamed the 2nd Virginia Cavalry and 40th Ohio Infantry, who were supposed to have posted their regiment on the hills across the Kanawha River from Buffalo to support him, of being late and failing to cover his flank. Grousing in his official report, Turley reasoned:

…had the forces sent to cooperate with us, as per your order, arrived at the scene of action in time to act in concert with my Regiment, the expedition would doubtless have accomplished all you desired – even the capture of Brig. Gen. Jenkins and his whole force, as he slept at a private residence in Buffalo, on the night previous. In conclusion, permit me to say that not a single officer or soldier of the Ninety-first faltered, and, as this is a new regiment never before under fire, I cannot refrain from saying that they acted like veterans and elicited my admiration. I returned to camp last night, after having marched 45 miles in thirty hours, skirmishing four hours of that time, without the loss of a man.[69]

Elsewhere in Putnam County, Sarah Young's family was marked due to their father's Union service, as she penned on September 29, 1862: "Three mean looking rebels came today and searched our house for guns. They did not find any but seemed to think we had some hidden somewhere. We heard that the Rebels and Federals had a skirmish yesterday near Buffalo. The Rebels reinforced, and the Federals were compelled to retreat. I sincerely hope that our dear soldiers will soon be here. Ah! gladly would I meet them. Gladly would I say, "Welcome dear soldiers! We have missed you and have longed for your return." Not all Confederates behaved aggressively toward Young's family, as one paid a visit on October 4, 1862, whom Sarah noted was the "politest and most gentlemanly Rebel I have seen since they came to our Valley." Two Confederates from guerrilla James Nounan's outfit also came by her house later that evening in search of one of Young's horses, but somehow Sarah and her mother had managed to hide it in the bushes nearby. On October 3, 1862, Major General William Loring issued a proclamation to the citizens of the Kanawha Valley area, warning them:

We do not intend to punish those who remain at home as quiet citizens, in obedience to the laws of the land, and to all such clemency and amnesty are declared; but those who persist in adhering to the cause of the public enemy, and the pretended State Government he has erected at Wheeling, will be dealt with as their obstinate treachery deserves.[70]

Union Re-occupation: The Kanawha Expedition

As usual, speculation flooded the Kanawha Valley area that Union forces would return any day. Despite the incessant flow of rumors, Union troops garrisoning Point Pleasant continued to organize regular patrols into the Buffalo, Winfield, and Red House areas. On an unrecorded date during the first two weeks of October 1862, according to Sergeant J.D. Sedinger of Company E, 8th Virginia Cavalry Border Rangers, his company led an attack on Union pickets posted at Red House Shoals and drove them back. The Border Rangers paused to wait for Colonel Milton J. Ferguson's battalion to arrive en force; when they arrived, Ferguson decided to ride forward accompanied by three troopers to reconnoiter the Federals' location. This proved to be a dangerous mistake, as when they came to within a few yards of a pawpaw patch, Federal infantry opened fire, slightly wounding Ferguson and killing Sedinger's horse.[71]

Meanwhile, at her home near Coalsmouth, Sarah Young was reeling from the constant flow of rumors and misinformation and was unsure what to believe, but she hoped the Union army would soon return. On October 14, 1862, she diarized: "Glorious news, if it be true! – The Federals are at Buffalo, and the Rebels have skedaddled across Gauley. May they never come to Kanawha in arms again. By the blessings of God our men will soon be home. We hear from Pa often now. He is very anxious to come home. Oh, what joy when we will be free from Rebels!" However, the Federal army was yet to return in force. Citizens learned to quickly dismiss such conjectural rumors, but many became despondent waiting for Union troops to retake the Kanawha Valley.[72]

The Union force at Point Pleasant was soon increased to approximately 20,000 troops as the Cumberland Division, under Major General George Washington Morgan, gradually arrived from eastern Kentucky during the last two weeks of October 1862. They had recently experienced hard service during the Cumberland Gap Campaign and were exhausted and ragged, not having received fresh supplies or uniforms in months. Morgan had three brigades in his division, comprised of troops from eastern Tennessee, Kentucky, Ohio, Indiana and Illinois. The majority of Tennesseans and Kentuckians had something in common with the western Virginians; they had all come from areas with large Secessionist populations and were intimately familiar with the kind of sufferings had by Union citizens in the Kanawha Valley. Confederate Major General William Loring learned of the massive Federal troop increase and quietly began his retreat from Charleston on October 9, 1862.[73]

Early in the morning of October 20, 1862, Major General Cox ordered Colonel Lightburn to move his division toward Putnam County. His first brigade included the 4th West Virginia Infantry and the 42nd, 91st, and 92nd Ohio Infantry, along with Captain John Young's Company G, 13th West Virginia Infantry. Lightburn led the first brigade toward Buffalo that morning on the northern bank of the Kanawha River, at what one soldier described as "the rapidity of a tortoise," though another soldier in the 92nd Ohio found that despite their slow pace, "Being raw troops and unaccustomed to marching, our boys have suffered greatly from sore feet." Lightburn's second brigade, also known as the "Provisional Brigade," was commanded by Colonel Edward Siber and comprised of the 34th, 37th, and 89th Ohio Infantry and moved toward Buffalo on the southern bank of the river. The 92nd Ohio was later placed in the second brigade when they reached Red House. Union advance to regain control of the Kanawha Valley was underway in Putnam County.[74]

Enroute to Buffalo, Private James M. Miles of the 91st Ohio Infantry recalled their movement toward the village:

Oct. 20th Morning comes. Its earliest streaks have scarcely appeared till the order come to be ready to move. 'Tis a welcome mandate. The humming of 3000 voices mingled with the crackling of burning barrels and boxes, and the glare of the conflagration, produces upon the spectator not accustomed to such scenes, a sensation of something wild and fantastic. "Fall in," is the cry, and now we have slung knapsacks, shouldered arms, and are in line of battle. Now we are doomed to wait under our heavy burdens, suffering not only from the pains of the body, but from an excruciating suspense till the whole brigade is ready to move.—The sun is getting higher and higher, still we are on a stand march, as the boys say when we don't march at all.—We move a short distance and are stopped. Suspense continues.

At length we are permitted to move without interruption, and that suspense is relieved. We turn up the Kanawha. Soon all begin to feel that traveling under knapsacks is not of little moment, and to some whose shoulders have for a long time been unused, it seemed almost intolerable. We march about twelve miles to-day, stop near two farmhouses, one of which is Union, the other not, and upon these "hangs a tale," simple and unadorned—a matter of fact. I'll tell you: Some three weeks ago, Jenkins, with some 200 of his men, encamped near said houses.—The disloyal family, of course claimed and received protection from the hands of Gen. J. from the despoliation that Southern soldiers visit upon the property of the loyal; but forgetting that retribution is sure to follow close upon the workers of iniquity, they informed upon the loyal house, and the bandits were permitted to plunder and destroy whatever they choose, leaving them in a state of almost utter destitution.

On our arrival, the boys were informed by the sufferers of what had transpired; a delegation, self-constituted, was not long in visiting upon them such punishment as they justly deserved, viz: The appropriation of every chicken, turkey, pig, and duck, as well as all the wine, fruit, honey, &c., they had. They pled loyalty, but they were too well known, and their pleadings were in vain.

Oct. 21st. At noon we are on our way again.—We reach Buffalo, the scene of our first skirmish, are met with the sweet smiles of its fair ones, and submissive countenances of its lords, but "the smile of a woman ever was deceitful," (only true in Dixie), and even men look submissive when they must. We bivouac just above town, eating for supper such food as our haversacks afforded. Went to bed on the ground, slept but little; it was so cold. We consoled ourselves that we had not seen hard times yet, that we would be doubly blest if we never suffer greater inconveniences.[75]

Lightburn arrives at Buffalo

On October 22, 1862, General Cox was at his headquarters in Gallipolis and received word that the Confederates had returned to Charleston, but he was skeptical. Once he arrived at Buffalo, Lightburn was informed that it was true; he also learned that General William Loring had been relieved of command for not following General Robert E. Lee's orders to join him in Maryland, and his 5,000 troops were given to Brigadier General John Echols, who immediately redirected his march toward Charleston. Brigadier General Albert Jenkins' cavalry had taken up position on Tyler Mountain, near modern Cross Lanes, with three pieces of artillery. Once Echols arrived in Charleston, Confederates immediately posted broadsides threatening to arrest any citizen suspected of disloyalty to the Confederacy. Cox was satisfied that his position near Red House was a tenable location to stage the upcoming movement on Charleston, but when he received confirmation that the Confederates had returned, he became anxious to concentrate his command before inclement weather caused the roads to become impassable. He ordered General William Morgan, who was then at Portland in Preston County, Virginia, to send his best troops toward Charleston, along with a battery of horse-drawn artillery as quickly as possible.[76]

Skirmish at Rock Branch

October 22, 1862 was unseasonably warm, with blustery winds blowing. The Confederates had sought to create a large obstruction blockading the Kanawha River near Red House Shoals, (the Rock Branch area was often cited as Rock Branch in period documents) and Cox directed Lightburn to act cautiously, not to allow the enemy to "become impudent," and proceed to Red House and clear the river to allow transport boats to operate in support of the expedition. Cox also admonished Lightburn not to allow Jenkins to get below him on the southern side of the Kanawha River, as that would allow an attack on the Union rear guard simultaneously with their advance on Charleston. Colonel Edward Siber's Provisional Brigade was in the advance and arrived near Red House at about 2 p.m., where they found a squad of Confederate cavalry videttes posted near the bridge some three miles north of the village. The 34th Ohio was sent along the hillside above the village, with the 4th West Virginia along the riverbank, hoping to entrap the Confederates. A brief skirmish occurred, but the 4th West Virginia had been too aggressive and prematurely gave away their position allowing the Confederates to escape the trap set for them. The remainder of Lightburn's force arrived at Red House that evening and encamped there overnight.[77]

The next day brought much cooler weather, as Lightburn began clearing obstructions in the river. He also combined a battery of Mountain Howitzers in the 47th Ohio Infantry with another battery, which became known as the Combined Mountain Howitzer Battery, having then eight guns. Lightburn further ordered his advance brigade under Colonel Edward Siber, the 34th Ohio, 91st Ohio, 92nd Ohio and 4th West Virginia Infantry, to move forward toward Poca, where they found the Confederates posted with three pieces of artillery in line of battle some three miles above Red House, in the vicinity of Rock Branch. A sharp skirmish occurred, resulting in the Confederates retreating down the Kanawha River toward Charleston. 2nd Lieutenant George F. Turner, Company F, 92nd Ohio described the action:

> We left camp at a few minutes notice and pressed on a few miles when a rebel force appeared. Our cannon was brought into position and ordered to fire, the Zouave regiment [34th Ohio] struck off into the hills to flank the rebel force, and our regiment climbed at the double quick one of the steepest Virginia hills, lying on the summit awaiting orders to rise, rush down the other side and support the battery. The prospect of a battle dwindled into the wish to see a few rebel horsemen, and, after some swearing because the rebels put spurs into their horses we moved on a short distance and encamped.[78]

Another soldier from the 89th Ohio Infantry coming up behind the advance brigade heard the firing begin and recalled: "As we approached this point last Thursday afternoon, the roaring of cannon and rattle of musketry told us in unmistakable terms that the ball had opened in earnest. On our arrival, we ascertained that the 34th Ohio (Zouaves) who were in our advance, had engaged the rebel cavalry under the notorious Jenkins, and after a few hours of 'How are ye's boys' in the shape of six-pounders, put them to flight." On October 25, 1862, the weather had changed dramatically and became cold and snowy; General Cox had left Point Pleasant and traveled to Pocatalico to join Colonel Lightburn, arriving there on October 27, 1862. He immediately sent out scouting parties to Scary Creek in Putnam County and to Tyler Mountain. Meanwhile, the Confederates had learned that a large Union force was approaching, and once more began their withdrawal from Charleston on October 28, 1862.[79]

General Cox sent a scouting party from the 8th West Virginia Infantry to Winfield on October 25, 1862, hoping to ascertain the Confederates' intentions in preparation for a general advance back into the Kanawha Valley. Word soon reached Sarah Young of the patrol, which was led by her beau, Captain Edgar Blundon. She wrote: "Our beloved soldiers are at Winfield, Captain Blundon is there. He sent word he would come out as soon as possible. We are so glad to know General Cox is commanding here again, and that the 8th Va. Vols. have come back to West Virginia. Yesterday five of the Rebellion thieves rode down the road as though no Yankees were this side of Ohio River; but I guess they went back double quick.....I hope we will never see them scouting here again. Such a pitiful set...."[80]

On the afternoon of October 29, 1862, Cox's Union advance troops reached a point some two miles from Charleston and once again encountered elements of General Albert Jenkins' cavalry, who retreated after a brief skirmish northeast of Poca. Meanwhile, the 37th and 89th Ohio regiments reached the mouth of the Coal River near Coalsmouth. At about 2 a.m., they reached Charleston and found the Confederates had left without a fight. The Kanawha Valley was once again in Union hands. Colonel Lightburn described the situation at the village of Poca on October 29, 1862:

> I arrived here about three o'clock. Found 3 or 4 hundred cavalry with one piece of artillery on the opposite side of Poca. A few shots from my artillery made them skedaddle. My position here I think is tenable. I have my entire command here the 8 Va and one battalion of cavalry on the opposite side of the river. I have thrown forward our regiment (the 4th Va) across Poca to occupy the hills on that side. My Bttn with subsistence are also here. I shall remain her until Gen Morgan's forces come up. In the mean time I shall feel the country on my left and on my right and as far in front as I can. Nothing

more from Chas except it is rumored that Floyd is at Coalsmouth with 1,000 infantry and some cavalry.[81]

On October 30th, 1862, Major General Cox ordered a large expedition of Union troops in the Guyandotte and Barboursville areas to reopen communication with Charleston, now that the Confederates had withdrawn from the area. One of those units was the 84th Indiana Volunteer Infantry Regiment, which was stationed at Guyandotte. They received Cox's orders to move toward Hurricane Bridge "scouting for Rebels who may be lingering in Putnam County." Once they arrived, Private Samuel Huddleston described the little village, noting it "…bore the marks of war. The bare chimney – monuments standing over the ashes of once peaceful and happy homes – and the absence of all able-bodied men told the sad story of a town which was one of the first to reap the bitter fruits of war. And this was only a sample of towns among the Western Virginia hills."[82]

Colonel Joseph Andrew Jackson Lightburn.
WV State Archives.

In late October 1862, General Cox was determined to re-establish communication with Union garrisons located at Barboursville in Cabell County and Ceredo in Wayne County via the James River and Kanawha Turnpike. This opened supply lines, and Union troops again maintained regular patrols operating through the area. Rumors abounded that the government would soon begin conscription, i.e. a military draft. Twenty-one-year-old Private David Burrows, Company F, 13th West Virginia, was stationed at Point Pleasant. He wrote to his wife on November 9, 1862, describing a recent scouting mission he went on covering more than forty miles into Putnam County. Burrows said they passed through Hurricane Bridge, where the soldiers interacted with several local citizens: "We was out to Hurricane, and it was a hard trip. There is a very hard talk down here of conscription, and I would like to know what people think about it here." Just four days previous, Burrows recalled witnessing several friends with "heavy hearts" enlist in the 9th West Virginia Volunteers during a rally held at a local Methodist church, in his hometown of Gallipolis, Ohio, in Meigs County; this prompted him to think he needed to do his part also, and he enlisted in the 13th West Virginia Infantry on September 9, 1862, at Point Pleasant. He served in the Shenandoah Valley Campaign of 1864, where he became ill with typhoid and died at Cumberland Hospital in Maryland, on August 6, 1864.[83]

On November 2, 1862, General Cox wrote to Colonel Jonathan Cranor, 40th Ohio Infantry, ordering him to post a detachment at Hurricane Bridge: "For the security of navigation on the Lower Kanawha, it is extremely desirable to keep some infantry and cavalry at Hurricane Bridge, with instructions to scour the country on both Mud and Hurricane Creeks, and over to Winfield, on the Kanawha. A force equal to that now in that region will probably be sufficient, and unless the condition of affairs in Eastern Kentucky requires your whole force, you will station part of your command as stated above." Colonel Cranor's regiment was then posted in eastern Kentucky working in concert with Colonel John Dil's 39th Kentucky Infantry, trying to drive Brigadier General John Floyd's Virginia State Line troops out of that region, along with flushing out Confederate guerrillas traversing the countryside.[84]

Horse Thieves and Soldier Shenanigans

On November 10, 1862, General Cox ordered Companies A, B, D and G of the 13th West Virginia to establish camp at Winfield along the southern bank of the Kanawha River, under command of Lieutenant Colonel James R. Hall. Companies C, E and F were then located at Point Pleasant. The regiment would remain so disposed until January 28, 1863. However, there were numerous Southern sympathizers in the area, and they were not pleased to learn that some 300 Union soldiers were now encamped in their midst. On January 21, 1862, Lieutenant Colonel Hall ordered Captain James W. Johnson, Company A, to take a detachment of twenty-two men from Winfield on a patrol to Mud Bridge, moving through Teays Valley along Midland Trail. Johnson returned to Winfield on November 24, 1862.[85]

During the late fall of 1862, General Cox was struggling to find solutions to protect the Union citizens in the Kanawha Valley and to maintain critical supply lines open from Charleston into Putnam and Cabell counties. He was dealing not only with Confederate guerrillas, but also with the constant accusations by angry Southern residents against his troops alleging they stole horses and other farm animals and harassed their families. One soldier in the 13th West Virginia, a young boy known as an excellent hunter, who was also quite lazy, devised a ruse one chilly day hoping to scare civilians into giving him a ride back to the army camp at Winfield, following a long trek into the woods looking for game. The cunning lad went to a farmhouse and told the family he was a Confederate and that a large rebel force was nearby, thinking they would take him prisoner and return him to camp. Instead, the family quietly fled and took their neighbors along, too. As his scheme failed, the youth had to walk some eleven miles back to camp anyway.[86]

He made it just in time to participate in evening drill. However, a large group of angry and terrified citizens soon arrived and informed Lieutenant Colonel James Hall of what had transpired. In the process, they identified the perpetrator, who was mortified when they recognized him. After a rather unpleasant interview with Lieutenant Colonel Hall, the guilty soldier confessed and was punished by being forced to carry a large load of bricks in his backpack during dress parade for the next ten days. As these often lasted two-to-three hours, he wasn't long to show remorse for his wrongdoing. According to eyewitnesses, his comrades witnessing the affair made no effort to restrain their laughter and insults, tormenting him as he loped along with his burden every evening at parade time.[87]

Lt. Col. James R. Hall.
St. Albans Historical Society.

General Jacob Cox was not as amused with the soldier's antics when he learned of the ruse, particularly when he received a letter from one of his subordinate officers stating that another irate citizen, who was also the local tax collector, had complained one of the locals requested he waive their taxes on an animal that was allegedly stolen by one of the Union officers, Captain John Young of Company G, 13th West Virginia Infantry. The citizen alleged that Young had wrongfully "pressed the animal" into Federal service without paying for it. The investigating officer wrote, "The pony claimed by Mrs. Thompson was found in his [Young's] possession. The pony is returned to its proper owner. This pony was taken...previous to his connection with the 13th Regt..."[88]

Cox referred the case to Brigadier General George Crook, one of his two immediate subordinates commanding troops in the Kanawha Valley. Annoyed with the accusations, which he did not believe, Cox responded:

Mr. [Dudley S.] Montague's wholesale assertion that Union men in the valley have "no more favors shown them than the meanest dogs" deprives the rest of his communication of reliability, as, if he knows anything of the matter, he knows he is making a misstatement, and it is quite probable that he is trying to cover up his neglect of duty in his department by such abuse of military officers. Any specific complaints will meet with prompt investigation. The troops stationed at Winfield are part of the 13th Virginia Volunteers, and I desire that you will require Mr. Montague to report at once whether he complains of them or of the general officers in command in the valley, giving full and specific details of the ground of his complaint, informing him that he will be expected to make good the charges, or be held responsible for a malicious effort to make trouble between civil and military authorities in West Virginia.[89]

Young defended himself by showing how he had no less than two horses stolen from his own farm by local Confederate guerrillas, and that the government failed to provide him with a replacement mount, to which he was entitled as a captain. General Crook thought formal charges ought to have been brought against Young when he learned of the issue, but the matter was eventually dropped. Young developed a strong resentment toward Crook during the process, however. An officer in Company D, 8th West Virginia Infantry, 1st Lieutenant, Isaac A. Wade, was captured by Confederates while patrolling along the Guyandotte River on November 25 1862. Wade was taken to the penitentiary at Richmond, Virginia, and forced into "confinement and hard labor." Virginia Governor John Letcher then attempted to hold him and another Union officer as hostages, as a "retaliatory practice," hoping to persuade Union officials to arrange the exchange of two Confederates who were recently captured in Jackson County for "stealing the mails." Wade was paroled at City Point, Virginia, on July 21, 1863, and returned to the regiment on July 23, 1863. Wade had initially enlisted as a private in Captain Isaac Rucker's home guard company at Buffalo in 1861.[90]

As 1862 drew to a close in the Kanawha Valley, the issues of emancipation and becoming the thirty-fifth state dominated the local newspapers. The former commander of the 9th West Virginia Infantry, Colonel Kellian V. Whaley, had formerly served in the United States Congress from 1860 until Virginia's secession caused him to lose his seat. He would later return to Congress, but in December 1860, he was stationed in the valley with his regiment. He sent an editorial to the *Weekly Register* on November 18, 1862, arguing in favor of statehood:

Mr. Editor: Permit me, through the columns of your paper, to call attention to the speech of Hon. K.V. Whaley, delivered during the last session of Congress, on the bill to admit West Virginia to the Union. But few of your readers have any idea of the tyranny exerted by the 40,000 slaveholders of Eastern Virginia, over the free white population of Western Virginia, by means of provisions of the Constitution of Virginia, and also the special legislation passed in pursuance thereof. Mr. Whaley sets out by showing the differences between the social organizations of Eastern and Western Virginia, and that this difference was developed to such a degree more than thirty-years ago, that John Randolph spoke in the Virginia convention in 1829, of the Valley and Western Virginia, as parts of the state which he might call alien to us, and forever separated from our interests and feelings.

Torn (the State) by factions, marked by lines which divide her into two different people – distinct in feeling, distinct in possession, different and antagonistic in interests. Mr. Baldwin, of Augusta, predicted that "if slave representation should be forced upon them, the final result will be the separation of the State. So oppressive had the legislation become, with no hope of relief, in the ordinary way, that Mr. Goode, in the convention of Virginia in 1851 proposed that the House of Delegates and the Senate should each be divided into two chambers, one composed of those east, and the other of the members west of the Blue Ridge, and requiring votes by chambers and a majority of each chamber necessary to appropriate or raise money by taxes, loans or otherwise. Mr. Wise said, "we, (the East) had kept their nose (the West) to the grindstone for the last seventy five years in agony." He then proceeds to show the unjust and monstrous system of taxation; that no slave, although worth $1,600 or $1,500, can be valued over $300 for taxation, and no slave under twelve years of age can be taxed, although worth seven or eight hundred dollars.

He thus shows, that over $200,000,000 worth of property, owned principally in Eastern Virginia, has never been taxed while every species of property in the West has been overburdened with taxation. To show the monstrous inequality of this system, I need only state, that in 1860 the number of slaves in Virginia was 490,887, of which number only 12, 771 were west of the Alleghenies. These are but a few of the evils inflicted upon Western Virginia, and the burdens under which she suffered, but my object is merely to call attention to the speech, and to express the hope that the people of Ohio, through their representatives in Congress, will, at the next session of Congress, welcome West Virginia into the sisterhood of States....[91]

In mid-December 1862, Captain James W. Bailey's home guard company on Hurricane Creek had yet to receive pay or commissions for their officers, but they received a shipment of Enfield muskets from Governor Pierpont on December 17, 1862. John Bowyer of Winfield petitioned Governor Pierpont on December 17, 1862 on behalf of Captain Bailey, noting they were doing "good business," having brought in several prisoners and were "proud of their arms." He requested a captain's commission on Bailey's behalf and a commission as 1st Lieutenant for George W. Leadmon of Hurricane Creek, promising he would "keep close watch that they obey such instructions as your Excellency may think proper, I think they are sound."[92]

At the end of 1862, President Lincoln found himself grappling with complex legal issues involved in admitting West Virginia into the Union as the thirty-fifth state, as well as his plan to release the final draft of the Emancipation Proclamation. Lincoln knew that to create a new state, he would need consent from the Virginia assembly under normal circumstances, but being war time, and with Virginia having seceded in 1861, he reasoned that since those serving in the Virginia assembly under the Confederacy were "engaged in open rebellion" against the government, the Restored Government of Virginia was not required to concern itself with consent of the mother state under such circumstances. Lincoln worked all night into the next morning at his office on December 31, 1862, deep in thought on the matter:

We can scarcely dispense with the aid of West Virginia in this struggle; much less can we afford to have her against us, in Congress and in the field. Her brave and good men regard her admission into the Union as a matter of life and death. They have been true to the Union under very severe trials. We have so acted as to justify their hopes; and we cannot fully retain their confidence, and co-operation, if we seem to break faith with them. In fact, they could not do so much for us, if they would. Again, the admission of the new State turns that much slave soil to free; and thus, is a certain, and irrevocable encroachment upon the cause of the rebellion, the division of a State is dreaded as a precedent. But a measure made expedient by a war, is no precedent for times of peace. It is said the admission of West Virginia is secession and tolerated only because it is our secession. Well, if we can call it by that name, there is still difference enough between secession against the Constitution, and secession in favor of the Constitution. I believe the admission of West Virginia into the Union is expedient.[93]

Chapter Three

1863: The Cost of Statehood

In many ways, January 1863 was a turning point of the war in Putnam County. President Lincoln issued the Emancipation Proclamation on New Year's Day, declaring all slaves held in Southern states "…are, and henceforward shall be free." Following the Battle of Antietam in September 1862, Lincoln had published the first edition of the Emancipation Proclamation, but afterward revised the document; it did not affect slavery in the Northern or border states and exempted those areas in the South already under Union control. While the freedom it promised depended upon Union military victory, Lincoln's proclamation reframed the Union political focus of the war. He faced another problem, as anti-slavery Congressmen were inflamed because he planned to admit West Virginia into the Union as a slave state. They argued it was a Pandora's Box to divide Virginia into two slave states, and that it was contradictory to the Emancipation Proclamation to do so. While Governor Francis Pierpont was opposed to slavery, he favored a gradual emancipation, asserting that since the Emancipation Proclamation only applied to Southern states in rebellion, an eventual emancipation was permissible in what would become West Virginia. He believed suddenly freeing thousands of slaves would result in chaos when the market became flooded with unskilled laborers. Nonetheless, Lincoln soon approved the statehood bill, thereby making West Virginia's admission into the Union as a slave state inevitable.[1]

As the year began, Captain John Young's Company G, 13th West Virginia Infantry, were posted at Winfield as garrison troops and remained there until then end of the month, when they were ordered to Coalsmouth. On January 23, 1863, Captain James W. Bailey, commanding the Union home guards on Hurricane Creek, was still waiting to hear from Governor Pierpont regarding a commission for his subordinate, George W. Leadman, who was earlier elected 1st Lieutenant. He wrote to Pierpont informing him the company had elected Leadman with "full attendance," and again requested a commission for him. On January 30, 1863, Putnam County Sheriff

Benjamin Morris was captured by a party of Confederates at Hurricane Bridge while on personal business; another man was with him but managed to escape. In response, Union troops there took several Southern citizens as hostages hoping to coerce the Confederates into releasing Morris. However, Southern authorities were aware that Lincoln wanted to make West Virginia a state soon and needed popular support from western Virginia in order to push the issue through Congress. As a result, they intended to capture as many Union public officials as possible, hoping to disrupt the process by making frequent raids and harassing Union citizens. This infuriated Union citizens in the area, as one resident quipped, "A little more wholesome hanging and a little less swearing is the only thing that will put an end to these raids. Whenever any of these rebel thieves, cutthroats and guerrillas are caught they should be immediately shot."[2]

The village of Hurricane Bridge had recently received much attention from both Union military and government leaders, despite the community being dominated by Southern supporters. The Unionists exerted a great deal of pressure on Governor Francis Pierpont and managed to persuade him to direct General Jacob Cox to send Federal troops there. The Southern contingent balked at the idea and were trying to pressure key Union citizens to relocate instead, hoping to remove the focus from their village. An editorial published in *The Weekly Register* on February 12, 1863, epitomized the political centrism exhibited by the small village, in a satirical piece ostensibly signed by Major Jack Downing. Downing was a fictional political commentator created by Seba Smith, the editor of the *National Intelligencer* newspaper. Downing was popularized in his often bittersweet, often stinging, oracles that quickly gained national notoriety. It is doubtful this piece was actually penned by Downing, as the author signed their name as Downing's junior. Once the fictional character became famous, many writers similarly published political satire using the same name. At any rate, the tongue-in-cheek editorial poked fun at the wartime residents of Hurricane Bridge:

Whereas, Secession seems to be the order of the day, and without here setting forth a long list of grievances, bill of rights or constitution for the new and independent state or Kingdom of Hurricane Bridge, heretofore a part of Putnam County, Virginia. The refined and talented citizens of the new government and within the following boundary to wit:

Beginning at the extremity of the north limb of the Moon, thence a straight line to the northeast corner of Purgatory, thence to the southwest edge of the Borealis in the north, and with the same to its intersection with the dog star, thence on an angular line to the beginning, claiming by Secession to the canopies above and the lowest mudsills of the bottomless pits, downward not to include any of Jupiter or other planets, and that a competent surveyor be appointed to run and mark the lines and courses thereof, and make a report of expenses & c., do hereby declare themselves free and independent of the County of Putnam, the state of Virginia, the United States and all the World, and any other World that may be created hereafter. Which boundary aforesaid, shall be known among the most favored nations of the earth, as the Kingdom of Hurricane Bridge.

The Constitution of which is to be democratic, however, glazed over with despotic and Monarchical features and no northern man with Southern feelings to rule the country and no person to be put in office, unless he is fond of strong, intoxicating liquors, bountifully mixed with strychnine, leaf tobacco and fish berries. The free port of entry to be established at Hurricane Bridge with suitable fortifications, custom houses, & etc., at the cost of the State, that a monarchical President with suitable cabinet, secretaries and foreign ministers, to be chosen by the elective franchise of the citizens thereof. That a strong and numerous naval force of Iron clad steamers be provided, and sail on and navigate the broad majestic waters of the Kingdom aforesaid, for offensive and defensive operations, that internal improvements progress and be completed, so as to avoid the laborious system of freighting heavy tonnage on horseback, over stupendous, high, rocky boundless mountains.

And the citizens of the State or Kingdom aforesaid, do further declare, that they can, when properly organized, with the large land and naval forces that can be brought to battle in the immense territory aforesaid, whip the world, which can be easily known by their vast numbers, great military skill, great wealth and means and wonderful facilities of travel, with stolen horses and by steam ships, rail roads and aerial voyages with balloons in the lower hemisphere. In a word, they are determined to protect themselves and their large and their numerous slave inhabitants against

Major Jack Downing.
Library of Congress.

the northern negro stealers and would greatly prefer to be annexed to South Carolina and Georgia, although they steal and smuggle more slaves or negroes from Africa ten to one than the Northern abolitionists among them. And the robbing of the public treasury and stealing horses is hereby tolerated, recommended, and legalized. And the Kingdom aforesaid when organized, will furnish more good and punctual officers, both civil and military, especially sheriffs and constables, than the Universe can start elsewhere.

And in the great territory above set forth, there are many distinguished and talented men, such as lawyers, physicians and statesmen, sufficient to control the bar of North America and the rest of creation and will in all probability practice in the courts of Exchequer and King's bench in the city of London, Paris, in France; Moscow and St. Petersburg in Russia; Warsaw in Poland, and all the large towns of Europe. And the many well-educated physicians, eminent and skillful, of great ability and moral worth, sufficient to cure all diseases except Secession, which is now an epidemic and can only be cured by powder and ball. And when the territory aforesaid becomes a monarchy which it will - the crown must be supplied by direct taxes, tithes, salvage and Royal perquisite common to crown-heads. The doctrine of the Democracy is to rule or ruin, they have done both, they have lost the rule and treasury, therefore, seceded. The coat of arms for said State, although ridiculous, a blue cockade, with a picture of a stolen horse, and battle smoke, fastened on the left side of that, with a tow-string, squatting position, and snake's mouth open. Should said state get into difficulty in their organization, write to the subscriber at Council Bluffs, and good advice will be freely and gratuitously given.

Maj. Jack Downing, Jr.[3]

Murder on Hurricane Creek: The Death of Calvary Gibson

Confederate guerilla activities continued in Putnam County throughout the winter of 1862-1863; local newspapers reported many incidents of Union citizens encountering their antagonists, usually with violent and brutal results, as in the case of Calvary Gibson of Hurricane Creek. Gibson was born there in 1818 to parents of Scotch-Irish descent and worked as a farmer. He married Lucretia Leadmon prior to 1850 and had five children with her. The 1850 Census shows him with three sons and two daughters: Thomas W. (b. 1840); James Jefferson (b. 1843); Martha J. (b. 1845); John H. (b. 1846); and Mary E (b. 1848). Another son, Francis Marion, was born in 1851. Gibson's son James later enlisted in the 7th Ohio Heavy Artillery, Company F and eventually became a sergeant. Gibson was unarmed and murdered by a group of Confederates led by 2nd Lieutenant William Keaton, on Sunday, February 8, 1863. Evidence indicates it was due to his membership in Captain Isaac Rucker's company of Union home guards. Late that evening, a band of Confederate guerrillas surrounded his house and:

> ...broke open a window sash, and then swarmed into the house. Mrs. Gibson recognized several of the assailants as former neighbors, including one who Mr. Gibson had raised in part...Gibson cried out, "for God's sake don't murder me," but the man crushed his skull with the butt of a gun, and seven shots were fired into his body, "blowing out every vestige of life, and mutilating the remains in a terrible and sickening manner." As Gibson's daughter ran into the room screaming to her mother, "they've killed Pa, they've shot Pa," and got in the way of a large lieutenant, he threw the child into the fire. The wife and mother sprang to the child exclaiming, "Don't burn up my child after killing my husband" and the officer responded, "Shut up, you damned union bitch, or I'll kill you too." They reportedly shot him seven times and bayoneted him several times, and "...to make the crime more hideous, they with the butts of their guns broke his skull in until the hammer of the lock was buried in his brains up to the barrel, all this was being done while he was begging for his life, and to make the crime of a deeper dye, caught the wife of the murdered man, and choked her until she was insensible....[4]

Word of Gibson's murder reached Union troops at Hurricane Bridge on February 8, 1863, where a detachment of the 2nd West Virginia Cavalry were posted under Captain John C. Witcher; he immediately took a company out in pursuit of the Confederates, riding into Barboursville in the pouring rain. Once at the village, Witcher's troopers dismounted, camped inside of a barn without dinner, and briefly rested. Later that evening, Witcher and his men rode some forty miles to the Keaton Settlement in Cabell County, speculating that Lieutenant Keaton's group would be hiding there. A detachment of the 13th West Virginia Infantry had recently been ambushed by guerrillas there, and in response, they burned two houses belonging to Southern sympathizers. Witcher's conjecture proved correct—he found Keaton's men there and quickly engaged in a brisk skirmish, capturing the lieutenant and three other men, who were hiding out in a small house. Witcher reported, "This proved to be a very important capture, as among the squad was the leader of the gang, Lieut. Keaton, a desperado, that has been annoying the citizens of this part of Virginia for twelve months past, and has eluded vigilance, heretofore of the military authorities." Keaton and the others were imprisoned at Wheeling on the next day.[5]

Battle at Hurricane Bridge: "We are in a bad place"

Not far from the village of Winfield, along the western bank of the Kanawha River in Putnam County, was the mouth of Hurricane Creek, so named by a group of early surveyors working for George Washington who came to the area in 1774. They discovered the effects of a recent thunderstorm had laid several large trees in a long, symmetrical pattern at the creek's mouth, resembling that found along the path of a large hurricane, and hence named it Hurricane Creek. Further south, there was a small, quiet village known as Hurricane Bridge located near the Cabell County line. This area was a busy trading and hunting post for Native Americans in the pre-colonial era, and when the first European migrants settled there around 1778, it became known as the Hurricane Settlement. Hurricane Bridge appears on Virginia maps as early as 1811, in the area where the James River and Kanawha Turnpike crossed Hurricane Creek. For reference, this is the same area where modern U.S. Route 60 intersects with Midland Trail. (i.e. State Route 34, in the city of Hurricane, West Virginia.) Hurricane Bridge was named such due to a large wooden, uncovered bridge spanning Hurricane Creek. That bridge was in the same spot as the modern bridge, and not where the modern bridge crosses U.S. Route 60, as some writers have erroneously asserted.[6]

The 1860 United States Census shows there were ninety-nine homesteads reported in the village of Hurricane Bridge and eight unoccupied dwellings. Other sources showed there were twelve large farmhouses, a tobacco barn, a flour mill, and a general mercantile business, as well as the Duke Tavern and a large log frame building used as a public meeting house and church building by Baptists and Methodists. George Duke ran a tavern from his home at Hurricane Bridge; his family found multiple bullet holes in the walls following the March 28, 1863, battle.[7] An 1815 map of Virginia shows a stagecoach station on the Kanawha and James River Turnpike about three miles southeast of the present railway in modern Hurricane. Most of the homes were found in the northwest area behind modern Hurricane First Baptist Church. A 2017 archeological study conducted by the City of Hurricane revealed the remains of several burned stone fireplaces and wood foundations from the mid-nineteenth century, corroborating Civil War era eyewitness accounts describing burnt homes located near the modern Hurricane Bridge Park; several were burned by Confederates in the March 28, 1863 battle, most of which are believed to have been the dwellings of Union supporters, as this area was well known for its strong Southern contingency.[7]

An affair often referred to as the "First Battle at Hurricane Bridge" by historians occurred on September 20, 1856. Cabell County resident and plantation owner Albert G. Jenkins of Green Bottom was running for Congress. He engaged in a day long public debate with his opponent, Congressman John S. Carlile, at Hurricane Bridge. A large crowd gathered and were fed barbecue under a "beautiful grove of trees near the town." Afterward, they gathered at the log frame meeting house to hear the debate. Congressman Carlile led off with a speech of an hour and a half, charging the Democratic Party with the responsibility for "slavery agitation" in the country, while Jenkins argued in favor of slavery and left quite an impression, as cited in the *Kanawha Valley Star* on September 30, 1856, "Mr. Carlile has heretofore been regarded by his friends in this quarter as the big gun of the know-nothingism.... toward the close of Mr. Jenkins' speech, it surpassed anything we have

Mary Elizabeth Gibson Billups, Calvary Gibson's daughter. Courtesy Bob Gibson.

Lucretia Leadmon Gibson, wife of Calvary Gibson. Courtesy Bob Gibson.

A. G. Jenkins.
Lea
134

General Albert Gallatin Jenkins.
Library of Congress

ever witnessed....He is a young man of superior intellect and is likely to make a statesman of the first order."[8]

A post-war recollection written by former slave Fred Conner refers to a fight occurring at Hurricane Bridge on March 28, 1863, as the "Engagement at Hurricane Bridge." Conner stated:

In the winter of 1863, a report became current within the Confederate lines that a vast quantity of government stores was deposited at Pt. Pleasant, Mason Co. also that a number of horses were corralled at the same places. Accordingly, about the 20th of March a detachment of about 800 men consisting of portions of the 8th and 16th Virginia Cavalry commanded by Gen Jenkins with Dr. Chas. [Charles] Timmons of Buffalo as Surgeon began to march from Dublin Depot to Pt Pleasant over the mountains two hundred miles distant. On the 28th of the same month reached Hurricane Bridge in the southern part of Teays Valley....[9]

Brigadier General Albert G. Jenkins commanded a battalion of cavalrymen comprised of the 8th and 16th Virginia Cavalry. The majority of men comprising Company D, 16th Virginia Cavalry, along with more than seventy men in the 8th Virginia Cavalry, were recruited at Hurricane Bridge. Jenkins' men had spent the past few months near Salem and Giles Courthouse, Virginia, training as dismounted infantry because their horses were sent to North Carolina for the winter. Traveling on foot some 200 miles over rough mountain passes with many of his men lacking shoes, Jenkins arrived at the small village of Hamlin in what is now Lincoln County, West Virginia, on March 27, 1863. Jenkins then believed that the village was unoccupied by Federal troops. However, while at Hamlin his men intercepted a man carrying bacon to the Federal soldiers at Hurricane Bridge, who advised Jenkins there was now a garrison of roughly 300 Union troops posted there.[10]

Historians have long speculated as to why General Jenkins chose to fight at Hurricane Bridge, as it appears to have been a last-minute decision. When Jenkins approached Hurricane Bridge early in the morning of March 28, 1863, with his 500 to 600 dismounted troopers, he was aware his force outnumbered the Federals at least four to one; one writer concluded that Jenkins' decision to attack was "arrogant," noting the ultimate result was nothing more than a "sullen withdrawal." Some argue that Jenkins could easily have reached Point Pleasant without a fight, circling around the village out of sight of the Federal garrison. However, his immediate strategic objective was to distract attention from a series of raids conducted that spring by Generals William "Grumble" Jones and John D. Imboden in the northern area of western Virginia, known as the Jones-Imboden Raids, and to capture a large store of supplies and horses believed to be at Point Pleasant, as well as to receive the herd of beef cattle from Confederate sympathizers in Ohio. Jenkins knew if he did not attack on March 28, 1863, the Union garrison would have time to bring reinforcements in anticipation of his return, so he decided to risk a pre-emptory strike rather than having to fight later while potentially outnumbered and heavily encumbered with several wagons full of supplies and a large herd of beef cattle.[11]

In response to pressure from Union citizens at Hurricane Bridge to protect them, Brigadier General Jacob D. Cox, commanding Federal forces in the Kanawha Valley, ordered troops from the 13th West Virginia Infantry to establish an outpost there, with a view to both protect Unionists and to guard access to the James River and Kanawha Turnpike, a critical supply route from Charleston to the Ohio River. On February 10, 1863,

Companies B, D, G and H of the 13th West Virginia Infantry, under command of Captain James W. Johnson, arrived there and immediately began constructing a large earthen fort on the western heights above the village.[12]

Before this, the 13th West Virginia's only combat experience was going on patrols and scouting missions and disrupting guerilla operations. They would soon become hardened veterans, as the regiment later served under future U.S. President Rutherford B. Hayes in the Shenandoah Valley Campaign in 1864, where they fought at Lynchburg and Lexington and witnessed the Virginia Military Institute burn to the ground. The 13th West Virginia also fought in the battles at Kernstown, Berryville, Winchester (Opequon), Fisher's Hill, and Cedar Creek. Shortly after arriving at Hurricane Bridge, Private Jacob Shoemaker of Company D was "accidentally wounded in the hand" while cleaning a loaded rifle, bearing testimony to the inexperience of troops there. Colonel William Brown, who commanded the 13th West Virginia, had his headquarters at nearby Barboursville and was not present at the time of the March 28, 1863, battle. Although he was not a career army officer, Brown was known for his rigid, by the book discipline, and many soldiers dreaded having to deal directly with him.[13]

Captain James W. Johnson,
13th West Virginia Infantry.
West Virginia State Archives.

Weather conditions at Hurricane Bridge during February-March 1863 were cold and damp. According to one soldier, "…we have had a great deal of rain here for the last week…" thus making the roads muddy and wet. Many of the Union soldiers were very ill; there was a small field hospital at Hurricane Bridge, managed by Dr. Samuel G. Shaw, the 13th West Virginia Regimental Surgeon, in which at least seventy men sick with typhoid and pneumonia were treated between February 10 and March 28, 1863. As Jenkins stealthily approached Hurricane Bridge from Hamlin, he arrived early in the morning of March 28 and halted near where modern State Rt. 34 intersects with Route 60. Observing the Union pickets (sentries) posted near Hurricane Bridge, Jenkins also ordered his sharpshooters to take position on the heights to the south and east, each roughly four tenths to a half mile from the fort. Jenkins then ordered the main body of his force to position along the ridgeline near the Duke Tavern, extending southwest toward the base of the southern heights. He now had the Union fort in a dangerous trap, as the Union pickets guarding access to the earthen fort were completely unaware of the approaching Confederates.[14]

Sergeant James D. Sedinger described how events began to unfold at Hurricane Bridge on the morning of March 28, 1863:

We marched all night, nearly the next night, arriving at Hurricane Bridge about daylight. The General sent in a flag of truce demanding surrender. The Captain in command refused and moved into a fort that was nearby and held it against us as we had no artillery with us. John Payne of the Company was killed….[15]

According to one historian, Jenkins sent Major James Nounnan with a flag of truce bearing a message for Colonel William Brown, commanding the 13th West Virginia. Brown was not present, however, and Captain James W. Johnson, commanding the garrison, received the message from his pickets. A soldier in Company A, twenty-three-year-old Corporal Martin Van Buren Edens, indicated that it was thirty-three-year-old

Captain Milton Stewart.
West Virginia State Archives.

1st Lieutenant Alexander H. Samuels of Company D, 8th Virginia Cavalry, who actually carried the flag of truce and accompanied Major Nounnan. After the war, Fred Conner, who personally knew many of the soldiers in Jenkins' command, collected several accounts from men who fought at Hurricane Bridge and wrote that when Major Nounnan approached the Union pickets, he was taken under flag of truce with Lieutenant Samuels to Captain Johnson's headquarters, which were located in a field about one hundred yards to the north of the bridge.[16]

Upon receipt of Jenkins' note, Captain Johnson realized Jenkins expected to find Colonel William Brown inside the fort commanding. He later reported to Colonel Brown what took place that morning:

…I have the honor to make the following report of the assault made upon this post. The rebel Genl Jenkins and his command on the 28th inst. about 6 O.C. in the morning on the 28th Inst. our pickets brought in a flag of truce with the following from Jenkins: 'Col, I now have an overwhelming force so disposed as to completely surround you, and cut off your retreat, a humane desire to avert the loss of life, and this is need to demand your surrender, in the event of your compliance, and the surrender in good faith of all forces under your command, they shall receive the treatment warranted by the usages of War, and both officers and men will be paroled. Twenty minutes will be allowed for the consideration of this note and to return reply.'

On receipt of the above note I immediately sent him reply, that I should not surrender the forces under my command, unless forced to do so by an exhibition of his boasted strength. And immediately set about making the best possible disposition of the limited forces under my command. In fifteen minutes, we were ready for action. All available force remaining about 150 effectives and were drawn up inside our fortifications when the enemy appeared in force….[17]

Captain Milton Stewart, Company B, noted in his morning report that the battle began at about 5:45 a.m. Captain Johnson apparently either did not know Jenkins' actual strength, thought he was bluffing, or both. He may also have over-estimated his own firepower, but either way, he chose to fight. Once he declined to surrender, Johnson realized an attack was imminent. He quickly ordered the pickets inside the unfinished fort and gave the orders for the four companies to "fall in" to ranks, creating an organized formation of two battle lines posted on the interior walls of the fort. Corporal John H. Hess, Company H, wrote on February 18, 1863, that the soldiers were building the earthworks "as fast as we can," although Captain Johnson stated the condition of the earthen fort was "unfinished at the time of the battle, leaving their flanks exposed." Hess was aware of the risk fighting in an incomplete fort presented, and dryly informed his wife, "we are in a bad place."[18]

As the Union soldiers took their places along the roughhewn logs lining the muddy walls of the fort, and silently stood awaiting orders to open fire, they quietly thought of their wives, families, and friends at home. A few looked forward to the coming fight, wanting to prove themselves in their first real combat experience. Captain Johnson ordered twenty-three-year-old Sergeant Hezekiah Scott of Company D, the regimental color bearer, to raise the colors. Scott was appointed color sergeant in December, and he carried the colors

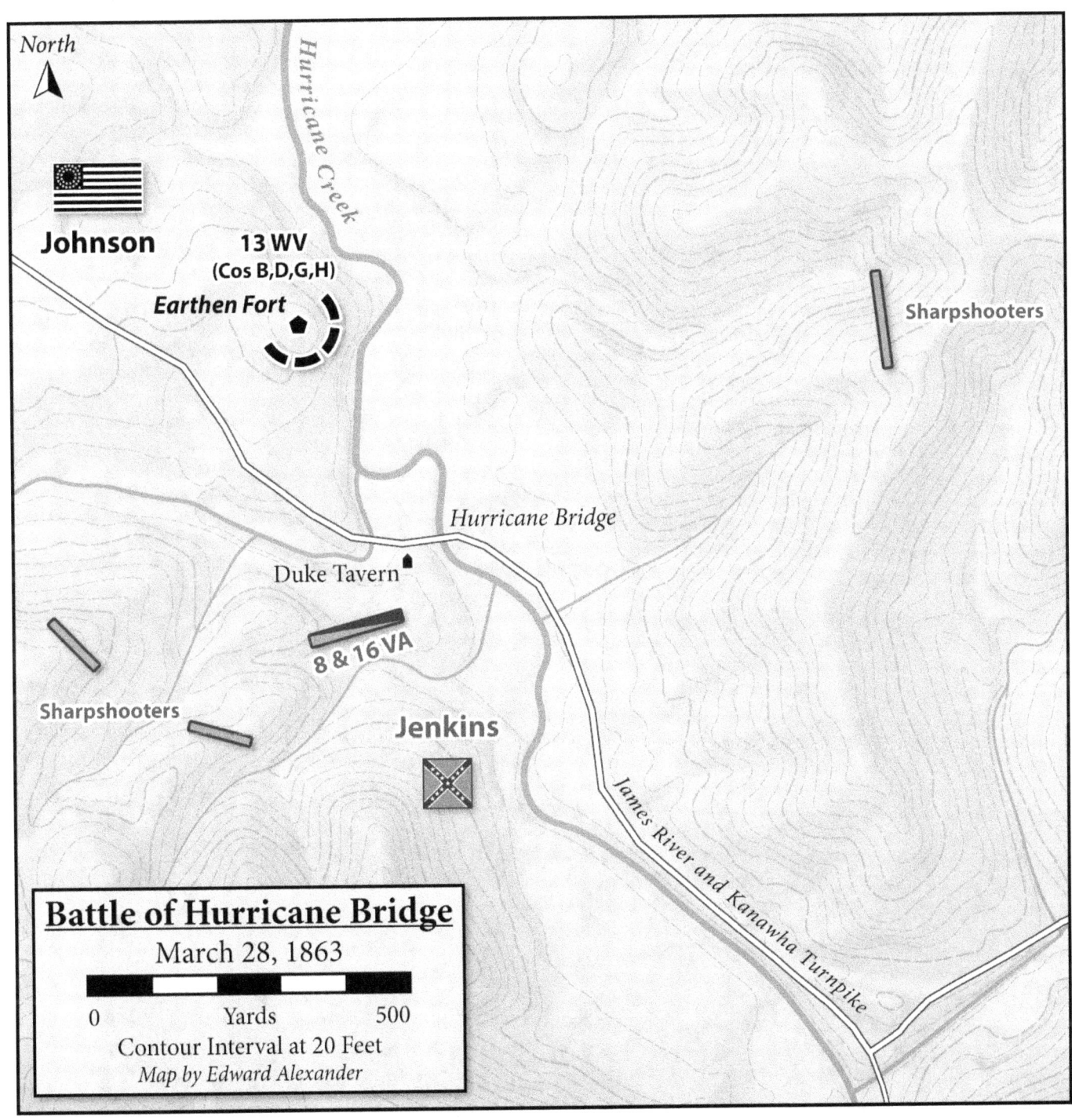

North

Johnson

13 WV
(Cos B,D,G,H)

Earthen Fort

Hurricane Creek

Sharpshooters

Hurricane Bridge

Duke Tavern

8 & 16 VA

Sharpshooters

Jenkins

James River and Kanawha Turnpike

Battle of Hurricane Bridge

March 28, 1863

0   Yards   500

Contour Interval at 20 Feet
Map by Edward Alexander

Elevations: Union Fort, camp, and hospital area 680-720 feet; Eastern Confederate Sharpshooter position 800-900 feet; Southern Confederate Sharpshooter positions 800-900 feet; Confederate lines near Duke Tavern: 640-720 feet. Note: modern Harbor Lane (known locally as Old Chicken Farm Road) is the route of the James River & Kanawha Turnpike in 1863. Modern US Route 60 now intersects with Midland Trail (Route 34) where James River & Kanawha Turnpike turned north along Hurricane Creek.

13th West Virginia Infantry in the earthen fort at the battle of Hurricane Bridge
Courtesy Donald Long, artist.
Used with permission.

until promoted to 1st Sergeant on February 7, 1864. He was later wounded at the Second Battle of Kernstown, Virginia, on July 24, 1864. Corporal Martin Van Buren Edens of Company A later remarked that the soldiers were "cool as ice" as they fell into ranks within the earthworks to repel Jenkins' attack. Hence, despite their inexperience, Companies B, D, G and H of the 13th West Virginia Infantry were about to "See the Elephant," a wartime colloquialism meaning to experience combat. Captain Johnson posted the color guard a few yards behind the line of battle. Near the center where Johnson stood were also two lieutenants, one of whom was 1st Lieutenant Emory J. Bridgeman, the regimental adjutant, who, unknowingly, was in his last few moments of life on this earth. Soon, the battle opened in earnest with sheets of flame erupting from the eastern and southern heights facing the Union position, and massed Union musketry roared in response.[19]

Though he was not present, after reading Captain Johnson's report, Colonel William Brown later succinctly summarized the events that morning:

On the morning of March 28th, a rebel force numbering eleven companies of the 8th and 11th [16th] Regiments of Virginia Rebel Cavalry (dismounted) under the command of General A.G. Jenkins, appeared before that place and demanded the surrender of the force, which was refused by Capt. James Johnson who commanded the post. A battle ensued which lasted from 6 am until 11 o clock am.[20]

Brown's estimate of Jenkins' companies was not far off; Jenkins had ten, not eleven, companies present at Hurricane Bridge. Captain Johnson left a more graphic picture of the Federals' predicament, recalling further that within about twenty minutes of his refusal to surrender, Jenkins' sharpshooters, posted on the three hills above and surrounding them, opened fire in force. Johnson had no idea the Confederates were on the surrounding hillsides, much less that they bore deadly "Globe sighted rifles." As five-to-six-hundred bullets zipped through the air around he and his men, Johnson knew it was time to fight. Jenkins' firing positions from the three surrounding heights created a triangular shaped killing zone and resulted in what Johnson described as a "galling crossfire."[21]

The "Globe sighted rifles" Johnson mentioned were the Whitworth Rifle, a .451 caliber, single-shot muzzle loader made by British armorer James Whitworth of Manchester, England. Whitworths had a telescopic rear sight adjustable to 1,200 yards, with a "globe" sight located on the muzzle, enabling the user to accurately estimate target distance based on its relative size observed through the sight. The bullets were also octagonal shaped. The Confederate army purchased several hundred Whitworth Rifles from England during the Civil War at a cost of $1,000 each. At such a price, it is doubtful there were more than a few present at Hurricane Bridge. Some writers have also mistakenly identified the Whitworth Rifles used at Hurricane Bridge as "scoped" rifles; globed sights were very much different than those employing a telescopic lens or scoped rifle. The latter were typically mounted on the top or side of the barrel and were much easier to operate than the complex sighting procedure required with globe sights.[22]

As his troopers were dismounted and had just marched over two hundred miles, Jenkins wisely kept his distance from the Union fort and deployed his troops as follows: on the eastern heights located roughly four tenths of a mile from the Union fort, he placed about one hundred sharpshooters armed with Whitworth Rifles. On the ridgeline to the immediate right of the fort, roughly three tenths of a mile south, he posted nearly four hundred troopers armed with Richmond .69 rifled muskets and 1855 Harpers Ferry rifles, also .69 caliber. A few researchers have conjectured that Jenkins' Confederates were carrying double-barreled shotguns in 1863; however, according to Private Thomas Copenshaver, Company A, 8th Virginia Cavalry, while many men earlier carried double-barreled shotguns from home when they volunteered in 1861, by 1863 those were replaced with arms "supplied by the Federals."[23]

Private Winfield S. Hobbs,
Co. H, 13th West Virginia Infantry.
Courtesy Gregg Abbott.

On Jenkins' upper far left, located on the hills some one to two hundred yards south (across modern U.S. Route 60 along Lower Coach Road) he posted roughly another one hundred sharpshooters. The four companies of the 13th West Virginia, on the other hand, were armed with 1861 Springfield Rifles, .58 caliber, which was the standard U.S. Army issue weapon at that time. However, Company A received a shipment of 1862 Austrian Lorenz Rifles on October 15, 1862, after turning in their old .69 caliber percussion conversion rifled muskets. Captain Johnson later recalled, "...the enemy appeared in force and opened a furious fire upon us simultaneously on three sides from as many different hills, owing to the high elevation of which and the unfinished condition of our works, exposed our men to a most galling crossfire." Dr. Samuel Shaw, the 13th West Virginia assistant surgeon, was thankful that he did not have to treat severe casualties from artillery wounds at Hurricane Bridge. He wrote to his daughter from Point Pleasant a few days later, "At the time of the fight the fort was not completed and would have been no protection from artillery...It certainly is a very difficult place to fortify against artillery, there are high hills all around it in nearly every direction commanding this place."[24]

When they saw Jenkins' men appear "in force" along the ridgeline located near the tavern some one to two hundred yards south, the Federals' firing was rapid and "animated," according to Captain Johnson. Soon, a dense smoke filled the air and hovered around the fort and adjacent heights, limiting the visual field of both the Union and Confederate soldiers. Companies D and H, the two center companies, were ordered to "fire at will" upon the sharpshooters located on the southern heights to their right. As the battle pitched, Jenkins' sharpshooters pinned the Federals down inside the earthen fort. Corporal George W. Fulwiller, Company H, could not stand the tension and deserted his post, running from the field during the fight. Fulwiller was later arrested and confessed, then confined in Charleston.[25]

Fighting lasted for five hours at Hurricane Bridge, eventually fading into desultory firing. The unusually long duration of this fight was most likely due to the use of earthworks, which provided a great deal of cover for the Union soldiers, as well as heavy smoke filling the small valley where the fort was located and limiting visibility. Sharpshooters posted along the hills had to take more time to zero in on targets, and those in the fort likewise had to be more deliberate in aiming their muskets. Another likely reason is that this was the first engagement the 13th West Virginia fought as a cohesive unit. Although they were well drilled and disciplined, the officers and men were still technically inexperienced when it came to actual combat. The Confederates, on the other hand, were physically exhausted and hungry, and many were without shoes. The weather had been rainy and quite cold, and the ground was still muddy. Jenkins' cavalrymen were also fighting dismounted. Captain Johnson was proud of his men and reported they had withstood the heavy, galling crossfire "...and returned with the firmness of Veterans."[26]

Around 11 a.m., Jenkins realized he was not able to capture the Union garrison and withdrew behind the hills located to the south, using them as cover while he retreated westward. Captain Johnson reported:

The enemy sharpshooters were so posted on the adjacent heights and armed with globe sighted rifles were constantly endeavoring to pick off officers and men. About 5 hours of brisk and animated firing from both sides the enemy suddenly withdrew his forces leaving few of his wounded who fell into our hands. From whom we learned that the enemy force engaged did not number less than 500 men. Our loss was 3 killed and 4 wounded, one of whom has since died. To both officers and men, I return my most sincere thanks for the bravery and gallantry displayed during the engagement where so many heroic deeds were performed; it would be unjust to mention individual acts of gallantry. It is enough to say that they all behaved in the most noble and gallant manner.[27]

Jenkins quietly reorganized his troops and moved "behind the hill to the south, flanking the Federal position and rejoining the James River Turnpike far enough west to be out of range of enemy weapons." Before leaving Hurricane Bridge, the Confederates burned several houses and buildings, including the log structure used as a church and meeting house. In the annals of warfare, civilians inevitably suffer loss of life, property, or both when the opposing armies are nearby. It is unknown whether Jenkins authorized the homes burnt or whether some of his men acted autonomously. While admittedly speculative, there were more than seventy men from the immediate vicinity of Hurricane Bridge present in the 8th and 16th Virginia Cavalry, who were doubtless familiar with the residents of the village. They were aware of who the Union supporters were, and likely used the opportunity to settle personal vendettas against them. While no civilian casualties were reported at Hurricane Bridge, the loss of their homes and church caused some twenty-four residents to scatter.[28]

Jenkins next turned his battalion northward along Benedict Road, went about one mile, and turned east. His next steps are not clear, but he likely crossed the dividing ridge line near Coon Creek or followed Poindexter until he came to Hurricane Creek. Then, he continued east toward his primary objective: the town of Point Pleasant. Colonel William Brown learned of the action at Hurricane Bridge that afternoon and telegraphed Brigadier General Eliakim. P. Scammon, his division commander, informing him that he believed "the troops are in trouble at Hurricane Bridge," and requested permission to send two companies to reinforce the garrison, leaving one at Point Pleasant. Scammon approved and directed Brown to keep him informed of the situation.[29]

Colonel Brown summarized casualties at Hurricane Bridge as follows: "...when the rebel force withdrew leaving 4 wounded who were taken prisoners. Our loss were 4 killed and 3 wounded." Captain Milton Stewart, Company B, reported, "our loss three men killed, eight wounded...Company B lost two men killed in action." However, those reports conflict with other records, including the morning reports for Companies A, B, D and H of the 13th West Virginia Infantry on March 28, 1863. Rather, there were four wounded and three killed in action, and one man mortally wounded, Adjutant Bridgeman, on March 28 at Hurricane Bridge.[30]

Although the Union earthworks were not finished, they still afforded a reasonable degree of protection. Union soldiers likely only had to expose their head and shoulder areas to fire for the most part, but there were clearly exceptions. Corporal Leroy Newman, Company H, was severely wounded in the right thigh as a musket ball passed through both legs, breaking his right femur. He was briefly treated at the field hospital, sent home afterward, and did not return to duty. From all accounts, he never fully recovered and later filed a claim for a pension due to disability.[31]

The Confederates mortally wounded one Union officer, twenty-one-year-old 1st Lieutenant Emory J. Bridgeman, who had initially enlisted in Company F during 1861. He was promoted to serve as the 13th West Virginia adjutant prior to the battle and received multiple gunshot wounds inside the earthworks. Bridgeman died in the Hurricane Bridge field hospital three days later, according to Dr. Samuel Shaw. He was from Meigs County, Ohio, and the war took a harsh toll on his family; his brother, Austin Bridgeman, who served in the 63rd Ohio Volunteer Infantry as a surgeon, was killed aboard the steamer Sultana when the engines exploded on April 27, 1865. That incident resulted in the death of 1,800 soldiers onboard who were returning home.

Known as the worst maritime disaster in the Civil War, the steamship traveled the Mississippi River and was rated maximum capacity for only 376 people.[32]

Heavy Confederate musketry also struck nineteen-year-old Private Henry Hoffman of Company D, who was "slightly wounded in the head." He was hospitalized at the Hurricane Bridge field hospital and eventually returned to duty in May 1863. Nineteen-year-old Corporal James [John] A. Rayburn, Company B, 13th West Virginia, was also "slightly wounded in the head in action" at Hurricane Bridge, attesting to the Confederates' marksmanship and their use of technology—the Whitworth Globe sighted rifles. Rayburn was taken to the field hospital and later examined by Dr. Shaw, who released him to duty. Others were not so fortunate as to survive their wounds; eighteen-year-old Private Jesse Hart of Company B died instantly from a gunshot wound at Hurricane Bridge. He enlisted on August 9, 1862, at Point Pleasant; his personal effects and extra uniform items were given to a friend in Company D.[33]

Private Henry Sands of Company A, who was twenty-five years old, was also killed in action at Hurricane Bridge. His brother, Matthew Sands, served in the 8th West Virginia Infantry and was stationed at Bull Town in March 1863. They were both friends with Captain Edgar Blundon, who commanded Company F of the 8th West Virginia Infantry, as well as several other soldiers in both regiments. Captain Blundon wrote to his fiancée, Sarah Young of Coalsmouth, on April 16, 1863, that his men were "indignant" toward Jenkins when they learned of Sands' death at Hurricane Bridge. Sands' body was recovered by family and later buried at the Mace Cemetery in Big Chimney, West Virginia. Private Altimus Young, of Company B, was also killed in action at Hurricane Bridge on March 28, 1863. He was eighteen years old and a resident of Point Pleasant, where he enlisted on October 18, 1862. Young's body was sent home to Mason County and buried in Greer Cemetery.[34]

There were no casualties reported from the 16th Virginia Cavalry at Hurricane Bridge. As was common in the Civil War, there were discrepancies in Union and Confederate casualty reports. For example, Captain William Johnson of the 13th West Virginia cited that "a few" wounded Confederates were captured, while Confederate records indicate there was one man killed and two men wounded, and both were captured. Sergeant James Sedinger of Company D, 8th Virginia Cavalry, also wrote in his diary that there was one man from his company killed, whom he identified as Private John Payne of Company E. It is presumed the body was buried in vicinity of the battlefield at Hurricane Bridge, since Jenkins left his casualties on the field.[35]

One historian stated there were two men killed in action and suggested there were several men wounded at Hurricane Bridge, and identified one of those killed as John Chapman, of Company D, 8th Virginia Cavalry. Chapman's service records indicated he was "killed in Putnam County in 1863." Two of Jenkins' wounded at Hurricane Bridge were relatives from the same extended family in Cabell County. Private Thomas H. Morris of Company D suffered a gunshot wound and was captured "at the same time" as Jordan Morris at Hurricane Bridge. Jordan Morris, who was twenty-two, was also "wounded at Hurricane Bridge and left at that place." Thomas Morris was afterward listed as "in the hands of the enemy" on Company D records. Both men received medical care by Dr. Shaw at the Hurricane Bridge field hospital, until taken to prison at Camp Chase, Ohio, in May 1863. They were moved to Fort Delaware, Maryland, in August and later transferred to Point Lookout in 1864. Jordan Morris died from acute dysentery there on January 28, 1865. As Captain Johnson indicated there were "a few" wounded Confederates, it is quite likely there were more, although military records do not identify them.[36]

Another incident related to Confederate casualties at Hurricane Bridge supposedly occurred during Jenkins' retreat, cited as local oral tradition by Mrs. Irene Ambler of Putnam County in the May 7, 1987 issue of the Hurricane Breeze: "Mr. Elmer Foster, a respected friend of mine, told me in the 1950's that his father saw the band of ragged Confederates with their wounded thrown across horses' backs marching down Hurricane Creek Road near Poindexter Road. Mr. Foster said, his father said, that one soldier slipped from the horse's back and rolled down the bank of Hurricane Creek, appearing to be dead. He said others picked him up and laid him again across the back of the horse." They then continued on their way, moving slowly down Hurricane Creek.[37]

Captain Johnson's Tribulations

One of the more intriguing figures who fought at Hurricane Bridge was Captain William J. Johnson. In May 1861, Brigadier General Henry A. Wise, commanding Confederate troops in the Kanawha Valley, had ordered him to enlist in a Confederate regiment. When Johnson refused, he was arrested and all of his property seized. He was released in June 1861 and later enlisted in the 13th West Virginia on August 15, 1862. Shortly after the battle at Hurricane Bridge, he again found himself in trouble, only this time with civilian authorities. Details are vague in extant records, although it apparently involved a civilian who made some unsavory accusations against him. Johnson later wrote to a friend on May 21, 1864, from Jacksonville, Florida, alluding to the situation, which he described as resulting from, "outside pressure alone; an unfortunate and sad occurrence for me, but I am not going to confess to you or anyone else."[38]

Despite somewhat sketchy circumstances, Jonson informed Colonel William Brown that he wanted to transfer into the 3rd United States Colored Troops (USCT) to accept a "higher post of authority" than he presently held, and on April 15, 1863, Brown petitioned the U.S. War Department to have Johnson transferred. Johnson then submitted his resignation on May 15, 1863, which was approved on July 25, 1863. Johnson was not actually given a higher position; rather, he was commissioned as a 1st Lieutenant in Company C, 3rd USCT. In May 1863, under the auspices of the War Department, the Bureau of Colored Troops was authorized, with the contingency that white officers must command the regiments. The 3rd U.S. Colored Regiment was organized at Philadelphia, Pennsylvania, on August 3, 1863, and served in the 10th Corps at South Carolina and Florida. Interestingly, Johnson later told a friend that one of the main reasons he had resigned was due to frustration with other officers in his regiment, grousing, "I don't think it's right to do the duty of half dozen officers…. they loaf around on the sick list or lazy list just as you please…."[39]

Johnson arrived in South Carolina to join the new regiment on July 21, 1863, where only four days previous they were in the attack against Fort Wagner, at Charleston Harbor, with the 54th Massachusetts. The 3rd USCT soon transferred to Florida in February 1864 and trained to become part of the heavy artillery service. Johnson was promoted to captain of Company C, 3rd USCT, on October 8, 1864. Johnson obviously had a knack for finding trouble, and again found himself in a whirlwind of strife in Florida. Immediately after his promotion to captain, he was appointed to serve as provost marshal at Gainesville. On the afternoon of December 22, 1864, he was accosted by two men at the 7th United States Infantry Regulars headquarters for insulting the wife of a young civilian, who then "used abusive language" toward him. Johnson apologized and asked to shake hands and resolve the matter. The civilian refused and asked him how he could request a handshake after that, and as they "exchanged words," the man threatened to do physical violence to Johnson. The ruckus awoke the garrison commander, who was asleep in his room. Meanwhile, a young lieutenant intervened and loudly ordered the crowd to disperse, warning them he would protect Johnson and demanded they leave; three soldiers then escorted the two men away from headquarters.[40]

A few minutes later, Johnson and a Federal cavalry officer rode off on their horses toward Newmansville. The two civilian men were waiting outside and followed Johnson, who was unaware. When the garrison commander learned that the two men went after Johnson, he immediately mounted his horse and rode off in search of him, knowing he was in danger. However, after riding all night he failed to locate Johnson, who had taken a different road. Johnson and the cavalry officer were attacked by the two men, who beat them severely, causing several injuries. Afterward, Colonel John T. Sprague, commanding the 7th United States Infantry, informed the

Jack and Parthenia Estes
at the 1913 Confederate Veteran's Reunion,
Huntington, West Virginia.
Courtesy Upper Vandalia Historical Society.

Judge Advocate General of the Eastern District of Florida on December 25, 1865 that he wanted the lieutenant who broke up the scuffle in the barracks arrested "for neglect of duty" and recommended a board of inquiry for failing to protect Johnson. As it turned out, the cavalry officer who accompanied Johnson to Newmansville was an accomplice of the two civilians and had led Johnson to them and helped in the assault. He was arrested and charged with assault and battery with intent to kill and sent to prison along with the other two assailants, and charges against the lieutenant were dismissed.[41]

That was not the end of Johnson's troubles, as while he was stationed at Jacksonville, Florida on January 7, 1865, he allowed another officer to go to St. Augustine on leave without approval by headquarters. The commander became angry and demanded to know by what authority Johnson had approved the leave, as the provost marshal did not possess that right. The incident was reported to Major General John General Foster, who required charges against Johnson on June 22, 1865 for overstepping his authority, though the charges were later dismissed. Also, on January 10, 1865, a board of inquiry was called against Johnson for failing to account for a large stockpile of government ordnance. Johnson produced records indicating proper accounting of the stores, and the charges were dropped. Johnson still managed to enjoy a sterling reputation with the command, as on January 25, 1865, he was recommended for promotion to major in the 3rd USCT.[42]

It has become a truism that many soldiers in border states or territories lost their friends, and in some cases their families, over partisan divisions in the Civil War. In western Virginia, it was not only commonplace for families to divide, but in many instances, it was more embittered when men joined military units on the opposing sides. Such a case occurred at Hurricane Bridge; Corporal John "Jack" Estes of Company D, 8th Virginia Cavalry was the elder of two brothers and the son of Thomas and Mary Estes, two of the earliest settlers in the Hurricane Bridge area. The family lived on a small farm near Cow Creek. Jack's parents died when he was fifteen years old, and when the war broke out in April 1861, the brothers agreed that the youngest, Erasmus, would stay home and tend to the farm while the older two served in the army. In May 1861, Jack enlisted in a local volunteer militia company, the Virginia Guards, and was captured by Union troops and held prisoner in Charleston for about two months. Upon release, he returned home and then enlisted in the 8th Virginia at Hurricane Bridge on September 12, 1862.[43]

Jack's younger sibling, James Monroe Estes, was eighteen when the war began. However, he quickly opposed the Confederacy and aligned himself with the local Union men of the area. This enraged Jack, and, knowing the danger a Unionist presented to local families, James left their farm to prevent bringing any harm to them. He enlisted in the 3rd Kentucky Infantry, Company E at Camp Robinson, near Louisville, on August 17, 1861. He saw heavy action in the western campaigns and was wounded in the shoulder at the battle of Murfreesboro, Tennessee, on January 6, 1863, and returned to duty. James was killed at the battle of Resaca, Georgia, on May 17, 1864, and his family had no idea what happened to him. Jack was eventually captured again by

Union soldiers in Wayne County, West Virginia in 1864. Specifically, he was arrested by 2nd Lieutenant John Harshbarger of the 3rd West Virginia Cavalry. As a sad epithet to the affair, after the war a family member asked Jack what he would have done if he had to face his brother James on a battlefield during the war, and he is said to have harshly and abruptly responded, "I would have shot him as quickly as I would have shot any other damn Yankee," adding a brutally honest perspective to the "brother against brother" cliché in Putnam County.[44]

As an epilogue, twenty-eight-year-old Martin van Buren Edens of Company A, 13th West Virginia, memorialized the Battle at Hurricane Bridge in a poem published in The Weekly Register on April 30, 1863. Edens enlisted as a private on August 15, 1862, at Charleston, West Virginia. He was promoted to corporal on September 23, 1862, then reduced to the ranks on June 1, 1864. He was severely wounded on September 19, 1864, at the Battle of Winchester and hospitalized at Chester, Virginia, until transferred to the army hospital at Gallipolis, Ohio, a few weeks later, where he remained until the end of the war.[45]

A Soldier's Poem: Skirmish at Hurricane Bridge!

Between a high hill and circuitous ridge,
Is the neat little town, known as Hurricane Bridge,
Or at least, 'twas a neat little village before -
The rebellion arose in the bright days of yore.

But rebellion has banished those pleasures, so sweet,
And the wail of despair is now heard in the street –
The many fine buildings in ashes are laid
The wealth of the inmates forever decayed.

The 13th Virginia is camped near this town,
Who in a late battle have won great renown.
The regiment is formed of a brave set of boys,
Who accomplish their work without making much noise.

But Albert G. Jenkins not aware of that fact,
Came early one morning to make an attack,
With a yard of white cotton unfurled to the breeze,
His staff came into camp, while Jenkins stayed behind trees.

'Twas Samuels who brought in the banner of truce.
Says Johnson, to surrender I this morning refuse.
In the time which is given to my works I'll repair.
And give you a battle on principles fair.

When cool as an iceberg we fell into line.
To defend the bright stars which on our banner doth shine,
And to hold our position at Hurricane Bridge,
In spite of the Rebs on each neighboring ridge.

For Jenkins marched forth with his menacing host
To capture or drive us away from our post,
He threw his men round on the top of each hill
To make us surrender or fly at his will.

He thought with his men on the left and the right,
He would capture our squad without having to fight,
And with Yankee clothing he his men would equip,
And thus would secure successful his trip.

But Albert was much disappointed to find
To surrender that morning we were not inclined
Then he told all his men to prepare for the blow
And soon they'd conquer the insolent foe.

From each hill top they fired on the 13th in vain,
For each at his post did boldly remain.
For the space of four hours he fought very hard
But his incessant firing we not much did regard.

Like Jeff. Davis' scrip that's more plenty than good,
They sent in their lead from each neighboring wood.
Like the insects that sing in the long days of June,
The balls from the Rebs almost whistled a tune.

But it was not sufficient to induce us to dance,
It was like Mason in England or Slidell in France,
Who after they made known their treacherous plan,
Have to end their hard labor just where they began.

With stomach's quite empty and feet without shoes,
Each felt like a bankrupt with a spell of the blues,
Like a dishonored guest ere the banquet is o'er
Arrives at the feast and is kept from the door.
They knew in our camp were crackers, coffee and meat,
And they longed to get in to get something to eat.
Like Cruse's man Friday, who on the mountain did stand,
And beheld in the distance, his own native land.

With obstacles in front which he could not surmount
Was not able to settle the lengthy account,
And fell ere he crossed o'er the dark rolling wave
And found in the deep sea a watery grave.

So Jenkins after giving us a hard shower of hail
And finding with muskets he could not prevail
Sent out his command to retreat from the field,
For the 13th Virginia was too stubborn to yield.

Being tired and hungry, they left in disgust,
Aware of the fact that Albert won't do to trust;
He promised to give them both food and attire,
In short everything that a reb could desire.

Except a good thrashing they left as they came
With nothing to brighten Jeff. Davis' fame;
And Jenkins found out that one blunder he made
In seeking for sunshine he found nought but shade.[46]

Companies C, E and F of the 13th West Virginia were at Point Pleasant on March 28, 1863; upon hearing of the attack at Hurricane Bridge later that day, Brigadier General Eliakim P. Scammon ordered Colonel Brown to send Companies C and F on a forced march to Hurricane Bridge to assist Captain Johnson's four companies—a distance of more than fifty miles. They arrived around 4 p.m. the next day, only to find Jenkins was nowhere to be found. Company E remained at Point Pleasant under the command of Captain John D. Carter, with sixty men present for duty. This company was originally recruited as an independent sharpshooter company in August 1862, but that organization "never was finished," according to Private George Rucker. General Jacob D. Cox thought Captain Carter had approximately two hundred fifty men present, but Colonel Brown later reported he only had about sixty men there and estimated Jenkins had about four hundred men. Later that day, Cox realized, "The force at Point Pleasant is weaker than I supposed, General Scammon had ordered most of it to sustain the post at Hurricane Bridge and only one company is left there."[47]

Attack on the Victor No. 2

On March 29, 1863, Jenkins' cavalrymen were still dismounted, marching through Putnam County toward Point Pleasant. After traversing Hurricane Creek Road to the Kanawha River the day previous, they moved northward and soon encountered the Union steamer *Victor No. 2* at Robert M. Hall's Landing near Frazier's Bottom, not far from the head of Knobb Creek. On board the steamer was an Army paymaster, Major Benjamin R. Cowan, some forty-five passengers, and about twenty soldiers, along with $86,000 in cash and about twenty disabled cavalry horses. The Kanawha River was narrow in this area, less than 200 yards wide, and crooked, requiring pilots to slow down and carefully navigate through the channel. Knowing this, Jenkins posted troops on both sides of the river—it is unknown where they crossed—attempting to create a "blockade" forcing them ashore. Some of Jenkins' men also persuaded a local farm hand to attempt to flag the steamer down, pretending to be a would-be-passenger, hoping to draw it close to shore.[48]

The Confederates hid in the weeds, and behind fences and houses on the riverbanks. According to Captain Fred Ford, when the *Victor No. 2* passed by, they poured a "streaming blaze of fire" across the bow and ordered the ship to pull over. Instead of complying, Captain Ford rang for full speed ahead and hunkered down behind the wheel, as a hail of bullets riddled the ship, shattering the glass in the wheelhouse. While passing by the Confederates on the "gauntlet of death," the Union soldiers gave "a loud shout of triumph" taunting their

Major Benjamin R. Cowan.
Library of Congress.

Captain Fred Ford.
Library of Congress.

tormentors, and several who had their rifles returned fire. The *Victor No. 2* escaped, although one soldier was killed, and several passengers and horses wounded. Ford stated: "Men and horses were struck by the deadly missles. The groans of the wounded, screams of the terrified women and children and the cries of the plunging animals filled the air, mixed with the constant whistling of bullets. Most of the passengers lay flat on the deck…the blood of men and animals was flowing freely on the deck, presenting a ghastly spectacle." Ford also mentioned the wheelhouse was especially bullet ridden with glass shattered, though the entire boat was splintered from heavy musketry. Afterward, Jenkins moved on toward Point Pleasant.[49]

Jenkins' Raid on Point Pleasant

Jenkins arrived at Point Pleasant early on the morning of March 30, 1863, where he attacked some sixty men from Company E, 13th West Virginia, and approximately 100 soldiers from the nearby army hospital at Gallipolis. The Federals put up a ferocious defense, fighting in the streets for nearly four hours. During the melee, the Confederates located a large storage of corn and some buildings containing army stores and set them on fire. The Union troops were forced into taking cover inside the courthouse and were nearly overtaken, until some 200 home guards and militia from Gallipolis arrived about 3 p.m. After another hour or so of fighting, Jenkins withdrew, unable to acquire the supply depot or herd of beef cattle, his primary objectives on this expedition.[50]

Following the battles at Hurricane Bridge and Point Pleasant, Companies E and F of the 13th West Virginia Infantry were sent to Mud Bridge in Cabell County in late April, where they quickly constructed earthworks in the vicinity of the Union Baptist Church. Meanwhile, Company G was at Coalsmouth, and Company C was sent to Winfield. The remaining companies A, B, D and H spent the next month at Hurricane Bridge improving the earthen fort; Dr. Samuel Shaw wrote to his daughter from the hospital there during a heavy rainstorm on April 6, 1863: "Today they have commenced enlarging and strengthening the fortifications, they have had eight yokes of oxen drawing up very large logs for this purpose. At the time of the fight the fort was not completed, it has been much improved since and will be still

The steamer *Victor No. 2.*
Library of Congress.

further improved...." The weather at Hurricane Bridge was unpredictable to say the least during March-April 1863. Dr. Shaw indicated that on March 30, 1863, it was "spring like" only to experience "one of the fiercest snowstorms of the season" the next day. On April 1, 1863, he noted "The temperature is that of January rather than April" and mentioned a heavy rainstorm occurred on April 6, 1863. The 23rd Ohio Infantry regiment arrived to strengthen the Union garrison at Hurricane Bridge on April 3, 1863.[51]

During Confederate General Albert Jenkins' retreat from Point Pleasant, he encountered Lieutenant Colonel John C. Paxton of the 2nd West Virginia Cavalry six miles west of Buffalo. Paxton reported to General E.P. Scammon that the Confederates were riding stolen horses and had some 400 to 600 troopers and requested a steamer to carry prisoners. Scammon responded by telegraph that afternoon informing Paxton to return to Charleston. The outpost at Hurricane Bridge quickly became known as very unpopular duty among the Union soldiers serving in the Kanawha Valley. Essentially a remote, isolated fort, there were persistent problems with disease plaguing the garrisons there throughout the war. According to Dr. Shaw: "There is no security here outside the camp. I spend a part of the day generally in camp. Yesterday we had general inspection and dress parade, the first since I have been here." Shaw told his daughter that on April 7, 1863, things were: "All quiet on the Hurricane as they say of the Potomac. We have a cool, chilly and disagreeable morning, a regular northern spell of weather."[52]

Private David Burrows, Company F, 13th West Virginia Volunteer Infantry, was one of the soldiers who became intimately acquainted with the hardships of garrisoning that isolated outpost. Burrows wasted no time expressing to his family his thoughts about what occurred there. He opined one of the reasons Jenkins had been able to easily attack the post was because, due to the remote location, Union officials were not aware of his approach until March 28, 1863, which is not accurate, as General Jacob Cox was aware of the need for a garrison there in December 1862. On April 4, 1863, Company F was still at Hurricane Bridge, and Burrows groused: "I don't know when we will get away from here. Some of the boys had a fight up here, but we did not get in on it...we have been on one big scout since we have been up here."[53]

Dr. Shaw was similarly convinced of the hardships at the lonely outpost of Hurricane Bridge, quipping, "This place seems to be cut off from all the rest of creation at present." Corporal John Hess of Company H wrote to his wife Samantha on April 10, 1863, "I set on my bed which is straw with a sad heart" and expressed intense homesickness, "I can't bear it," from the isolation at the lonely outpost. They were also having trouble getting enough food, as Hess told his wife, "Tell Leon to fit up the regiment with corn shocks." Soon, the boredom of camp led to mischief, as Hess also informed Samantha: " the boys is so bad that I can't write a lot...I expect that you can't read it – I can't rite it makes me feel bad…" Rations were mostly poor beef and hardtack crackers, even in the summer, as they rarely had time to cook while out on patrol. Their pay was also slow making it to camp, as Hess griped to his wife, "I had to eat raw meat and crackers for breakfast all the time I was glad to get it…I can't get no money we will get 4 months pay next week.[54]

Captain David Dove, 2nd West Virginia Cavalry, went on an expedition from Camp Piatt through Logan and Cabell counties, beginning on April 3, 1863. His battalion camped at Red House that night, then moved to Mud Bridge the next morning and were engaged in a small skirmish with Confederate cavalry under General Jenkins at Mud River. Dove found that several companies of cavalry belonging to Colonel James Sweeney's battalion were with Jenkins; he described the area as "one of the wildest sections of country in Western Virginia," and he captured thirty-three prisoners on the expedition. Dove reported, "After resting an hour, I started for Hurricane Bridge, arriving there at 8 o'clock, and remained there during the night." He also telegraphed General E.P Scammon from Hurricane Bridge, stating his detachment would be at the mouth of the Coal River the next morning at 9:30 a.m., with thirty-four Confederate prisoners and their stolen horses, and requested a steamer to transport them to Charleston. Dr. Shaw admitted seven of the prisoners to the field hospital at Hurricane Bridge, most of whom were seriously ill and walking barefoot.[55]

An editorial appearing in the *Gallipolis Journal* reflected the popular opinion of Unionists in the Kanawha Valley who were tired of the constant Confederate raids; many felt they had received little, if any, help from the state and Federal governments:

How much longer are the Union people of the Kanawha to suffer? Twice has Jenkins' gang of robbers visited our valley, and each time he has been able to accomplish his purpose, by the murdering of our citizens and stealing our horses & c. Each time his career could have been checked, if the commanders of the union troops, sent for our protection, had done their duty; but so much of their kindness and attention is given to the traitors with whom they are in daily intercourse, that they cannot attend to anything else, and still our brave troops with their officers are willing to do their duty, as is proved by the affair at Hurricane Bridge and the fight at Point Pleasant, wherein they were able to drive off the scoundrels who call themselves the Confederates.

The Unionists of the Kanawha valley have suffered much. They have shown great forbearance, if not destroying the villains who have invited these raids of Jenkins, but now they are desperate. They feel that they cannot live any longer with the authors of their ruin, and a new era is about to be initiated, which may possibly open the eyes of the Government and their agents. The Unionists feel that they never had any protection from the Government of Wheeling or Washington. They feel that they have done their duty as citizens, in paying the heavy taxes assessed upon them, and in sending their sons to fight the battles of that Union which they hold so dear.

They feel moreover that they have been wronged by the army that they had reinforced, while on its way through their territory to the seat of the war, in destruction of their farms, the robbery of their crops, & c., and now they feel that unless the Government does them justice, they must find out the means of protection. Deprived of their cattle and horses, they are unable to cultivate their land, and they foresee starvation before them.

While thus suffering, they see their traitorous neighbors fully protected, getting rich by selling their produce to the Government, and if this Government will not protect them and repair their losses by confiscation and imposts on the secessionists, then they are determined to act for themselves, to plunder as they have been plundered, and to defend themselves. The time has come. The army will be on their side, for the army is right. Either the Government must act for the Union, or the Unionists will act for themselves.

A Sufferer[56]

Lincoln Proclaims West Virginia a State

The citizens of West Virginia voted to ratify a revised state constitution, allowing the gradual emancipation of slaves within its territory, in March 1863, which enabled President Abraham Lincoln, after two years of debate on the question of constitutionality, to sign a proclamation admitting West Virginia into the Union as the thirty-fifth state on April 20, 1863. This would not take effect for sixty days, on June 20, 1863. Lincoln's six-member cabinet was equally divided on the question of whether it was constitutional to admit West Virginia without the consent of the mother state, Virginia, but Lincoln maintained his position that the act was made expedient by a war, arguing that since Virginia had seceded and was no longer entitled to the protections afforded by the United States Constitution, it had no say in the matter.[57]

Also on April 20, 1863, attorney Arthur Ingram Boreman was elected as the first governor of West Virginia, to be sworn into office on June 20, 1863, with Wheeling as the first capital. A former member of the Virginia House of Representatives from 1855 to 1861, and an anti-abolitionist, Boreman was a strong Union supporter who tried to prevent Virginia from seceding in 1861. He served as president of the Second Wheeling Convention in 1861 and played a key role in establishing the Restored Government of Virginia. Francis H. Pierpont continued to serve as governor of the Restored Government of Virginia, though only for counties under Federal control, until 1865. While still recognizing Richmond as the official capital, his de facto seat of government moved to Alexandria, Virginia, until the war's end, and then moved to Richmond where he served until 1868. Pierpont's nephew, Francis P. Pierpont, an officer in the 12th West Virginia Infantry, was appointed as the new state adjutant general of West Virginia by Governor Boreman in mid-1864.[58]

Lincoln's bold announcement of West Virginia statehood caused a great deal of anxiety among Southern citizens, and Confederate military leaders began to increase the frequency and intensity of raids into the Kanawha Valley in response. West Virginia Adjutant General H. P. Samuels subsequently ordered all state militia to begin drilling daily, on May 3, 1863, and required officers unfamiliar with the mechanics and nuances of organized drill and tactics to acquire manuals and begin studying at once. Captain James W. Bailey, who commanded a Union home guard company from Hurricane Creek, was captured by Confederate cavalry on February 8, 1863 and imprisoned at Richmond. He escaped sometime in early June 1863 and returned to resume command of his company. Despite the ire of Southern citizens, however, Congress finally agreed with Lincoln, and West Virginia was admitted into the Union as the Thirty-fifth state on June 20, 1863. On June 24, 1863, militia officers from Wayne and Cabell counties reported to the state adjutant general that there were roughly 700 men enrolled in the county militia available for duty, though Putnam County failed to file a report. A year earlier, Cabell County militia officers reported that while there were 700 men on the rolls, only 120 were actually available for duty; however, in nearby Mason County, the 106th Regiment Virginia Militia reported 671 men available for duty, reflecting a dramatic increase in Union men enlisting in those companies during the interim since the draft began in 1862.[59]

July 1863 was a time of major setback and disappointment for the Confederacy. General Robert E. Lee's Army of Northern Virginia was defeated at Gettysburg July 1-3, and on July 4, the siege of Vicksburg ended in a Union victory when Lieutenant General Ulysses S. Grant accepted the surrender of embattled Confederates who had been under siege since May 1863. At Point Pleasant, Sergeant Joseph Brumley of Company F, 13th West Virginia Infantry, was ordered to march with twenty men to Buffalo in Putnam County and establish a recruiting station. Traveling from Barboursville through Mud Bridge and Hurricane Bridge, and passing through Winfield, Brumley and his detachment arrived at Buffalo late in the afternoon of July 4, 1864. While the town was busily celebrating Independence Day, Brumley quickly located a suitable building to use as a recruiting office near the old Union Mill on Main Street. By the end of the day, he had seven new volunteers signed up. When news of Union victories at Gettysburg and Vicksburg reached Captain Isaac Rucker's home guard company, who were then posted at Winfield, they were much encouraged. Rucker was in the process of selling off captured horses and mules to locals, and on July 27, 1863, paid an auctioneer a hefty fee of $1.00.[60]

Similar to his predecessor Francis Pierpont, Governor Boreman received frequent complaints from residents of Putnam County about Confederate guerrillas raiding farms and stealing horses, bacon, and flour, among other supplies. Many citizens also griped that the local home guards had been "of little benefit in repelling the enemy." One irate citizen also pointed out that many of the home guards had moved their families across the river into Ohio and were hiding out there with them to avoid regular military service. In response, Boreman issued a proclamation on August 20, 1863, identifying by name more than one hundred men from Putnam County, who in 1861 had:

> …deserted their homes and are actively engaged in aiding the so called Confederate States of America, and the rebel State Governments at Richmond, in their attempt to objurgate the good people of this State, but in consequence of the war evidence of their rebellious and criminal acts cannot be obtained; Now therefore, I, Arthur I. Boreman, Governor of the state of West Virginia, do issue this my proclamation declaring the said…enemies of this State, unless they shall within sixty days from the date of this proclamation take and file in the Clerk's office of the Circuit Court for the said county of Putnam an oath to support the Constitution of the United States and the Constitution of the State of West Virginia, and thereafter demean themselves as good citizens.[61]

Brigadier General Joseph Lightburn ordered the 13th West Virginia to move from Winfield and Coalsmouth to Point Pleasant immediately, while Captain John Young's company was directed to remain at Barboursville. This temporarily left Winfield open to Confederate raids, but fortunately for anxious Union citizens there, nothing occurred at this time.[62]

Brigadier General Eliakim P. Scammon's Crisis

On October 1, 1863, U.S. Secretary of War Edwin Stanton received a letter written by John A. Wells, on letterhead from the 3rd Division Headquarters, Department of West Virginia, located at Washington City, informing him that at the request of Mrs. Madeline V. Goddard, a cousin of Dr. Edward Naret, that Brigadier General Eliakim P. Scammon, who commanded the Kanawha Division, charges be brought against him "for his conduct towards Dr. Edward Naret, late of Buffalo, W.Va., now of Gallipolis, Ohio." Wells continued:

> The facts of the case are these: Dr. Naret addressed a private letter to his cousin, Mrs. Goddard, describing the conditions in the Kanawha Valley, and complaining of the way in which that department was managed by our officers, and many others…that he has been robbed by [Brig. Gen. Albert G.]

Jenkins, and had his property taken by our Quarter masters, he has been a devoted friend of the Union, and has been more anxious for the triumph of the cause, than for the concerns of his private fortune. Knowing this, Mrs. Goodard, knowing the Government ought to be informed of the way things were managed in the Kanawha Valley, requested me to lay Dr. Naret's [letter] before you, for the information of General Burnside, their commander at Cincinnati. By her request I took the letter to the Department, and showed it to Genl. Cumby, there acting as your substitute. He read it and asked if he might retain it. I told him he might. It turns, from subsequent events, that the letter of Dr. Naret was sent to Cincinnati, and in consequence of the charges of conditions there, fell into the hands of Genl. Scammon, instead of Genl. Burnside.

Genl. Scammon finding himself the subject of complaint by Dr. Naret, took advantage of his position, as commander, for in the course Dr. Naret to be answered, at the dread of myself, and dragged to Cincinnati, to answer the desirous officer of not being satisfied with his conduct in the Kanawha Valley. After inflicting this indignity upon him, the Genl. dismissed him "with an apology"! The facts of this outrage are detailed in a subsequent letter of Dr. Naret, which I have the honor herewith to submit; with this request that such an abuse of power as it exhibits, shall not go without the censure and punishment of the War Department; with great respect, I have the honor to be,

Yours truly,
John A. Wells[63]

Eliakim Parker Scammon was born at Whitfield, Maine, on December 27, 1816. He matriculated to West Point in 1833 and was ranked fifth in his class of fifty-two at graduation in 1837. Scammon attended the military academy with Ulysses S. Grant and William S. Rosecrans. Commissioned as a 2nd Lieutenant of Artillery, Scammon taught mathematics at West Point until July 7, 1838, when he was assigned to the Topographical Engineers and sent to Florida during the Seminole War until 1840. Afterward he returned to West Point, serving as a professor of geography, ethics and history. He served in that post until September 21, 1846, when promoted to 1st Lieutenant and was sent to Massachusetts as a surveyor. During the Mexican War, Scammon served on Major General Winfield Scott's staff and was cited for bravery in battle. Scammon submitted his resignation to the War Department on March 13, 1856; before that processed through channels, however, he was accused of being intoxicated with alcohol on duty by subordinate officers while stationed in Santa Fe, New Mexico. This severely tarnished his career, as he was court martialed out of the army for "Conduct Unbecoming an Officer and Drunkenness on Duty" on June 4, 1856. Future Confederate President, Jefferson Davis, was then the U.S. Secretary of War and signed the order removing him from service on July 18, 1856. Once a civilian, Scammon returned to teaching and became a professor at Mount St. Mary's College in western Virginia until the Civil War began in 1861.[64]

On June 14, 1861, a little more than five years after dismissal from the army, Scammon obtained a commission as Colonel of Volunteers by the Governor of Ohio. When Colonel William S. Rosecrans, who then commanded the 23rd Ohio Volunteer Infantry, was promoted to brigadier general, Scammon was given command of the regiment. This regiment became known as the "President's Regiment," because two future U.S. presidents, Rutherford B. Hayes and William McKinley, were members. When Hayes first met Scammon, he described the colonel as "irritating but interesting," and further described him as intelligent, although he thought he lacked "vigor of nerve." Hayes also privately confided that he thought Scammon was unfit to command a large volunteer force. Despite Hayes' apprehension, Scammon was quite knowledgeable of military matters

General Eliakim P. Scammon.
Maine Department of Archives.
Used with Permission.

and rapidly transformed the rough volunteers into a highly disciplined regiment. Scammon's regiment was initially assigned to Camp Chase, Ohio, where he was in charge of training new volunteers. The 23rd Ohio was next assigned to western Virginia; he was then placed in command of the 1st Brigade of the Kanawha Division in September 1861. Captain Russell Hastings, an officer from Ohio who later served on Rutherford B. Hayes' staff, recalled of Scammon: "He was something of a martinet, or rather seemed so to us at that time. We thought he was fussy and particular as to little details of drill and camp life. Later when we saw him under fire, how cool and collected he was, we forgave him."[65]

In September 1862, the Kanawha Division joined the 9th Corps of the Army of the Potomac in the bloody Maryland Campaign. Scammon's brigade was heavily engaged at South Mountain on September 14, 1862. 9th Corps commander Major General Jesse Reno was mortally wounded there; command of the corps fell upon Brigadier General Jacob D. Cox of the Kanawha Division, and Scammon was given command of the division. At the battle of Antietam on September 17, 1862, his 2nd Brigade under Colonel George Crook attacked Confederates at Burnside's Bridge and supported the Union advance toward Sharpsburg. For his calm demeanor and gallantry under fire, Scammon was promoted to brigadier general in October 1862. When the Kanawha Division returned to western Virginia after the Maryland Campaign, Scammon had command of the Kanawha District, where he remained through early 1864.[66]

The 8th West Virginia Infantry, with many men from Putnam County, including Company D which organized at Buffalo, became mounted infantry on June 20, 1863, the same day West Virginia officially entered the Union. The regiment took part in the last major battle of the Civil War in West Virginia at Droop Mountain, near Hillsboro in Pocahontas County, on November 6, 1863. Union General William W. Averell had earlier launched a series of raids in that area during August 1863, hoping to disrupt the Virginia and Tennessee Railroad in southwestern Virginia. Averell encountered a brigade commanded by Colonel George S. Patton at White Sulphur Springs and was defeated on August 26 and 27, 1863. He afterward devised a plan to trap Confederates near Lewisburg but failed. Averell next attacked 1,700 Confederates under Generals John Echols and William Lowther "Mudwall" Jackson at Droop Mountain, which ended in vicious hand-to-hand combat when the Federals forced their way through the Confederate left flank and routed the Confederates. While there would still be raids and bushwhackers to deal with in the Kanawha Valley, this action essentially put a halt to any future chance of larger scale Confederate operations in the region.[67]

Captain David Dove, 2nd West Virginia Cavalry, was at Coalsmouth on November 14, 1863, with two companies. He telegraphed General E.P. Scammon that "One hundred Rebel Troops infantry were at Coal last night - fifty crossed the Kanawha & are now on the lower side the other squad of 50 are on the upper side and have gone up to Poca." Captain John V. Young and his Company G were ordered to garrison Hurricane Bridge in early December 1863; at that time, he had approximately ninety to one hundred men in the company. After receiving orders from the War Department in November that Company G was being assigned to the 11th West Virginia, Colonel William Brown promptly recalled forty-seven of Young's men to Barboursville on December 3, 1863, and shrewdly ordered them to fill in ranks of the other companies in his own regiment. Brown argued it was his regiment's presence in the Kanawha Valley area that initially attracted those men to enlist in the first place, and he was therefore entitled to them. This infuriated Young, who had recruited those men after his initial affiliation with the 13th West Virginia in August 1862.[68]

Young wrote to his wife on December 3, 1863, stating he did not think there was imminent danger at Hurricane from Confederates; however, when he wrote to Colonel Brown on December 11, 1863, he had dramatically changed his mind on the issue, as during their first days at the outpost, Company G sent patrols into the village and surrounding areas and arrested several Confederate citizens. Young became acutely aware of the strong Confederate support present in the village and began to suspect there would soon be contact from Confederate troops. When he received a new dispatch from Union headquarters in Charleston on December 10, 1863, ordering him to send a lieutenant and twenty-six men to Coalsmouth—leaving him with about fifteen men at Hurricane Bridge—he became furious.[69]

The reason this occurred was because the state assistant adjutant general, George C. Bowyer of Winfield, had recently advised Lieutenant Colonel James R. Hall of the 13th West Virginia Infantry that if he thought it necessary to "send a Lieut. and 25 men of Capt Young's Company to Coalsmouth, do so." Bowyer further indicated, "From representations made to me by Mr. Benedict I do think it is necessary…" The Mr. Benedict referred to was Samuel Benedict of Coalsmouth, father-in-law of 13th West Virginia adjutant, 1st Lieutenant John Cunningham, who had recently replaced 1st Lieutenant Emory Bridgeman, who was killed in action at Hurricane Bridge. Benedict was a wealthy and influential attorney and strong Unionist. Benedict sent several letters to both the governor and the state adjutant general during the war, complaining that Coalsmouth was not secure from Confederate raids. In October 1863, he sent another letter requesting arms for the Coalsmouth citizens. A stark reminder that even in wartime, political influence is not to be dismissed, Benedict, who had no prior military training, received a shipment of new Enfield short-rifles, .58 caliber, with cartridge boxes with slings, cap boxes, and waist belts and buckles, with one hundred rounds of ammunition from the state ordnance supply, on November 3, 1863.[70]

Meanwhile, Captain John Young, finding he had only fifteen men left to defend Hurricane Bridge, wrote to Colonel Brown on December 11, 1863 from that outpost:

"I have the honor wherein to enclose copies of orders received today, and you may surmise on their receipt, to think that I have been placed here on this rebel thoroughfare with my Company, where we are in danger day & night and then by other representation to have the company divided so as to be sure that some of us may be captured or killed. (It makes me indignant) You know that I never have flinched from duty since I have been in the service but this trys my patience and I think the request is beyond precedent. I suppose that you have not learned that Provost Marshall has arrested a great number of rebel women and men in Putnam, this week, and taken them to Charleston and they are now in the Guard House, and the rebels here says they will have revenge in a few days. I understand today that they are threatening that they will have Union women taken as hostages and that in a few days. I learned yesterday that notorious horse thief Wake Dudding is in, I had Sergt McDaniel and 12 men after him last night, and but for this order would have at him tonight."[71]

Second Battle at Hurricane Bridge

Young's fears of a Confederate attack on his post at Hurricane Bridge became reality on December 13, 1863. At that time, Young only had about twenty-five men from his company available for duty, as the others were still Coalsmouth. On the bitter cold afternoon of Sunday, December 13, Young was alerted by his pickets that a large force of enemy cavalry was rapidly approaching the post. The Confederates were later identified as some 300 to 500 men from the 16th Virginia Cavalry, who belonged to Brigadier General Albert Jenkins' cavalry brigade, one of the same units that had attacked the outpost with the 8th Virginia Cavalry on March 28, 1863. Young received a written demand for surrender prior to the assault, which he promptly declined, just as the former garrison commander, Captain James W. Johnson of the 13th West Virginia, had done nine months previous. Recalling the majority of the 13th West Virginia were then stationed at nearby Barboursville some thirty miles west, and realizing he was significantly outgunned, the contentious Young decided to fight anyway rather than surrender, knowing not only his men's fighting tenacity, but that he had a great deal of protection afforded by the improved earthworks.[72]

The Confederates attacked, and while it is not known whether they deployed sharpshooters along the heights as in the previous battle there, it seems very likely they would have taken advantage of the terrain available to them, having fought there before. Regardless, Young's small company fiercely resisted the Confederate attack until just after dark, when Young realized he had to decide whether or not to evacuate his post. It is not known who retired first, but the only official report on the matter indicates Union officers believed Young's account that "The enemy left, probably about the same time in great haste…It is doubtful whether they discovered that our force had left." There were no casualties, but in his retreat toward Barboursville, Young found he had two men missing. The Confederates withdrew and likewise moved toward Barboursville, where there was no telegraphic communication with the Union troops' brigade headquarters at Point Pleasant to call for reinforcements if needed.[73]

When Confederates retreated from Hurricane Bridge, Young's company traversed the James River Turnpike as far as Mud Bridge, searching for them but finding nothing. A few days later, Young received orders to join the Union garrison located at Barboursville, commanded by Lieutenant Colonel James R. Hall of the 13th West Virginia Volunteer Infantry. Hall immediately organized a search party of approximately 200 infantrymen, including Young's company, and scouted throughout Cabell and Wayne counties looking for the Confederates— and this time ran into them. Hall reported:

We passed through the country between this and Wayne-Court House and found that they were camping in the neighborhood of Wayne-Court House. I found it impossible to force them to fight, as they were well mounted and appeared to be only disposed to interrupt us by harassing our advance and rear guards…I would have remained out longer but for the want of rations and the sudden change in and inclemency of the weather, which rendered it impossible for the men to march.[74]

Captain Isaac Rucker's company, the "Putnam Scouts," were at Winfield on December 14, 1863, when he received an order from Colonel William Brown, who was at Barboursville: "There is a detachment of our troops at Mud Bridge and a detachment at Hurricane Bridge. You had better place yourself in communication with them if you have any information and can do anything. Spare no means to inform [Lt. Col.] Col. [James R.] Hall as he marched from here last night at about 10 O.C. to Mud Bridge and keep him advised." Rucker, on the other hand, wrote to former governor and State Adjutant General Francis P. Pierpont, nephew of Governor Francis H. Pierpont, the next day requesting pay for his company, noting they had not received pay in more than eleven months, "I have to keep them on duty near all of the time and some of their families or some of them are in destitute circumstances." Rucker also requested permission to recruit up to seventy-five men in his company.[75]

On December 15, 1863, news of the most recent fight at Hurricane Bridge reached Major General B.F. Kelley, who then commanded the Union forces in West Virginia, via Lieutenant Colonel James R. Hall, 13th West Virginia, who telegraphed:

General: Kelley's dispatch just received. The information of the approach of the enemy came from Camp Piatt, Gallipolis, and Barboursville simultaneously. I had no force with which to make any attempt to cut them off. Two gunboats were extemporized-one here, to patrol down the river, and one at Gallipolis, to patrol up. One small party succeeded in crossing during the night and cut the wire near Red House. No other damage has been done. The lines are now up. The enemy attacked a small force at Hurricane Bridge Sunday (13th) afternoon. That night our forces escaped, with 2 missing. The enemy left, probably at about the same time in great haste, going toward Barboursville, taking nothing with them. It is doubtful whether they discovered that our force had left. Our force was only half a company, Under Captain Young, of the Eleventh [West] Virginia Infantry. The enemy's force was about 300. The Thirteenth [West] Virginia is at Barboursville, not under my command. They may intercept the enemy's retreat. It cannot be done from here. I have no telegraphic communication with Barboursville. Colonel Brown is in command there. Boats will commence running again to-morrow, accompanied by sufficient guards.[76]

Captain Isaac Rucker encountered a group of Confederate cavalry from Wayne County near Buffalo, around the same time Captain Young's garrison was attacked at Hurricane Bridge. He reported the affair to Francis P. Pierpont, nephew of the former governor, who was then serving as the state adjutant general, on December 22, 1863:

I have the honor to you a complete roll of my company with ranks attached. I would have made my returns before this but for a Rebel raid that was made by one Maj. Smith…. from Wayne [County] but this raid was intended to be on Point Pleasant and Gallipolis, but I claim the honor of having turned their course. They came within a mile and half of me, but learning I had a piece of artillery, they retreated on the double quick. I sent message to Col. [William R.] Brown you will please find enclosed his orders to me.[77]

In late December 1863, Lieutenant Colonel James R. Hall, 13th West Virginia Infantry, learned that a large body of Confederate cavalry were recently sited near Hurricane Bridge and appeared to be moving toward Wayne County. Hall led a battalion of two hundred of his men from Barboursville to Wayne County on December 30, 1863, where they encountered the 16th Virginia Cavalry, although due to lack of rations to sustain a lengthy expedition and inclement weather, they returned to Barboursville after only minor skirmishing by his rear guard. Thus, as the year 1863 ended in Putnam County, there would be many more skirmishes and raids until the end of the war, but none as intense as those occurring 1861-1863. However, the new year would bring many other events of significance, including the capture of a Union general.[78]

The Devil's Tea Table

This is a rock formation near Cross Creek in Buffalo. Seated on the left is
J.H. Collins, Mayor of Buffalo. He was a Union Civil War Veteran of Co. H
12th Ohio Volunteer Infantry.

Courtesy Buffalo Academy Museum.

Chapter Four

1864: Incessant Raids

During January 1864, Captain Isaac Rucker wrote to the state quartermaster requesting rations and reported he had fifty-two men present in his company. The former 8th West Virginia Mounted Infantry was officially redesignated as the 7th West Virginia Cavalry on January 23, 1864. On February 10, Rucker signed a receipt for 2,000 rounds of "rifle musket cartridges" for the Putnam Scouts from the army ordnance depot at Clarksburg. Captain Rucker soon made a decision to leave the company, however, as on March 1, 1864, he tendered his resignation to state Adjutant General Francis P. Pierpont, son of Governor Francis H. Pierpont. He recommended John M. Ball of Buffalo to replace him as captain in his company, noting: "He is the best qualified man in the company. He will make an energetic officer and is the unanimous choice of the men." Rucker also requested "full authority" to recruit a full company of seventy-five men. Before he left, Rucker ensured his men were paid when he received $2,426.42 from the state. His request to recruit a full company was granted, and on April 27, 1864, he was commissioned as 1st Lieutenant, Company L, 7th West Virginia Cavalry. He was promoted to captain of Company D on May 24, 1864, and served in that regiment until the end of the war. However, it appears that Ball was already serving as captain, possibly because Rucker was planning to depart soon. Earlier on January 9, 1864, Ball was in the Putnam Scouts camp located at Union Ridge in Mason County and wrote to state quartermaster General William Brown as "Captain" John M. Ball, requesting the appropriate forms to complete his quarterly muster rolls, and requested pay for his men, whom he mentioned had not received any funds for their service in almost one year.[1]

George Washington Smith.
Courtesy Vickie Wood.

George Washington Smith of Buffalo

George Washington Smith was born at Liberty, Virginia, on November 30, 1837, and raised as the eldest of ten siblings. His family moved to Leon in Putnam County in 1850. Smith was semi-famous in the region after he discovered a natural gas source burning at the mouth of Two-Mile Creek in Kanawha County in 1854 and was the first person to use it for cooking—without knowledge that it was being used to boil salt in the saline mines above Charleston. Smith worked as a farmer and as a salt boatman on the Kanawha River before he joined the army. Smith's family owned a slave named Ned; when Smith was sixteen years old in the fall of 1863, he went swimming in a small pond on the family farm and nearly drowned. Ned, who had been severely abused by Smith's family, was nearby and had one of his legs in a splint from a recent accident working on the farm. He saw Smith struggling and could have easily allowed him to drown. Instead, Ned jumped into the pond and pulled Smith out, heroically saving his life. For this, Smith became ardently opposed to slavery and later said the incident motivated him to enlist in the army at Leon, West Virginia, on January 1, 1864.[2]

Smith literally had to force his way into the army, instead of avoiding the draft as many young men were then attempting to do. Standing only four feet, five inches tall and weighing 110 lbs., Smith only wore a sized four boot. The recruiting officers refused him, saying he was too young and too small, and mocked him saying he would make a better mascot than a soldier. The spunky lad abruptly informed the officer he could not keep him out of the army that was fighting for the Union. He immediately walked to the 13th West Virginia camp at Point Pleasant, a distance of thirteen miles, and found some soldiers he knew in Company K. He simply acted as if he had been formally enlisted and ate, slept, drilled, and did camp duties along with the soldiers; the officers assumed that he had been sworn into service along with other new recruits who arrived that month. It did not take long before Smith was discovered, but due to his tenacity and courage shown during his first skirmish with some bushwhackers while on patrol, the officers allowed him to stay with his company as he had proven his worth as a soldier. Smith was then officially mustered into Federal service on March 11, 1864.[3]

Smith paid a dear price for his enlistment; his family disowned him, and two of his younger brothers had joined the Confederate army. For years after the war, his brother William refused to converse with him under any circumstances and would simply turn his head away when George spoke, although they remained neighbors. William was near death when he called for George to come to his bedside, and they agreed to forgive and forget the past just before William passed away. After the war, Smith resided in Liberty, Putnam County. He rarely talked about his wartime experiences, preferring instead to tell his family about his exploits hunting rabbits and fishing as a youth. In 1867, he became constable and served for fifteen years. Smith also married twice; he had one child with his first wife Sarah B. Smith (Jividen), 1842-1866, and seven children with his next spouse Margaret Thornton, whom he married in 1868. Smith died in 1934 at age ninety-seven.[4]

View of Red House Shoals from Winfield.
Photo by author.

Brigadier General E.P. Scammon Captured at Red House Shoals

By January 1864, many of the new pro-Union county governments in West Virginia were beginning to function. Confederate authorities desired to dismantle the organization of Union leaders in Putnam County and made frequent raids into the area searching for them. This called for action on the part of the Union officials at Charleston; Brigadier General Eliakim Parker Scammon, who commanded the Kanawha Division, made a trip from Charleston to Gallipolis, Ohio, to meet with General Jacob D. Cox to develop counterstrategies to quench the Confederate operations against local governments in the region.[5]

Around 5 p.m. on the evening of February 2, 1864, after meetings with General Cox and other Union officials, Scammon ordered Captain Charles Regnier to take him to Charleston on the government steamer *B.C. Levi*. However, Captain Regnier warned him it was not a good idea due to the dangerously stormy weather and because the area was swarming with Confederate cavalry and guerrillas. Scammon insisted but would soon regret his unwillingness to heed the boat captain's warning. When they reached Red House Shoals across from Winfield, Captain Regnier found it impossible to navigate the chutes and refused to go any further. The steamer was docked at Red House Shoals for the night, though Scammon failed to post pickets on the shore and retired to his quarters to sleep. Overnight, a party of Confederate scouts entered Winfield and learned of Scammon's presence from some Southern residents. They got into a boat and "with muffled oars moved cautiously over to the boat and boarded her with drawn revolvers" and quietly snuck aboard the *Levi*, as the entire crew was asleep. Some of the Union soldiers onboard were armed with muskets and revolvers, although when the Confederates confronted Scammon, he showed no "disposition to fight," according to one source. The *Levi* was then taken across the river to Winfield and docked, where Confederates unloaded several bags of mail and gave them to soldiers waiting there. Then they forced the pilot to take the steamer downriver toward Point Pleasant.[6]

Captain Regnier, of the *B.C. Levi*, reported the following account of the fateful events transpiring that night:

…Soon after coming on board the general asked me if I could run up that night. I told the general it was too dark and stormy a night to run farther than Red House Shoals, there being a dug chute there, and could not run that without it being light enough to see the walls. I insisted upon not leaving that night, as I remarked to him before leaving we could not run the chute unless it was light enough to see. The general thought we could make time by leaving that night. I told him we could leave at 1 or 2 o'clock in the morning and make as good time as we could by leaving that night.

Capt. G.J. Stealey, assistant quartermaster, also did not wish him to start that night, and tried to persuade him otherwise. The general thought it best to go, and so ordered. I left the mouth of the river about 7 p.m.; run to Red House Shoals and tied up. I gave instructions to the watchman on the boat to have the pilot called at 2:30 o'clock. After giving these instructions to the watchman of the boat, I went back in the cabin to retire; had some moments of conversation with the general. He asked what time I thought of starting from there. I told him just as soon as the pilot could see; if moon would rise and not cloudy we would leave at 2:30 o'clock. The pilot was called at that time, and said it was entirely too dark and could not see. While waiting for it to clear up some, so as he could see, the boat was captured.

A Lieutenant and 13 men came aboard with a rush and secured all arms that were in the boat. There were some soldiers aboard; to best of my knowledge, some 16 or 17. No sentinel or picket was placed on shore. At the time of the capture of the boat I had steam up, pilot was at the wheel, the mate on the hurricane deck, engineer at his post. On arriving at Red House that night could learn of no rumor or hear of any rebels. After some little time, with a guard over the pilot and engineer, the boat was run over to the Winfield side; remained there until about 10 o'clock. On landing on that side more of the enemy came on board, making them number 38. Were taken some minutes after 5 a.m.

About 10 o'clock, with the guard over pilot and engineer, the boat was ordered to run down to the mouth of Hurricane Creek and landed about half mile below at Vintroux's Landing. At twenty minutes after 12 o'clock, the general and officers were taken ashore, and ten minutes given to crew and all to get ashore; they were going to burn the boat. The boat was burnt at 12:30 p.m. At that time is the last I saw of the general. After the capture of the boat, and during the morning, the general tried to induce the soldiers to stand and retake the boat but could not. The above are facts, as I will testify to.[7]

Captain Charles Regnier.
Courtesy Larry Strayer.

Once the *Levi* was docked at Vintroux's landing, all on board were given six minutes to get on shore with their baggage before the boat was set afire. The soldiers who were willing to accept a parole were then released.

The *B.C. Levi* was carrying 110 tons of cargo, including military stores, several bags of U.S. mail, $100,000 worth of medical supplies, and one piece of artillery and ammunition. After the Confederates plundered the cargo, they abandoned the boat, "retreating by way of Hurricane Bridge." The steamer was also carrying a load of green timber, which burned slowly; the charred hull eventually drifted to the opposite side of the Kanawha River. After the Confederates left, some of the officers and crew who accepted paroles managed to cross the river in small skiffs they found and succeeded in putting out the fire, so as to save the hull and some of the machinery. The *Levi* was later raised after the war, restored, and renamed the *Cuba No. 2*.[8]

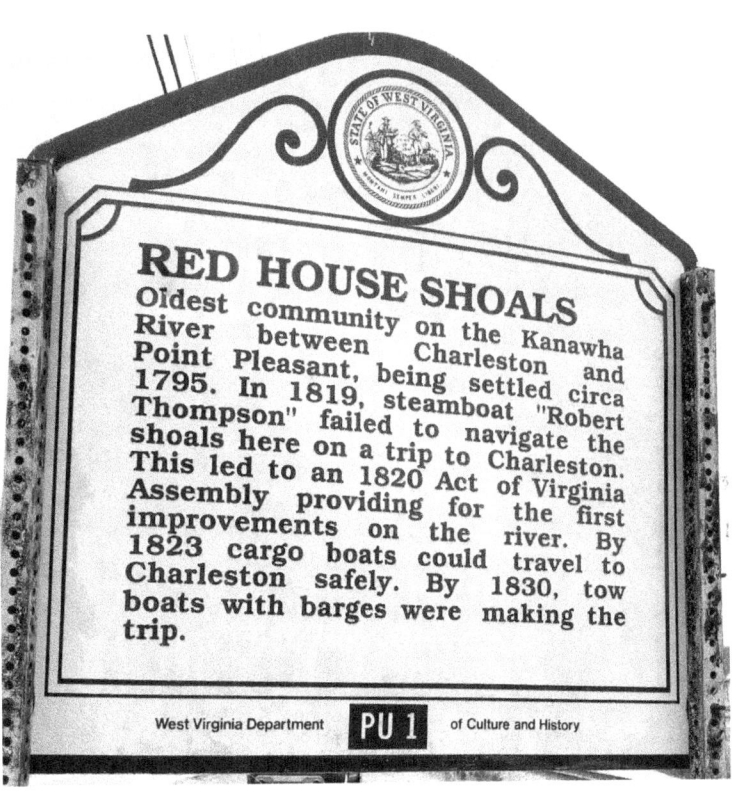

Red House Shoals historical marker.
Photo by author.

The Confederates captured not only General Scammon, but also a quartermaster captain, two lieutenants, and Sergeant Thomas McCormick of the 9th West Virginia Infantry. He stubbornly refused to take a parole and told the Confederates they could "take him to Richmond or shoot him, or do as they pleased, but he would take no parole from a damned rebel." McCormick's resistance proved effective, as he was unharmed, and continued on with the other prisoners. Once the boat was engulfed in flames, Scammon was placed "on a miserable old white horse, without either saddle or bridle," while the defiant McCormick and the other prisoners moved off on foot. Enroute, Scammon confided among the Union soldiers he was willing to organize a party and attempt to escape and try to recapture the steamer, but being unarmed, his suggestion was wisely "not acceded to."[9]

Initially following Scammon's capture, there was a great deal of confusion as to who was responsible. Military authorities originally thought it was a band of guerrillas, while rumors spread across the Winfield area that it was local Southern sympathizers. One newspaper openly accused the infamous guerilla Peter Carpenter. None were correct, however, as it was actually a former schoolteacher, 1st Lieutenant George S. Vertegans, a member of the famed Border Rangers, Company E, 8th Virginia Cavalry, along with Major James Nounnan of the same regiment, leading the boarding party comprised of twelve men that captured Scammon. Vertegans was formerly in the Fairview Rifle Guards from Wayne County and fought at the battle of Scary Creek in July 1861. Earlier, in August 1862, he was captured and sent to Camp Chase, Ohio. He later published an account of Scammon's capture while living at Saltville, Virginia:

> During the winter months, while our horses were recruiting, it was customary for twenty-five or thirty of us to get permission to visit the border, and we would locate isolated squadrons of the Yankee forces, a regiment, or a company, as might be the case. Then, selecting some favorable night, we would divide the little squad and, attacking all at once from different sides, usually succeeded in stampeding them after killing, wounding, or capturing many.

> ....my brother, Ed. G. Vertegans, was detailed to select eight men and go across the country east until

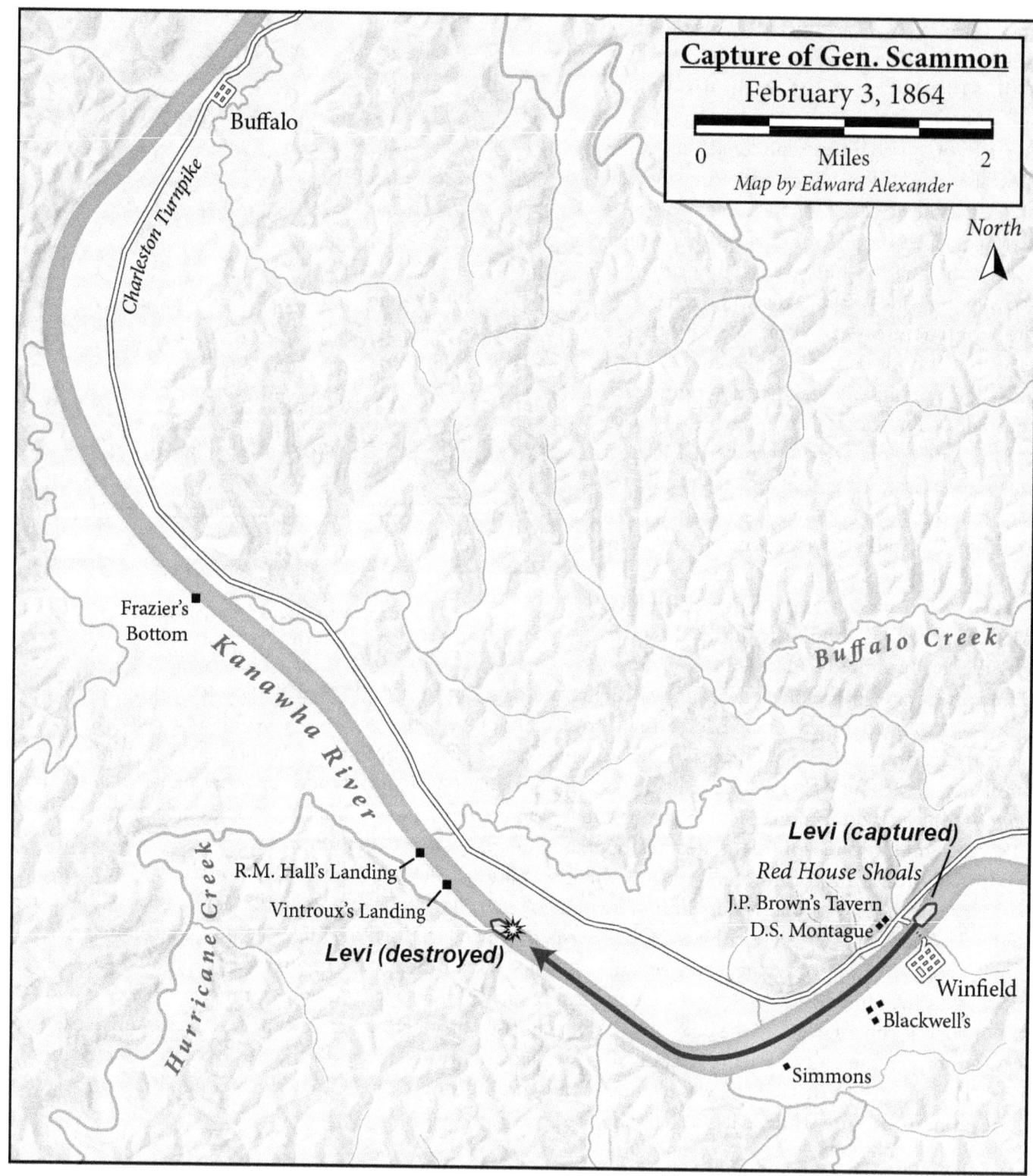

The James Vintroux farm was located near the mouth of Hurricane Creek
in District 4 per the 1860 U.S. Census.

he struck the Kanawha River, about seventy-five miles. He took with him that I recall of the eight: Charles Lalin (a Vermonter), Al West, Ralph Templeton, Dave Richards, John Tormey (an Irishman) and myself. We traveled at night, as were entirely in the enemy's country. At daylight on the 5th of January my brother sent me into the town of Winfield, Putnam County, to get information. At the house of a friend it was learned that the United States Steamer *R.C.* [B.C.] *Levi* was tied to the bank on the opposite side of the Kanawha River, which was about three-eighths of a mile wide at that point.

I learned also that she had on board Brigadier General Scammon and staff and that the boat carried one twelve pound brass piece and thirty marines. On getting this information my brother instantly ordered us to the river, where we found a coal barge, and in this barge was a Joe boat about twelve feet long. We got some pieces of board and paddled across to the other side. There we found the telegraph office, which we gutted in five minutes and then ran to the boat. By this time we were discovered. My brother jumped on the gangplank and was pulled aboard. Threatening the fireman and deck hands with his pistol, he ordered them to shove the plank out again. We then ran upstairs, where General Scammon met us, and the following amusing dialogue took place:

Lieutenant Vertegans: "Who is the commanding officer here?"
General Scammon: "I suppose I am, sir."
Lieutenant Vertegans: "And who do you suppose you are, sir?"
General Scammon: "I suppose I am General Scammon, of the United States Army. Who the devil do you suppose you are, sir?"
Lieutenant Vertegans: "I suppose I am Lieutenant Vertegans, of the Confederate Army, and more than that, I suppose you are my prisoner, sir."
General Scammon: "Well sir, I suppose I am, sir."

In the meantime, I and a few others were hunting the Yankee soldiers. We found them hidden in all kinds of places, disarmed them, and marched them to the bow, where they were guarded by some other men. I then paid a visit to the clerk's office, where I found fifteen hundred dollars in gold and greenbacks. The clerk swore that this was all private funds which had been given to him to deposit in the bank in Charleston. Upon this my brother ordered me to return it, which I did very reluctantly, and it was afterwards proved that their clerk pocketed it and made out that we had taken it.

As we had both and engineer and a pilot with us, the boat was cast off and we steamed down the river. For fear of meeting another boat, the charge was drawn from the gun and it was freshly loaded. As we went down I explored the lower deck, and among other things, I found a hogshead of medicines; but since we were all on foot and completely surrounded by Yankees, I took only fifty-seven ounces of quinine and thirty-six ounces of morphia and tumbled the rest overboard. We ran on to the mouth of Scary Creek, where we had our first fight in May, [July] 1861, with Ohio troops under Tyler, we being under Jenkins. We beat them badly in a two hours fight. Having landed at the mouth of the creek, we battered the gun with sledges and then burned the boat to the water's edge. Counting our prisoners, we found that we had thirty armed soldiers, one brigadier general, one paymaster with the rank of lieutenant colonel, two first lieutenants, and one sergeant major. The private soldiers we paroled, then started west for the James River and Kanawha Turnpike, which we reached at dusk....[10]

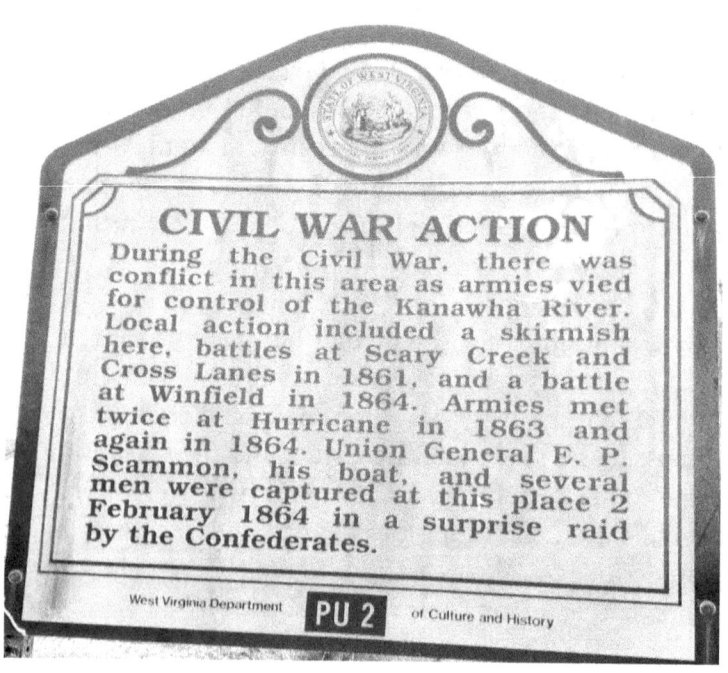

Red House Shoals historical marker.
Photo by author.

Note that it was not at the mouth of Scary Creek where Lieutenant Vertegans and his men burned the *Levi*, but rather it was at the mouth of Hurricane Creek, near the Vintroux family landing on the Kanawha River. Major James Nounnan was Lieutenant Vertegans' immediate superior. He also wrote an account of the capture on February 7, 1864:

I left Colonel [Milton J.] Ferguson in Wayne County on the 26th ultimo with indefinite orders and discretionary powers, and moved in the direction of the Kanawha River, along which stream I maneuvered in the counties of Mason and Putnam until the 3d instant. I entered Winfield (Putnam Court-House) on the morning of the 3d instant at 3 o'clock with 40 men, and found a number of Government officials there, whom I failed to secure, and a Government steamer with a strong guard and a piece of artillery lying upon the opposite side of the river. With great difficulty I secured a small craft, capable only of carrying four men, with which I crossed a small party of 12 men, under Lieut. E.G. Vertegans, who obeyed my instructions as speedily as possible in cutting the telegraph and assaulting the boat, which surrendered without firing a gun, although having moored several yards from the shore.

I found a valuable cargo on board, consistently chiefly of medical stores and tarpaulin, a lot of arms, & c., and Brig. Gen. E.P. Scammon, Capt. William G. Pinckard, and Lieut. Frank Milward, of his staff, and Lieut. William C. Lyons, Twenty-third Ohio Volunteers, and 25 non-commissioned officers and privates. I secured about 20 horses and some of the most valuable medicines, demolished the telegraph office, instruments, and wire & c., and moved to the mouth of Big Hurricane [Creek], where I burned the boat and cargo of over $100,000 worth of medicines, destroyed the piece of artillery, and a quantity of ammunition, paroled all the non-commissioned officers and privates except one, and determined to make my way through with the most valuable prisoners with as much speed as possible. The enemy pressed me heavily at all points in their efforts to recover the prisoners and compelled me to come to this point. I herewith send you General Scammon, Captain Pinckard, Lieutenants Millward and Lyons, and Sergt. Thomas McCormick, who refused to take a parole....[11]

The Union troops that Major Nounnan mentioned were under 2nd Lieutenant John J. Ball, who commanded the "Independent Scouts," a company of home guards from Hurricane Creek. Shortly after Scammon was captured, word reached Ball, who was in his camp near Union Ridge close to the Cabell County line. An unidentified man ran some six miles and entered the camp "breathless" informing Ball of what had transpired on the river. The Confederates were then heading toward Hurricane Bridge, and Ball and twenty-two men "double quicked," literally running some twelve miles along the backroads attempting to get between them and that village. According to an unidentified member of the home guards known only as *Quick Step*:

…when they finally saw the rebels, Ball's men "raised the yell, gave chase, run them two miles, and being entirely exhausted, came to a halt, and then returned, picking up what their flying enemies had thrown away in the race. They gathered up arms, tobacco and dry-goods, to the amount of about $1,000, and about sixty rebel letters directed to residents of Mason and Putnam counties and arrived safe in camp about 7 P.M....[12]

General B.F. Kelley commanded Union troops in West Virginia in 1864. He was notified of the capture by telegraph at his headquarters in Gallipolis, Ohio, the same morning. Kelley then informed the U.S. War Department that while the entire crew and passengers were asleep, Scammon was captured and the Union troops aboard had not offered any resistance. The next morning, General Kelley learned Lieutenant John Ball's company of Independent Scouts had caught up to the Confederates, but failed to re-capture Scammon. Kelley then ordered Colonel Rutherford B. Hayes, 23rd Ohio Infantry, to take 100 men along with two mountain howitzers on board the steamer *Victress* and pursue the Confederates. Frustrated, Kelley telegraphed the following message: "If I do not succeed by this way my cavalry will recapture him if my orders are fully carried out. The officer at Hurricane Bridge, who has allowed the enemy to cross Hurricane Creek, is placed in arrest. I shall again call your attention to my request that a gun-boat should be sent here to protect the river."[13]

According to 1st Lieutenant Barnabas Powell, adjutant of the 3rd West Virginia Cavalry, a squad of cavalry were in the area when Scammon was captured and arrived at Winfield about an hour afterward. Once they learned what transpired, the troopers started off toward Hurricane Bridge in pursuit, entertaining hopes that General Scammon "would be retaken." Brigadier General Alfred N. Duffie, who commanded a division of cavalry in West Virginia, was greatly annoyed with General Scammon for failing to post pickets that night. He later wrote to Major General B.F. Kelley requesting all boats in the Kanawha district be placed under his command, "in order to regulate the hour of their departure and avoid by this means all kinds of disaster."[14]

1st Lieutenant George S. Vertegans, 8th Virginia Cavalry, recalled his attempt to elude Union troops after capturing General Scammon:

By this time the whole country was aroused. We were within twelve miles of the Ohio River and one hundred miles from our own lines. After reaching the turnpike we waited until dark; then I was sent down the road, and another was sent up to guard the crossing. After being there ten minutes I heard a courier coming. My orders were not to fire until he got within twenty yards, when I halted him with "Who comes there?" he answered, "Messenger to the 34th." I knew this to be [Colonel] Don Piatt's regiment, quartered at the Hurricane Bridge, four miles above, so I dallied him as to the nature of his message. He told me that the Rebels had captured a steamer, and his order to Piatt was to send a force on every road. I said to him, "I have got all those Yankees here, and I'll have you in a minute." I heard him turn his horse, which was what I wanted, and away he went. That night the paymaster got a chance to talk to his guard. He had on a belt in which there was four hundred dollars in gold, which he offered to his guard to let him escape. But the guard told my brother, who took the money away from the paymaster and returned it to him in Richmond in the presence of General Winder, who gave him a receipt for it.

Our little camp was surprised one night on our way out, and one of the lieutenants was killed; his name was Millward, from Ohio. We made our way out with little trouble. In Wytheville, Va., I went and brought General Williams of our army. He and General Scammon were old comrades. General Jones, commanding the Department of Southwest Virginia, gave me and my brother a blank furlough, and we took our prisoners to Richmond on their parole. The last I saw of General Scammon he was playing chess....[15]

After word reached Washington, D.C. that General Scammon was captured, politicians responded with a flurry of blame toward Brigadier General B.F. Kelley, who commanded the Department of West Virginia. Several senators demand his replacement with a major general, although Governor Arthur I. Boreman supported General Kelley. Despite this, the senate passed a resolution calling for President Abraham Lincoln to replace Kelley with Major General Franz Sigel as department commander in March 1864. The incident damaged Scammon's already tenuous credibility with the U.S. War Department. Colonel Rutherford B. Hayes indicated he felt sorry for him, but also quipped in a letter to an uncle that his capture was "the greatest joke of the war. It was sheer carelessness, bad luck and accident...He bored us all terribly with his extreme vigilance. The greatest military crime in his eyes was a surprise. Here he is caught in the greatest and most inexcusable way."[16]

Even though it was Scammon who failed to post pickets on the shoreline on the night of his capture, the newspapers were equally merciless toward General Kelley and bristled with armchair commentary, offering advice on everything from local troop placements to points of key strategy. The *Wheeling Intelligencer* printed an example on February 25, 1864: "Winfield has been subject to raids ever since the war commenced except a few weeks that troops have been stationed there, we have always considered this town an important point. Hurricane Bridge is the right place for troops to protect Mason and Putnam counties, we hope our General who succeeds Scammon will go down and view the country and see the necessity of troops at Hurricane to prevent another raid soon. Troops at Winfield are no protection to the Union citizens of Putnam or Mason County."[17]

An unidentified soldier in the 13th West Virginia Infantry posited an editorial discussing recent events, defending the Union high command and putting the blame where it belonged—on Scammon himself. The letter was written from the Union camp at Barboursville on February 18, 1864:

Since I wrote to you last, we have had a shadow to cross our little circle. I send you the enclosed report which explains it all with the exception that Lt. Griswold was an exemplary man and an excellent officer; he was captured on the 7th inst., in Wayne County, and was killed on the 15th inst. Captain Pinckard too was a superior officer; he was captured on board the *B.C. Levi*, with General Scammon...I regret that the Legislature has seen fit to create a bone of contention about the command of this department and ventilate their opinions publicly in regards to the ability of General officers.

If General Kelley has been negligent of his duties, it is very probable the Government at Washington would know it and correct them, or if the Legislature thought grave errors were committed, a quiet representation in a becoming way to the General-in-Chief would, in my opinion, be a surer way to have the errors corrected, at all events it would not give cause of rejoicing to our enemies. The capture of General Scammon cannot be attributed to the fault of General Kelley, or to any possible negligence on his part. If any is in fault, I think it would be General Scammon himself. I believe the latter General is a careful officer, but it so happened in an unguarded moment he was captured, and I feel it is a disgrace upon our division that the rebels succeeded in eluding pursuit. I do not think from all information I could gather here at camp, or whilst I was out on his trail, that it was designed upon the part of the enemy, but by mere accident that they captured him.

There was in corral near Buffalo about two hundred government horses on the upper side of the Kanawha the rebels were after. The horses were sent up to Charleston the day before the General was captured. The rebel Captain [Hurston] Spurlock was captured in this vicinity and sent to Charleston; the rebels guarded the road between this place and Coalsmouth with the view of recapturing him, but found he was sent up via the river. I have no doubt the rebels thought while the boat was tied up they would attempt his release, thinking he was on board, and instead of Spurlock took General Scammon.[18]

Scammon's Fate as Prisoner of War

General Scammon was sent to Libby Prison at Richmond, Virginia, and later relocated to Charleston, South Carolina. He was replaced by Brigadier General George Crook, in command of the Kanawha Division. Scammon also received a public flogging from the regional newspapers; the *Gallipolis Journal* editor taunted: "With the Commanding General of the Department and his Quarter Master in Libby Prison, captured by rebels within 35 miles of Gallipolis-a government steamer burned at the same time, it might seem to an unpracticed eye that the State of West Virginia was not so intensely loyal as some persons wished it to be considered. The fact is that region of the country is just as well stocked with rebels both armed and unarmed as any other portion of the South."[19]

According to one historian, "Scammon was held in high esteem by Charleston [S.C.] people," but that is not why he was taken there; the purpose was much more sinister. The reality was that Scammon, along with some forty-nine other high-ranking Federal officers, including five generals, were to be used as hostages to prevent Federal artillery from firing into the city. The situation at Charleston, South Carolina was intense. On April 20, 1864, Major General Samuel Jones arrived in Charleston to take command of the Department of South Carolina, Georgia, and Florida. Jones was a career army officer and West Point alumni, class of 1841. Jones previously commanded the Department of West Virginia in 1862–1863. Charleston was battered, having endured eight months of bombardment, causing much destruction throughout the city. Not long after Jones took command, Major General John G. Foster, a Mexican War veteran and career army officer, was placed in command of the Union forces there on May 26, 1864. He was at Fort Sumter as a captain when it fell in April 1861. Foster desired to avenge Fort Sumter and occupy Charleston but knew he did not have sufficient troop strength to take it by land, so he decided to continue the bombardment strategy. Foster had earlier determined that because of the Charleston Arsenal, which manufactured arms and equipment supplying the Confederate army, it was a military target and maintained a heavy fire upon the city for several weeks.[20]

Desperate to stop the bombardment, Jones resorted to drastic measures. On June 1, 1864, he requested authorization from President Jefferson Davis to send him fifty high ranking Federal prisoners, five of them brigadier generals, including E.P. Scammon. His intention was to hold the Federal officers hostage, placing them in a large house located in a civilian area that took heavy fire from Union batteries. Davis approved, and the prisoners from Camp Oglethorpe in Macon, Georgia, arrived in Charleston on Sunday, June 12, 1864. The prisoners were taken to a large home converted into a prison in the south side of Charleston. The home was a lovely antebellum structure, but as planned, it was also in the area exposed to the heaviest artillery fire. Jones sent word to Foster that if he continued the bombardment, it would be at the prisoners' peril.[21]

Foster was furious and demanded the War Department send him fifty Confederate officer prisoners from Fort Delaware to be placed in front of the Union forts on Morris Island as his retaliation. He sent a letter to Jones under flag of truce, stating his objective was to destroy the munitions factories and wharves where blockade runners delivered their goods, as a means of weakening the Confederate war effort—not to involve prisoners of war. Jones did not budge and responded with an angry letter chastising Foster for the bombardment, stating that Confederate authorities had not been given adequate time to evacuate the city, and he noted that the bombardment had been ongoing since August 1863. The clash between Jones and Foster drew both governments' and the media's attention, and General Scammon wrote to Jones asking to release him because of rapidly declining health under such duress and to travel to Washington and try to persuade the War Department to allow the prisoner exchange. Jones refused, claiming he did not have the authority to allow the exchange as the governments had ceased that practice a year previous.[22]

An irony of this incident was Scammon had earlier written to Major General Samuel Jones, who commanded the Confederate forces in southwestern Virginia, on January 25, 1864, requesting a prisoner exchange; he had no idea this would soon be an omen for his own fate. Scammon wrote:

> I send by flag of truce to your lines by the Lewisburg Turnpike a Mr. C.W. Maupin, who has been detained at the military prison at Charleston as a hostage for Mr. Shaw, Sheriff of Putnam County in the state of West Virginia, who was taken from his home in Putnam County and conveyed as a prisoner to some place within the Confederate lines. Mr. Maupin leaves here under a pledge to procure the release of Mr. Shaw. He is bound by oath to give no military information, and also to return to the custody of the U.S. authorities at Charleston unless he shall procure the release of Sheriff Shaw within twenty days of this date. The capture of Mr. Shaw, cannot, I think, have been authorized by you. His detention can serve no end, save that of provoking retaliation upon such civilians as may sympathize with his captors, and who, but for such useless acts, would be permitted to remain in tranquility.[23]

This was not the first time Jones and Scammon dealt with each other over the fate of prisoners; Jones wrote to Scammon on April 4, 1863 regarding the fate of two Union deserters who were recently captured, "They will be tried by the proper tribunal, and if it appears on the trial that they were not deserters from the C.S. service they will be paroled." Jones further mentioned some Union officers had also written him, threatening "if they are not paroled...some four influential southern men will have the debt to pay...." Jones responded: "....I need hardly say that the threats of those men will have no weight whatever...I do not doubt that you will promptly take such steps, as will effectually prevent those lawless men from executing their threats. The presence on the border of men who entertain such lawless ideas and purposes, and who act by authority of your government, is calculated still further to exasperate the feeling on the border, and to provoke lawless retaliation, which you so much depreciate." Apparently, Jones learned a lesson from his earlier encounters in such scenarios and refused to give in to Foster's demands at Charleston.[24]

General Scammon's health eventually deteriorated to the point where he was able to obtain a surgeon's certificate of disability. He wrote to the Confederate War Department requesting to be exchanged. The Confederate Secretary of War declined his request on July 31, 1864, stating: "My own view is that if we yield in one case of special exchange we are overwhelmed. Moreover, the Federal authorities would not so far respect the parole mentioned by General Scammon as to let him return....If General Scammon's conduct was such as to entitle him to special favor he might be sent off on a general parole, but I more than doubt the policy of naming his equivalent. If we did, how could we refuse to do the same in other equally meritorious cases?"[25] President Lincoln soon learned of what was transpiring at Charleston and authorized General Foster to make an exception to War Department policy. Foster notified General Jones, who agreed now that Lincoln had intervened, and they began making plans for the exchange on August 3, 1864. General Ulysses S. Grant objected to an exchange, but despite this, it appeared the transfer would soon occur—at least until the Confederate government sent hundreds of other Federal prisoners to Charleston and a yellow fever epidemic quickly broke out. Jones ordered all prisoners who were not sick to return to Andersonville, Georgia. In response, General Foster built a large wooden stockade in front of Battery Wagner on Morris Island, directly in the path of

Southern artillery, and in September 1864, he had 600 Confederate officers brought there from Fort Delaware to increase the ante against Jones. These men became known as the "Immortal 600."[26]

Throughout the month of September, the shelling continued, and both Union and Confederate captives remained in their prisons amidst the unbearable summer heat, with yellow fever spreading through the area and food in short supply. In October, the Union prisoners were finally moved further inland and out of the line of fire. Shortly afterward, the Confederate prisoners were transferred to Fort Pulaski at Savannah, Georgia. This became one of the most controversial incidents of the Civil War; no matter who was responsible, it was no doubt one of the darkest periods of the war, and for General Scammon, it began in Putnam County. Although large scale prisoner exchanges ceased during the summer of 1863, Scammon's case eventually made its way to President Lincoln, and he was exchanged along with the forty-nine other Union officers on August 3, 1864. General Scammon was granted a brief convalescence until October 1864; then, he was ordered back to South Carolina and given command of the Northern District of the state. In one of the most bizarre twists in the Civil War, less than two weeks after his return, the luckless Scammon was again captured and taken to one of the Confederate prison camps at Charleston, South Carolina. However, this time his confinement only lasted five days, and he was again exchanged. He returned to duty and was next ordered command of the District of Florida where he served until the war's end.[27]

As his appointment of brigadier general of volunteers was terminated when the war ended, he no longer held an official military role; however, Scammon wanted to continue in service, and he wrote to the U.S. adjutant general in April 1866 requesting a commission as a colonel or a lieutenant colonel but was declined. Military documents reflect Scammon was not only court martialed in 1856 for being drunk on duty, but there was also a second incident occurring in July 1863 when his subordinates accused him of being intoxicated while in command of troops. Despite his reputation as a stoic and reliable combat commander, the War Department did not overlook either of the two former incidents and his request was denied. In June 1866, Scammon was appointed United States consulate at Prince Edward Island. He stayed there until 1870, when he resigned and became an engineer under General Newton in New York harbor as a civilian employee of the U.S. Government. Scammon later accepted another professorship of mathematics and history, this time at Seton Hall college in New Jersey from 1875 to 1885, and afterward entered his retirement. E.P Scammon died of stomach cancer at his daughter's home on Friday, December 7, 1894, at age seventy-eight.[28]

It's a Small World: Two Putnam Men Collide

Twenty-year-old John Gilbert Cartmill enlisted in Company A, 22nd Virginia Infantry, on October 26, 1862. While on patrol in Boone County on February 9, 1864, his squad encountered a group of Federals also patrolling the area looking for them, led by another Putnam County resident, Captain John Young of Company G, 13th West Virginia Infantry, who took Cartmill prisoner in a small skirmish. Cartmill was then sent to Fort Delaware until paroled June 9, 1865.[29]

Post-war image of John Gilbert Cartmill, Company A, 22nd Virginia Infantry, and wife Virginia Helen McGuire Cartmill Courtesy Gilbert Casto.

Incessant Raids

The village of Hurricane Bridge continued to be a hotspot for frequent raids by Confederate cavalry and guerilla parties. On February 20, 1864, a scouting party of twenty Union troopers led by 2nd Lieutenant Henry A. Wolf, Company K, 3rd West Virginia Cavalry, was sent out from the Union camp there and encountered a Confederate cavalry patrol nearby. During the ensuing skirmish, Wolf was killed in action, and the Confederates retreated into Cabell County. This prompted Captain John S. Witcher, 3rd West Virginia Cavalry, to write to Congressman Kellian V. R. Whaley, former colonel of the 9th West Virginia Infantry, informing him of several recent skirmishes in Putnam and Cabell counties with Captain Hurston Spurlock's cavalrymen from the 16th Virginia Cavalry and asking for support to gain increased Union troops in the area.[30]

Witcher observed the Confederates seemed "very determined to put down their own bogus government," by committing a multitude of depredations against local Union citizens during that winter. The village of Buffalo was also the site of what seemed to residents to be continual skirmishes and raids, as one resident described yet another visit from Confederate raiders two days following the skirmish near Hurricane Bridge: "The incendiaries who have been holding high carnival the month past firing barns, after firing four different tenements last night, culminated their villainy in firing the Union elevator, which was burned to its foundation. The bark *William Treat*, lying in the slip in front of the elevator, had her rigging, masts and bulwarks considerably damaged. The elevator was owned by D.S. Bennett & Sherwood & Co., and valued at $30,000; insured for $13,750, principally in the New York companies. The bark *William Treat* was valued at $25,000 and was insured for $13,000 in Eastern companies."[31]

Captain James M. Ball's company of Independent Scouts had thirty-five men present on April 20, 1864; on this date Ball requested the state quartermaster send "one thousand and eighty-five" rations for his men and groused that they had yet to receive any pay. According to one observer, by March 24, 1864, Ball's company had been paid: "We understand that this company, so long and shamefully kept out of their money have at last been paid. This company has been a great protection to the people of Putnam and Mason." However, pay was inconsistent for Union troops in West Virginia, even as late as 1864. Captain Ball wrote to former governor Francis Pierpont, who was then serving as adjutant general, on August 13, 1864, indicating his company had yet to receive their pay.[32]

During the first week of May 1864, Captain John Witcher, 3rd West Virginia Cavalry, took a part of his company, along with a squad of the 13th West Virginia Infantry from Point Pleasant, and started in pursuit of a band of "rebel horse thieves who were stealing horses in the lower end of Mason and Putnam counties." Witcher's detachment was hot on their trail, and followed them into Confederate territory in Cabell County, capturing several Confederates, including five men who had lived at Point Pleasant, one of whom was severely wounded and sent to the Army hospital at Gallipolis, Ohio. Captain Ball's company of Independent Scouts were frequently found in Putnam County; he wrote to the West Virginia state quartermaster on May 25, 1864, requesting a supply of canteens, which were much needed because the "weather is getting warm."[33]

During late May through June 1864, Company K, 141st Ohio National Guard, was posted at Hurricane Bridge, along with elements of the 3rd West Virginia Cavalry. The 13th West Virginia Infantry previously held that outpost, although it departed for the Shenandoah Valley in Virginia on May 23, 1864. Prior to leaving, Colonel William Brown warned the 141st Ohio National Guard officers that it was unsafe to travel alone into Cabell County from there, due to frequent attacks by Confederate guerrillas and cavalry who were a constant threat to Union residents of Putnam County. One frustrated Unionist griped that they had "been very bold and murderous in their attacks of late." Hence, in June 1864, Major General David Hunter, who commanded the Department of West Virginia, published a stern warning to "bushwhackers and guerrillas" who were "swooping out on the roads to plunder and outrage loyal residents, falling upon, and firing into defenseless wagon trains" and harassing soldiers posted to guard the trains. Hunter admonished the partisans they were acting illegally and were not afforded protections of civil or military laws, and if apprehended, he would order Union troops to destroy every home and farm belonging to them, and the same for any citizens aiding the partisans, whom he viewed as "spies...pirates and outlaws." Hunter also stated that any public property "jay hawked or destroyed by these marauders, an assessment of five times the value of such property will be made upon the secession sympathizers...."[34]

Private William A. Whiting of Buffalo, Company F, 7th West Virginia Cavalry, wrote to his mother Nancy Whiting on June 28, 1864, from Cumberland, Maryland. His regiment had garrisoned Buffalo in 1861 to 1862 as the 8th West

John S. Witcher, 3rd West Virginia Cavalry. National Archives.

Virginia Infantry, and Company D was comprised of many men from that area of Putnam County. They had recently participated in heavy fighting at the battles of Cloyd's Mountain, Lexington, and Lynchburg, and returned to the Kanawha Valley shortly after the following letter was penned. He mentions Captain John Young, whose company transferred into the 11th West Virginia Infantry in March 1864 after serving two years with the 13th West Virginia Infantry:

Dear Mother,

A part of our command is at Cumberland but I do not know how long we will stay. Capt [Edgar] Blundon is here sick and I saw John today [Capt. John V. Young] he was in our camp the first time I saw him since he left the Buffalo, he is in the 11th W Va Inf. Part of his regiment is hear and going to Cab K ___. Well mother I will borrow ten dollars to send you and the balance that I draw. Well, I have no more to write. This letter leaves me well and I hope finds you in good health and I will come home as soon as I can get a furlough.[35]

A Deadly Scuffle

On July 9, 1864, the Union steamer *Victress No. 1* was moving down the Kanawha River loaded with Union soldiers from the 14th West Virginia Infantry. Most were standing on the upper deck, enjoying the balmy summer weather, and observing the beauty of the surrounding hills on shore. As the boat moved into Red House Shoals and was preparing to go down the chute, a fight broke out between two soldiers, Privates John W. Miller and Nelson Steele of Company C. It became an all-out fistfight. As they battled, both accidentally broke through the upper deck railing and fell overboard, tumbling into the rocks and rapids below. No trace of either was found that day, and the Army simply declared them dead and closed out their service records. However, in February 1886, the Kanawha River froze over, and several weeks later, during a warmer period, the river thawed, creating a large ice-jam on both banks of the river along Red House Shoals. There, two skeletons were discovered amidst large chunks of ice floating along the river's edge. The remains were identified as Privates John W. Miller and Nelson Steele, the two soldiers who fell overboard and vanished on July 9, 1864. Private Miller enlisted at Wheeling on August 25, 1862 and was a farmer prior to the war. He was nineteen years old when he volunteered for the army, and stood five feet, ten inches tall, with brown hair and blue eyes. Little is known of Private Nelson Steele, although he apparently enlisted around the same time as Miller. It is unknown whether they were chums prior to the altercation, or what started it.[36]

Despite the important role played by Union home guards in Putnam County, they only infrequently received pay, as well as adequate supplies of ammunition, equipment, and sustenance. On July 25, 1864, Captain John Ball, commanding the Putnam Independent Scouts, wrote to state quartermaster General William Brown once again insisting his men receive their pay, stating, "I have paid some of these claims to convince the citizens that they will be recompensed…" Ball admonished Brown to look into the matter as soon as possible, for "the men are needy." On August 13, 1864, Ball indicated his company had recently been "…very busy scouting. I have taken many prisoners of late who had been hiding in the bushes. There has been several who give themselves up to me wishing to take the oath [Oath of Allegiance]." Ball also stated his company was "poor" in ammunition and requested their pay for state service, which they had yet to receive, noting they were in a "detestable condition." Ball lost one of his men to disease sometime during the interim of April to July 1864 and informed the state quartermaster that his thirty-four men then were in dire straits for more ammunition. Despite the paucity of supplies, Ball's company continued to fight and had recently captured several "…bushwhackers that has bin [been] hiding in the bushes…." who were waiting for a chance to ambush on his men, but Ball had gotten behind them and turned the element of surprise in his favor.[37]

By early fall 1864, Union residents of Putnam County were fed up with Confederate guerilla-partisan raids on their farms and properties and the effects of the Confederate Conscription, which caused hundreds of citizens from Logan, Boone, Fayette, Wyoming, and Raleigh counties to seek asylum in the area, because at this point in the war, desperate Southern authorities were literally forcing all able-bodied males into military service, regardless of their claimed political affiliation. One citizen wrote to Governor Arthur Boreman quarreling about the guerilla attacks, "Our outposts from Guyandotte to Gauley are now threatened and pressed by heavy and strong parties," and groused that the flood of refugees represented the "great energy" with which the Confederates were asserting to carry the Conscription Act into "full execution." This meant increased work for Captain Ball's home guards, which was taking a significant toll on them. He wrote on September 9, 1864 that, "My company is almost broke down, troops have been very scarce in this section where my company operates and horse thieves and bushwhackers [are] very numerous…" Ball also queried the state quartermaster as to whether he should procure medical care for his men at the expense of the state, noting he had two men who had been quite ill for several weeks who were "faithful to their country & cause" but were without means to pay for care and had still not received their pay.[38]

Further evidencing the vicious and personalized nature of warfare in Putnam County during the Civil War, on September 14, 1864, a Confederate deserter, Private William H. Meeks, a.k.a. Meek, was shot and killed instantly by Private James J. Hall, Company D, 7th West Virginia Cavalry, at Buffalo. Meek enlisted in Company B, 34th Battalion Virginia Cavalry, Colonel Vincent A. Witcher's Battalion, at Logan on April 4, 1862, and deserted in Wayne County, West Virginia on October 15, 1862. His former company commander, Captain William Stratton, wrote that Meeks was "supposed in Jenkins' command" after deserting, which proved correct as Meeks enlisted in Company A, 8th Virginia Cavalry, at Lewisburg on June 10, 1863. Apparently, he was dissatisfied in that regiment also, and deserted again on September 20, 1864, and returned to Buffalo. James J. Hall was a resident of Buffalo, and initially enlisted in Company D, 8th West Virginia Infantry there on October 31, 1861. He was captured by Confederates on November 24, 1862, while scouting near his home, and imprisoned. Hall's conflict with Meek had its origins during the time he was in Confederate custody, as reported by an observer when the shooting occurred:

It seems that in the beginning of the war, when the rebels were organizing a camp at Buffalo, this fellow Meeks had ran over Hall a great deal, and had succeeded in getting him arrested, and while a prisoner made several attempts to kill him because he would not join the rebel army. A few days ago, Meeks deserted from the rebel army, and returned to Buffalo, and learning that Hall was in town and thinking that he could "crow" over him as he had done heretofore, hunted him up. Finding Hall, he said in an insulting manner, "Hall, how do you like to hear of your brother being hung and his mouth stuffed full of sheep's wool, by the Confederates?" Hall, without saying a word, immediately drew his pistol and shot him dead in his tracks, as a true Union soldier should. We say he done perfectly right. We trust he may never be arraigned for a trial, and that he may be permitted to go on in the even tenor of his way.[39]

On September 18, 1864, a Southern sympathizer from Poca, Elliott Thomas, was arraigned and tried in Putnam County Court for horse theft. When the jury had heard all evidence, they broke for dinner. At that time, Thomas heard from some people in attendance that he was likely going to be found guilty, and he eloped, breaking his $2,000 bond posted by his father-in-law. Thomas crossed the Kanawha River at Red House and left "for parts unknown."[40]

In October 1864, Captain John M. Reynolds, Company D, 7th West Virginia Cavalry, was ordered to establish a fortified position at Winfield overlooking the chute on the Kanawha River across from Red House Shoals. His objective was to prevent Confederates from accessing the shoals to navigate the river, thereby protecting government steamers passing through the chute. Shortly after arriving at Winfield, Company D began digging earthworks with rifle pits along the riverbank near a flour mill, capable of protecting them from attacks on the river and from the road approaching the town. They also dug rifle pits and put up earthen entrenchments around their campsite in the vicinity of the brick courthouse building, upon a small ridge overlooking the village toward the Kanawha River. Locals were pleased to see the cavalrymen arrive, as one Winfield resident wrote on September 16, 1864, "Through a kind providence, and the protection afforded by Captain [John] Reynolds and his brave men, the people of this county are once more permitted to attend the September term of our circuit court." A day later, there was a public meeting of Putnam citizens at the courthouse; they nominated John Bowyer as a candidate for state senate.[41]

Shortly afterward, on September 30, 1864, a Federal detachment posted near the mouth of the Coal River came under attack by one hundred Confederates commanded by Major James Nounnan, 16th Virginia Cavalry, along with a detachment of fifty men from the 64th Virginia Infantry. Nounnan was on a reconnaissance sortie, with orders to ascertain the number of Federal troops in the area. Around 9 p.m. that evening, the Confederates attacked the Union garrison but were met with stubborn resistance and were eventually driven off, with one killed and five men wounded. The Confederates retreated on the James River and Kanawha Turnpike toward Hurricane Bridge and were pursued by a company of Union cavalry from the post at Winfield, although no further action occurred. Nounnan encamped there until October 1, 1864, when they left for Wyoming Courthouse to rendezvous with Colonel Vincent Witcher's 34th Virginia Cavalry battalion. Oddly, Nounnan's brief encampment went undetected by the daily Union patrols operating from the garrison at Hurricane Bridge.[42]

On the same day, Captain John Ball wrote to state Adjutant General Francis Pierpont apologizing for the delay in his quarterly report, noting that for the past two months, the rebels had been "very troublesome" and that his former orderly sergeant, who was typically responsible for compiling the reports, had joined the regular Army. Ball indicated his company was in a "bad condition" from constant scouting and patrols, and he had little time to complete paperwork as they had recently "taken a good many prisoners of war." Ball wrote that he had recruited three new men only because they were promised they would receive new uniforms, but that his company was still "very small and scouting very hard to convince you that this is a very troublesome and dangerous place." Ball pleaded further they were in dire need of new uniforms and blankets, as the men were "broke down" and a few had "left the state or went into the U.S. service" because they were unable to draw new uniforms.[43]

As it turned out, a major reason why Captain Ball's Putnam Scouts were not paid consistently was because they were never officially mustered into state service and had been operating as an unofficial home guard company in the eyes of the U.S. War Department, the apex of all things pertaining to military bureaucracy. Ball wrote to Adjutant General Pierpont on October 21, 1864, indicating he had thirty-four men who were desirous to officially organize and muster into state service, but he only had two men fit for duty. Ball indicated that for the previous month, his scouts were in pursuit of a former Confederate guerilla, Peter M. Carpenter, also of Putnam County, who at that time was a captain in the 34th Battalion Virginia Cavalry. Ball wrote that Carpenter's gang of "horse thieves and robbers" had "been very troublesome in this section" and advised Pierpont a group of citizens residing in Cabell County wished to organize a home guard unit to protect themselves from Confederates.[44]

During the summer and fall of 1864, dozens of men from Putnam County serving in Union and Confederate regiments left the Kanawha Valley to serve in the bloody Shenandoah Valley Campaign. Captain John Young, who earlier raised a company of Union men at Coalsmouth and had been temporarily attached to the 13th West Virginia Infantry, was re-assigned to the 11th West Virginia Infantry in March 1864. Because of the frequent Confederate raids near their home on the eastern base of Coal Mountain, as well as harassment from Southern supporters at Coalsmouth, Young moved his wife and children to a new home in Winfield in July 1863, thinking they would be safer there due to the large number of Unionists in the village and knowledge of Union troops posted there. Young fought in the battle of Cloyd's Mountain, which included many of his former adversaries from the Kanawha Valley in the 22nd and 36th Virginia Infantry, and was also in battles at Lynchburg, Lexington, Winchester, Berryville, Charles Town, and Cedar Creek. During late summer, he decided to run for the House of Delegates in Putnam County. Being away with the army, Young had little time to campaign, however, and hoped his reputation as a soldier and solid Union supporter would carry the election against his opponent, Dudley S. Montague, a popular local tavern and hotel owner from Red House. Young informed the *Weekly Register* of his intent to run in September 1864, and the editor supported him in a commentary published on September 22:

> It will be seen by our announcements, that Captain J.V. Young, a tried and brave soldier of the 11th Virginia V.V.I., is a candidate for the House of Delegates in Putnam County. Captain Young has been in the service of his country since the beginning of the war. He will make a good delegate. D. S. Montague is a candidate for the same office, though we are not yet authorized to announce him. He will get a large vote.[45]

Young wrote to his daughter, Emily Young, on October 30, 1864, just days after the battle of Cedar Creek. In this engagement, several of his men were killed or wounded, and he barely escaped being trampled to death in the early morning surprise attack when Confederates routed the Federals. Emily had sternly warned her father not to have high hopes of winning the election, which came as little surprise to Young, given his circumstances. His response reveals a sanguinary glimpse into life on campaign, but also into his character, evidenced by his devotion to his men:

You said something about my being a candidate and my proverbial defeat. My dear child, this concerns me the least of anything else at present. I am sorry that my name was used as a candidate, but my greatest trouble now is the safety and comfort of my brave men. Even if I had been elected, I don't know how I could leave them in the hands of another man. It is just as much as I can do to keep them from being imposed upon, and I with them; and I know if I were away from them, I could not enjoy myself under any circumstances whatever. My time will soon be out, and how I can leave my men in the field is more than I can conjecture. But we will see…. Well, Emma, I have just eaten dinner. Salt Pork, Coffee and Crackers is our regular living….we enjoy it very well…We have a very comfortable shanty built out of Cedar logs, and covered with our shelter tents…Yes, Emma, we are like you – we think we have done enough fighting for one campaign, and I assure you that we are tired enough to haul down this year and go into winter quarters. But if the Rebels still insist, we will give them another trial and another good flogging if they desire it….[46]

There were several Southern sympathizers suspected of being guerrillas in Putnam County that fall, and Young was in favor of their execution. One local resident, William Harvey Bowyer, had enlisted in the 36th Virginia in 1861, deserted, and taken the Oath of Allegiance, only to later return and become captured in October 1864 by men from the 7th West Virginia Cavalry, was being held for trial. Rumors were circulating that he was to be executed, which Emily had informed her father about in her most recent letter. Young responded: "You spoke of Harvey Bowyers' sentence to be shot. I do wish there were more of the same kind of sentences in Putnam. John Crawford ought to have been shot three years ago. There are many who will be shot without Court Martial when the soldiers get home, in retaliation for their lost comrades, and the insults given to their families and friends while they have been doing their duty in service of their country."[47]

Recollections of a Putnam County resident of the Shenandoah Valley Campaign

Fred Conner, a servant to Colonel William Fife of the 36th Virginia Infantry during the war, collected numerous personal accounts written by soldiers of battles that men from Putnam County fought in. Long after the war ended, Conner received a letter from Fife's daughter, Julia, requesting information about battles her father was in during the Shenandoah Valley Campaign of 1864. Conner was present with the 36th Virginia Infantry during the entire campaign as part of Major General Jubal Early's army. Early also had ties to Putnam County. Conner recalled some events transpiring in September 1864 and shared them with the colonel's daughter:

Dear Miss Fife,

After such a long delay, I take great pleasure in answering your letter which I received some time ago. I was more than glad to hear from you. You said you would like for me to tell you something about the war. The fight you asked me about was at Cedar Creek and we were camped at Fisher's Hill. The Colonel told me the day before the fight to cook two days rations and said he was going to have a little fun. We did, and about 4:00 A.M. the next morning they started off the fight and the Confederates got between the Federals and their camp. I stayed behind with the wagon train and it lasted until about 7:00 o'clock. The Confederates drove the Yankees back and captured 15 pieces of artillery and took about 500 prisoners and several horses. They drove them back down the Shenandoah Valley about 15 miles to a town called Woodstock.

They came to a halt there at which time Yankee General Sheridan was at Winchester. He rode up and said to his men, "We will sleep on the ground tonight that we came in on." After that he told his boys to raise three cheers and come on back up the valley and they came too. Now Colonel Fife was wounded in the morning while they were chasing Yankees. Old Uncle Al Gatewood waited on Mr. Peter Nickle, a quarter master. He went on down to Strasburg with the troops that day while I stayed up on Fisher's Hill. He came back and told me that the Colonel wanted me to come down to Strasburg where he was wounded. I hurried and went as quick as I could. When I got there, he was lying on the floor at Ms. Jenny Keister's. He said "Fred, they came very near getting me." And I looked back at him and I couldn't help but to bust into tears.

About 3:00 o'clock that evening, I kept hearing cannons and I said, "The Yankees are coming," and he said, "Ah, hell, they ain't a commin." I said, "Look here, Mars Will, we better get out of here." About 5:00 o'clock here come the Yankee cavalry into Strasburg. It wasn't 15 minutes until the cavalry was there shooting at everyone they seen. I went out among them and asked whose cavalry they was but they didn't pay no attention to me. Colonel said to me, "Fed, what will we do," and I said, "I told you so and now they've got us." Mrs. Keister said to me, "I can hide the Colonel, but I don't know what I can do with you." She said, "Oh, if they catch you all here, they will burn our house down." They searched the house several times while we were there but couldn't find us. We stayed up there three weeks and a day and had a good time and Mrs. Keister brought our meals to us. After that the Yankees fell back and we came down and got a furlough and came away. I will tell you more the next time. Colonel gave Mrs. Keister a watch that cost $150. I will close now hoping to hear from you soon.

From Fred[48]

Raid on Winfield

In mid-October 1864, Colonel John Oley, commanding the 7th West Virginia Cavalry, learned of a large Confederate force operating near Guyandotte, under Colonel Vincent A. "Clawhammer" Witcher. On October 22, 1864, Oley notified Captain John Reynolds at Winfield: "Lieutenant Colonel Polsley reports that Witcher, with 500 men, passed Raleigh, in the direction of Coal River, the evening of the 20th. Keep your men well in hand, ready to act....defend your post at all hazards."[49]

Confederates soon learned of the Federal garrison at Winfield, and Colonel Witcher brought some 400 to 425 men, including two companies led by thirty-eight-year-old Captain Philip J. Thurmond of Monroe County, to attack the Union troops posted there. Known as "Thurmond's Rangers," those two companies were an independent partisan group operating with Witcher and had a tough reputation. Witcher's battalion fought at Gettysburg in 1863, and in the East Tennessee campaign, as well as the bloody Shenandoah Valley campaign earlier in 1864. Witcher's battalion had recently merged with Thurmond's Rangers at Tazewell, Virginia, and devised a plan to conduct a series of raids on Union outposts in northern and central West Virginia. Witcher attacked Federal troops at Bull Town and Buckhannon, capturing some 300 prisoners, and afterward rode to Greenbrier County. From there, Witcher moved into the Mud River Valley in mid-October, just prior to the raid at Winfield.[50]

Company D, 7th West Virginia Cavalry, was comprised of eighty-three men in October 1864, many of whom were locals from Hurricane Creek, Buffalo, and Winfield. As such, they had a strong personal interest in their mission of protecting Union citizens and guarding the courthouse, as well as Red House Shoals on the Kanawha River. Shortly after arriving at Winfield, Captain John Reynolds ordered Company D to construct earthworks and

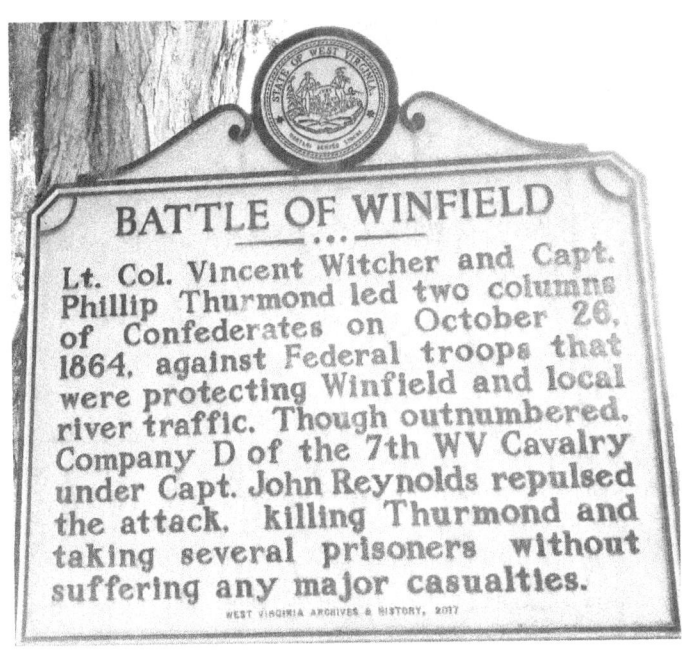

Winfield historical marker in front of court house. Photo by author.

rifle pits around their encampment near the courthouse. According to one historian: "No sooner had Captain Reynolds taken position, then he began the construction of a rifle pit around his encampment. This included the present site of Pioneer Hills [Mills] and the present residence of Captain Lawrence A. Cristy, a steamboat pilot on the Kanawha River. The ditches then dug are yet plainly visible." Unfortunately, the earthworks and rifle pits were later destroyed, but their approximate location was just west of the modern Putnam County courthouse along the ridge rising above Route 34. There were also rifle pits constructed near the corner of modern Main Street and Second Street. This company earlier served under Major General John Pope during the 1862 Valley Campaign, fighting against General Thomas J. "Stonewall" Jackson, as Company D, 8th [West] Virginia Volunteer Infantry, and were veteran troops by this point in the war. Witcher's forces arrived on the outskirts of Winfield on October 26, 1864, just one week after the battle of Cedar Creek in the Shenandoah Valley of Virginia. They took position along the northwestern edge of the village around 9 p.m., after riding through Teays Valley by way of Hurricane Bridge.[51]

Under cover of darkness, Witcher divided his force into two columns, one led by himself, the other led by Captain Thurmond, who posted his column along the Kanawha riverbank from the lower end of town. Meanwhile, Witcher's column would approach the Federals posted in the earthworks near the Putnam County Courthouse, with Thurmond intending to proceed "down a small stream known as Ferry branch, [adjacent to Ferry Street] which enters into the Kanawha at the upper end of the town," in hopes of attacking the Federals from the rear. As the Confederates stealthily approached, Thurmond was surprised to find Federal videttes posted along the Kanawha riverbank. The Union soldiers were similarly unaware the Confederates had moved in so closely to their position, but quickly opened fire once they realized the threat. Thurmond's column charged their position at about 10 p.m., and according to Captain John Reynolds, "They drove in my pickets and surrounded my Co. quarters."[52]

An account later written by Dr. John P. Hale, a resident of the Kanawha Valley, also described the action:

2nd Lt. Harvey Reynolds,
Co. D, 7th West Virginia Cavalry.
Brother of Captain John Reynolds.
West Virginia State Archives.

Thurmond ordered a charge, leading it in person, and just as the head of the column reached the corner of Ferry and Front streets, it received the first fire and Col. Thurman [Thurmond] fell mortally wounded. He was carried to the rear where he soon after expired. The firing now became general and continued for an hour, several being killed and wounded on both sides.[53]

Captain Thurmond was reportedly shot in the abdomen, causing heavy blood loss. As fighting pitched in the streets of Winfield, visibility was limited due to darkness and heavy smoke filling the air. In the melee, eighteen Union cavalry horses panicked, breaking their halters, and ran into the Confederate lines, where they were captured.[54]

An unidentified correspondent published the following account of the raid in *The Weekly Register* on November 3, 1864:

The rebels had detailed about 40 men to take a circuit towards the river to attack our forces in the rear, behind their defenses, while the main body were to charge, simultaneously, in front. They confidently expected to capture the entire company, but they met with a resistance they little expected. In the very outset of the attack, Captain Thurman [Thurmond] was mortally wounded. The rebels immediately gave way and after a desultory fire of about twenty minutes retreated, carrying off about sixteen horses and two or three prisoners.[55]

A Winfield resident identified only as "Citizen" also described the action:

On the night of the 25th about 11 o'clock, we were aroused from our slumbers by the firing of guns, the yelling of Rebs and Yankees. Before time had elapsed sufficient to offer up prayer or sigh for those we love, the Rebel Col. Witcher rushed into town with 425 men. Capt. Reynolds (co D) 7th WVVC had part of his men in the fortification which were partly finished. The rebels charged on the fortifications several times but were repulsed with the loss of one captain. The name of Captain Reynolds and men will ever be cherished by the citizens of Winfield, while memory lasts. They are brave, they are gentlemen.[56]

Realizing the attack had failed, the Confederates were "handsomely repulsed" and began to withdraw from town. According to one historian, "Then the Confederates, having secured a number of horses, withdrew, and fell back to Mud River Bridge, leaving the Federals in possession of the town...." Captain Reynolds indicated he then ordered a squad to pursue the Confederates, whom he wrote "commenced a hasty retreat." Reynolds stated the Union troopers gave chase for several hours and went as far as Loup Creek in pursuit, but were unable to re-engage the Confederates, noting, "...I have heard nothing of the enemy since they passed Hurricane Bridge."[57]

Captain Thurmond's wound was mortal, and his younger brother, Elias Thurmond, remained behind with him and was captured. Later that morning, one of Thurmond's officers, Captain William Bahlman, approached Federal pickets with a flag of truce and requested permission to bury him, which was granted by Captain Reynolds. Although not all historians and researchers agree on the location, Thurmond was reportedly buried in an unmarked grave in the hollow behind the courthouse, near the modern location of Judge James W. Hoge's house with the understanding that his family would reinter the body after the war. This has been the subject of some local controversy, however, as no action was taken until 2010, when a body many believed to be Thurmond was reinterred to a marked military grave located behind the Hoge House, although some researchers are doubtful that was actually the body of Captain Thurmond.[58]

Colonel John Oley, commanding the 7th West Virginia Cavalry, later summarized the affair in his official report:

> Witcher, with 400 men, attacked Winfield at 3 this a.m., where one company of the Seventh Virginia Cavalry was stationed. He was repulsed and is retreating. Capt. Philip J. Thurmond fell into our hands mortally wounded and has since died. Detachment of the Seventh are in pursuit. The enemy have retreated....[59]

Captain Philip Thurmond's grave site, adjacent to the Hoge House, Winfield, WV. Photo by Steve Cunningham.

Colonel Oley also requested more troops be sent to the Winfield area; Major General George C. Crook, who had only recently returned from the Shenandoah Valley Campaign, was then commanding Union forces in the Kanawha Valley. He received Oley's report and responded by admonishing him to: "Hold out, fight, clean out and destroy all in your front....as there can be nothing but bushwhackers in that country. You must not permit yourself to be frightened by them. You have force enough; none can be spared from here."[60]

As was common in the Civil War, casualty reports of Witcher's raid on Winfield conflicted among various sources. For example, Captain Reynolds stated, "My loss is one man wounded, four horses killed, and eighteen horses captured." He also mentioned that 2nd Lieutenant Andrew Hix of Thurmond's Rangers had given himself up to the Union as a deserter. On the other hand, his commander, Colonel John Oley, stated the loss was "...three or four killed and several wounded." A newspaper article published in the *West Virginia Journal* claimed: "Our men took five prisoners, among them Elias Thurmond, who is here in the guard house and wounded seven of the Rebels besides killing Phil Thurmond. Our loss was two slightly wounded." Despite the inconsistencies, the raid on Winfield was a Union victory, which, according to one citizen, largely "...put an end to the active military operations in the immediate valley."[61]

Local newspapers similarly printed varying accounts of casualties as well as the action at Winfield. The *Charleston Daily Bulletin*, a strongly pro-Union organ, reported:

> Capt. Reynolds and his men deserve great credit for the determined bravery with which they defended the post of Winfield, last Wednesday morning. Eighty men fought for one hour, and kept at a respectful

distance, four hundred and twenty-five of the Virginia "chivalry!" Will Col. Witcher go back this time and boast of his victories? But we must not forget, in our exultation over the heroic valor of our own men, as compared with the miserable cowardice of Witcher's land-pirates, of how much real importance the defeat of the guerrillas was to us, and to give due credit to the gallant band who saved our communication below from being cut off, and possibly one or two of our boats from being captured and burnt. We have the principal facts last week. Our men took five prisoners, among them Ed Thurman, who is here in the guard house, and wounded seven of the rebels, besides killing Phil Thurman. Our loss was two, slightly wounded.[62]

The Weekly Register in Point Pleasant, meanwhile, published the following version of the raid on Winfield:

None of our men were killed. Six horses were killed inside the defenses. The rebel Captain Thurman [Thurmond] was left in our hands and died in a few hours. His brother who remained with him, was taken prisoner, and from the appearances of blood in various places many rebels were wounded. Our men deserve great credit for their bravery. They were attacked by four times their number, but handsomely repulsed the enemy. There are rumors of the appearance of rebels at other points on the Kanawha, and also at Guyandotte but we cannot learn any reliable particulars.[63]

On October 30, 1864, General George Crook further directed Colonel Oley:

Pursue your good work and show them no mercy. Send expeditions to the sections of the country where these bushwhackers are harbored and destroy all subsistence for man or beast. Drive off all their stock but destroy no houses. In this way, you will make a belt of devastation between your lines and the enemy's all around your front, which will prevent these frequent incursions of theirs. It is cheaper and more humane for us to feed these people than to fight their bushwhackers. You must carry out sound judgment in carrying out these instructions.[64]

Following the raid at Winfield, the Confederates were no longer able to sustain any significant offensive operations against Union forces in Putnam County beyond occasional raids. Despite this, General Crook was deeply concerned about the ease by which Confederates and guerilla units conducted frequent raids in the Kanawha Valley. Knowing that much of the problem had to do with the 5th, 9th and 13th West Virginia Infantry regiments still being deployed to Virginia's Shenandoah Valley, the general realized the areas west and south of Charleston were left vulnerable to Confederate raiders. Crook wrote to Governor Arthur Boreman on October 29, 1864, asking for more troops:

I feel it my imperative duty to call your attention to the defenseless condition of the Kanawha Valley and the southern portion of the state generally. It seems to be the general impression, and I am inclined to think it a correct one, that that section of the country is being threatened and will be overrun by a considerable rebel force unless aid is speedily afforded....it is my purpose, as it is my duty, to persevere in my efforts to have our loyal people saved from the ruinous consequences of these rebel incursions for the future....[65]

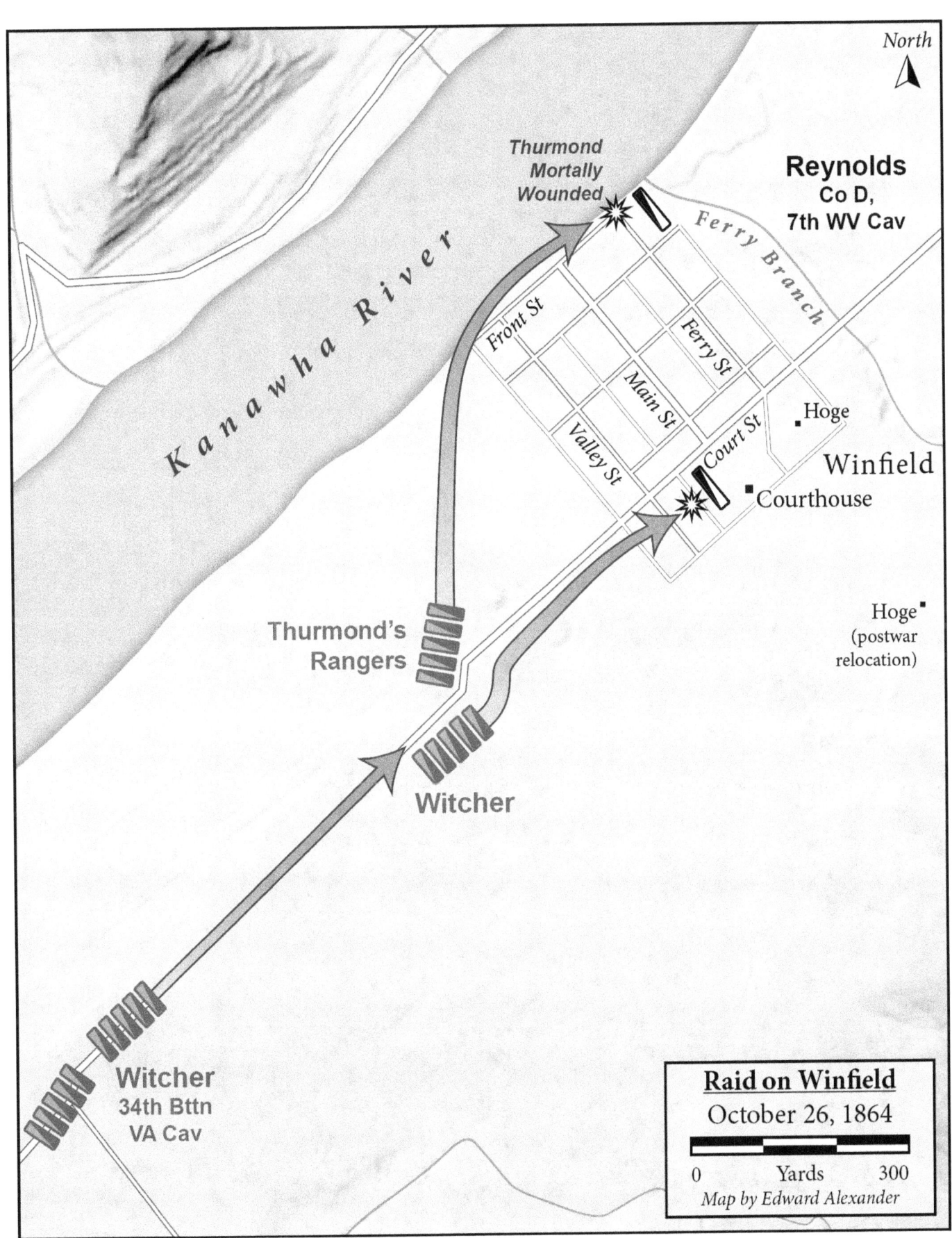

North

Kanawha River

Thurmond Mortally Wounded

Reynolds
Co D,
7th WV Cav

Ferry Branch

Front St

Ferry St

Main St

Valley St

Court St

· Hoge

Winfield

· Courthouse

Hoge ·
(postwar relocation)

Thurmond's Rangers

Witcher

Witcher
34th Bttn
VA Cav

Raid on Winfield
October 26, 1864

0   Yards   300

Map by Edward Alexander

Bullets recovered from the site of the raid on Winfield,
near the courthouse.
Courtesy Steve Cunningham

Sharps Pepperbox pistol recovered from the site of the raid on Winfield, near the courthouse.
Courtesy Steve Cunningham

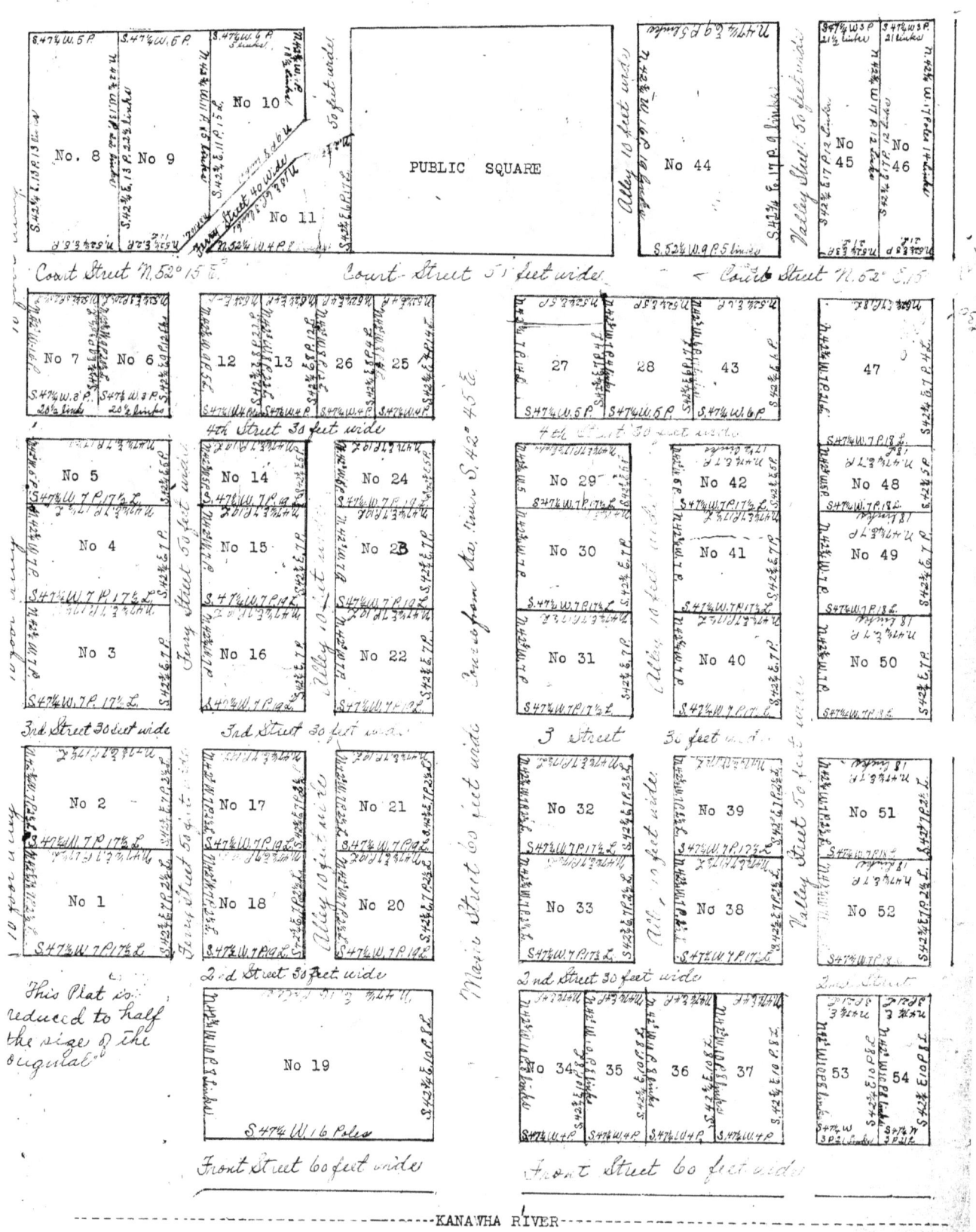

1862 plot map of Winfield showing private homes and street layout.
The home of Capt. John V. Young, Co. G, 11th West Virginia Infantry, was located on plot number two on Ferry Street.
Putnam County Clerk of Court Records, Winfield, West Virginia.

Crook closed by requesting that Boreman "take such action as will ensure the safety of the section of the state....If you have not the means in your power to comply with my request, please inform me to whom it would be best to make application."[66]

Rebel Spy at Winfield

One of the means Southern citizens utilized to pass information to their respective government and military authorities was spying. As with any period of history, such was common during the Civil War, and there were spies among residents of Putnam County. A letter to a friend in the Virginia legislature, Samuel L. Miller, written by an unknown Confederate spy at Putnam Courthouse identified only as "Rebel Spy," was discovered and published in the *West Virginia Journal*, a Union news organ, on October 25, 1864. The letter reveals modes of operation and maxims, including a rather arrogant and contemptuous view of West Virginians, along with a conspiracy to hold them in ignorance under the control of the wealthy Eastern elite:

I will commence by saying, that we have another maxim, which we carefully conceal from people of the *New State*, which runs as follows: It is a self-evident truth that no West Virginian ought to hold any office whatever, because "he has neither words nor worth nor utterance, to make it respectable;" but all offices should be conferred on Eastern Virginians, who have lived in the west long enough to make them eligible, because of their high birth, superior manners and superior cunning. Another maxim of this class, is that West Virginians should be kept in ignorance, lest they should become intelligent enough to throw off the yoke....

It has long been a rule with us in Eastern Virginia, to send our restless office seekers, who are always stirring up contentions at home, out west, where, after a short residence, they become eligible for office, and where, by loud professions, and a kind of mock dignity which would not pass for good manners in the east, they always obtain a position amongst the clod-hoppers, or rather, a position above them. Now it is not hard to conceive the course taken by those Eastern Virginians, once they are installed in office. They live in the west for the purpose of making money, but their real homes, as well as their friends, interests, are in the east; and in all their acts of legislation, they lean to the east, and find it easy to make their mud-sill constituency believe they are doing the very best thing possible for their interests.

It might be thought that since the commencement of the war this *mode of procedure* would be broken up, but this is not the case. When some wild, embryonic politician has failed of preferment in the east, and is in a fair way to be conscripted, he obtains permission to go through the lines on private business, where at once he falls deeply in love with the old flag, tells of the thousand and one hardships he has undergone in the east for the sake of the Union cause, and begs protection of the Yankees: and in an incredibly short time he becomes one of the most prominent leaders in the New State; he is elevated to office and every honor paid him that could be bestowed upon a political martyr. He will indeed make a useful man, but it will be to Eastern Virginia, not to his stupid constituency, who by a blind veneration for religion....

Again, it has always been our policy to keep the people of West Virginia in ignorance, and when they became clamorous for a school system, we so shuffled all the cards so as to cause all the counties but two or three to reject it: and we succeeded in getting it broken down in all these counties except Kanawha, where it was continued because some of our friends could make their living by it who could not do it otherwise. But I will here observe that this system, which has only been operation for twelve or fifteen years, has done our cause incalculable injury. It has raised up a set of young politicians who think and act for themselves and refuse to be controlled by us: and that is the reason that Kanawha could not be got to go with us into the Southern Confederacy as easily as the other counties of the west....As to our mode of operating at elections, we resolve to carry the day at all hazards....[67]

Execution of William Harvey Bowyer

William Harvey Bowyer was twenty-one years old when he enlisted as a private in Captain Albert Beckett's Company on May 16, 1861, at Hurricane Bridge. Beckett's company mustered into Confederate service as Company A, 36th Virginia Infantry, at Buffalo on the same date. Bowyer was the nephew of John Bowyer, son of Peter Bowyer, Jr., of Winfield. On November 21, 1861, he deserted from the Army and returned to Winfield, where he voluntarily surrendered to his uncle, and took the Oath of Allegiance on November 27, 1861. He remained at home until rumors began circulating he was a Confederate spy, and he became fearful for his life. In late November, he encountered some Confederate officers who persuaded him to "return south, where, they told him, he would be safe." Bowyer left home and when he had reached the rebel lines, he was quickly informed that he "must return to the service."[68]

He complained to the Confederate authorities he had taken the Oath of Allegiance to the United States but was told it "made no difference," and he was forced to return to the Army on April 8, 1862. Another account states he "remained at home a while, stole a horse from his uncle, Capt. John Bowyer, and went into the rebel army." Regardless of the circumstances, Bowyer served until he was captured on February 19, 1864, by the 3rd West Virginia Infantry near Boone Courthouse, and was imprisoned at Camp Chase, Ohio. Once Major General George Crook learned of his capture, he ordered a military tribunal to hear the case on March 22, 1864.[69]

Bowyer pled guilty and was sentenced to death by firing squad for violating the Oath of Allegiance. During the interim, more than 110 letters were received at Union headquarters in Charleston, petitioning for his case to be commuted to life in prison, from his friends, many of whom were prominent Union men at Winfield and Buffalo, including Judge George Summers, a Union supporter who had gained a reputation for advocating the release of Southern sympathizers. Generally, those who knew Bowyer claimed he was "uneducated and ignorant" and argued that made him especially vulnerable to the coercion of the Confederate officers who had persuaded him to return to Confederate lines. General Crook forwarded the case to President Lincoln for review. Lincoln declined commutation, and Bowyer was summarily executed by troops led by Colonel John Oley, 7th West Virginia Cavalry, on November 4, 1864.[70]

1864 Presidential and Gubernatorial Elections

Major General George B. McClellan, known as "Little Mac" by Union soldiers, was a West Pointer and career soldier. Having commanded troops in western Virginia during the early campaign of 1861 against General Robert E. Lee, he was well known to residents of Putnam County as well. However, after the battle of Antietam in September 1862, Lincoln removed McClellan from command, resulting in quite a jolt for McClellan, who was known for being overly self-confident but gained an arduous reputation as being too cautious as a field commander. He decided to run against Lincoln in the 1864 presidential election and won the Democratic party nomination. McClellan was opposed to the popular notion of making peace with the South, and for his platform vowed to do a better job of continuing the war than the Lincoln administration had done. The Democratic party chose George Hunt Pendleton, an Ohio attorney and U.S. senator, who was also the leader of the Ohio Copperheads, a group in favor of making peace with the South, as his vice presidential running mate.[71]

This election was unique in many ways, primarily because it was the first time that Alabama, Arkansas, Florida, Georgia, Virginia, Louisiana, Mississippi, North and South Carolina, Tennessee, Arkansas, and Texas had not participated in the vote, in favor of Jefferson Davis, the Confederate president as their own choice. Lincoln had become rather unpopular in many areas and was deeply concerned about losing the election against McClellan, especially after the Union army failed to capture Richmond thus far. His opponents accused him of being a tyrant for imposing a military draft and then announcing emancipation. Even with Union victories at Gettysburg and Vicksburg in 1863, the draft riots that summer further polarized many factions against him. Despite his fears, the pendulum of popular opinion again swung in Lincoln's favor on September 1, 1864, just one day after the Democrat party announced their endorsement of General McClellan to run for president, when Atlanta fell to Major General William T. Sherman's army.[72]

Lincoln then swept the election, taking fifty-five percent of the popular vote and 212 electoral votes to McClellan's twenty-one; despite his former popularity among the troops, Little Mac only received thirty percent of the military vote. In the new state of West Virginia, Arthur I. Boreman won the election for governor with 204 votes in Putnam County, and citizens voted for Lincoln over McClellan 338 to 109. Also in Putnam County, Captain John Young, who ran for House of Delegates against local Red House tavern owner Dudley S. Montague, had only thirty-two votes while his opponent had fifty-one. Young was then stationed in the Shenandoah Valley and had recently been in heavy combat at the battle of Cedar Creek on October 19. Additionally, attorney John Bowyer, who ran for a seat in the U.S. Senate, was defeated by Kanawha County resident Greenbury Slack.[73]

Despite earlier fears Confederates would attempt to disrupt voters in the presidential election in Putnam County, it "passed off quietly," and according to one surprised citizen, "If ever there an election was held in this country at which rows and riots would be expected, it was that of last Tuesday….To govern oneself during such an election day is evidence enough that the individual is fit for freedom." Captain John Ball wrote from camp on Union Ridge near the Mason-Cabell County line on November 18, 1864 that his company of home guards finally received a few uniforms and equipment, and two loads of "stores," including rations and ammunition. He described their current condition as "very good," although he groused that because that "I have understood you could not pay the company until the legislature is convinced my men has had to go into debt to keep up their families from suffering…" Ball pled further for them to receive the pay due his men before the legislature convened, stating that many had gone into debt while they were in the army, and it was critical in order to "keep their families from suffering for their services," admonishing General George Brown, "You will please speak to the governor about it." At that time, more than half of his company had enlisted primarily because they were able to draw blankets and overcoats, as "my company is holding one of the outposts [Union Ridge] and it's very probable the duties will be very hard the present winter."[74]

Ball again wrote to the state quartermaster on December 9, 1864, thanking him for sending a few blankets and overcoats, but noted he had promised the company could draw more "if they needed it." Ball insisted, "Well they need it bad," and requested sixteen more overcoats and blankets. It was not sufficient, however, as on December 9, 1864, Ball again asked for sixteen more blankets and overcoats, which he said the needed "very bad" due to the harsh winter weather. Ball noted many of them had been without coats for several weeks. At this point, Federal troops had maintained control of the Kanawha Valley since 1862, although Putnam County continued to suffer occasional guerilla raids and bushwhacking. At the end of 1864, the war was beginning to wind down in West Virginia, and many residents still had loved ones serving in the larger armies in the eastern and western theatres of war.[73]

Chapter Five

1865: The Shadow of Slavery

Two years after the Emancipation Proclamation was released, the new state of West Virginia had yet to determine an answer to the ultimate question of slavery, though the state constitution now afforded gradual emancipation. Many residents wanted "total and immediate" abolition, however, and wanted to drop Article 11, Section 7, known as the Willey Amendment, ratified on March 26, 1863. This stated that children of slaves born within state limits after July 4, 1863 were free, and that all slaves within the state under age ten would be free at the age of twenty-one; those between ten and twenty-five years old would not be free until they reached twenty-five. The Wiley Amendment also prevented any enslaved person from taking up residence in the state who did not already live there. This meant no slaves would be free until 1867, as there was no provision for freedom of slaves over age twenty-one, and it should be noted the Emancipation Proclamation only applied to states in Confederate territory not under Federal control. In statistical terms, this meant the Willey Amendment would leave some 6,000 slaves in bondage, roughly forty percent of the state's slave population.[1]

Proponents of total abolition argued the state constitution in its present form rendered the institution of slavery unprofitable, but still left the shadow of the "burdensome" practice. One citizen quipped: "As the case now stands, we hold an anomalous position. Our state is neither a free nor a slave state. Unfortunately, we have just enough of the institution to clog the wheels of our advancement as a free state, without any compensating advantages" Such opinions were commonly found in period newspapers and other printed mediums in the state and are important for modern readers to grasp, because they contradict many inaccurate, albeit popular, notions that West Virginia was a completely free state following emancipation, as well as that the new state government had wanted complete abolition when the war began. Both ideas are apocryphal, as the question of slavery was not fully settled in West Virginia until after the war ended; while Congress passed

Union Ridge Road sign on Route 2, Cabell County.
Photo by author.

the Thirteenth Amendment completely abolishing slavery on January 31, 1865, and West Virginia ratified it on February 3, 1865, the amendment was not fully ratified by the necessary twenty-seven of thirty-six states until December 6, 1865.[2]

Private Brian S. Kesterson, Company C, 44th New York Infantry, was passing through Winfield and Red House Shoals aboard the steamer *B.C. Levi* on Sunday, January 11, 1865, and made mention in his diary that the boat he was on was "once captured by the Rebs with General Scammon and staff." When Kesterson arrived at Charleston, he found it "muddy and dilapidated." On February 20, 1865, Captain John M. Ball, Putnam Scouts, finally received pay for his company, in the amount of $4,071.07 for the men and officers. Ironically, the West Virginia Legislature had only recently passed a new law authorizing pay for state scouts/ home guards on January 27, 1865.

On March 1, 1865, Ball was given leave and arrived safely at home. Prior to this time, he had only been home to Buffalo three days since the war began. He informed Francis P. Pierpont, the state adjutant general, that his company had recently captured two rebels whom he expected to "turn over as horse thieves." Ball also mentioned some of his men had been drafted, and he was uncertain as to how many more he would lose. Despite Ball's efforts, however, Confederate partisans continued to sneak about Putnam County even this late in the war. On February 17, 1865: "...a band of rebel thieves entered the town of Buffalo, and robbed the store of Mr. Dan Carr, of some five or six hundred dollars' worth of goods, consisting of shirts, pants, vests, drawers, boots, shoes, blankets, hats, caps, and stockings. These scoundrels are supposed to have retreated into Jackson County. Something ought to be done to rid the country of these thieves and murderers."[3]

Despite its unpopularity, the military draft continued, and on February 22, 1865, sixty-five men from Putnam County were conscripted into the Union Army. Guerilla raids continued in neighboring counties of Putnam and Wayne, prompting the state legislature to call for stronger organization of the "state guards," as according to one delegate: "every part of the county of Wayne, on the Ohio River, was held by guerrillas. In the county of Cabell, only one town, Guyandotte, was held by Federal troops. The Rebels have their headquarters up in Logan County, and they make forays down toward the Ohio River, stealing, murdering, and devastating the country. They enter houses of loyal citizens and steal household furniture and bed clothing, and frequently strip women and children of wearing apparel and leave them in an actual state of nudity...."[4]

On March 5, 1865, Major Edgar Blundon, 7th West Virginia Cavalry, commanded the Union garrison at Guyandotte in Cabell County and regularly sent patrols through Putnam County. Blundon was also the son-

View of area believed to be Ball's camp on Union Ridge.
Photo by author.

in-law of Captain John Young of Putnam County. He reported on that date guerilla activity was beginning to diminish in the region: "There is but one organized band of guerrillas, consisting of Bill Smith and fifteen or twenty men, in Wayne or Logan Counties, and no organization in Mason, Cabell or Putnam. The depredations committed by them are relatively few contrasted with the past." William "Rebel" Bill Smith was notorious in southern West Virginia, Virginia and Kentucky for ambushing Union troops and harassing Union citizens. Although not officially recognized by the Confederate government, Smith's battalion is thought to have had as many as four hundred men, including William Anderson "Devil Anse" Hatfield of Logan, who later became a national icon in the famous Hatfield and McCoy Feud.[5]

With the war drawing to a close, Captain John Ball had thirty-seven men present at camp on Union Ridge, near the Mason-Cabell County line, on March 7, 1865, having recently lost two men to the draft, but he also managed to recruit six new men. A few days later, on March 11, 1865, Ball held public auction to sell off six government horses and mules his company had used on patrols. He obtained $437.40 for three horses and three mules. He also had a fourth horse that a Winfield resident claimed belonged to them and would not release it until proof was provided. On April 7, 1865, Ball again requested new clothing, noting it was "time" after a hard winter. He also nudged the state quartermaster general that if his company had breech-loading rifles (carbines), they would be "of much greater service to the state." Ironically, even at this late point in the war, Ball's company still suffered from poor supplies from the Army. While he had adequate rations for his men, his company only received "one suit" of the thirty-six sack coats, trousers, hats and bootees, and seventy-two pairs of stockings, drawers and flannel shirts on April 24, 1865. [6]

Appomattox: Lee's Surrender

On April 9, 1865, General Robert E. Lee surrendered the Army of Northern Virginia to Lieutenant General Ulysses S. Grant at the village of Appomattox, Virginia, essentially ending the war in the eastern theatre. Putnam resident Captain John Young, Company G, 11th West Virginia Infantry, was present, having participated in the final siege at Petersburg and was in the Union Army's pursuit of Lee to the final conflict at Appomattox. Young described those harrowing last few days of the war in a letter to his wife on April 17, 1865:

Since my last writing we have had hard fighting and harder marching. We have taken Richmond and Petersburg, followed old Lee to Appomattox Court House and whipped and captured his whole forces. Then we went to Lynchburg and captured that Rebel hole. Remained there three days and destroyed all the Rebel property and are this far back on our way to Richmond where, it is said, we will remain until our time is out. We have had a hard time of it but we have cleared Virginia of the Rebel army. Never did men fight harder than the West Virginia boys did in storming the Rebel forts before them on the 2nd of April…Company G was the first in the Fort at Hatcher's Run and captured one stand of colors and several cannon and horses. Our division charged on Forts Whiting [Fort Whitworth] and Gregory, [Fort Gregg] and the hardest fighting in the war was done there. There was at least three hundred men lying dead on the ground when we took the fort. [Fort Whitworth] Out of two hundred Rebels who were in the fort, only about eighteen came out alive; and our officers could hardly save them. After we had taken the place, General Grant said that the men who took that Fort took Petersburg and Richmond. But we are done fighting in Virginia.[7]

On April 14, 1865, President Abraham Lincoln was assassinated by John Wilkes Booth at Ford's Theatre in Washington, D.C. and was succeeded by Vice President Andrew Johnson. By May 6, 1865, Captain Ball was aware that the war was practically over at a national level, although locally: "This section of the country there is many deprivations in the way of thieving, I have been for one week arresting and turning over to civil authorities' men who is committing these depredations. I am thinking we will have a great deal of trouble yet bringing into action the laws of this state – nothing but a signed enforcement of civil law will ever better our condition. The health of my company is rather bad, through exposure in the past winter and spring, the duties was too hard for the strength of my company." On May 10, 1865, Ball again held a public auction and sold three horses and mules for $486.50. West Virginia Assistant Adjutant General George C. Bowyer of Winfield wrote on May 11, 1865:

I do not think there is any necessity of continuing Capt. Ball's company in the service, the Rebels in this sector – to use a common term, are completely "played out" and are so well pleased with the terms granted to them by our government that I apprehend no trouble with them. There is now a store back of this place at Hurricane Bridge, one of the worst neighborhoods in this valley, and almost as bad as any place in Rebeldom, has been in operation almost two weeks and has not been interfered with.[8]

Did the Last Battle of the Civil War in West Virginia occur in Putnam County?

Although otherwise undocumented, Civil War veteran Reverend William A. Byus claimed that the last engagement of the Civil War in West Virginia was fought in Putnam County on April 18, 1865. This account appeared in the April 9, 1927 edition of the *West Virginia News*, and is based solely upon a story provided by eighty-three year old Mason County resident and minister. As Byus aged, had grown "blind and feeble" but was still said to be quite cognizant. Byus was born in Putnam County on October 7, 1843, and resided there until the war began. He enlisted as a private in Company D, 8th West Virginia Infantry at Buffalo on October 14, 1861, and served with the regiment throughout the war. The 8th West Virginia became the 7th West Virginia Cavalry in 1864, and Byus fought in eleven engagements, some of them being major battles, including the second Bull Run in August 1862. Byus worked his way up in rank to First Sergeant, and in 1863 was commissioned as 2nd Lieutenant, and was promoted to 1st Lieutenant on February 23, 1865, and had command of Company D until discharged on August 5, 1865. However, from there, the story becomes sketchy as no other contemporaneous sources similarly document the fight he claimed occurred at Winfield. Nonetheless, the story is included herein only as part of the local tradition, but the reader is cautioned that it is apocryphal as the Raid on Winfield Byus described was fought on October 26, 1864. As such, many of the otherwise factual details of the fighting, etc., likely apply to that action, but it simply did not occur in April 1865 as Byus claimed.

Byus claimed that final action of the war in West Virginia was fought at Winfield on April 19, 1865, and involved an attack on the small Union garrison of Company D, 7th West Virginia Cavalry, by the 44th Battalion, Virginia Cavalry, (a.k.a. Morris' Rangers, Hounshell's Battalion, Thurmond's Partisan Rangers) under command of Captain William D. Thurmond, brother of Colonel Philip James Thurmond, who formerly commanded the battalion and was killed at the raid on Winfield on October 26, 1864. William D. Thurmond enlisted as captain of an independent partisan company August 26, 1862 at Sweet Sulphur Springs, Virginia and was mustered into Confederate service by Major General William Loring. The battalion was assigned to Brigadier General John Echols's brigade in April 1864. As his service records show that Colonel William D. Thurmond took the Oath of Allegiance at Charleston, WV on June 29, 1865. There is no evidence he was ever wounded, much less killed in action, in his service records. Hence, Byus must have either confused the alleged death of William D. with his brother Philip J. Thurmond from his recollection of the October 1864 raid, of which he was also part.[9]

Byus reported that the Union garrison was quartered in an old hotel located on Front Street in Winfield in April 1865, and were not expecting an attack as the war had all but drawn to a close, and "everyone knew that General Robert E. Lee had surrendered" the Army of Northern Virginia just nine days previous. Byus stated, "On the night of April 18, I had just gone to bed, and was sound asleep, when about 10 o'clock I was suddenly awakened by a shot from the camp. I jumped out of bed, and put on a few clothes, calling for the men to form a line. The Confederates were coming down Front Street toward us, led by Col. Thurmond. (Thurmond's service records shows his rank as captain in June 1865) They were firing, I had only 45 men, since we were not expecting any trouble, some of the men having gone home on furloughs. The Confederates had about 425 men, and had slipped through the fields around our outposts, led by some guides who were familiar with the town and surroundings. They were in the town and almost upon us when the guard heard them and fired. We began firing and were giving them as much lead as our guns would give. They advanced steadily upon us and were near, when I heard a man say, 'Boys, I'm shot.' It was Col Thurman, and he had been fatally wounded. Finding their leader shot, the Confederates retreated. We afterward learned that 15 of their men had been wounded. Only one of my men was hurt. They carried Col. Thurmond into a house, and I went into see him. I said, "Col. Thurmond, you have got things mixed a little." "I have got things mixed for myself," he replied. I said, "Didn't you know that Lee had surrendered? "Yes, but I was persuaded to attack you, so as to get your horses." He died about four hours after he had been shot." Byus continued, "The retreating Confederates took 23 of our horses with them. The animals were in a barn away from the camp. During the battle an old coal house owned by John Dudding, had 84 bullets fired into it from our guns."[10]

One day later, April 20, 1865, Colonel John H. Oley, 7th West Virginia Cavalry, was advised by the War Department via the West Virginia Adjutant General to, "Post yourself up as thoroughly as possible. If necessary, you can let Colonel Hounshell (Houndshell) and others go home and collect their men and make arrangements. You can inform them that all can be paroled - Thurmond, Witcher, and everybody. This is by order today received from General Grant. All those whose homes were in the States that never passed the ordnance of secession have forfeited their homes and can only return under the amnesty proclamation by taking the Oath of Allegiance.... Men can return to West Virginia on parole. Oley was referring to Captain William Thurmond, Colonel Vincent Witcher, 34th Battalion Virginia Cavalry, and Lieutenant Colonel D.S. Hounshell, (Houndshell) who at one point commanded the 44th Battalion Virginia Cavalry and then had command of an independent partisan cavalry battalion surrendered at Appomattox, Virginia on April 9, 1865. On April 29, 1965, Colonel Oley ordered Major Edgar Blundon, 7th West Virginia Cavalry posted at Guyandotte, that all of the parolees who were not considered dangerous, being held in the region could go home. As for the Confederate deserters who had not been with their commands, however, Oley ordered that they "receive no mercy."[11]

Captain Ball's company of home guard scouts finally received their first full shipment of uniforms on April 25, 1865, with Ball noting his company had heretofore received only "one full suit of clothing last fall," and several new men who "joined me last winter" still had no uniforms at all. The shipment was comprised of thirty-five sack coats, trousers, and caps, seventy-two pairs of drawers and flannel shirts, and stockings. Ball wrote to the state quartermaster on that date apologizing for not sending more timely reports, noting he had injured his right hand, which was very "sore" and prevented him from writing. Ball also wrote that his "ammunition is getting scarce" and requested more uniforms.[12]

On June 3, 1865, Captain Ball received orders from the state adjutant general to formally disband his company. He requested a few days to "fix up my business" and promised to ship all arms and accoutrements to the state quartermaster as soon as possible. Ball did not accomplish the latter, however, as he took ill at Parkersburg and was out of duty until July. He wrote to Adjutant General Pierpont on June 11, 1865, stating he was boarding a boat to Gallipolis, Ohio. He noted on July 5, 1865 he was still sick and had been so "ever since I left Wheeling." Despite Assistant Adjutant General George Bowyer's recent belief that guerilla activity had slowed in the Kanawha Valley, there were in fact significant Sectionalist tensions yet in the region, and Pierpont decided to order Ball to stay in service a while longer through August 1865. Ball recovered from his illness in July and returned to duty; he immediately requested twenty new rifles for his company, along with cartridge boxes and cap boxes, noting "Other equipage will be of little advantage." Ball also completed a company muster roll on that date containing the following men:

John M. Ball, Captain. Enlisted: M.V. Deal, John C. Deal, James McWharter, A.B. Campbell, Henry Byrd, William Goff, William Forth, Pascal Hawthorne, William Hawthorne, C.C. Deal, James H. Taylor, William F. Lunsford, David Lykins, James N. Rowley, James C. Rowley, Wallis Andrew, John Walls, Alfred Gillespie, and George Holly.[13]

Epilogue – Life after the Civil War in Putnam County

A sad testament to the nature of service in a Union home guard company in Putnam County during the Civil War is best said as *Too little, too late,'* as by August 1865, the war was officially over, and yet, Captain John Ball had not received the new arms he so often requested, complaining, "There a great many thieves and robbers in the country, and armed men is necessary for protection of the county." Others echoed Ball's concern, as found in a Buffalo resident's observation of how the Union and Confederate veterans alike adjusted upon their return to Putnam County in the summer of 1865:

They are farmers today, statesmen tomorrow, and soldiers always. The performance of the Valley men lent honor to their ancestral heritage and maintained the soldiery background of the Great Kanawha Valley. With the return of peace, these men came home, laid by their military trappings, donned citizen's garb and united in an effort to secure the intellectual and industrial development of their beautiful valley." In reality, however, it wasn't always that easy. Many veterans from the Eighteen Mile Creek area returned and found it extremely difficult to adapt to the mundane routine of civilian life after war. They began meeting on weekends to play cards and consume alcohol heavily, and many were soon arrested for stealing local farmers chickens and pigs. Before long, there was a petty crime wave cited in that part of the county and was attributed largely to the veteran's intoxicated behavior. Known as the "Red Legs" this band of comrades in arms were dreaded and even feared, before most if not all of them were apprehended and wound up in prison. It should not be surprising that some men had trouble adjusting to what amounts to a boring life compared to the Civil War; area guerrillas that operated in the mountainous region of western Virginia often lost their focus and became lawless renegades who answered to neither military nor civil authorities during the Civil War. For some men, it was an opportunity to simply engage in violence, as many wreaked havoc on even their own neighbors and friends in nocturnal raids, sacking homes, barns, and looting....[14]

Not only the soldiers, but also most civilians in the region experienced a great deal of tension when trying to resume life together among former enemies, which continued throughout much of the Reconstruction era. One citizen observed:

Among us they are like their master Jeff Davis. They blow and bluster, and curse like a drab, but when a Union soldier comes about, they take to their petticoats and speak of "Mrs. Davis' mother." Some of them don't believe that Jeff has been taken at all, any more than they do that Booth has been killed. They all seem to be very sorry that Lincoln was killed, but we think they will mourn much more sincerely, if Jeff stretches hemp. A good many of them talk now about the shame of striking a man when he is down & c. Well in an ordinary stand up fight this might do, if your opponent was a man of honor. But when he happens to be a murderer aiming at your life, or a thief, at your property, a little killing is justifiable, particularly if you know that you don't kill, your chances of being killed are good. When I tap a rattlesnake or copperhead, (animal I mean) that strikes at me, so as to break his back, I think it my duty to kill him outright, and not leave him to crawl off and practice his game on somebody else....[15]

Not all the veterans were so unruly, however, as many sought to live peacefully and try to return to some sense of normality, as one Union veteran identified only as "Hardtack" opined:

The paroled rebel soldiers from West Va., are returning to their homes and living as peaceably as their more loyal neighbors will permit. In Cabell County, very little hostility has thus far manifested itself on (the) part of the Union men toward these repentant rebs. A meeting was lately held at Barboursville, at which Judge [H.J.] Samuels made a speech, counselling moderation on the part of loyal, and quietness on part of those who had earned for themselves the reputation of disloyal men. In Kanawha and Putnam counties there seems to be considerable ill feeling, toward the rebels, nor is it likely to be allayed by the course adopted...the result is now history.[16]

Captain John Young arrived at his home in Winfield around 9 p.m. on the evening of July 7, 1865, after being discharged from the army at Richmond a few days earlier. Exhausted, Young wanted to spend as much time with his family as possible, but soon learned he had acquired an illness known as consumption (tuberculosis) while serving in the Shenandoah Valley Campaign of 1864. Young's health rapidly deteriorated, and it is doubtful he felt like socializing, but some of the men in his company soon paid him a visit while on their way home on July 19, 1865. One was former 11th West Virginia Infantry Quartermaster Sergeant John Hall, a resident of Coalsmouth, who "put on clean shirts" to go see the captain after boarding a steamer and traveling from Parkersburg. He ate dinner with Young and his family that evening. Hall soon discovered another comrade, former Lieutenant Van Morris, had also arrived at Winfield. They met up and went on a "drinking spree" to celebrate surviving the war, which lasted several days; Hall recalled in his diary, "Van was very tight." One morning after a night of celebrating, both were quite hungover and Hall penned, "I feel very bad today from the effects of our spree yesterday." He and Morris spent the day "very dryly" and mowed the grass together— though "very slowly." When Hall finally made it home to Coalsmouth on July 22, 1865, he found that it too was "...a very drunken place-some considerable fighting at Coal today."[17]

Summarily, the years 1861 to 1865 in Putnam County witnessed a bloody civil war that, for everyone involved, was a true fratricide as former friends, neighbors, school mates, and families divided. Historian Boyd Sutler once wrote that every county in the area that became West Virginia had its own story to tell of the Civil War in "actions and incident," and certainly Putnam County shared in the cost. Ultimately, with such strongly divided loyalties to Virginia and the Federal Union, the differences could only be settled by force of arms, and it was in consequence that many of the most ruthless events of the war occurred in this unstable border region, as residents suffered through four years of the terrors of guerilla and irregular warfare and smaller battles, often in their own homes. Indeed, when the area known as western Virginia became the thirty-fifth state admitted into the Union on June 20, 1863, it was truly a child of the storm, and although the Civil War officially ended in August 1865, Sectionalist tensions from the war era would remain unsettled in the region for decades, if at all.[18]

Appendix A
Captain John H. Ball's Company
Putnam County Scouts
Muster Roll May 31, 1865

Name	Rank	Enlisted	Comments
John H. Ball	Captain	Dec. 29, 1862	Formerly 2d Lt. in James W. Bailey's Co. 1861
Martin W. Deal	1st Sergeant	July 1, 1864	
John C. Deal	Ordnance Sgt.	July 1, 1864	
James Reedy	3d Sergeant	Mar. 15, 1864	
Addison Ballard	Private	Oct. 1, 1864	
Anderson Byas (Bias)	Private	June 20, 1863	Home sick per Dec. 31, 1863, roll. Also appears on Rucker's roll Co. A
Bennett Byas (Bias)	Private	July 1, 1864	
Archibald B. Campbell	Private	May 1, 1864	
Bradford Campbell	Private	1864	Died March 22, 1864
Jonathan Chapman	Private	July 1, 1864	
John M. Chapman	Private	July 1, 1864	
Hawen Cremeans	Private	May 1, 1864	
Preston K. Cremeans	Private	July 1, 1864	
Janotterege (Barrottege) Cremeans	Private	May 6, 1864	
Alfred Doss	Private	July 1, 1864	
William C. Doss	Private	July 1, 1864	

Name	Rank	Enlisted	Comments
Samuel Dunn	Private	May 25, 1864	
Martin R. Edmunds	Private	Oct. 8, 1864	
William Forth	Private	July 1, 1864	
John R. Fossett	Private	July 1, 1864	
Edward Fowler	Private	July 25, 1864	
Charles D. Gatewood	Private	May 25, 1864	
Benjamin P. George	Private	May 25, 1864	
Richard S. George	Private	Mar. 15, 1864	
Alfred Gillespe (Gillespie)	Private	July 1, 1864	
William E. Green	Private	May 25, 1864	
Columbus Hawthorne	Private	Sept. 28, 1864	
Pascal Hawthorne	Private	July 1, 1864	
William Hawthorne	Private	Sept. 28, 1864	
George Holley	Private	Mar. 15, 1864	
George W. Holley	Private	July 1, 1864	
James C. Holley	Private	Mar. 15, 1864	
John R. Holley	Private	Mar. 15, 1864	
William W. Holley	Private	Mar. 15, 1864	
John W. Hughes	Private	Mar. 15, 1864	

Name	Rank	Enlisted	Comments
Andrew M. Jordan	Private	July 1, 1864	
Andrew G. Jordan	Private	July 1, 1864	
James L. Jordan	Private	July 1, 1864	
John H. Jordan	Private	July 1, 1864	
Samuel Jordan	Private	May 1, 1864	
Thomas V. Jordan	Private	July 1, 1864	
Frederick Lewis	Private	July 1, 1864	
Samuel Lock	Private	July 1, 1864	
James Lunsford	Private	Aug. 12, 1864	
John Lunsford	Private	July 1, 1864	
William F. Lunsford	Private	July 1, 1864	
David Lykins	Private	Jan. 15, 1865	
Lawrence B. McCoy	Private	Mar. 10, 1864	
John B. McGinnis	Private	July 1, 1864	Aged 67 years
Jacob F. McWhorter	Private	June 30, 1864	
James McWhorter	Private	July 1, 1864	
Robert McWhorter	Private	Mar. 10, 1864	
Hezekiah Morrison	Private	1864	Enl. 7th WV Cavalry Sept. 9, 1864
William Reedy	Private	Mar. 15, 1864	
James W. Rowsey	Private	Jan. 15, 1864	

Name	Rank	Enlisted	Comments
James C. Rowsey	Private	Jan. 15, 1864	
Samuel Sturgeon	Private	Mar. 10, 1864	
James H. Taylor	Private	July 1, 1864	
Andrew J. Wallis (Wallace)	Private	Jan. 10, 1865	
John Wallis (Wallace)	Private	Mar. 1, 1865	
John R. Williams	Private	July 1, 1864	
John Wright	Private	Jan. 15, 1865	
John F. Young	Private	July 1, 1864	
Jeremiah Young	Private	July 1, 1864	

Source: WV Union Home Guards, AR 373, Box 21, WV State Archives.

Appendix B
Captain James W. Bailey's Company
Hurricane Creek Home Guard
Muster Roll June 13, 1863

Name	Rank	Enlisted	Comments
James W. Bailey	Capt.	1861	Mustered in Dec. 29, 1862. Captured Feb. 8, 1863, spent four months in prison. Bailey organized the company in 1861.
George W. Leadmon	1st Lt.	Aug. 1862	Commissioned 2d Lt. Aug. 6, 1862; promoted to 1st Lt. Dec. 23, 1862. Later served in Co. G, 13th WV Infantry
Robert Forth	2d Lt.	Dec. 29, 1862	Formerly 1st Sgt. Paid as private in Dec. 1862 because the company census was below minimum 84 for pay as 2d Lt.
William (Williams) T. Gibson	2d Lt.	Dec. 29, 1862	Elected 2d Lt at Hurricane Creek
Edward C. Bailey	Private	1862	
James Bailey	Private	Dec. 1, 1862	Capt. Bailey's brother
Isham Bailey	Private	Dec. 1, 1862	
James M. Ball	Private	Aug. 1862	Killed by rebels 1863
John H. Ball	Private	Aug. 1862	
John Bowyer	Private	Dec. 29 1862	
Joseph Chapman	Private	Dec. 1861	
Stephen Davis	Private	Aug. 1862	
James C. Forth	Private	Aug. 1861	
Joseph Forth	Private	Aug. 1861	
William S. Forth	Private	Aug. 1861	
Monroe Foster	Private	Aug. 1861	
George Frederick	Private	Aug. 1861	Captured, exchanged at Wheeling Dec. 12, 1861
Cavalry Gibson	Private	Aug. 1861	Killed by the rebels Feb. 8, 1863

Name	Rank	Enlisted	Comments
James F. Gibson	Private	Aug. 1861	
Joseph Holley	Private	1861	
William T. Lunsford	Private	1861	Enl. Co. E, 5th WV, as cook, Aug. 7, 1861, at Ceredo, Va.
Albert Luarles (Laurels)	Private	1861	
Allen Luarles (Laurels)	Private	1861	
Charles Luarles (Laurels)	Private	1861	
George W. Luarles (Laurels)	Private	1861	
Henry Rowsey	Private	1861	
Daniel P. Sarine	Private	1861	
John M. Sarine	Private	Aug. 1861	
Joseph S. Sarine	Private	Aug. 1861	
William H. Sarine	Private	Aug. 1861	
Bartley Smith	Private	1862	
John H. Smith	Private	1861	
George Taylor	Private	1862	
George Thomas	Private	Aug. 1861	

Source: WV Union Home Guards, AR 373, Box 21, WV State Archives.

Appendix C
Captain E.H. Ferguson's Company
First Company
Muster Roll Sept. 4, 1861

Name	Rank	Enlisted	Comments
E.H. Ferguson	Capt.	Sept. 4 1861	
John W. Harrison	1st Lt.	Sept. 4 1861	Elected Sept. 9 1861
Trent Littleberry	2d Lt.	Sept. 4 1861	Elected Sept. 9 1861
Tobias Althouse	1st Sergeant	Sept. 4 1861	
Frank H. Turner	2d Sergeant	Sept. 4 1861	
Henry Hedrick	1st Cpl.	Sept 4 1861	
William Cartwright	2d Cpl.	Sept. 4 1861	
George H. Ferguson	3d Cpl.	Sept. 4 1861	
William Hall	4th Cpl.	Sept. 4 1861	Elected Sept. 4 1861
James Blake	Private	Sept. 1 1861	Not sworn
H.H. Burch	Private	Sept. 1 1861	
Samuel Conaway	Private	Sept. 1 1861	Not sworn
Alfred Doss	Private	Sept. 1 1861	Not sworn
Jordan Dunfield	Private	Sept. 1 1861	Not sworn
William Ferguson	Private	Sept. 4 1861	
Gideon Fisher	Private	Sept. 1 1861	Not sworn
Henry H. Fisher	Private	Sept. 1 1861	Not sworn
V. Gillespie	Private	Sept. 1 1861	Not Sworn
Samuel Hall	Private	Sept. 1 1861	Not Sworn
Henry Harris	Private	Sept. 4 1861	

Name	Rank	Enlisted	Comments
Robert Harris	Private	Sept. 4 1861	
William Harris	Private	Sept. 4 1861	
Josiah Harrison	Private	Sept. 4 1861	
George W. Hedrick	Private	Sept. 1 1861	Not sworn
Frances Hedrick	Private	Sept. 4 1861	
Jacob Hedrick	Private	Sept. 4 1861	
George Higginbotham	Private	Sept. 1 1861	Not sworn
John D. Higginbotham	Private	Sept. 4 1861	Not sworn
Samuel Higginbotham	Private	Sept. 5 1861	Not sworn
George Jones	Private	Sept. 4 1861	
William Jones	Private	Sept. 4 1861	
Columbus Jordan	Private	Sept. 4 1861	
George W. Karnes	Private	Sept. 4 1861	Not sworn
D.F. Kirkpatrick	Private	Sept. 4 1861	
John Knapp	Private	Sept. 4 1861	
James Novell	Private	Sept. 1 1861	Not sworn
L.E. Pierce	Private	Sept. 1 1861	Not sworn
V. Pierce	Private	Sept. 4 1861	
William Pogue	Private	Sept. 4 1861	
John Preddy	Private	Sept. 4 1861	
Thomas Renner	Private	Sept. 4 1861	
C.M. Shank	Private	Sept. 4 1861	Not sworn
R.H. Shank	Private	Sept. 4 1861	
J. Tucker	Private	Sept. 4 1861	

Name	Rank	Enlisted	Comments
William J. Tucker	Private	Sept. 4 1861	
Frances Turner	Private	Sept. 4 1861	
J.J. Walker	Private	Sept. 4 1861	
Wiley W. Walker	Private	Sept. 4 1861	
Thomas Whittington	Private	Sept. 1 1861	Not sworn
William Whittington	Private	Sept. 1 1861	Not sworn
Samuel Woodall	Private	Sept. 4 1861	

Source: WV Union Home Guards, AR 373, Box 21, WV State Archives.

Appendix D
Captain Isaac M. Rucker's Company
Rucker's Second Company
Muster Roll June 20, 1863

Name	Rank	Enlisted	Comments
Andrew H. Blake	Capt.	Aug. 5, 1862	Elected Aug. 16, 1862, crippled Aug. 28, 1862
David Allen Ford	Capt.	Dec. 5, 1861	Elected Dec. 7, 1861, commissioned Feb. 24, 1862
Everett P. Hodges	Capt.	Sept. 5, 1861	Elected Aug. 16, 1862
William H. Hudson	Capt.	Sept. 3, 1861	Elected Aug. 28, 1862
James H. Mines (Mynes)	Capt.	Aug. 11, 1862	Elected Aug. 11 1862
B.P. Morris	Capt.	July 3, 1862	Adjutant, commissioned as mustering officer July 3, 1862
Dr. Edward Naret	Capt.	Aug. 26, 1861	Adjutant. Resigned June 12, 1862. 22nd Brigade, 3rd Div.
Isaac M. Rucker	Capt.	Sept. 5, 1861	Elected Sept. 5, 1861
Clarington D. Sanders	Capt.	Sept. 5, 1861	Elected Sept. 3, 1862, but not commissioned
Anderson Byas (Bias)	1st Lt.	Sept. 3, 1861	Elected Dec. 7, 1861, commissioned Feb. 24, 1862
Samuel C. Robinson	1st Lt.	Aug. 23, 1862	Elected at Buffalo Aug. 23, 1862, comd. Sept. 3, 1862
Robert A. Shank	1st Lt.	Sept. 3, 1862	Elected Sept. 3, 1862
John H. Smith	1st Lt.	Aug. 17, 1862	
Noah H. Young	1st Lt.	Aug. 16, 1862	
Isaac A. Wade	1st Lt.	Sept. 5, 1861	Elected Sept. 5, 1861
John H. Ball	2d Lt.	Sept. 5, 1861	Initially elected 2d Cpl. Sept 5, 1861. Elected 2d Lt. Dec. 28, 1861, commissioned Feb. 24, 1862
James Carr	2d Lt.	Aug. 1862	Elected & commissioned at Buffalo Sept. 3, 1862
William L. Raynes	2d Lt.	Aug. 23, 1862	Elected Sept. 3, 1862

Name	Rank	Enlisted	Comments
Zachariah Scott	2d Lt.	Sept. 5, 1861	Elected Sept. 5, 1861
Alexander S. Young	2d Lt.	Aug. 16, 1862	
Thomas E Ball	1st Sgt	Sept. 5, 1861	
William T. Lunsford	3d Sgt	May 1, 1861	Elected Sept. 5, 1861
Andrew D. Ballinger	4th Sgt	Sept. 5, 1861	
James W. Ball	1st Cpl	Sept. 5, 1861	Elected Dec.
A.M. Ballinger	1st Cpl	Sept. 5, 1861	
James Doss	2d Cpl	Sept. 5, 1861	
Jackson Forth	4th Cpl	Sept. 5, 1861	
James W. Ball	Private	Sept. 5, 1861	Killed by rebels Feb. 1, 1863
Martin Barbour	Private	Sept. 5, 1861	
John Barnes	Private	Sept. 5, 1861	
Allen Bayley (Bailey)	Private	Sept. 5, 1861	
Andrew W. Blake	Private	Sept. 5, 1861	
Jackson W. Blake	Private	Sept. 5, 1861	
William M. Cameron	Private	Sept. 5, 1861	
John H. Chapman	Private	Sept. 5, 1861	
James Coe	Private	Sept. 5, 1861	
Reuben Cox	Private	Sept. 5, 1861	
Thomas C. Davis	Private	Sept. 5, 1861	
Hezekiah Dunn	Private	Sept. 5, 1861	
James T. Dunn	Private	Sept. 5, 1861	
John Dunn	Private	June 20, 1863	

Name	Rank	Enlisted	Comments
Richard Escue	Private	Sept. 5, 1861	
William H. Escue	Private	Sept. 5, 1861	
A.H. Ferguson	Private	Sept. 5, 1861	
Robert Forth	Private	Sept. 5, 1861	
Steven Garten	Private	Sept. 5, 1861	
James W. Gibson	Private	Feb. 1, 1863	
Thomas Gibson	Private	Sept. 5, 1861	
William F. Gibson	Private	Sept. 5, 1861	
Alfred Gillespie	Private	---- 1861	
Sampson Gillespie	Private	---- 1861	
Flemmings Griffith	Private	Sept. 5, 1861	
Isaac H. Hall	Private	Sept. 5, 1861	
Thomas Hall	Private	Sept. 5, 1861	
Edwin Pillow	Private	Sept. 5, 1861	
William D. Pillow	Private	Sept. 5, 1861	
Maryat F. Richards	Private	----- 1861	Not mustered in
George W. Roach	Private	Sept. 5, 1861	
John P. Smith	Private	Sept. 5, 1861	

Source: WV Union Home Guards, AR 373, Box 21, WV State Archives.

Appendix E

Campaigns and Battles Involving Putnam County Soldiers

Antietam/Sharpsburg
Appomattox
Atkeson's Gate
Averell's Raids
Berryville
2nd Bull Run/Manassas
Carnifex Ferry
Cedar Creek
Cedar Mountain
Charleston
Chancellorsville
Cheat Mountain
Cloyd's Mountain
Cross Keys
Cross Lanes
Droop Mountain
Fayetteville
Fredericksburg
Fisher's Hill
Gauley Bridge
Gettysburg
Raid on Guyandotte
Hatcher's Run
Hurricane Bridge
1st & 2nd Kernstown
Lexington
Lewisburg
Lynchburg
McDowell
Petersburg Campaign
Piedmont
Port Republic
Scary Creek
Waynesboro
White Sulphur Springs
1st, 2nd & 3rd Winchester
Raid on Winfield

Notes

Prelude

1. "The First Compromise." *Gallipolis Journal*, August 8, 1861, https://chroniclingamerica.loc.gov.

2. Wintz, William D. *History of Putnam County*. Vol. 1. (Charleston, West Virginia: Pictorial Histories Publishing, 1999), 1-4; 17; 48-51; 56 (hereafter Wintz, Vol. 1); Hubbard, Robert E. *Major General Israel Putnam: Hero of the American Revolution.* (Jefferson, North Carolina: McFarland & Company, 2017), 255-256.

3. *Ibid.*, Wintz, 48-51; 56; 1810 United States Census, National Archives Microfilm Publication M252, Mason & Kanawha County, Virginia schedules, Records of the Bureau of the Census, Record Group 29; Roll 69, National Archives, Washington, D.C.

4. "A Great Lost River Gets Its Due." *New York Times*, November 29, 1983, Online: https://www.nytimes.com/1983; Online: e-WV: The West Virginia Encyclopedia.

5. Wintz, Vol. 1, 160.

6. *Ibid.*

7. The Seventh United States Census: 1850; National Archives Microfilm Publication M432, Putnam County, Virginia schedules, Records of the Bureau of the Census, Record Group 29; Roll 0992, National Archives, Washington, D.C. (s 1850 US Census); The Eighth United States Census: 1860: National Archives Microfilm Publication M653, Putnam County, Virginia schedules, Records of the Bureau of the Census, Record Group 29, Roll 1373, National Archives, Washington, D.C. (hereafter 1860 US Census).

8. Letter from Lawrence Washington to his mother-in-law, Mrs. Comfort Wood, August 27, 1816. Mount Vernon, Virginia: Mount Vernon Ladies Association, 1816. Cited in Wintz, Vol. 1., 53-54.

9. 1850 U.S. Census, Putnam County, Virginia Slave Schedule; 1860 U.S. Census, Virginia Schedules, Putnam County, District 5, RG 29, M653, Roll 1373, National Archives.

10.   Atkeson, Thomas C. & Atkeson, Mary M. *Pioneering in Agriculture: One Hundred Years of American Farming and Farm Leadership*. (New York, NY: Orange Judd Publishing, 1937), 48-49 (hereafter Atkeson, *Pioneering in Agriculture*); Wintz, Vol. 1, 54-56.

11.   *Star of the Kanawha Valley*, May 21, 1860 & July 23, 1860, Newspapers on Microfilm, M-126, WV State Archives; *Official Records of the War of the Rebellion, Series 1*, Vol 2, 59. (hereafter *OR, Series 1*)

12.   *Ibid.*

13.   *Ibid.*, Oct. 18, 1856. Misc. Reels M-54; Wintz, Vol. 1, 67.

14.   *Gallipolis Journal*, December 26, 1861.

15.   *Ibid.*, August 15, 1861.

16.   *Ibid.*, September 12, 1861.

17.   *Star of the Kanawha Valley*, June 4, 1860, Newspapers on Microfilm, M-52, WV State Archives.

18.   *Ibid.*, March 19, 1861. Vol 6, 2. Online Library of Virginia: https://virginiachronicle.com.

19.   *Ibid.*, April 9, 1861, Newspapers on Microfilm, M-52, WV State Archives.

20.   Wallenstein, P. *Cradle of America: Four Centuries of Virginia History*. (Lawrence, Kansas: University Press of Kansas, 2007), 169-173. (hereafter Wallenstein)

21.   *Ibid.*

22.   Williams, John A. *West Virginia: A History*. (Morgantown: WVU Press, 2001), 35-43; 46 (hereafter Williams); *Daily Intelligencer*, December 25, 1860, Chronicling America, Library of Congress (hereafter *Daily Intelligencer*); Mellott, D. W. and Snell, M.A. *The Seventh West Virginia Infantry: An Embattled Union Regiment from the Civil War's Most Divided State*. (Lawrence, Kansas: University of Kansas Press, 2019), 8; 35-43. (hereafter Mellott & Snell)

23.   *Grafton Guardian*, April 24, 1861, Chronicling America, Library of Congress.

24.   Mellott & Snell, 46.

25.   Biographical information for Sarah Harris Dickerson Froe. Tazewell Library Photographs Collection, Album Part 1, (1999), Call No. V210227, 227. Library of Virginia, Richmond, Virginia.

26.   Miller, O.R. "Go Where, this is my Home." Unpublished manuscript, October 1998. Courtesy Sandy Miller Larch; The Ninth Decennial Census of the United States: 1870; Records of the Bureau of the Census, Putnam County, West Virginia Population Schedules, Record Group 29, Microfilm Publication M593, Roll 1702, (T132, 255B), National Archives (hereafter 1870 US Census); The Tenth Decennial Census of the United States: 1880; Records of the Bureau of the Census, Putnam County, West Virginia Population Schedules, Record Group 29, Microfilm Publication T9, Roll 1412, National Archives (hereafter 18870 US Census).

27.   Conner, Fred. "The Part Taken by Putnam Co. W.Va. During the War 1861-65 by Fred Conner, faithful servant of the 36th Virginia Infantry." Civil War Manuscripts, MS 79-18, No. 6, WV Archives, 1-3; 6-7. (hereafter Conner)

Chapter 1

1.   *Acts of the General Assembly of the State of Virginia passed in 1861*. No. 1. Resolutions upon the subject of the Coercion of a State. Adopted January 8, 1861. (Richmond, VA: William F. Ritchie, public printer, 1861).

2.   Wintz, Vol. 1, 67; *Acts of the General Assembly of the State of Virginia passed in 1861*. No. 3. *Joint Resolutions inviting the other States to send Commissioners to meet Commissioners on the part of Virginia and providing for the appointment of the same. Adopted January 19, 1861*. (Richmond, VA: William F. Ritchie, public printer, 1861) (hereafter Acts of the General Assembly 1861).

3.   West Virginia Sesquicentennial Online: http://www.wvculture.org.

4.   Wintz, Vol. 1, 67; "Judge Summers of Kanawha." *Gallipolis Journal*, January 9, 1862.

5.   Solomon Minsker Family Letters, Civil War Manuscripts, PL 2004-109, West Virgina State Archives (hereafter Minsker); National Register of Historic Places Registration Form: (June 14, 2007), James W. Hoge House. US Department of the Interior, National Park Service, 2-9. (hereafter Hoge House National Register)

6.   Governor John Letcher Executive Papers, Letter to Letcher from Robert Trigg Harvey of Buffalo, April 22, 1861. Accession No. 36787, Box 30, Folder 1, Correspondence April 1861. Library of Virginia.

7.   Squires, Duane J. "Lincoln and West Virginia Statehood." *West Virginia History*, Vol. 24(4), (July 1963). Online article: http: www.wvarchives.gov.; Granville Parker. *The Formation of the State of West Virginia*. (Wellsburg, WV: Glass & Son Publishers, 1975), 1-5.

8.   DeGruyter, Julius. *The Kanawha Spectator*, Part 2: Backdrop. (Charleston, West Virginia: Willard H. Ervin, Publisher, 1976), 28-37.

9.   Conner, 7-8.

10.   Boatner, Mark M. *The Civil War Dictionary*. (New York: McKay, 1959; revised 1988), 123-124; Sutherland, Daniel E. *A Savage Conflict: The Decisive Role of Guerrillas in the American Civil War*. (Chapel Hill, NC: UNC Press, 2009), 65-67; 319-325; OR, Series 1, Vol. 2, 195-196; Curry, R. O. & Ham, G. "The Bushwhacker's War: Insurgency and Counter-Insurgency in West Virginia." *Civil War History*, Vol. 10(4), (December 1964), 416-433.

11.   *United States. War Department. The War of the Rebellion: A Compilation of the Official Records of the Union and Confederate Armies*. Washington, 1894. Series 1, Vol. 2, Part 1, 674; 679. (hereafter OR)

12.   Turk, Daniel S. *The Union Hole: Unionist Activity and Local Conflict in Western Virginia.* (Bowie, Maryland: Heritage Books, 1994), 28-29, 30-32. (hereafter Turk)

13.   *OR, Series 1*, Vol. 2, Part 3, 673.

14.   *Ibid.*, Part 1, 674; 679; Records of Colonial Militia through World War I, circa 1936. MS80-22, West Virginia State Archives, 5-11 (hereafter Records of Colonial Militia through WW1); Militia Called into Service: June 11, 1861: An Ordinance of the Convention Assembled at Wheeling, June 11, 1861. Cited in Records of Colonial Militia through World War 1, 46-47.

15.   West Virginia Adjutant General Papers, Union Regiments 1861-1865, AR 383; Box 36; Broadsides and Oversized Items, No. 3. House Bill No. 5 Broadside, June 1861, West Virginia State Archives. (hereafter WV AG Papers)

16.   John V. Young Pension Files: Pauline Young, Widow of Captain John V. Young, testimony for Pension Claim, February 1, 1871: filed by C. Mollohan, Attorney At Law, Gallipolis, Ohio, with the U.S. Department of the Interior Veteran's Pensions Claims Office. Union Soldier Pension Files, MT288 Roll 542, US National Archives; Young's Pension File contains a letter from C. Mollohan, Attorney, of July 22, 1867 stating that he was already in active service for several months on date of his commission, November 15, 1861; Griffith, Joe. *History of Company G, 11th West Virginia Volunteer Infantry From Coalsmouth to Richmond, 1862-1865.* (Roswell, GA: Self-published monograph, 1995), 225 (hereafter Griffith); Diary of Sarah Francis Young 1861-1862. West Virginia Regional History Collection, Roy Bird Cook Collection, Call No. AM 1651, WVU Library. Morgantown, WV. (hereafter Sarah F. Young Diary)

17.   *OR, Series 1*, Vol. 2, Part 1, 679.

18.   WV AG Papers, AR 373, Union Militia, 1861-1865, Captain Edward Naret Letters, Box 21, Folder 1, 181st Regiment Virginia Militia. West Virginia State Archives (hereafter Naret Letters); Griffith, 225-226; Virginia Adjutant General's Office Papers, Call No. Mss12, Adjutant General's Order dated Feb. 3, 1849 establishing the 181st Regiment Virginia Militia in Putnam County. Copy of original document courtesy of John Edmondson Norvell, Richmond, Va., 28 October 1968. Virginia Historical Society, Richmond, VA.

19.   Callahan, James M. *History of West Virginia: Old & New and West Virginia Biography.* (Chicago, IL: American Historical Society, 1923), 114; Birth record, 2 fructidor an VIII (20 August 1800), Montceaux-lès-Provins, Seine-et-Marne, France; Death record, April 18, 1812, Montceaux-lès-Provins, Seine-et-Marne, France; Death record, September 26, 1815, Montceaux-lès-Provins, Seine-et-Marne, France; 1820, 1830 and 1860 United States Census; Commencement records, University of Pennsylvania, March 24, 1831; West Virginia Marriages 1853-1970 and Death Records: www. pilot.familysearch.org; Family record of marriage contract drawn up between Edouard Naret and Benoite Henriette Pitrat was dated March 25, 1843; Naret Letters; Gallia County Ohio Probate Court, probation of Last Will and Testament of Benoite Henriette Naret, August 20, 1862; National Register of Historic Places Registration Form, dated June 26, 1991, "Buffalo Townsquare Historic District," Section 8, p. 2. Library of Congress.

20.   *Ibid.*

21. *Ibid.*, Naret Letters: Captain Naret to H. J. Samuels, February 17 & 28, 1862.

22. *Ibid.*, Letter from S. H. Grose to H. J. Samuels August 19, 1862, September 2 & 4, & 26, 1861; Naret Resignation Letter, June 12, 1862.

23. WV AG Papers, AR 373, Box 34, Miscellaneous Files, Folder 9, WV State Archives.

24. WV AG Papers, AR 373, Union Militia 1861 to 1865, Box 21, Folders 1-5; 9 & 10, 181st Regiment Virginia Militia, Captain E. Naret letter to H.J. Samuels, February 17, 1862, WV Archives; Linger, James C. *Confederate Military Units of West Virginia.* (Tulsa, OK: Self-published Monograph, Revised Ed., 1990), 2-23; 59-82; WV AG Papers, Union Militia, AR373, Box 33, Misc. 1, Folder 14, WV State Archives.

25. Hoge, James C. "Who He Was: James W. Hoge, Putnam Judge." Unpublished Manuscript, Hoge House National Historic Site, Winfield, West Virginia, 1-3; James W. Hoge House, National Register, West Virginia Landmarks, January 21, 2007. ID No. 86536037. National Archives, Washington D.C.; United States Department of the Interior, National Register of Historic Places Registration Form 10-900 for Putnam County Court House, May 31, 2000, ID No. B3fea499-74ca-45c3-8fb7-f49921f279c5. National Park Service, National Register of Historic Places Collection, Lakewood, CO (hereafter Hoge House National Register); 1860 U.S. Census Slave Schedules, Putnam County, Virginia.

26. Wintz, William D. "Putnam County." Online: e-WV: The West Virginia Encyclopedia. 03 June 2013. Web. 18 May 2020. https://www.wvencyclopedia.org; Rowe, Alan R. & Jim Hines. (Nov. 19, 1999); Hoge House National Register; "The Putnam County Court House Story, Installment I." *The Putnam Democrat*, July 25, 1958. Newspapers on Microfilm, Misc. Reels, Roll M101, WV State Archives.

27. Naret Letters: Naret to H. J. Samuels, February 17 & 28, 1862; WV AG Papers, AR 382, Box 2/2, Militia Muster Rolls. WV State Archives; WV AG Papers, Union Regiments, 13th West Virginia Files, AR 382, Folder 7, WV State Archives (hereafter 13th WV Files); 1860 US Census.

28. Records of the Colonial Militia through World War I, 50-53; Wallace, L.A., Jr. *A Guide to Virginia Military Organizations 1861-1865.* (Lynchburg, VA: H.E. Howard, 1986), 234-235.

29. Egan, Michael. *The Flying Gray-Haired Yank or the Adventures of a Volunteer.* (Leesburg, VA: D.L. Phillips (Ed.), Gauley Press, 1992), 19-38. (hereafter Egan)

30. Naret Letters: Naret to H. J. Samuels, September 6, 1861.

31. *The Weekly Register*, March 24, 1864; WV AG Papers, Union Militia, AR 373, Captain Isaac

Rucker's Company Muster Roll, Drawer 158 & Box 21, Folders 11-13. WV State Archives; CSR, RG 94, M508, Roll 80, National Archives.

32. WV AG Papers, Union Militia, AR 373, Box 21, Folders 3, 5-7, 11, WV State Archives; WV AG Papers, AR 382, Box 2/2, Militia Muster Rolls. WV Archives; 13th WV files.

33. *Ibid.*, Union Militia, Folder 7.

34.   Governor Francis Pierpont Telegrams, 1861-1865. Lucien Loeser to Pierpont, December 30, 1861, Collection No. 19W86&67, West Virginia Regional History Center, WVU Library, Morgantown, WV; Lang, Theodore F. *Loyal West Virginia 1861-1865*. (Baltimore, Maryland: Deutsch Printing Co., 1895), 226-227; *History of Buffalo*, Vol. 1, 11.

35.   William A. Whiting of Buffalo was captured at the second battle of Bull Run on August 30, 1862, and listed on muster rolls as missing in action, but was later paroled. Whiting was again captured in action at Covington, Virginia, on December 19, 1863, and taken to the prison at Andersonville, Georgia, on February 10, 1864. According to the affidavit of William W. and James H. Garnett of Jackson County, West Virginia, two brothers who were sergeants in the 8th West Virginia Infantry, Whiting's capture occurred, "while in the line of duty on foot with the ambulance and wagon train, coming back from Salem and near the bridge on Jackson's River in the state of Virginia, was with a large number of other soldiers taken prisoner by the Rebels, and the said William A. Whiting never returned." William Whiting died in prison of dysentery on July 25, 1864. Whiting was born in Allegheny County, Virginia, to James and Nancy Whiting, who married in March 1830 at White Rock Gap, Virginia. James left Nancy just prior to the birth of their youngest child in 1851. According to the testimony of Abraham Armentrout and Ruth M. Rose, who knew the family well for fifteen years, James had abandoned his family in the company of a "woman of ill repute." Whiting's father later moved to one of the western territories and died several years later. His mother afterward took her four children to Monroe County, Virginia, then relocated to a small cabin located on the farm of Thomas H. Markham in Putnam County in 1858, near the eastern base of Coal Mountain. At that time, William was fifteen. Markham hired him as a laborer on his farm and paid his mother his wages. In 1860, they moved to the farm of John Young, about one mile distant. Nancy Whiting filed to receive a government pension for William's military service in May 1865. Nancy was awarded a pension of $8 per month. CSR, RG 94, M508, Roll 83, National Archives; US Pension Files 1861-1934, Box 33900, Microfilm T288, Roll 514, Application for Pension No. 95.545, Nancy Whiting for William Whiting. Washington, DC: National Archives.

36.   Raines, Matthew J. "Progress Mill." Clio Guide to History. May 3, 2017. Online: https://www.theclio.com/tour. See also Hale, John P. *History of the Great Kanawha Valley*. (Madison, WI: Brant, Fuller & Co., 1891, Reprint, Gauley & New River Pub. 1994) (hereafter Hale, *History of the Great Kanawha Valley*); James Hardesty. *Hardesty's Historical and Geographical Encyclopedia*. Vol. 1. (Chicago: H. H. Hardesty, 1883, Reprint, Richwood: Comstock, Hardesty West Virginia Counties, 1973), 223-224.

37.   *Ibid.*, Raines. "Buffalo Presbyterian Church" and "Buffalo Academy"; Wintz, William D. *Annals of the Great Kanawha*. (Charleston: Pictorial Histories Publishing Company, 1993), 73-78. (hereafter Wintz, *Annals of the Great Kanawha*)

38.   Wintz, Vol. 2, 69.

39.   CSR, RG94, M322, 16th Missouri Infantry, Roll 166, National Archives; Bronaugh, W.C. *The Younger's Fight for Freedom: A Southern Soldier's Twenty Year's Campaign to Open Northern Prison Doors – with Anecdotes of War Days*. (Columbia, Missouri: E.W. Stephens Publishing, 1906), 15-18, 27-35, 246-250; "Gen. Warren C. Bronaugh, U.C.V." *Confederate Veteran*, (1923), Vol. 31, 225.

40.   Abel Propst Sinnett Collection, 1880-1991 Letters, Notebook, MS2002-050, Box 3, Folder 26, WV State Archives; Jubal A. Early. *Major General Jubal Anderson Early, C.S.A. Autobiographical Sketch and*

Narrative of the War Between the States. (Philadelphia, PA: J.B. Lippincott & Co., 1912), xxii-xxiii; See also: Benjamin Franklin Cooling III, *Jubal Early: Robert E. Lee's "Bad Old Man"* (Lanham, MD: Rowman and Littlefield, 2014), 6-7; "Jubal Anderson Early and his ties to Putnam County."

41.   Jubal Anderson Early Papers: Chronological File, 1829-1911; 1841, Dec. 2-1861, Jan. 21. Manuscripts Division, Collection No. MSS19356, Box 2. This collection contains several letters written by Jubal Early and his father, Joab Early mentioning the plantation known as Westview in Mason County; this area became part of Putnam County in 1848.

42.   *Ibid.*; *Charleston Gazette*, August 28, 2003; *Hurricane Breeze*, November 20, 2003.

43.   Lowry, Terry. *22nd Virginia Infantry*, (Lynchburg, VA: H.E. Howard, 1988), 6-7, 127; 5-6 (hereafter Lowry, *22nd Virginia Infantry*); Michael J. Pauley. *Unreconstructed Rebel: The Life of General John McCausland, C.S.A.* (Charleston, WV: Pictorial Histories Publishing, 1993), 1-3.

44.   Harden, James. A. Civil War Letters, 1861-1865 [Digital]. Virginia Military Institute Archives. https://archivespace.vmi.edu/repositories/3/digital_objects/150 Accessed December 25, 2020.

45.   Lowry, *22nd Virginia Infantry*, 5-6; Pauley, 3-5; McMurray, Richard M. *Virginia Military Institute in the Civil War.* (Lynchburg, VA: H.E. Howard, 1999), 27, 165 (hereafter McMurray).

46.   Foster, Jack. Letter to former Confederate General John McCausland, December 13, 1883. (Ms2008-018), Virginia Tech Special Collections and University Archives Online, accessed Dec. 25, 2020, http://digitalsc.lib.vt.edu/AmericanCivilWar.

47.   Lowry, *22nd Virginia Infantry*, 5-6; OR, Series 1, Vol. 2, 788.

48.   *Ibid.*, Lowry, 2-3; Pauley, 6.

49.   Scott, James L. *36th Virginia Infantry.* (Lynchburg, VA: H.E. Howard, 1987), 4-6 (hereafter Scott); Ezra J. Warner (hereafter Warner, Generals in Gray) *Generals in Gray: Lives of the Confederate Commanders.* (Baton Rouge, LA: Louisiana State University Press, 1959, Reprinted 1987), 197-198; CSR, 36th Virginia Infantry, RG 94, M324, Roll 827, National Archives; Pauley, 77.

50.   *Ibid.*, Scott, 3-4, 43-44; Pauley, 6-8, 77-91; Warner, 197-198; Confederate Military Records, 1859-1865, Accession No. 27684, Series II, Infantry Regiments: 36th Virginia Infantry, Box 25, Folder 1, Library of Virginia, Richmond, VA (Hereafter 36th Virginia Infantry Records, Library of Virginia); *Kanawha Valley Star*, May 11, 1861. Vol. 7, SN 85059862, Newspaper Reading Room, Library of Congress, Washington DC.

51.   *Ibid.*

52.   Lowry, *22nd Virginia Infantry*, 5-6; "Death of Colonel George Patton." *Richmond Daily Dispatch.* October 3, 1864, Chronicling America, Library of Congress; Bruce Allardace. *Confederate Colonels: a Biographical Register.* (Columbia, MO: University of Missouri Press, 2008), 300; Letter from Lieutenant Colonel John McCausland to Governor John Letcher, May 28, 1861. Civil War Manuscript Collections, Governor John Letcher Papers, 1770-1970, Mss1-L5684 a FA2, Series 6, Folders 364-431, Virginia

Historical Society, Richmond, Virginia. (hereafter McCausland Letter to Governor John Letcher, May 28, 1861). George Smith Patton was born on June 26, 1833, in Fredericksburg, Virginia and grew up in Richmond. His father, John Mercer Patton, was a well-respected politician. George attended the Virginia Military Institute and graduated in 1852 ranked second in a class of twenty-four cadets. Afterward, he studied law in Richmond, and was admitted to the bar in 1855 prior to relocating to Charleston, [West] Virginia.

53.   CSR, RG 94, M324, Roll 830, National Archives; Cadet Fife, William E. Quarterly Grade Report, April 1, 1852, MS-0345, Virginia Military Institute Archives, Lexington, Virginia.

54.   *Ibid.*, CSR; "L.J. Timms." *Confederate Veteran*, (January 1918), Vol. 26, 261.

55.   CSR, RG 94, M324, Roll 823, National Archives; "James D. Farrar." *Confederate Veteran*, (1921), Vol. 29, 309.

56.   CSR, RG 94, M324, Roll 821, National Archives; Hitner, J.K. "The Bryan Boys." *Confederate Veteran*, (1923), Vol. 31, 108.

57.   Harlan H. Hinkle. *Grayback Mountaineers: The Confederate Face of Western [West] Virginia.* (New York: Universe, Inc. Publishing, 2003), 165-166; CSR, RG 94, M324, Rolls 821 and 823, National Archives. Alfred Beckett was hospitalized at Lynchburg Virginia July 5-12, 1862 for an unspecified Illness. https://about.usps.com/who/profile/history/postmaster-finder/postmasters-by-city.htm

58.   Letter to the Editor by Alfred Beckett written May 8, 1861 at Hurricane Bridge. *Star of the Kanawha Valley*, May 14, 1861, M-52, WV State Archives.

59.   CSR, RG94, M324, Roll 821, National Archives; 36th Virginia Infantry Records, Buffalo Guards (Co. A); Box 25, Folder 1, Library of Virginia; Confederate Military Records, 1859-1865, Accession No. 27684, Series I, Cavalry Regiments: 8th Virginia Cavalry, Box 15, Folders 36-45, Library of Virginia, Richmond, VA. (hereafter 8th Virginia Cavalry Records, Library of Virginia)

60.   Peter W. Fizer, Jr.: CSR, RG94, M324, roll 823, National Archives; William Fizer: CSR RG 94, 36th Battalion Virginia Cavalry (Sweeney's Battalion), M324, Roll 194, National Archives. Peter Fizer, Jr. was born November 7, 1822 at Pulaski County, Virginia and died on March 3, 1907; Sowards, Gloria E. Family Interviews with Peter W. Fizer, Jr., Beckett's Company, 36th Virginia Infantry regarding his wartime experiences left for his descendants. (1947. Unpublished typescript), courtesy Melissa Fizer Conley. (hereafter Interview with Peter W. Fizer, Jr.) James Tackett enlisted in Company G, 13th West Virginia Volunteer Infantry on April 17, 1862 at Coalsmouth. Company G was later affiliated with the 11th West Virginia Volunteer Infantry in March 1864; See: CSR, RG 94, 11th West Virginia Infantry, M508, Roll 195, National Archives.

61.   Scott, James L. *36th and 37th Battalions Virginia Cavalry.* (Lynchburg, Virginia: H.E. Howard, 1986), 1-2; 1860 US Census.

62.   CSR, RG 94, M324, Roll 830, National Archives; Sterrett Family Records, 1807-1884, Accession No. 1982/09.0368, Marshall University Library Special Collections, Huntington, WV; Sterrett Family

Collection, Civil War Manuscripts, AR373, Ms81-30, Box 2, Folder 27, WV State Archives; *Charleston Daily Mail*, August 13, 1973: Clipping from Carolyn H. Frazier Collection, Ms84-210, WV State Archives.

63.   *Ibid.*

64.   CSR, RG 94, M508, Roll 81, National Archives; Buffalo Historical Society. *History of Buffalo, Volume 1: The Beginning to 1900.* (St. Albans, West Virginia: Harless Printing, 1993), (hereafter History of Buffalo, Vol. 1) Note some sources erroneously place Charles E. Shank in Company D, 7th West Virginia Cavalry.

65.   CSR, RG 94, M324, Roll 650, National Archives.

66.   Benaniah F. Handley: CSR, RG 94, M324, Roll 650, National Archives; Wintz, Vol. 2, 127-128; Henry G. Handley: CSR, RG 94, M324, Roll 83, National Archives.

67.   Wintz, William D. "The Fabulous Handley Family." *The Vandalia Journal*, (Charleston, WV: Upper Vandalia Historical Society, October 1996), 4-12.

68.   Wintz, William D. (Ed.). *Recollections and Reflections of Mollie Hansford: 1828-1900.* (Charleston, WV: Quick Copy Press, 1976), 26-27 (hereafter Hansford Recollections); Wintz, *History of Putnam County*, Vol. 2, 127-130.

69.   *Ibid.*, Wintz, Vol. 2, 69-71; 1860 United States Census; McCausland Letter to Governor John Letcher, May 28, 1861.

70.   Lowry, *22nd Virginia Infantry*, 6-7, 127; CSR, RG 94, M324, Roll 647, National Archives; Confederate Military Records, 1859-1864, Accession No. 27684, Series II, Unit Records, Subseries 3, Infantry, 22nd Virginia Infantry, Folders 52, 53, 59 and 62. Library of Virginia, Richmond, Virginia (hereafter 22nd Virginia Infantry Records, Library of Virginia); Wintz, Vol. 2, 70-71; "From Charleston." *Daily Intelligencer*, August 2, 1861, Vol. 10(4), 2.

71.   *Ibid.*, Wintz Vol. 2, 70-71.

72.   CSR, RG 94, M324, Roll 647, National Archives; 22nd Virginia Infantry Records, Library of Virginia; Lowry, *22nd Virginia Infantry*, 6-7, 127.

73.   Hale, *History of the Great Kanawha Valley*, 20; Wintz, Vol. 2, 70-71; *The Weekly Register*, October 15, 1874.

74.   Lowry, *22nd Virginia Infantry*, 6-7; John Morgan. *The Last Dollar.* (St. Albans, WV: St. Albans Historical Society, 2002), 2-3 (hereafter Morgan, *Last Dollar*); CSR, RG94, M324, Roll 827, National Archives. John Morgan was killed in action near Fayetteville, Virginia, on September 10, 1862, as Major General William Loring's force of some 6,000 Confederates advanced on Charleston.

75.   8th Virginia Cavalry Records, Library of Virginia; Confederate Military Records, 1859-1864, Accession No. 27684, Series II, Unit Records, 16th Virginia Cavalry, Boxes 35-45, and, Company D, Box 58, Library of Virginia, Richmond, VA (hereafter 16th Virginia Cavalry Records, Library of Virginia);

Jack L. Dickinson, *8th Virginia Cavalry* (Lynchburg, VA: H.E. Howard, 1986), (hereafter Dickinson, *8th Virginia Cavalry*); Jack L. Dickinson, *16th Virginia Cavalry* (Lynchburg, VA: H.E. Howard, 1989), (hereafter Dickinson, *16th Virginia Cavalry*).

76.   Lowry, *22nd Virginia Infantry*, 6-11; Terry Lowry. *The Battle of Scary Creek*. (Charleston WV: Pictorial Histories Publishing, 1982), 22-29; 33 (hereafter Lowry, *Scary Creek*).

77.   *"Star of the Kanawha Valley."* Online Library of Virginia: https://virginiachronicle.com; Munn, Robert F. Index to the Press of the Kanawha Valley 1855-1865. Unpublished Monograph, 1966, 115. West Virginia Regional History Collection, Call Number PN899.K33M8. WVU Library, Morgantown, WV.

78.   *Ibid.*

79.   *Ibid.*; CSR, RG 109, M324, Roll 828, National Archives; 36th Virginia Records, Library of Virginia.

80.   *OR, Series* 1, Vol. 2, 48-49.

81.   *Ibid.*, 49.

82.   *Ibid.*, 908-909; *Ironton Register*, June 19, 1861; Geiger, Joseph Jr. *Disorder on the Border: Civil Warfare in Cabell & Wayne Counties, 1856-1870*. (Charleston, WV: 35th Star Publishing 2020), 45-46 (hereafter Geiger, *Disorder on the Border*).

83.   Lowry, *22nd Virginia Infantry*, 2-3; Otis K. Rice. *The Hatfield's & McCoys*. (Lexington, Kentucky: University Press of Kentucky, 2010), 10-11; Virginia Infantry, Logan County Wildcats, Logbook, 1830-1900. Accession No. 1977/11.0206 (MS-59) Marshall University Special Collections (MUSC), Marshall University Library, Huntington, WV; Scott, 2-3; 36th Virginia Records, Library of Virginia; CSR, 36th Virginia Infantry, RG 94, M324, Roll 824, National Archives; 36th Virginia Infantry Records, Library of Virginia; Pauley, 6-8; CSR, RG 94, M324, Roll 827, National Archives.

84.   *OR*, Series 1, Vol. 2, Part 1, 674; 679.

85.   *Ibid.*, 673. Militia Called into Service: June 11, 1861. An Ordinance of the Convention Assembled at Wheeling, June 11, 1861. Cited in Records of Colonial Militia through World War 1, 46.

86.   *Ibid.*, *OR*, 673.

87.   *Ibid.*, *OR*, 679; WV AG Papers, Union Regiments 1861-1865, AR 383; Box 36; Broadsides and Oversized Items, No. 3. House Bill No. 5 Broadside, June 1861, WV Archives (hereafter House Bill No. 5).

88.   *Ibid.*, House Bill No. 5.

89.   *OR, Series* 1, Vol. 2, 713.

90.   Records of Colonial Militia through WW1, 5-11.

91.   *OR, Series* 1, Vol. 2, 196.

92.   *Ibid.*, 723-724.

93.   WV AG Papers, AR 382, Box Number 2. Letter from S. H. Grose to H. J. Samuels August 19, 1862; Naret Letters: Resignation June 12, 1862; September 2 & 4, & 26, 1861.

94.   *OR, Series 1*, Vol. 2, 293.

95.   Cox, Jacob D. *Military Reminisces, of the Civil War, Vol. 1, April 1861–November 1863.* (Great Britain: Hard Press Books, 2016), 119-122; (hereafter Cox, Vol. 1) Jacob Dolson Cox. *Military Reminiscences of the Civil War, Vol. 5.* (Cincinnati, OH: Cochran Publishing, October 1900, Reprinted by Kessinger Publishing, Whitefish, MT, 2008), 26; 34; 58; (hereafter Cox, Vol. 5); Eugene D Schmiel. *Citizen-General: Jacob Dolson Cox and the Civil War Era.* (Athens, Ohio: Ohio University Press, 2014), 225-248; (hereafter Schmiel) CSR, RG 94, M508, Roll 206, National Archives.

96.   *Ibid.*, Cox, Vol., 1, 120-121.

97.   Burdette, William A. "Burdette Family History." Unpublished manuscript delivered to the Hon. Joe F. Burdette, West Virginia Secretary of State, February 25, 1959. Courtesy Imogene Burdette, Hurricane WV.

98.   Diary of Sarah F. Young, July 13, 1861.

99.   *Ibid.*

100.   Mansfield, William L. "History of the Civil War in Wayne County." Lambert Family Papers, Ms-76A, Box 1, Marshall University Special Collections, Huntington, WV; Geiger, *Disorder on the Border*, 65-66.

101.   Wintz, Vol. 2, 2-3, 79.

102.   *Ibid.*; Thomas C. Atkeson Biography: attached to a portrait of him held at the West Virginia University Library, Regional History Collection, Call. No. A&M 1010, ID No. 027038.

103.   *Biographical Directory of the United States Congress 1774-1903, House Doc. 108-142*, (Washington, DC: U.S. Government Printing Office, 1903), 654; Biography Online: www.poplarheightsfarm.org; 1870 US Census.

104.   Wintz, *Annals of the Great Kanawha*; Wintz, William D. "Putnam County." Online: e-WV: The West Virginia Encyclopedia. 03 June 2013. Web. Accessed 18 May 2020. https://www.wvencyclopedia.org.

105.   *Pomeroy Weekly Telegraph*, July 19 & 26, 1861. Vol 4(33), 2-3. Chronicling America Series, Library of Congress.

106.   Cox, Vol. 1, 121-122; Vol. 5, 26-30.

107.   "Men of Kanawha." *Gallipolis Journal*, Thurs. Aug. 15, 1861.

108.   Hamblinton, James P. *A Biographical Sketch of Henry A. Wise*. (Richmond, VA: J.W. Randolph, 1856), xxvi-xxviii, xxxiv-xxxviii, 8-28; Warner, 341-342.

109.   Cox, Vol. 1, 119-122; Vol. 5., 26; 34; 58; Schmiel, 225-248; CSR, RG 94, M508, Roll 206, National Archives.

110.   Lowry, Scary Creek, 45-46, 98.116-117; Richard Andre, Stan Cohen, & William Wintz. *Bullets and Steel: The Fight for the Great Kanawha Valley 1861-1865*. (Charleston, WV: Pictorial Histories Publishing, 1995), 54-60 (hereafter Andre, et al., *Bullets and Steel*)

111.   Diary of Victoria Hansford Teays, September 22, 1861. Boyd Stutler Collection, MS78-1, Series 1, No. 8, WV Archives. (hereafter Hansford Diary).

112.   Lowry, Scary Creek, 104; Hansford Diary, July 8, 1861; William D. Wintz. *Civil War Memoirs of two Rebel sisters*. (Charleston, WV: Pictorial Histories Publishing, 1989) 25-26. (hereafter Wintz, *Memoirs*); Wintz, Vol. 2, 220.

113.   Sarah F. Young Diary, July 17, 1861.

114.   Thompson, Cameron L. "The Battle of Scary Creek, and Some incidents of it." (April 1917). Manuscript Collection, Ms80-307, 2. WV State Archives (hereafter Thompson, Scary Creek); CSR, RG 94, M324, Roll 654, National Archives; Ward, James E.D. *Twelfth Ohio Volunteer Infantry*. (Ripley, OH: NP, 1864), 27. Original copy in private collection. (hereafter Ward, *Twelfth Ohio*)

115.   Letter from First Sergeant John U. Hiltz, Co. C, 12th Ohio Volunteer Infantry, *Clermont Courier* (Ohio), August 7, 1861, Vol. 123(32), 3. SN 83035427, Library of Congress.

116.   Atkeson-Morgan Family Papers, A&M 3372, Box 1, Folder 1a, Civil War Letters, West Virginia & Regional History Collection, West Virginia University Library, Morgantown, WV (hereafter Atkeson-Morgan Family Papers); Wintz, Vol. 2, 191-192; CSR, RG 94, M324, Roll 652, National Archives, Washington, DC; Lowry, 22nd Virginia Infantry, 178-179; 22nd Virginia Infantry Records, Library of Virginia; Morgan, *Last Dollar*, 1-2.

117.   *Ibid*.

118.   "The Kanawha Campaign: 18 miles from Charleston." *New York Times*, July 27, 1861. *New York Times* archive online: https://timesmachine.nytimes.com. Accessed December 20, 2020.

119.   "From the Kanawha." *Western Reserve Chronicle*, July 31, 1861. Chronicling America Series, Library of Congress.

120.   *Thompson, Scary Creek, 3; Western Reserve Chronicle*, July 31, 1861.

121.   *Roster of Ohio Soldiers*, Vol. 1, 733-744; Sedinger, James D. "Diary of a Border Ranger." *West Virginia History*, Vol. 51, 1992, 55-78; (hereafter Sedinger Diary); Wartime Reminiscences of James D. Sedinger, Company E, 8th Virginia Cavalry, (Border Rangers), July 17, 1861 & April 20, 1861. West Virginia Archives Manuscript Collection, MS78-1, Series 1, WV State Archives. (hereafter Sedinger Wartime

Reminiscences); Mervin R. Shirey. (Edited by Neil Richardson), *The Battle of Scary Creek: July 17, 1861.* (St. Albans Historical Society, St. Albans, WV: Dawson Printing Company, 1932, Reprinted 2014, 17. (hereafter Shirey, *Scary Creek*); *New York Times*, July 27, 1861.

122. *Western Reserve Chronicle*, July 31, 1861; Thompson, *Scary Creek*, 4.

123. *New York Times*, July 27, 1861.

124. Letter from First Sergeant John U. Hiltz, Co. C, 12th Ohio Volunteer Infantry, *Clermont Courier*, August 7, 1861, Vol. 123(32), 3. SN 83035427, Library of Congress.

125. *Ibid.*

126. Elijah Beeman Letters, 1861-1862. Marshall University Special Collections, Civil War Manuscripts, Accession No. 1979/03.0250, Marshall University Morrow Library, Huntington, WV. Elijah Beeman enlisted in Company A, 12th Ohio Volunteer Militia on April 20, 1861 as a private, at age nineteen years, for three months service at Camp Jackson, Ohio. The regiment mustered into United States Service for three years on May 30, 1861 as the 12th Ohio Volunteer Infantry at Camp Dennison Ohio. Beeman died on September 23, 1862 and is buried at Whitacre Cemetery in Warren County, Ohio; Ward, *Twelfth Ohio*, 28; Howe, James C. Adjutant General. CSR, RG 94, M552, Roll 66, National Archives; *Roster of Ohio Soldiers*, Vol. 3, 21st-36th Regiments Infantry, 585; William Ludwig, Correspondence & Record Book, 1861-1865, Collection No. A&M2318, West Virginia Regional History Collection, WVU Library, Morgantown, WV. Sergeant William Ludwig re-enlisted and mustered into service on September 13, 1864, at the expiration of his first three year term. (hereafter Ludwig); *Roster of Ohio Soldiers*, Vol. 2, 255; 258.

127. "Battle of Scary Creek as told by Kanawha Rifleman Levi Welch." *West Virginia Historical Quarterly*, Vol. 1(1), (January 1901), 12-13. (hereafter Welch, Battle of Scary Creek)

128. Civil War Correspondence of Captain William S. Williams, Independent Battery, Ohio Volunteer Artillery (Three Months Volunteers). Civil War Manuscripts, Series 147-9: 181, 3. Ohio State Archives. (hereafter Williams Correspondence)

129. Sedinger Diary, 56-57; Sedinger Wartime Reminiscences July 17, 1861; Shirey, *Scary Creek*, 18.

130. Welch, Scary Creek, 12-13.

131. *OR, Series 1*, Vol. 2, 289; Letter from Corporal Jeroboam "Jerry" B. Creighton, Gunner in the Independent Ohio Artillery Battery, July 18, 1861, *Tiffin Weekly Tribune*, July 26, 1861.

Chronicling America Series, Library of Congress.

132. "The Fight on the Kanawha." *Daily Ohio Statesman*, July 21, 1861. Chronicling America, Library of Congress.

133. Shirey, *Scary Creek*, 19; Lowry, *Scary Creek*, 122-123; "Millard Phillips of Huntington was Youngest Soldier in Southern Army." *Huntington-Herald Advertiser*, July 8, 1928. Newspapers on Microfilm, Misc. Reels, WV State Archives; Thompson, Scary Creek, 4.

134.   *Western Reserve Chronicle*, July 31, 1861.

135.   Collins, J.H. "The Irrepressible." Letter, May 3, 1894, cited by William Wintz in "More on the Battle of Scary Creek" in *Upper Vandalia Historic Society Journal*, (July 1973). Note sources sometimes conflict as to whether Companies B and D of the 21st Ohio or Companies A & B present; however, regimental records indicate it was Companies B and D.

136.   Thompson, *Scary Creek*, 4-5.

137.   *New York Times*, July 27, 1861.

138.   *Western Reserve Chronicle*, July 31, 1861.

139.   *Clermont Courier*, August 7, 1861.

140.   Letter from Private James A. Gorsuch, Co. I, 12th Ohio Volunteer Infantry, *Darke County Democrat* (Ohio), July 24, 1861, Online: Newspapers.com.

141.   *Western Reserve Chronicle*, July 31, 1861

142.   Lowry, *Scary Creek*, 137-138; Ward, *Twelfth Ohio*, 31-32.

143.   Williams Correspondence 3-4.

144.   *New York Times*, July 27, 1861.

145.   Lowry, *Scary Creek*, 125-126.

146.   *Clermont Courier*, August 7, 1861.

147.   Lowry, *Scary Creek*, 125-126; *Western Reserve Chronicle*, July 31, 1861; *Daily Intelligencer, August 2, 1861.*

148.   *Ibid.*, Lowry; Shirey, *Scary Creek*, 19-20; CSR, RG 94, 1st Kanawha Rifles-22nd Virginia Infantry, M324, Roll 653; CSR, RG 94, 8th Virginia Cavalry, M324, Roll 83, National Archives; 8th Virginia Cavalry Records, Library of Virginia; 22nd Virginia Infantry Records, Library of Virginia; CSR, RG 94, 3rd Kanawha Infantry, M324, Roll 1019, National Archives. James F. Sweeney of the 3rd Kanawha Regiment later served in 60th Virginia Infantry.

149.   Sedinger Wartime Reminiscences, April 20, 1861; Lowry, *Scary Creek*, 125-126; Shirey, *Scary Creek*, 19.

150.   Thompson, *Scary Creek*, 5.

151.   Sedinger Diary, 56-57; Sedinger, Wartime Reminiscences, July 17, 1861.

152.   Lowry, *Scary Creek*, 126; Shirey, *Scary Creek*, 19; Ferguson, M. J. "The Battle of Scary Creek, W.VA." *Confederate Veteran*, (1917), Vol. 25, 503. (hereafter Ferguson) Lt. Col. Carr B. White was born in Mason

County, Kentucky, and grew up in Ohio. After service in the Mexican War, he became a physician. White was later promoted to Colonel after Colonel Lowe's death at the battle of Carnifex Ferry on September 19, 1861 and saw heavy action during the Antietam Campaign. He was later breveted as a brigadier General in 1863. He died at Georgetown, Ohio in 1871.

153.   *Ibid.; Western Reserve Chronicle*, July 31, 1861; Ferguson, 503.

154.   *Daily Ohio Statesman*, July 21, 1861.

155.   *New York Times*, July 27, 1861.

156.   Ferguson, 503; Warren, R.A. "3rd to 5th and 7th to 13th Regiments, Ohio Volunteer Infantry,1861." *Company of Military Historians*, Vol. 57 (Fall 2005), 151.

157.   Welch, *Scary Creek*, 12-13.

158.   CSR, RG 94, 22nd Virginia Infantry, M324, Roll 647, National Archives; 22nd Virginia Infantry Records, Library of Virginia; Lowry, 22nd Virginia Infantry, 6-7, 127.

159.   *Ibid.*, Lowry, 125-127; Canfield, Silas S. *History of the 21st Regiment Ohio Volunteer Infantry in the War of the Rebellion.* (Toledo, Ohio: Vrooman, Anderson & Bateman, Printers, 1893), 9 (hereafter Silas); Shirey, *Scary Creek*, 19.

160.   *Ibid.*, Lowry, 135; *Western Reserve Chronicle*, July 31, 1861; *Daily Ohio Statesman*, July 21, 1861; CSR, RG 94, M324, Roll 652, National Archives. James H. Mays was a private in Company F, 1st Kanawha Infantry (22nd Virginia Infantry) during the battle.

161.   Welch, Scary Creek, 13.

162.   Lowry, *Scary Creek*, 136-138.

163.   *Ibid.*, 137; *Western Reserve Chronicle*, July 31, 1861.

164.   *Daily Ohio Statesman*, July 21, 1861; Lowry, *Scary Creek*, 126; Williams Correspondence, 4.

165.   *Tiffin Weekly Tribune* July 26, 1861.

166.   Shirey, *Scary Creek*, 20-21; *OR, Series 1*, Vol. 12; Part 2; 288; 757-761.

167.   Diary of Sarah F. Young, July 17, 1861, 1-2; *OR, Series 1*, Vol. 2, 288; 292; 1011-1012.

168.   Lowry, *Scary Creek*, 23; Andre et al., Bullets and Steel, 57; 129th Regiment Virginia Militia. 129th Regiment Virginia Militia, Series 2, Unit Records, Subseries 8, Militia, Box 36, Folder 15, Library of Virginia, Richmond, Virginia; CSR, RG 109, 129th Regiment Virginia Militia, M324, Roll 1056, National Archives; "Devil Anse Tells the True History of the Famous Hatfield-McCoy Feud." *Wheeling Intelligencer*, November 23, 1889. Vol. 38, 1. Chronicling America Series, Library of Congress; Thompson, R.M. *Twelve Pole Terror: The Legend of Rebel Bill Smith.* (Wayne, WV: R.M. Thompson Books, 2015),

47-48; 22nd Virginia Infantry Records, Library of Virginia; 36th Virginia Infantry Records, Library of Virginia; 8th Virginia Cavalry Records, Library of Virginia; Confederate Military Records, 1859-1864, Accession No. 27684, Series II, Unit Records, 60th Virginia Infantry Records, Box 28, Folders 45-52, Library of Virginia; CSR, M324, Roll 650; CSR, RG 94, M324, Roll 824; CSR RG 94, M324, Roll 1014; CSR, 94, M324, Roll 83, National Archives; William Anderson 'Devil Anse' Hatfield does not appear on any of the 8th Virginia Cavalry muster rolls, nor those of the 36th or 22nd or 60th Virginia Infantry, and each of those regiments had companies at Scary Creek in the 1st, 2nd, and 3rd Kanawha Infantry. The exact date the Sandy Rangers became part of the 8th Virginia Cavalry is unknown, but was likely on or about May 15, 1862.

169.   "Evacuation of Scary Creektown by the Rebels." *New York Times*, July 28, 1861. *New York Times* archive online: https://timesmachine.nytimes.com. Accessed December 26, 2020. (hereafter Scary Creektown, *New York Times*, July 28, 1861)

170.   Lowry, *Scary Creek*, 141-145; 146.

171.   Andre *et al., Bullets & Steel*, 64-69; OR, Series 1, Vol. 2, 1011-1012; *Gallipolis Journal*, August 15, 1861. Vol. 26(37), 3.

172.   *Ibid.*; *Daily Intelligencer*, August 2, 1861.

173.   *OR, Series 1*, Vol. 2, 1011-1012.

174.   *Ibid.*, 766.

175.   *OR, Series 3*, Vol. 1, 431.

176.   *Gallipolis Journal*, Aug. 15, 1861.

177.   WV AG Papers, AR 382, Box Number 2. Letter from S. H. Grose to H. J. Samuels August 19, 1862. WV State Archives; Naret Letters: Naret to H. J. Samuels, September 2, 1861.

178.   Naret Letters: Naret to H.J. Samuels, September 4 & 6, 1861.

179.   *Ibid.*, September 6, 1861.

180.   Sarah F. Young Diary, September 3, 1861; OR, Series 1, Vol. 5, pp. 118-119; 128-132; 136-139; 144-165; 616; Brigadier General John B. Floyd, was the former U.S. Secretary of War from March 1857 to December 1860, and a former governor of Virginia from January 1849 to January 16, 1852.

181.   *Ibid.*, Sarah F. Young, September 23 & 24, 1861

182.   *Ibid.*, October 5, 6, & 8, 1861.

183.   Naret Letters: Naret to H. J. Samuels, September 11, 1861.

184.   Wintz, Vol. 2, 13

185.   *Ibid.*, 27.

186.   Hansford Diary, September 22, 1861; Wintz, Memoirs, 25-28.

187.   *Ibid.*

188.   WV AG Papers, Union Militia, AR 373, Box 21, Folders 1, 4, 14-16. WV State Archives; WV AG Papers, AR 373, Union Militia, 1861-1865; Naret Letters: Naret to H. J. Samuels, September 26, 1861.

189.   *Ibid.*

190.   *Gallipolis Journal* October 17, 1861.

191.   *Cincinnati Daily Times*, October 21, 1861. Newspaper Reading Room, SN 83045113, Library of Congress; Civil War Diaries of Francis G. Hale, 34th Ohio Volunteer Infantry. Accession No. MSS 13405, Albert & Shirley Small Special Collections Library, University of Virginia Libraries.

192.   *Gallipolis Journal* October 17, 1861.

193.   *Cincinnati Daily Gazette*, October 19, 1861. Microfilm, Hamilton County Ohio Public

Library, Cincinnati, Ohio.

194.   *Ibid.*

195.   CSR, RG 94, M552, Roll 66, National Archives; Roster of Ohio Soldiers, Vol. 3, 21st-36th Regiments Infantry, 585; Ludwig, October 27, 1861.

196.   *Ibid.*, Ludwig, October 27, 1861.

197.   Dickinson, *8th Virginia Cavalry*, 10-11, 97; CSR, 8th Virginia Cavalry, RG 94, M324, Roll 84, National Archives. John A. Miller was five feet, six inches tall with blue eyes. After the war, he had "many whiskers" and married Frances Woods; they settled on Sycamore Road near modern Hurricane. Miller cleared the land himself, and built his own home, and earned his income as a farmer; he also made extra money selling timber shaped into square logs to the railroad. He and his wife had nine children. Miller was known as honest, hardworking and a good neighbor.

198.   Executive letter book of Governor Francis H. Pierpont, 1861-1864. Accession 37226, Misc. Microfilm reel 6191. State government records collection, The Library of Virginia, Richmond, VA.

199.   Wintz, Vol. 2, 55-56.

200.   *Ibid.*

201.   Wintz, Vol. 2, 55-56; Hale, *History of the Great Kanawha Valley, Vol. 2,* 288.

202.   *Ibid.*, Wintz, 57.

203.   CSR, RG 94, M508, Roll 195, National Archives; Geiger, Joseph Jr. "The Tragic Fate of Guyandotte." *West Virginia History*, Vol. 54, 1995, 28-41; Naret Letters: Naret to H. J. Samuels, November 11, 1861.

204.   WV AG Papers, Union Militia, AR 373, Box 21, Folder 8. WV State Archives.

205.   1860 US Census; Morgan, *Last Dollar*, 15-16; CSR, RG 109, 34th Battalion Virginia Cavalry, M324, Roll 0193.

206.   *Ibid.,* Morgan.

207.   Osborne, Randall & Weaver, Jeffrey C. *The Virginia State Rangers and State Line*. (Lynchburg, VA: H.E. Howard, 1994), 47, 164; Virginia. Dept. of Confederate Military Records, 1859-1996. Accession No. 27684, State Records Collection, Series 2, Unit Records, Subseries 7: Virginia State Line, 4th Regiment, Box 34Folders 1&7, Drawer 12, Library of Virginia, Richmond, Virginia.

208.   *OR, Series 1*, Vol. 5, 674-675.

209.   Naret Letters: Naret to H. J. Samuels, December 7, 1861. WV Archives; "Kanawha

Volunteers." *Richmond Daily Dispatch,* December 3, 1861.

210.   *Ibid., Richmond Daily Dispatch*, "Western Virginia," 2.

Chapter 2

1.   Minsker Family Papers, Solomon Minsker to John Minsker, March 12, 1862. Civil War Manuscripts, Ms2004-109, WV State Archives; Blundon & Matthews Family Papers, Edgar Blundon Civil War Diary and Letters 1861-1920, typescript, Blundon to Sarah Young, January 8, 1862. Civil War Manuscripts, Ms 89-94, WV State Archives; David H. Donald. *Lincoln.* (New York: Simon & Schuster Publishers, 1996), 266-267; Noah Brooks. *The Nation's Leader.*(New York: Putnam & Sons, 1888), 425-429.

2.   Records of Districts, Department of West Virginia, District of the Kanawha, Record Group 393.5, Telegrams, Microfilm 1193, National Archives.

3.   *Ibid.*, CSR, Roll 80; Naret Letters, February 17 & 28, 1862.

4.   *OR Series 1*, Vol. 12, Part 3, 8-12; Sarah Young Diary, March 9, 11, & 28, 1862; Griffith, 44-45.

5.   Online: https://www.findagrave.com; Papers of and Relating to Military and Civilian Personnel, compiled 1874 - 1899, documenting the period 1861 – 1865. CSR, RG 109, M347, Roll 0174, National Archives; Meeting in Putnam County, Va." *Gallipolis Journal*, April 3, 1861; "A Returned Traitor." *The Weekly Register*, March 27, 1862.

6.   *Ibid., The Weekly Register*, April 17, 1862 & March 27, 1862; *Gallipolis Journal*, April 3, 1861; John J. Polsley Papers, 1862-1879, Letter to Nellie, April 8, 1862. Collection No. A&M.1601, West Virginia and Regional History Center, West Virginia University Libraries, Morgantown WV; CSR, 22nd Virginia

Infantry, RG 94, M324, Rolls 650, National Archives; 22nd Virginia Infantry Records, Library of Virginia; CSR, 36th Virginia Infantry, RG 94, M324, Roll 824, National Archives; 36th Virginia Infantry Records, Library of Virginia; Virginia Militia Commission Papers, 1777-1858, Accession No. 42222, Subseries A, Microfilm 6443-6614, Putnam County, Virginia (1849-1852), Box 131, Folders 12-19, Library of Virginia.

7.   Wood, Andrew J. "Biographies of West Virginia Statehood Leaders." 2010. Marshall University Graduate College Humanities Program, unpublished manuscript, South Charleston, West Virginia; "A State of Convenience: The Creation of West Virginia, Chapter 13: Congressional Debate on the Admission of West Virginia, The Willey Amendment." Online: www.http.wvculture.org; Ambler, Charles H; Atwood, Frances H; Matthews, William B. (Eds.). *Debates and Proceedings of the First Constitutional Convention of West Virginia, 1861-1863. (Huntington, WV:* Gentry Brothers Printers), 80-81. 1850 and 1860 US Census; https://www.findagrave.com. The 1850 U.S. Census shows Dudley S. Montague employed as an Inn keeper with real estate valued at $100.00. The 1860 U.S. Census showed him at the same residence, employed as a Bar owner, with $2,500 worth of real estate. After the Civil War, he relocated to the Hutton Township in Putnam County, and later lived in Union District. The 1880 U.S. Census indicated his occupation was Whiskey Retail. Montague died on January 31, 1886, and is buried at Spring Hill Cemetery in Charleston, West Virginia.

8.   "Meeting in Putnam County, Va." *Gallipolis Journal,* April 3, 1861.

9.   WV AG Papers, Union Militia, 80th Regiment Virginia Militia; AR 373, Misc. File, Letter from A.I. Waterson, May 2, 1862, WV State Archives. (hereafter Waterson); *Wheeling Daily Intelligencer,* April 15, 1862. Vol. 11, SN 84026845, Newspaper Reading Room. Library of Congress; *The Weekly Register,* April 17, 1862.

10.   "Letter from the Camp." *Pomeroy Weekly Telegraph,* April 11, 1862, Vol. 5(14), 1.

11.   *The Weekly Register,* April 17, 1862; Cabell-Wayne Historical Society Collection, No. 778, Marshall University Library Special Collections, Huntington, WV. After the Civil War, Robert T. Harvey relocated to Huntington, West Virginia, and established a clothing store, Harvey & Sons Clothing and Dry Goods, with his sons Harry C. and Clayton Harvey. He died in 1893 and is buried in Spring Hill Cemetery in Huntington.

12.   "Letter from the Camp." *Pomeroy Weekly Telegraph,* April 11, 1862.

13.   *Ibid.*

14.   Sarah Young Diary, April 15, 1862; Cunningham, Steve. 1992; "From Buffalo." *The Weekly Register,* May 22, 1862; Edgar B. Blundon Papers, A&M 0895, Roy B. Cook Collection, WVU Library.

15.   J.V. Young Letters, Company G Non-Commissioned Officers to U.S. War Department May 24, 1862; Sarah Young Diary, June 5, 1862. WV AG Files, AR 383, 11th West Virginia Infantry, Boxes 1 & 2, Folders 7; 41; 42; & 43; Muster and Descriptive Rolls and Morning Reports; Letter from C. Mollohan, Attorney, to Pierpont, January 10, 1864, on behalf of Lt. Robert Brooks; WV AG Papers, Pierpont Samuels Collection, Telegraphs May 11 & 20, 1862, & Boxes 1 & 7, WV Archives; Roy Bird

Cook Collection, Box 1, Folder 2, Call No. A&M 0895, Series 1, Correspondence; Letter from Non-Commissioned officers to Governor Francis Pierpont, May 24, 1862, WV Regional History Collection, WVU Library; Brookes resignation: CSR, RG 94, M508, Roll 186, National Archives. See also: WV AG Papers, AR382, Union Militia Oversized Muster Rolls, 1861-65, Drawers 80-87. WV Archives; Blundon Letters, June 7, 1863.

16.   *Ibid.*

17.   *Gallipolis Journal,* April 3, 1861.

18.   *OR, Series 1*, Vol. 12, Part 3, 100.

19.   256Francis H. Pierpont Papers, Series 6, Telegrams 1861-1869. A&M 0009, West Virginia Regional History Collection, WVU Library. (hereafter Pierpont Telegrams, WVU)

20.   "West Virginia Volunteers." *The Weekly Register,* May 15, 1862. Vol. 1, 2 & June 12, 1862, 2.

21.   "From Buffalo." *The Weekly Register,* May 29, 1862 & June 5, 1862; Lewis, Virgil A., *Second Biennial Report of the Department of Archives and History of the State of West Virginia,* (no publisher, 1908), 180-181.

22.   "Buffalo Items." *The Weekly Register,* June 12, 1862.

23.   WV AG Papers, AR 373, Union Militia, 1861-1865, Box 21, Folder 1, 181st Regiment Virginia Militia Correspondence. Edward Naret to H. J. Samuels, June 12, 1862. WV Archives.

24.   Transcript of letter by Mary Higginbotham, Grayson, Kentucky, to her sister-in-law, Mary Sproul Higginbotham of Buffalo, dated June 18, 1862. Civil War Manuscripts, Anna Lutz Collection, Ms2003-141, Folder 3, West Virginia State Archives; CSR, RG 94, M508, Roll 175, National Archives; 1860 US Census.

25.   "Buffalo Items." *The Weekly Register,* June 19, 1862.

26.   *Ibid., The Weekly Register,* July 3, 1862. Vol. 1(17), 2.

27.   "Admission of West Virginia" and "Putnam County." *The Weekly Register,* July 10, 1862.

28.   *Ibid.,* "West Virginia" cited from the Utica, *New York Herald, undated.*

29.   *OR Series 1*, Vol. 12, Part 2, 52; "A Good Order from General Pope." *The Weekly Register,* July 31, 1862.

30.   "Buffalo Items." *The Weekly Register,* July 24, 1862.

31.   *OR, Series 1*, Vol. 24, Part 3, 513-515; WV AG Papers, Union Militia, AR 373, Putnam County, Box 2, Folder 1. Letters to H.J. Samuels, August 11 & 15, 1862; CSR, RG 94, M508, Roll 192, National Archives.

32.   *Ibid.*

33.   *OR, Series 1*, Vol. 12, Part 3, 560-561, 567, 570, 572.

34.   *Ibid.*, 407; 534; 540; 543; 577; 619; 629; 698-699; 712; 722; 726; also Part 1, 738; 742; 754; Part 2, 405-411; OR, Series 1, Vol. 19, Part 1, 419; 424-426; 427-431; 458-474; Cox, *Military Reminisces of the Civil War.* Vol. 1, 77-79; 80-81; 96-98; 114-115; 118-122. General Jacob Cox's promotion to Major General expired in March 1863 due to Congressional reports indicating there were too many general officers of that rank. Cox was later re-commissioned as Major General in 1864.

35.   WV AG Papers, Pierpont-Samuels Memory Project, Telegraphs, Box 6, WV State Archives; WV AG Papers, AR 654, Folders 10-11, Part 1, Field History of the 13th West Virginia Volunteer Infantry, WV State Archives (hereafter 13th WV Field History); OR, Series 1, Vol. 19, Part 1, 1069-1071; Warner, Generals in Gray, 193-194.

36.   OR Series 1, Vol. 12, Part 2, 757; Robertson, James I. *Soldier of Southwestern Virginia: The Civil War Letters of Captain John Preston Sheffy.* (Baton Rouge, LA: Louisiana State Press, 2004), 174-187. (hereafter Robertson)

37.   *Ibid.*; Lowry, Terry. *The Battle of Charleston and the 1862 Kanawha Valley Campaign.* (Charleston WV: 35th Star Publishing, 2016), 77-78. (hereafter Lowry, *Battle of Charleston*)

38.   Pierpont Telegrams, September 8, 1862; WV AG Papers, Union Regiments, 4th West Virginia Infantry, AR 382, Box 12, Folder 4, J.A.J. Lightburn letters September 1862 (hereafter Lightburn Letters); Robinson, 186-187; *Journal of the Congress of the Confederate States of America, 1861-1865*, Vol. 5. (Washington DC: Government Printing Office, 1905), 340-341; Joseph J. Sutton. *History of the 2nd Regiment, West Virginia Cavalry Volunteers in the War of the Rebellion.* (Portsmouth Ohio: 1892, reprinted by Blue Acorn Press, 1992), 60-61. (hereafter Sutton)

39.   *Ibid.*

40.   *Ibid.*

41.   Wintz, *History of Putnam County, West Virginia.* Vol. 2., 175-176; Cabell County West Virginia Deed Books, Vol. 4, 178-181. Deed to Richard McCallister, September 4, 1825 dividing his land to heirs including John McCallister; 1870 & 1940 U.S. Census.

42.   *Ibid.*

43.   Sarah Young Diary, September 12, 1862; Dickinson, Jack L. *16th Virginia Cavalry.* (Lynchburg, VA: H.E. Howard, 1989), 9-10; 109. (hereafter Dickinson, *16th Virginia Cavalry*)

44.   Sarah Young, September 13, 1862.

45.   *Ibid.*

46.   Lightburn Letters, September 7 & 16, 1862; Lowry, Battle of Charleston, 84-85.

47.   *OR, Series 1*, Vol. 12, Part 2, 756-764; *The Weekly Register,* September 18, 1862; January 22, 1863, WV Archives; OR, Series 1, Vol. 19, Part 1, 1060; Sutton, 60.

48.   Sarah Young Diary, September 8 & 9, 1862; Shanklin, Harry L. *History of Putnam County*. (Charleston, WV: Upper Vandalia Historical Society, 1967), 55-56. Note that the date of the skirmish on Coal Mountain occurring on September 12, 1862, is erroneously cited as September 9 or 10, 1862, in Sarah Young's diary.

49.   *The Guerilla*, Vol. 1, September 28, 1862, SN: 85059834. Newspaper reading room, Library of Congress.

50.   "Buffalo Items." *The Weekly Register*, September 4 1862.

51.   CSR, RG 94, M508, Roll 209, National Archives; Civil War Recollections of George Rucker, Company E, 13th West Virginia Infantry. West Virginia Civil War Manuscript Collection, Rucker Family Papers, Call No. MS-94-95. WV Archives. (hereafter Rucker)

52.   Rucker, George. "A Discourteous Enemy." *National Tribune*, June 10, 1909. Vol. 29(31), 1. https://www.loc.gov/item/sn82016187/1909-06-10/ed-1/.

53.   Pierpont Telegraphs, September 19, 1862, Gen. George Bowyer to Pierpont; "To Arms! To Arms!" *The Weekly Register*, September 18, 1862.

54.   *Ibid.*, *The Weekly Register*, "Matters at Home."

55.   *The Weekly Register*, October 2, 1862.

56.   CSR, RG 94, M508, Roll 208, National Archives; Butler Generations in America. Unpublished Manuscript. Compiled by Joseph Martin Butler, Jr., and later descendants, Courtesy Terry Lowrey, n/d. (hereafter Butler Generations) Note that the story of Butler meeting General Jenkins is unverified outside of family oral tradition.

57.   *OR, Series 1*, Vol. 12, Part 2, 759-760; Series 1, Vol. 24, Part 2, 756-757; Perkins, Charles. "Battle of Atkeson's Gate (1862) Historical Marker." Clio Guide to History. May 6, 2018. Accessed January 26, 2020. https://www.theclio.com/entry/56321; "Skirmish Near Buffalo Va." *The Weekly Register*, October 2, 1862; CSR, RG 109, M324, Rolls 131 & 206.

58.   *Ibid.*, *OR*, 761; 1860 U.S. Census, Putnam County, Virginia, District 4; CSR, RG 94, M324, Roll 829, National Archives.

59.   Allen, James C, 91st Ohio Volunteer Infantry. "Letters Home from Point Pleasant." Newspaper clippings without date or references, Courtesy Penny Clagg. Cited in Lowry, *Battle of Charleston*, 280.

60.   *OR, Series 1*, Vol. 19, Part 2, 6-7.

61.   *Ibid.*; OR, 1074; Windsor, Anthony W. *History of the Ninety-first Regiment, O.V.I.* (Cincinnati, OH: Gazette Steam Printing House, 1865), 122-123.

62.   CSR, RG 109, M324, Roll 85, National Archives; Robertson, 132-133. Rosinante was Don Quixote's horse in the novel by Cervantes.

63.   *Ibid.*, CSR; Robertson, 127, 133. Captain John P. Sheffey was most likely referring to *The Weekly Register* from Point Pleasant, a decidedly pro-Union news organ popular among Union residents at Buffalo.

64.   Conner, 8.

65.   Atkeson, *Pioneering in Agriculture*, 163-164.

66.   Wintz, Vol. 2, 2-3; *The Weekly Register* September 18, 1862.

67.   "Skirmish Near Buffalo Va." *The Weekly Register*, October 2, 1862 & September 18, 1862.

68.   "Affairs in the Kanawha valley." *Richmond Daily Dispatch*, October 9, 1862.

69.   *OR, Series 1*, Vol. 19, Part 2, 6-7.

70.   Sarah Young Diary, September 29, 1862, October 4 & 6, 1862; Lowry, *Battle of Charleston*, 292-293; *The Guerilla*, October 3, 1862.

71.   Sedinger Diary, October 1862.

72.   Sarah Young Diary, October 14, 1862.

73.   Lowry, *Battle of Charleston*, 335-355.

74.   *Ibid.*; "Headquarters 13th V.V.I." *Pomeroy Weekly Telegraph*, November 28, 1862.

75.   *Gallipolis, Journal*, November 16, 1862.

76.   *Ibid.*; Lowry, *Battle of Charleston*, 338; OR, Series 1, Vol. 19, Part 2, 462-463.

77.   *Ibid.*; *OR, Series 1*, Vol. 19, Part 2, 462-463, 475; "Rambling Correspondence from a Piatt Zouave." *Pomeroy Weekly Telegraph*, November 21, 1862. The Zouave correspondent noted they had two "little brushes" with the rebel cavalry outposts near Red House; however, as noted in the text, that area was actually the vicinity of modern Rock Branch near Poca.

78.   *Ibid.*

79.   *Ibid.*; Lowry, *Battle of Charleston*, 342; George B. Turner Papers, 92nd Ohio Volunteer Infantry, Call No. MS75-1210. Ohio Historical Society, Columbus, Ohio; Online: Lee Fenner's web page: http://www.89thohio.com.

80.   WV AG Papers, Union Regiments, AR383, 4th West Virginia Infantry, F&S, Box 12, WV State Archives; Sarah Young Diary, October 23, 1862. Captain Edgar Blundon commanded Company F, 8th West Virginia Infantry, and had only recently returned from his deployment with Major General John Pope's army during the summer.

81.   *Ibid.*, WV AG Papers.

82.	Huddleston, Samuel B. Papers 1843-1917. Rare Books and Manuscripts Collection, Folder S694. Indiana State Library, Indianapolis, Indiana. A Civil War History of the 84th Indiana Regiment as Recorded by Samuel Huddleston. (2007). Transcribed by Sharon Ogzewalla. Cambridge City, Indiana. (hereafter Huddleston)

83.	*OR, Series 1*, Vol 19, Part 2, 534-535; Roush, Herbert L., Sr. *If Thou Wilt Remember: A Historical Narrative*. Lowell, Michigan: Modern Printing, 1995, 26. The story of David M. Burrows, Company F, 13th West Virginia Volunteer Infantry. Call No. 973.781 R863, WV Archives. (hereafter Roush)

84.	*Ibid., OR, Series 1.*

85.	13th West Virginia Field History, Part 1; Records of the Adjutant General's Office, Record Group 94, Book Records of Union Organizations, 13th West Virginia Infantry, Vol. 3, Morning Reports, Companies A-D, F-K, October-December 1862. Accession No. E112-115, PI-17, National Archives, Washington DC. (hereafter 13th WV Morning Reports)

86.	Washington, Davis. *Camp-fire Chats of the Civil War: Being the incidents, adventure and way-side exploit of the bivouac and battle-field, as related by the Veteran soldiers themselves.* (Detroit, MI: W.H. Boothroyd and Co., 1887), 204-209.

87.	*Ibid.*

88.	CSR, 11th West Virginia Infantry, RG 94, M594, Roll 196, Letter from Captain Robert P. Kennedy, December 22, 1862.

89.	*OR, Series 1*, Vol. 19, 857; *OR Series 1*, Vol. 21, Part 1, 880-881; 997, 1902; WV AG Files, AR 383, 11th West Virginia Infantry, Boxes 1 & 2, Folder 42, Company G Muster Rolls.

90.	*Ibid;* Records of Districts, Department of West Virginia, District of the Kanawha, Record Group 393.5, Telegrams, Microfilm 1193, National Archives; *The Weekly Register*, February 19, 1863; CSR, RG 94, M508, Roll 83, National Archives.

91.	"WV Statehood." *The Weekly Register*, November 13, 1862.

92.	WV AG Papers, Union Militia, AR 373, Box 21, Folder 7. WV State Archives.

93.	Abraham Lincoln Papers, MSS30189, General Correspondence, Reel 42: Lincoln, Abraham. Opinion on the Admission of West Virginia, December 31, 1862, Library of Congress.

Chapter 3

1.	First Edition of Abraham Lincoln's Final Emancipation Proclamation. Alfred Whital Stern Collection of Lincolniana, Library of Congress; D. Shaffer. "Lincoln and the Vast Question of West Virginia." *West*

Virginia History, Vol. 32(2), (January 1971), 86-100; B.F. Wade Papers, 1800-1878, Letter from A.W. Campbell, June 26, 1862. Manuscripts Division, Control No. MM 78044263. Library of Congress; R. Morris. "The *Wheeling Daily Intelligencer* and the Civil War." (Unpublished doctoral dissertation. West Virginia University, 1964), 36-55; Diary of Orville H. Browning. Historical Collections, Part I, 1933. (Illinois State Archive, Springfield, Illinois), 550-551; 596-599; Robert Todd Lincoln Family Papers, 1864-1938. Control No. MM 97084148, Letter from Francis H. Pierpont, December 30, 31, 1862. Library of Congress; Curry, R. O. A. *A House Divided*. (Pittsburgh, PA: Univ. of Pittsburgh Press, 1964), 100-115; Salmon P. Chase Letters, General Correspondence 1810-1989: Letter from E. W. Crittenden July 21, 1861, MSS 15610, Reel 14, Library of Congress.

2.   13th West Virginia Field History, Part 1; CSR, RG 94, M507, Roll 208, National Archives; WV AG Papers, AR 382, 13th West Virginia, Box 2/2, Folder 72, December 17, 1862 Co. G Muster Roll, WV Archive; WV AG Papers, Union Militia, AR 373, Box 21, Folder 7. WV State Archives; "Putnam Sheriff carried off by Rebels." *The Weekly Register*, February 12, 1863.

3.   "Hurricane Bridge Declared an Independent State." *The Weekly Register*, February 12, 1863.

4.   Wintz, Vol 2., 115; *Gallipolis Journal*, February 26, 1863.

5.   *Ibid.*; *Ironton Register*, March 26, 1863; *Wheeling Intelligencer*, February 24, 1863 & March 25, 1863; Geiger, *Disorder on the Border*, 189-190.

6.   Hurricane Centennial Committee. *Centennial History of Hurricane, WV: A History of Hurricane 100 Years, 1888-1988*. (Salem, WV: Walsworth Press, 1988), 6; 197. (hereafter Hurricane Centennial) Hurricane Bridge was later known as Hurricane Station upon completion of the single railroad track in 1873 and was re-named as the town of Hurricane by an act of the Putnam County Court after the results of a general election on October 30, 1888.

7.   Weiss, C.M., Weiss, V.W. & Collins, R.L. Revised Phase – 1 Archeological Survey of the Proposed Hurricane Bridge Park, Putnam County, WV. (December 2017). Manuscript prepared for City of Hurricane. Fairmont, WV: Allstar Ecology, LLC, 39-42; 51- 59; 63-65; 73-77; (hereafter Weiss, *et al*, Archeological Survey). Hurricane Centennial, 4-6; 197; Harry L. Shanklin. *History of Putnam County*. (Charleston, WV: Upper Vandalia Historical Society, 1967), 8-9; Personal interview by the author with Mrs. S. Duke, Culloden WV, February 15, 2019; Jim. Comstock. *Hardesty's History of Early West Virginia: Monroe, Putnam, and Tyler Counties*. (Richwood, WV: Privately published, 1973), 138-142. (hereafter Comstock, *History of Monroe, Putnam and Tyler Counties*)

8.   Dickinson, Jack L. & Dickinson, Kay S. *Gentleman Soldier of Green Bottom: The Life of Brig. Gen. Albert Gallatin Jenkins, C.S.A.* (Huntington, WV: Self-published, 2011), 38; *Kanawha Valley Star*, September 30, 1856; Wintz, Vol. 1, 87.

9.   Conner, 6-8. Conners estimate of Jenkins' strength is likely too high, as other sources demonstrated his battalion numbered closer to 500-600.

10.   8th Virginia Cavalry Records, Company D, Library of Virginia, Richmond, VA; Dickinson, *8th Virginia Cavalry*, 37-38; Dickinson, *16th Virginia Cavalry*, 17-18; Flora S. Johnson, The Civil War

Record of Albert Gallatin Jenkins, C.S.A. *West Virginia History*, Vol. 8(4) (July 1947), 392-404 (hereafter Johnson); 13th WV Morning Reports, March-February, 1863.

11.   Brownlee, Kimberly Ball Hieronimus. "The Thirteenth Regiment, West Virginia Volunteer Infantry." Unpublished Senior Thesis, University of Toledo, 1996. Call No. 973.7454. WV State Archives, 6-7 (hereafter Brownlee); 13th West Virginia Field History, Part 1; Conner, 6-8; Miller, O.R. "Skirmish at Hurricane Bridge." Unpublished Manuscript, 1996, Courtesy Sandy Miller Larch (hereafter Miller, Skirmish at Hurricane Bridge); Hurricane Centennial, 4-5; 197; *Hurricane Breeze* Newspaper, March 25, 1998, 1; Dickinson, *8th Virginia Cavalry*, 28, 37-38, 44-56; Dickinson *16th Virginia Cavalry*, 20-32; Johnson, 398-399. Note that several historians have supposed Company G of the 11th West Virginia was also present, but this is inaccurate.

12.   *Ibid.*, 13th West Virginia Field History; OR, Series 1, Vol. 19, 857; OR Series 1, Vol. 21, Part 1, 880-881; 997; CSR, 13th West Virginia Infantry, RG 94, M508, Roll 207, National Archives. James William Johnson enlisted in the 13th West Virginia Infantry on August 15, 1862, at Coalsmouth, Virginia, at age twenty-four years, and was soon elected captain of Company A. He resigned on May 15, 1863, to accept a commission as 1st Lieutenant in Company C, 3rd U.S. Colored Troops on July 20, 1863. Johnson was later promoted to captain on October 8, 1864, while stationed in Jacksonville, Florida, by Brigadier General E.K. Scammon, former commander of the Kanawha Division.

13.   *Ibid.*, 13th WV Field History; 13th WV Morning Reports, Vol. 4, Companies A-D, F-K, March-February 1863.

14.   *Ibid.*, 13th WV Field History, Part 1; Hess, John H., Corporal, Company H, 13th West Virginia Infantry. Civil War Letters to his Wife, February 18, and April 10, 1863. Originals in author's collection (hereafter Hess Letters); Letters of Dr. Samuel Glover Shaw; Assistant Surgeon, 13th West Virginia Infantry, 1862-1865. Transcript copy from originals held in private collection of Irene "Cookie" Ambler, March 31, 1863; April 1, 1863; April 2, 1863; April 6, 7 & 8, 1863; and May 6, 1863; Transcribed by Irene "Cookie" Ambler and Ron Allen. Courtesy Betsy Allen and Ron Allen, (hereafter Dr. Shaw Letters); 13th WV Morning Reports; James B. Wiggins Papers, 1861-1919. Virginia Sesquicentennial of the American Civil War Collection, Call Number 44358, Manuscripts, Library of Virginia; Miller, O.R. Skirmish at Hurricane Bridge; OR, Series 1, Vol. 19, 1083.

15.   Sedinger Diary, 7; Sedinger Wartime Reminiscences, 18.

16.   Dickinson, *16th Virginia Cavalry*, 18-19; Edens, Martin Van Buren. Battle of Hurricane Bridge! Poem published in *Point Pleasant The Weekly Register*, April 30, 1863, WV Archives (hereafter Edens, Battle of Hurricane Bridge); CSR, RG 94, M324, Roll 85, National Archives; Conners, 6-8. Corporal Martin Van Buren Edens was from Mason County, Virginia, and enlisted on August 15, 1862, at Charleston, Virginia. He was promoted to Corporal on September 23, 1862 and was later "slightly" wounded at the battle of Winchester on September 19, 1864. He afterward spent the remainder of the war at the army hospital in Gallipolis, Ohio.

17.   13th West Virginia Field History, Part 1.

18.   13th West Virginia Morning Reports, Company B, March 28, 1863; Hess Letters February 18, 1863.

19. *Ibid.*, Hess Letters, April 10, 1863; CSR, 13th West Virginia, RG 94, M508, Rolls 204 & 209, National Archives; Edens, Battle of Hurricane Bridge.

20. *OR, Series 1*, Vol. 19, 1083.

21. 13th WV Field History, Part 1 and Appendix A; Miller, Skirmish at Hurricane Bridge; Sedinger, Diary of a Border Ranger, 55-78; Edens, Battle of Hurricane Bridge.

22. Dupuy, Trevor N. *The Evolution of Weapons and Warfare.* (Boston, MA: DaCapo Press, 1990); James B. Whisker, *U.S. and Confederate Arms and Armories During the American Civil War: Arms Imported from Europe During the American Civil War, 1861-1865.* (Lewiston, NY: E. Mellen Press, 2002); *OR, Series 1*, Vol. 25, Part 2, 657-658.

23. *OR, Series 1*, Vol. 25, Part 2, 657; Civil War Letters of Thomas P. Copenshaver, 8th Virginia Cavalry. Stuart A. Rose Library Manuscript and Archives, MSS-20, Emory University, Atlanta Georgia. Jenkins received 600 .69 Richmond muskets shortly after March 7, 1863, sent by order of Maj. Gen. Samuel Jones.

24. 13th West Virginia Infantry Morning Reports, Vols. 3 & 4, October 15, 1862: 13th West Virginia Field History, Part 1; Dr. Samuel G. Shaw letters, April 6, 1863.

25. CSR, 13th West Virginia, RG 94, M508, Roll 205, National Archives; WV AG Papers, 13th West Virginia, AR 382, Box 23, Company H Muster Rolls, WV Archives. Colonel Brown reduced Corporal George W. Fulwiller, Co. H, to the ranks, but he eventually returned to duty. Fulwiller became ill in July 1864 and was hospitalized until the end of the war.

26. 13th West Virginia Field History, Part 1, Appendix A.

27. *Ibid.*; *OR, Series 1*, Vol. 25, Part 2, 657.

28. *Ibid.*; 13th West Virginia Field History, Part 1; Hurricane Centennial, 5-6.

29. Papers of Eliakim Parker Scammon (1816-1894). Telegraph from W.R. Brown to Scammon, March 30, 1863. Manuscripts Collection, Accession No. GLC02414.127. The Gilder Lehrman Institute of American History, New York. (hereafter E.P. Scammon Papers)

30. WV AG, Union Regiments, 13th West Virginia, AR 382, Box 20, Muster Roll April 10, 1863, WV Archives; West Virginia Adjutant General's Report. December 1, 1864. (Wheeling, WV: J.F. M'Dermot Publishing, 1864) 364-366 (hereafter WV AG Report, 1864); 13th West Virginia Morning Reports, Co.'s A-D, F-K, March-April 1863.

31. CSR, RG 94, M508, Roll 207, National Archives; WV AG, Union Regiments, 13th West Virginia, AR 382, Box 20, Muster Roll April 10, 1863, WV Archives; WV AG Report, 1864, 364-366; 13th West Virginia Morning Reports, Co.'s A-D, F-K, February –March 1863.

32. CSR, 13th West Virginia, RG 94, M506 Roll 204, National Archives; Dr. S.G. Shaw Letters, March 31, 1863; WV AG Papers, 13th West Virginia, AR 382, Box 20, Muster Roll April 10, 1863,

WV Archives; Potter, Jerry. *The Sultana Tragedy: America's Greatest Maritime Disaster.* (Baton Rouge, LA: Pelican Publishing, 1992).

33.   13th West Virginia Field History, Part 1; OR, Series 1, Vol. CSR, 13th West Virginia, RG 94, M507-M508, Rolls 204, 206, 208, 209 and 211, National Archives; WV AG Papers, Union Regiments, 13th West Virginia, AR 382, Box 20, Muster Roll April 10, 1863, WV Archives; Comstock, 131; Blundon Family Papers, Letter to Sara F. Young, April 16, 1863, WV Archives.

34.   *Ibid.*

35.   Dickinson, *8th Virginia Cavalry*, 33-37; 77; Dickinson, *16th Virginia Cavalry,* 18; 13th WV Field History, Part 1, Appendix A; CSR, 8th Virginia Cavalry, RG 94, M324, Rolls 81-86, National Archives; 1860 US Census.

36.   *Ibid.*

37.   *Hurricane Breeze,* May 7, 1987.

38.   CSR, RG 94, M508, Roll 207, National Archives; E.P. Scammon Papers, Accession No. GLC02414.390, Letter from W.J. Johnson to Scammon June 27, 1865; Original Letter written by Captain James W. Johnson to Captain Greenbury Slack, May 21, 1864 from Jacksonville, Florida. Transcribed by the author. Used with permission from the private collection of Charles N. Slack, descendent of Greenbury Slack. Courtesy Steve Cunningham.

39.   *Ibid.*; Dobak, William. Freedom by the Sword: The U.S. Colored Troops 1862-1867. (Carlisle, PA: U.S. Army Military History Center, 2007) (hereafter Dobak); E.P Scammon Papers, Telegraph from W.R. Brown to Scammon, March 30, 1863.

40.   *Ibid.*

41.   *Ibid.*, CSR.

42.   *Ibid.,* Dobak.

43.   *Ibid*, CSR.

44.   CSR, Records of Volunteer Union Soldiers who served with the United States Colored Troops (USCT), RG 94, M1820, Roll 22, National Archives.

45.   CSR, 8th Virginia Cavalry, RG 94, M324, Roll 82; CSR, 3rd Kentucky Infantry and 3rd West Virginia Cavalry, M397, Roll 170 and M508, Roll 25, National Archives; Wintz, Vol. 2, 102-104.

46.   *Ibid.*, Edens, Battle of Hurricane Bridge; CSR, RG 94, M508, Roll 205, National Archives.

47.   13th West Virginia Field History, Part 1; Civil War Recollections of George Rucker, Co. E, 13th West Virginia Infantry, Letter of September 19, 1862, Rucker Family Papers, MS-94.45, WV State Archives; OR, Series 1, Vol. 25, Part 1, 76-77.

48. *Gallipolis Journal*, April 23, 1863; "A Perilous Voyage." *National Tribune*, June 3, 1886, Vol. 5(43), 1.

49. *Ibid.*

50. Conner, 7-8; Wintz, Vol. 1, 88; "The services of Capt. Fred. Ford, in the Late War." *The Weekly Register*, December 3, 1868; *Gallipolis Journal*, April 2, 1863; Captain Frederick Ford Navy Pension File, Feb. 15, 1882. Letter by Major B.R. Cowan, Army Paymaster, to Brig. Gen. B.F. Scammon, June 5, 1863, Claim No. 7945, Microfilm T288, Roll 157, National Archives. (hereafter Frederick Ford Pension file); Comstock, Jim. *Hardesty's Atlas of West Virginia Counties: Mason, Pleasants, Lewis Roane.* (Richwood, WV: Comstock, 1973), 27; OR Series 1, Vol. 25, Part 1, 75-76; Sedinger Diary; Sedinger Wartime Reminiscences, 55-78; *The Weekly Register*, April 16, 1863; *Gallipolis Journal* April 2, 1863. Online: www.galliagenealogy.com. Known as a strong Unionist and emancipation supporter, Frederick Ford was once sued by James Ruffner in Kanawha County Court for transporting a runaway slave valued at $1,500.00 on May 13, 1862. The case was heard in Kanawha County Court on January 6, 1883, and Ruffner won the case.

51. 13th West Virginia Field History, Part 1; Dr. Shaw Letters, March 30, 1863; April 3 & 6, 1863.

52. E.P. Scammon Papers, Telegraph from J.C. Paxton to Scammon, April 2, 1863; Dr. Shaw Letters, April 4, 6 & 7, 1863.

53. Roush, Herbert L., Sr. "If Thou Wilt Remember: A Historical Narrative." (Lowell, Michigan: Modern Printing, 1995), 26. The story of David M. Burrows, Company F, 13th West Virginia Volunteer Infantry. Call No. 973.781 R863, WV Archives, 12-13; 29.

54. Dr. Shaw Letters, April 7, 1863; Hess Letters, April 10 and June 7, 1863.

55. *OR Series 1*, Vol. 25, Part 1, 70-80. Dr. Samuel G. Shaw Letters, November 6, 1862; E.P. Scammon Papers, Telegraph from Captain David Dove to Scammon, April 5 1863.

56. *Gallipolis Journal*, April 16, 1863.

57. Basier, R.P. (Ed.). *The Collected Works of Abraham Lincoln.* Vol. 5. (New Brunswick, NJ Rutgers Univ. Press, 1953), 35-38; 166; Vol. 2, 255-256; Vol. 6, 26-28; 181; Bruce Crawford. *West Virginia: A Guide to the Mountain State.* (New York: Works Progress Administration, 1941), 8; Squires, 27; Otis K. Rice. *West Virginia: The State and its People.* (Parsons, West Virginia: McClain Printing, 1972), 202-203. (hereafter Rice, *West Virginia*)

58. *Ibid.*, Rice.

59. WV AG Papers, Union Militia, AR373, Box 21, Folder 14, WV State Archives.

60. *Ibid.*; CSR, RG 94, M508, Roll 204, National Archives. Special Order No. 106 signed by Colonel William R. Brown ordered Sergeant Joseph Brumley to take twenty men to Buffalo in Putnam County for recruiting duty on July 25, 1863, but oddly was not recorded in company record books until January 4, 1864.

61.   *The Wheeling Intelligencer,* August 20, 1863.

62.   *Ibid.*; 13th West Virginia Field History, Part 2.

63.   Original Letter in author's collection. John A. Wells to Edwin Stanton, U.S. War Department, October 1, 1863. Dr. Edward Naret of Buffalo relocated to Gallipolis, Ohio in late 1863.

64.   "A Veteran of the Mexican War and the Union." *New York Evening World, Evening Edition,* December 10, 1894. Newspapers on Microfilm, SN 83030384, Library of Congress; Letters and their Enclosures Received by the Commission Branch of the Adjutant General's Office, 1822-1860; 1861-1870. General Order No. 7, 1856, Special Order No. 15: Record Group 94, M1064, Rolls S112, 0223, National Archives.

65.   Hastings, Russell. The Civil War Memoirs of Russel Hastings. From Birth to July 25, 1861. Transcript of Chapter One. Hayes-25, No. 594031, Rutherford B. Hayes Presidential Library, Spiegel Grove, Ohio; Charles R Williams. *The Life of Rutherford Birchard Hayes, Nineteenth President of the United States.* (New York, NY: Houghton-Mifflin Company, 1911), 215.

66.   Hoptak, John D. *The Battle of South Mountain.* (Cheltenham, UK: History Press, 2011), 45-47; Francis Heitman. *Historical Register and Dictionary of the United States Army 1789-1903.* (Washington, DC: U.S. Government Printing Office, 1903), 218-219; Warner, Ezra J. *Generals In Blue: Lives of the Union Commanders.* (Baton Rouge, LA: University of Louisiana Press, 1992), 421-422.

67.   *OR, Series 1,* Vol. 29, Part 1, 498-450.

68.   E.P. Scammon Papers, Telegraph from Captain David Dove to Scammon, November 14, 1863; WV AG Papers, Union Regiments, AR 382, 13th West Virginia, Folders 10 & 11, WV State Archives; 13th West Virginia Field History, Part 1; Civil War Muster Rolls, RG 94, Loose Letter files, 13th West Virginia Volunteer Infantry, National Archives. (hereafter 13th WV Loose Letter Files)

69.   *Ibid.*, 13th West Virginia Field History; WV AG Papers; J.V. Young letters, December 3, 1863.

70.   *Ibid.*, WV AG Papers; G.W. Atkinson and A.F Gibbens. *Prominent Men of West Virginia.* (Wheeling, WV: W.L. Callin, 1890), 419-421; WV AG Papers, Union Militia, AR373, Box 21, Folder 17, WV State Archives.

71.   *Ibid.*, WV AG Papers, 13th West Virginia, Folder 10.

72.   *Ibid.*, WV AG Papers; J.V. Young letters, December 3, 1863; 13th West Virginia Field History, Part 1; OR, Ser. 1, Vol. 29, Part 1, 977; 13th West Virginia Loose Letter Files.

73.   *Ibid.*

74.   *OR, Ser. 1,* Vol. 51, Part 1, 1139.

75.   WV AG Papers, Union Militia, AR373, Box 21, Folder 14, WV State Archives.

76.   *OR, Series 1,* Vol. 30, Part 1, 977-978.

77.   WV AG Papers, Union Militia, AR373, Box 21, Folder 14, WV State Archives.

78.   WV AG Papers, 13th West Virginia Infantry, AR 382, Box 20, Folder 4. James R. Hall to W.R. Brown, January 10, 1864. WV State Archives.

Chapter 4

1.   WV AG Papers, Union Regiments, AR373, Box 21, Folder 11, WV State Archives; CSR, RG 94, M508, Roll 80, National Archives.

2.   CSR, RG 94, M508, Roll 209, National Archives; William D. Wintz & Patricia A. Slater. *Life and Times of George Washington Smith 1837-1932: The Putnam County Yankee, 1837-1932.* (Monograph published by Upper Vandalia Historical Society, 1986), 1-10 (hereafter Smith, *The Putnam County Yankee*); *Charleston Daily Mail,* April 26, 1979; Wintz, Vol. 2, 223. According to family tradition, George W. Smith supposedly remained in Company K until August 24, 1864, when he transferred into the elite Blazer's Scouts unit; however, service records state he was present with Company K until he mustered out on June 22, 1865. Smith's youngest child, Sheridan Smith, became a brigadier general in the United States Army.

3.   *Ibid.*

4.   *Ibid.*

5.   Roy Bird Cook. "The Civil War Comes to Charleston." *West Virginia History.* Vol. 23(2) (January 1962), 153-167; *OR, Series 1*, Vol. 33, 110-111; *Wheeling Daily Intelligencer,* February 8, 1864; *Gallipolis Journal,* February 11, 1864; *The Weekly Register,* February 11, 1864.

6.   *Ibid.*

7.   *OR, Series 1*, Vol. 33, 109-111.

8.   "Capture of Gen. Scammon and Burning of Steamer B.C. Levi." *Wheeling Daily Intelligencer,* February 8, 1864; 1860 U.S. Census, Putnam County, Virginia, District 3, Catalogue ID No. 2353568, RG 29, M653, Roll 29, National Archives. The Vintroux family migrated to Putnam County from France in the 1850's. The patriarch, L.E. Vintroux, was a forty-eight-year-old farmer with land valued at $25,000.00, who lived at Frazier's Bottom. His eleven-year-old son, Charles Vintroux would later have a son named Kendall Vintroux, (b. 1896) who became a regionally famous political cartoonist for the Charleston Gazette newspaper in the 1930's-1960's; Craig W. Gaines. *Encyclopedia of Civil War Shipwrecks.* (Baton Rouge, LA: University of Louisiana Press, 2008), 1866; *Gallipolis Journal,* February 11, 1864; *Wheeling Daily Register,* February 25, 1864. Vol 6, Newspapers on Microfilm, Misc. Reels M-94, WV Archives.

9.   *Ibid.,* Gallipolis Journal; The Weekly Register, February 11, 1864; E.P. Scammon Collection; CSR, RG 94, M508, Roll 118, National Archives.

10. Vertegans, G.S. Capture of Brigadier General E.P. Scammon at Red House, February 2, 1864. *Confederate Veteran,* Vol. 26, 1918, 389-390 (hereafter Vertegans); *OR, Series 1*, Vol. 33, 109; CSR, RG

94, M324, Roll 86, National Archives. Other sources indicated the *B. C. Levi* landed at Vintroux landing near the mouth of Hurricane Creek: "Capture of the Steamer B. C. Levi - Independent Scouts. *The Weekly Register*, February 11, 1864, and "Capture of the B.C. Levi." *Gallipolis Journal*, February 11, 1864; E.P. Scammon Collection.

11.   *OR, Series 1*, Vol. 33, 112. Major James Nounann's report of Scammon's capture.

12.   "For the Register: Capture of the Steamer B.C. Levi – Independent Scouts." *The Weekly Register*, February 11, 1864; CSR, RG 94, M508, Roll 69, National Archives; *The Weekly Register*, February 11, 1864. 2nd Lt. John J. Ball later enlisted in Company B, 7th WV Cavalry, on August 1, 1864.

13.   *OR*, 109-110; *Gallipolis Journal*, February 11, 1864.

14.   *Ibid.*; "Capture of Gen. Scammon and Burning of Steamer B.C. Levi." *Wheeling Daily Intelligencer*, February 8, 1864; CSR, RG 94, M508, Roll 38, National Archives; *The Weekly Register*, February 11, 1864.

15.   Vertegans, 390.

16.   Duncan, Richard R. *Lee's Endangered Left: The Civil War in Western Virginia, Spring of 1864*. (Baton Rouge, LA: University of Louisiana Press, 2004), 12-13; R.B. Hayes to S. Richards, February 19, 1864. Sardis Richards Papers, Coll. No. Hayes-15, Description ID 595666, Box 5. Rutherford B. Hayes Presidential Library, Spiegel Grove, Ohio. (hereafter Hayes)

17.   "Rebel Raid in the Kanawha Valley." *Wheeling Daily Register*, February 25, 1864. Vol 6, Newspapers on Microfilm, Misc. Reels M-94, WV Archives.

18.   *The Wheeling Intelligencer*, March 4, 1864

19.   *Gallipolis Journal*, February 18, 1864.

20.   *Ibid.*; Cook, 153-167; E. Milby Burton. *Siege of Charleston 1861-1865*. (Columbia, SC: University of South Carolina Press, 1981), 284-295; Douglass W. Bostick. *Charleston Under Siege: The Impregnable City*. (Charleston, SC: The History Press, 2010), 122-124.

21.   Burton, 296-299; Bostick, 124-128.

22.   *Ibid.*; Burton; Bostick, 128-132.

23.   *OR, Series 2*, Vol. 6, 875.

24.   *OR, Series 2*, Vol. 6, 875; Cunningham, 18-22; E.P. Scammon Papers: Samuel Jones to Eliakim Parker Scammon, April 4, 1863.

25.   *Report on the Treatment of Prisoners of War by the Rebel Authorities during the War of the Rebellion.* Congressional Serial Set, 40th Congress, 3rd Session, Report No. 45. (Washington DC: Government Printing Office, 1869), 683.

26.   *Ibid.*; OR, Series 1, Vol. 35, Part 2, 254; Cunningham, Tim. "The Immortal 600: Prisoners Under Fire at Charleston Harbor During the American Civil War." *America's Civil War*, Vol. 15, (January 2003), 18-24.

27.   *Ibid.*; Cunningham, J. *The Immortal Six Hundred: A story of Cruelty to Confederate Prisoners of War* (Winchester, VA: Eddy Press, 1905), 67-68; Warner, 421-422.

28.   Letters and their Enclosures Received by the Commission Branch of the Adjutant General's Office, 1822-1860; 1861-1870. General Order No. 7, 1856, Special Order No. 15: Record Group 94, M1064, Rolls S112, 0223, National Archives; Warner, 422.

29.   CSR, RG 94, M324, Roll 648, National Archives; *OR, Series* 1, Vol. 33, 109.

30.   *OR, Series 1*, Vol. 33, 158; Kellian Van Rensalear Whaley Papers. 1863-1879, Ms80-126, Folders 1&2, WV State Archives; "From Buffalo." *Wheeling Daily Register,* February 24, 1864.

31.   *Ibid.*

32.   *The Weekly Register,* March 24, 1864; WV AG Papers, Union Regiments, AR373, Box 21, Folder 11, WV State Archives.

33.   "Rebels Captured." *The Wheeling Weekly Intelligencer,* May 7, 1864, Vol. 12, Newspapers on Microfilm, M-91, WV State Archives; WV AG Papers, Union Regiments, AR373, Box 21, Folder 11, WV State Archives.

34.   *OR, Series 1*, Vol. 37, Part 1, 609-610; 623-624; *Charleston Daily Bulletin*, June 13, 1864, Vol. I, Newspapers on Microfilm, M-52, WV State Archives.

35.   William A. Whiting Pension file, Box 33908, Certificate No. 173609, National Archives. See also: Union Pension Index, Microfilm T288, Roll, 514, National Archives and RG 94, M594, Roll 195, National Archives. Captain Edgar Blundon was married to Captain John V. Young's eldest daughter Sarah F. Young.

36.   "Trouble in the Ranks." *Clarksburg Telegram*, February 27, 1886. Newspapers on Microfilm, Misc. Reels, M-1, West Virginia State Archives; CSR, RG 94, M508, Rolls 215 & 217, National Archives.

37.   WV AG Papers, Union Regiments, AR373, Box 21, Folder 11, WV State Archives.

38.   Weaver, Jeffrey C. *Thurmond's Partisan Rangers and Swan's Battalion of Virginia Cavalry*. (Lynchburg, VA: H.E. Howard, 1993), 57 (hereafter Weaver, Thurmond's Rangers); WV AG Papers, Union Militia, AR 373, Box 21, Folder 11. WV State Archives.

39.   CSR, RG 94, 8th Virginia Cavalry, M324, Rolls 84 & 189, National Archives; CSR, RG 94, 7th West Virginia Cavalry, M508, Roll 74, National Archives; *The Weekly Register*, September 22, 1864. Note that it is unclear whether William Meek was killed or wounded and captured, as his service records indicate he was captured while AWOL, on or about October 21, 1864. Meek was taken to Camp Chase, Ohio and exchanged on February 1, 1865.

40.   *The Weekly Register*, September 22 1864.

41.   Weaver, *Thurmond's Rangers,* 56; Cole, Scott C. *34th Battalion Virginia Cavalry*. (Lynchburg, VA: H.E. Howard, 1993), 95 (hereafter Cole); Hale, John P. History of the Great Kanawha Valley; with Family History and Biographical Sketches. Vol. 1, (Madison, WI: Brant, Fuller and Co., January, 1891), 273 (hereafter Hale); OR, Series 1, Vol. 43, Part 2, 443, 449, 461; Steelhammer, Rick. "Confederate Troops fought, died to take Winfield 150 years ago today." *Charleston Gazette*, October 27, 2014. (hereafter Steelhammer); *Weekly Register*, September 22 1864.

42.   *OR, Series 1*, Vol. 43, Part 2, 256.

43.   WV AG Papers, Union Militia, AR 373, Box 21, Folder 11. WV State Archives.

44.   *Ibid.*

45.   *The Weekly Register*, September 22 1864.

46.   John V. Young Letters: Young to daughter Emily Young, October 30, 1864.

47.   *Ibid.*

48.   Conner, 7-8; Wintz, Vol. 2, 94-95.

49.   Weaver, *Thurmond's Partisan Rangers*, 58-59; Cole, 95; Hale, 273; OR, Series 1, Vol. 443, 449, 461; Steelhammer, *Charleston Gazette*, October 27, 2014.

50.   *Ibid.*

51.   *Ibid.*; *Charleston Gazette*, October 27, 2014. Note that some accounts claim the attack began around 3:00 a.m. although Captain John Reynolds indicated it began at 10:00 p.m. Comstock, Jim. Hardesty's West Virginia Counties, Vol. 1, (Parkersburg WV: H.H. Hardesty, 1882, reprinted 1973), 168-170. Captain Lawrence Alvin Christy was a steamboat captain during the Civil War, and later worked for the U.S. Post Office in Winfield, WV. He was born at Malden, WV, and died in Charleston in 1941. Ibid.; Charleston Gazette, October 27, 2014. Note that some accounts claim the attack began around 3:00 a.m. although Captain John Reynolds indicated it began at 10:00 p.m.; Comstock, History of Monroe, Putnam and Tyler Counties.

52.   *Ibid.*, Hale; John M. Reynolds, Miscellaneous Papers. Report of attack at Winfield. October 27, 1864. RG 94, M594, Roll 195, National Archives. (hereafter Reynolds)

53.   *Ibid.*, Hale.

54.   Weaver, *Thurmond's Partisan Rangers*, 58-59; Hale, 273; Reynolds; "Phil Thurmond Killed!" *West Virginia Journal*, October 26, 1864, Vol. 1, Chronicling America, Library of Congress; Hale, 273; Reynolds; Steelhammer.

55.   "Rebel Raid upon Winfield, W.VA." *The Weekly Register,* November 3, 1864.

56.   *Ibid.*

57.   Reynolds; *OR, Series 1*, Vol. 43, Part 2, 256.

58.   Rush, Bonny. "Confederate Soldier buried with Fanfare, Military Rites." *Herald Dispatch*, November 12, 2010; *Putnam Herald*, November 5, 2010; *West Virginia Journal*, October 26, 1864; Hale, 273; Reynolds; Steelhammer.

59.   *OR, Series 1*, Vol. 43, Part 1, 645-646.

60.   *Ibid.* Part 2, 473.

61.   Ibid., Part 2; Reynolds; *OR, Series 1*, Vol. 43, Part 1, 645-646; Cole, 95; Weaver, *Thurmond's Partisan Rangers, 58;* Hale, 273; CSR, Captain Thurmond's Partisan Rangers, RG 94, M324, Roll 212, National Archives. Andrew Hix enlisted in Captain Philip J. Thurmond's company on March 13, 1863 as a private. The newspaper article published in the *West Virginia Journal is* cited in the 34th Battalion Virginia Cavalry regimental history.

62.   The Attack on Winfield." *Charleston Daily Bulletin*, November 2, 1864, Vol. 1, No. 2, 2. Newspapers on Microfilm, M-52, WV State Archives.

63.   "Rebel Raid upon Winfield, W.VA." *The Weekly Register,* November 3, 1864.

64.   *OR, Series 1*, Vol. 43, Part 2, 497.

65.   *Ibid.*

66.   *Ibid.*

67.   "Important Revelations: Letters of a Rebel Spy No.2." *West Virginia Journal*, November 9, 1864.

68.   CSR, RG 94, M619, Letters Received, Compiled 1805-1889, Roll 392, National Archives; CSR, RG 109, M324, Roll 821, National Archives; "The Execution last Friday." *West Virginia Journal*, November 9, 1864. Note the account published in The West Virginia Journal erroneously lists William H. Bowyer as a private on Company H, 36th Virginia Infantry, when he was in Company A.

69.   *Ibid.*; *OR, Series 1*, Vol. 43, Part 2, 473; Adjutant General Papers, General Court Martials, Special Orders No. 282, September 2, 1864, National Archives.

70.   *Ibid.*

71.   Long., David E. *The Jewel of Liberty: Abraham Lincoln's Re-Election and the End of Slavery.* (Mechanicsburg, PA: Stackpole Books, 1994), xvii, 20-23, 40, 124-134, 233-234, 245-248, 266-267 (hereafter Long); See also: John C. Waugh,. *Reelecting Lincoln: The Battle for the 1864 Presidency.* (New York: Crown Publishers, 1997).

72.   *Ibid.*, Long, xvii; *Gallipolis Journal*, November 10, 1864; *The West Virginia Journal*, November 16, 1864.

73.   "Putnam County Aggregate Vote." *Gallipolis Journal*, November 10, 1864; "An Encouraging Lesson." *The Weekly Register*, November 17, 1864; WV AG Papers, Union Militia, AR 373, Box 21, Folder 11. WV State Archives.

74.   *Ibid.*, WV AG Papers.

Chapter 5

1.   Fast, Richard E. & Maxwell, H. *The History and Government of West Virginia.* (Charleston, SC: Nabu Press, 2010), 109-110; Richard O. Curry. *A House Divided: Statehood, Politics, and the Copperhead Movement in West Virginia.* (Pittsburgh, PA: University of Pittsburgh Press, 1964), 91-131. (hereafter Curry)

2.   "West Virginia Slavery." *The Weekly Register*, January 19, 1865; Allain, Jean. *The Legal Understanding of Slavery: From the Historical to the Contemporary.* (New York: Oxford University Press, 2012), 115-135; Curry, 129.

3.   Kesterson, Brian S. *Soldier of Courage, Soldier of Compassion: The Story of Captain Bennett L. Munger, Company C, 44th New York State Infantry.* (Washington, WV: Nighthawk Press, 2017), 95; WV AG Papers, Union Militia, AR 373, Box 21, Folder 11. WV State Archives; *Acts of the Legislature of West Virginia, at its Third Session commencing January 27, 1865*: Chapter Five: An Act to pay State Scouts (Wheeling, WV: J. Frew, Public Printer, 1865), 4; "Raid on Buffalo." *The Weekly Register*, February 23, 1865.

4.   "A List of Men from Putnam County in the Draft." *The Weekly Register*, March 2, 1865, Vol. 3(48), 1; *The Weekly Register*, March 2, 1865.

5.   OR, Series 1, Vol. 43, Part 2, 738-739; Jeffrey C. Weaver. *45th Battalion Virginia Infantry, Smith & Count's Battalions of Partisan Rangers.* (Lynchburg, Virginia: H.E. Howard, 1994); 137-138; James M. Prichard. *The Devil At Large: Devil Anse's War.* In William Davis. *Virginia at War*, 1863. (Lexington, KY: University of Kentucky Press, 2008), 66-68, 82; Dr. Coleman C. Hatfield and Robert Y. Spence. *Tale of the Devil: The Biography of Devil Anse Hatfield.* (Charleston, WV: Quarrier Press, 2003), 81; *Wheeling Intelligencer*, November 23, 1889. Prichard cited two letters written by William S. "Rebel Bill" Smith of August 16, 1864, and October 12, 1889; In the former, Hatfield was not listed among Smith's company commanders in the letter to Confederate Adjutant and Inspector General Samuel Cooper; however, he reported Hatfield had led a company in his partisan battalion during 1864-1865. See also: Records of the Adjutant and Inspector General's Department, Letters and Telegrams Sent & Received, 1861-1865. RG 109, M410, National Archives. (August 16, 1864, Letter); See also: Public Records Division, Governor Simon B. Buckner Papers, Records pertaining to Applications for Requisitions (Returning Fugitives to Kentucky), Identifier No. 04538-RG1189, KDLA.

6.   WV AG Papers, Union Militia, Ball's Company, AR 373, Box 21, Folder 11, WV State Archives. (hereafter Ball's Company Records)

7.   John V. Young Letters, April 17, 1865.

8.   Ball's Company Records.

9.   *Ibid.*, *West Virginia News*; *Fayette Journal*; CSR, Captain William D. Thurmond, 44th Battalion Virginia Cavalry (Thurmond's Partisan Rangers) RG 109, M324, Roll 207, National Archives.

10.   *Ibid.*, *West Virginia News*; *Fayette Journal*.

11.   *OR*, *Series 1*, Vol. 48, Part 2, 873, 1014-1015; *West Virginia News*; CSR, Lieutenant Colonel D.S. Hounshell, Hounsell's Battalion, Partisan Rangers, RG 109, M324, Roll 206, National Archives.

12.   Ball's Company Records.

13.   *Ibid.*

14.   *Ibid.;* Wintz, Vol. 2, 96-98.

15.   *Gallipolis Journal*, June 1, 1865.

16.   *Ibid.*

17.   J.V. Young Diary, July 5-7, 1865. Roy Bird Cook Collection, Call No. A&M 0895, Series 1, Correspondence, Box 1, Folder 1, West Virginia Regional History Collection, West Virginia University Library, Morgantown WV; CSR, 11th West Virginia Infantry, RG 94, M508, Roll 195; John H. Wood. Wartime Diary, January 1, 1865 to August 22, 1865. Civil War Collection, Series 1, MS 79-18, WV Archives; July 19-August 21, 1865.

18.   Stutler, Boyd. *West Virginia in the Civil War*. (Charleston, WV: Education Foundation, 1966), v-vii.

BIBLIOGRAPHY

Books

Andre, Richard, Cohen, Stan & Wintz, William. *Bullets and Steel: The Fight for the Great Kanawha Valley 1861-1865.* (Charleston, WV: Pictorial Histories Publishing, 1995).

Basier, R.P. (Ed.). *The Collected Works of Abraham Lincoln.* Vol. 5. (New Brunswick, NJ Rutgers Univ. Press, 1953), Vols. 2 &6.

Boatner, Mark Mayo, III. *The Civil War Dictionary.* (New York: McKay, 1959; revised 1988).

Bronaugh, W.C. "The Younger's Fight for Freedom: A Southern Soldier's Twenty Year's Campaign to Open Northern Prison Doors – with Anecdotes of War Days. (Columbia, Missouri: E.W. Stephens Publishing, 1906).

Callahan, James M. *History of West Virginia: Old & New and West Virginia Biography.* (Chicago, IL: American Historical Society, 1923).

Canfield, Silas S. History of the 21st Regiment Ohio Volunteer Infantry in the War of the Rebellion. (Toledo, Ohio: Vrooman, Anderson & Bateman, Printers, 1893).

Centennial History of Hurricane, WV: A History of Hurricane 100 Years, 1888-1988. Hurricane Centennial Committee. (Salem, WV: Walsworth Press, 1988).

Comstock, Jim. Hardesty's History of Early West Virginia: Monroe, Putnam and Tyler Counties. (Richwood, WV: Privately published, 1973).

Cox, Jacob D. *Military Reminisces, of the Civil War, Vol. 1, April 1861-November 1863.* (Great Britain: Hard Press Books, 2016).

----- *Military Reminiscences of the Civil War, Vol. 5.* (Cincinnati, OH: Cochran Publishing, October 1900, Reprinted by Kessinger Publishing, Whitefish, MT, 2008).

Crawford, Bruce. *West Virginia: A Guide to the Mountain State.* (New York: Works Progress Administration, 1941).

Curry, R. O. A. *A House Divided.* (Pittsburgh, PA: Univ. of Pittsburgh Press, 1964).

DeGruyter, Julius. *The Kanawha Spectator*, Part 2: Backdrop. (Charleston, West Virginia: Willard H. Ervin, Publisher, 1976).

Dickinson, Jack. *8th Virginia Cavalry.* (Lynchburg, Virginia: H.E. Howard, 1986).

Dupuy, Trevor N. *The Evolution of Weapons and Warfare.* (Boston, MA: DaCapo Press, 1990).

Egan, Michael. *The Flying Gray-Haired Yank or the Adventures of a Volunteer.* (Leesburg, VA: D.L. Phillips (Ed.), Gauley Press, 1992).

Geiger, Joseph, Jr. *The Civil War in Cabell County 1861-1865.* (Charleston, WV: Pictorial House Publishing, 1991).

Griffith, Joe. *History of Company G, 11th West Virginia Volunteer Infantry From Coalsmouth to Richmond, 1862-1865.* (Roswell, GA: Published by the author, 1995).

Hale, John P. *History of the Great Kanawha Valley.* (Madison, WI: Brant, Fuller & Co., 1891, Reprint, Gauley & New River Pub. 1994).

Hamblinton, James P. *A Biographical Sketch of Henry A. Wise.* (Richmond, VA: J.W. Randolph, 1856).

Hardesty, James. *Hardesty's Historical and Geographical Encyclopedia.* Vol. 1. (Chicago: H. H. Hardesty, 1883, Reprint, Richwood: Comstock, Hardesty West Virginia Counties, 1973).

Heitman, Francis. *Historical Register and Dictionary of the United States Army 1789-1903.* (Washington, DC: U.S. Government Printing Office, 1903).

Hinkle, Harlan H. *Grayback Mountaineers: The Confederate Face of Western [West] Virginia.* (New York: Universe, Inc. Publishing, 2003).

Hoge, James C. "Who He Was: James W. Hoge, Putnam Judge (1830-1882). Unpublished Manuscript, Hoge House National Historic Site, Winfield, West Virginia, n/d.

Hoptak, John D. *The Battle of South Mountain.* (Cheltenham, UK: History Press, 2011).

Hubbard, Robert Ernest. *Major General Israel Putnam: Hero of the American Revolution.* (Jefferson, North Carolina: McFarland & Company, 2017).

Lang, Theodore F. *Loyal West Virginia 1861-1865.* (Baltimore, Maryland: Deutsch Printing Co., 1895).

Linger, James C. *Confederate Military Units of West Virginia*. (Tulsa, OK: Self-published Monograph, Revised Ed., 1990).

Lowry, Terry. *The Battle of Scary Creek*. (Charleston WV: Pictorial Histories Publishing, 1982).

----- 22nd Virginia Infantry. (Lynchburg, Virginia: H.E. Howard, 1st Ed., 1988).

Mellott, D. W. and Snell, M.A. *The Seventh West Virginia Infantry: An Embattled Union Regiment from the Civil War's Most Divided State*. (Lawrence, Kansas: University of Kansas Press, 2019).

Minsker, Solomon. Family Letters, Civil War Manuscripts, PL 2004-109, WV State Archives.

Parker, Granville. *The Formation of the State of West Virginia*. (Wellsburg, WV: Glass & Son Publishers, 1975).

Pauley, Michael J. *Unreconstructed Rebel: The Life of General John McCausland, C.S.A.* (Charleston, WV: Pictorial Histories Publishing, 1993).

Potter, Jerry. T*he Sultana Tragedy: America's Greatest Maritime Disaster*. (Baton Rouge, LA: Pelican Publishing, 1992).

Rice, Otis K. *The Hatfield's & McCoys*. (Lexington, Kentucky: University Press of Kentucky, 2010).

----- *West Virginia: The State and its People*. (Parsons, West Virginia: McClain Printing, 1972).

Scott, James L. *36th Virginia Infantry*. (Lynchburg, Virginia: H.E. Howard, 1987).

----- *36th and 37th Battalions Virginia Cavalry*. (Lynchburg, Virginia: H.E. Howard, 1986).

Schmiel, Eugene D. *Citizen-General: Jacob Dolson Cox and the Civil War Era*. (Athens, Ohio: Ohio University Press, 2014).

Shanklin, Harry L. *History of Putnam County*. (Charleston, WV: Upper Vandalia Historical Society, 1967).

Sutherland, Daniel E. *A Savage Conflict: The Decisive Role of Guerrillas in the American Civil War*. (Chapel Hill, NC: UNC Press, 2009).

Turk, Daniel S. *The Union Hole: Unionist Activity and Local Conflict in Western Virginia*. (Bowie, Maryland: Heritage Books, 1994).

Wallenstein, P. *Cradle of America: Four Centuries of Virginia History*. (Lawrence, Kansas: University Press of Kansas, 2007).

Ward, James E.D. *Twelfth Ohio Volunteer Infantry*. (Ripley, OH: NP, 1864).

Warner, Ezra J. *Generals In Blue: Lives of the Union Commanders.* (Baton Rouge, LA: University of Louisiana Press, 1992).

----- *Generals in Gray: Lives of the Confederate Commanders.* (Baton Rouge, LA: Louisiana State University Press, 1959, Reprinted 1987).

Whisker, James B. *U.S. and Confederate Arms and Armories During the American Civil War: Arms Imported from Europe During the American Civil War, 1861-1865.* (Lewiston, NY: E. Mellen Press, 2002).

Wintz, William D. Annals of the Great Kanawha. (Charleston, West Virginia: Pictorial Histories Publishing Company, 1993).

----- *Civil War Memoirs of two Rebel sisters.* (Charleston, West Virginia: Pictorial Histories Publishing, 1989).

------ *History of Putnam County, West Virginia.* Vol. 1. *Upper Vandalia Historical Society.* (Charleston, West Virginia: Pictorial Histories Publishing, 1999).

------ *History of Putnam County, West Virginia.* Vol. 2. *Upper Vandalia Historical Society.* (Charleston, West Virginia: Pictorial Histories Publishing, 2001).

----- (Ed.). *Recollections and Reflections of Mollie Hansford: 1828-1900.* (Charleston, West Virginia: Quick Copy Press, 1976).

Williams, Charles R. *The Life of Rutherford Birchard Hayes, Nineteenth President of the United States.* (New York, NY: Houghton-Mifflin Company, 1911).

Williams, John A. *West Virginia: A History.* (Morgantown: WVU Press, 2001).

Manuscripts

Atkeson-Morgan Family Papers, A&M 3372, Box 1, Folder 1a, Civil War Letters, West Virginia & Regional History Collection, West Virginia University Library, Morgantown, WV.

Beeman, Elijah. Letters 1861-1862. Marshall University Special Collections, Civil War Manuscripts, Accession No. 1979/03.0250, Marshall University Morrow Library, Huntington, WV.

Buffalo Historical Society. Monograph. *History of Buffalo, Vol. 1: The Beginning to 1900.* (St. Albans, West Virginia: Harless Printing: 1993).

Creighton, Jeroboam "Jerry" B., Corporal, Independent Ohio Artillery Battery. Letter written July 18, 1861, published in *Tiffin Weekly Tribune*, July 26, 1861. Vol. 13(42), 3. Chronicling America Series, Library of Congress.

Civil War Collection, 1859-1911. [artificial]. Ms79-18. Four boxes -misc original and photostatic copies of letters, diaries, journals, muster rolls, discharges, enlistments, passes, currency, bonds, broadsides, clippings, and other assorted material relating to the Civil War. WV State Archives.

Craig Family Papers ca. 1861-1960. *Sc86-201.* Scrapbooks (mostly of Putnam County, West Virginia interest) kept by Lucy and Mary Craig, including clippings, correspondence, photographs, programs, Confederate currency, and miscellaneous. WV State Archives.

Davison, William. Scrapbook 1860-1861. Civil War Manuscripts, MS80-275. Letter by Maj. William Rucker, Putnam Home Guards, to Capt. Julius Lesage, August 22, 1864. WV State Archives.

Fred Conner. "The Part Taken by Putnam Co. WV. During the War 1861-65 by Fred Conner, faithful servant of the 36th Virginia Infantry." Civil War Manuscripts, MS 79-18, No. 6, WV Archives, 1-3; 6-7.

Gorsuch, James A. Gorsuch. Letter from a Private, Co. I, 12th Ohio Volunteer Infantry, *Darke County Democrat* (Ohio), July 24, 1861, Vol. 7(8), 2. Online: Newspapers.com.

Foster, Jack. Letter to former Confederate General John McCausland, December 13, 1883. (Ms2008-018), Virginia Tech Special Collections and University Archives Online, accessed Dec. 25, 2020, http://digitalsc. lib.vt.edu/AmericanCivilWar.

Frazier, Carolyn Hall. Collection. 1851-1967. Folder 26, Ms84-210. Newspaper clippings, postwar photos of Samuel A. Sterrett, Co. A, 36th Virginia Infantry, CSA, and the Sterrett farm which was used as a camping area by troops during the war. WV State Archives.

Frazier Family Collection. 1859. Ms90-96. Original commission for Allen Frazer, Jr. as 1st lieutenant, 181st Militia, 22nd Brigade, 5th Division, dated May 25, 1859. Signed by Henry A. Wise, governor of Virginia and later brigadier general in the Confederate army serving in the Kanawha Valley region in 1861. WV State Archives.

Froe, Sarah Harris Dickerson. Biographical information. Tazewell Library Photographs Collection, Album Part 1, (1999), Call No. V210227, 227. Library of Virginia, Richmond, Virginia.

Harden, James A. Civil War Letters, 1861-1865 [Digital]. Virginia Military Institute Archives. https://archivespace.vmi.edu/repositories/3/digital_objects/150 Accessed December 25, 2020.

Hiltz, John U. Letter by member of Co. C, 12th Ohio Volunteer Infantry, to *Clermont Courier* (Ohio), August 7, 1861, Vol. 123(32), 3. SN 83035427, Library of Congress.

Lutz, Anna. Collection. 1862-1982. Ms2003-141. Folder 3, Transcript of letter by Mary Higginbotham, Paint Lick, Garrison Co., KY, dated June 18, 1862, stating "Lincolnites" killed her son. WV State Archives.

Miller, O.R. "Go Where, this is my Home." Unpublished manuscript, October 1998. Courtesy Sandy Miller Larch.

Morgan, John. *The Last Dollar*. (St. Albans, WV: St. Albans Historical Society, 2002, Originally published 1909).

Putnam County. n.d. Ms2004-141. Historical information, photos and clippings on Putnam County, WV, compiled by Charles Ray Harper. Included is a postwar photo of James Harvey Nuckles, Co. A, 8th Virginia Cavalry, CSA, and accompanying article; an article on Gen. John McCausland. WV State Archives.

Sterrett Family Collection. 1865-1970. Ms81-30. Collection includes miscellaneous material on Samuel Alexander Sterrett, (born Aug. 21, 1841; died May 11, 1937), a veteran of Co. A, 36th Virginia Infantry, CSA. Box 2: typed literary manuscript of Sterrett's Civil War record (1861-1865); Box 3: Receipt book for Lt. Boyd B. Sterrett, Co. A, 36th Virginia Infantry, C.S.A. for 1865, containing a roster of the company and assorted cooking recipes; Memorandum Book (1854-1868) contains September 14, 1862 remarks about retreat of Federal army from Kanawha Valley. WV State Archives.

Pierpont, Francis H. Executive letter book of Governor Francis H. Pierpont, 1861-1864. State Government Records Collection, Accession No. 37226, Mis. Microfilm Reel 6191. Library of Virginia, Richmond, VA; Poffenberger, Livia Simpson. Genealogical and historical papers of Mason County, West Virginia. Ms80-287, Folder 34, Information on Lt. Col. Andrew R. Barbee, 22nd Virginia Infantry, CSA. WV State Archives.

Polsley Family. Papers and Correspondence. 1860-1890. Ms82-274. Five folders of photocopies, primarily Civil War letters and service of Lt. Col. John J. Polsley, 8th (West) Virginia Infantry (later 7th West Virginia Cavalry), and James Polsley, Co. A, 116th Regiment Militia (Mason County). WV State Archives.

Rife, Jacob Marvin. Collection. Ms78-2. Captain Jacob Marvin Rife, (born Nov. 11, 1838 Piketon, OH), served in the 7th West Virginia Cavalry (formerly 8th West Virginia Infantry and 8th West Virginia Mounted Infantry) and 18th Ohio Regiment during the Civil War. WV State Archives.

Sedinger, James D. "Wartime Reminiscences of a Border Ranger: Company E, 8th Virginia Cavalry, April 20, 1861." Typescript. West Virginia Archives Manuscript Collection, MS78-1, Series 1, WV State Archives.

Shirey, Mervin R. *The Battle of Scary Creek: July 17, 1861*. (St. Albans Historical Society, St. Albans, WV: Dawson Printing Company, 1932. Reprinted 2014, Edited by Neil Richardson).

Thomas, Jean. Collection. 1720s-2003. Ms2010-154. Box 1, No. 32: Recollections of Col. John W. Blizzard in the Civil War (36th Virginia Infantry, CSA). WV State Archives.

Thompson, C. L. Manuscript. 1917. Ms80-307. Typescript literary manuscript "The Battle of Scary Creek and Some Incidents of It" describing the July 17, 1861 battle of Scary Creek, Putnam County, WV. WV State Archives.

Virginia Infantry, Logan County Wildcats, Logbook, 1830-1900. Accession No. 1977/11.0206 (MS-59) Marshall University Special Collections (MUSC), Marshall University Library, Huntington, WV.

Young, Sarah Francis "Sallie" Young. Diary, 1861-1862. West Virginia Regional History Collection, Roy Bird Cook Collection, Call No. AM 1651, WVU Library. Morgantown, WV.

Newspapers

Cincinnati Daily Gazette, Microfilm, Hamilton County Ohio Public Library, Cincinnati, Ohio.

Daily Intelligencer, Chronicling America, Library of Congress online: https://chroniclingamerica.loc.gov.

Daily Ohio Statesman, Chronicling America, Library of Congress online: https://chroniclingamerica.loc.gov.

Gallipolis Journal, Chronicling America, Library of Congress online: https://chroniclingamerica.loc.gov.

Grafton Guardian, Chronicling America, Library of Congress online: https://chroniclingamerica.loc.gov.

Huntington-Herald Advertiser, Newspapers on Microfilm, Misc. Reels, WV State Archives.

Ironton Register, June 19, 1861. SN84028882 Newspaper Reading Room, Library of Congress, Washington, DC.

Kanawha Valley Star, SN85059862, Newspaper Reading Room, Library of Congress, Washington DC.

New York Times, online: https://www.nytimes.com/1983.

Pomeroy Weekly Telegraph, Chronicling America Series, Library of Congress online: https://chroniclingamerica.loc.gov.

The Putnam Democrat, Newspapers on Microfilm, Misc. Reels, WV State Archives.

The Weekly Register, Chronicling America, Library of Congress online: https://chroniclingamerica.loc.gov.

Western Reserve Chronicle, Chronicling America, Library of Congress online: https://chroniclingamerica.loc.gov.

Wheeling Daily Intelligencer, SN 84026845, Newspaper Reading Room. Library of Congress.

Wheeling Intelligencer, Chronicling America, Library of Congress online: https://chroniclingamerica.loc.gov.

Periodicals

Civil War History, Vol. 10(4), (December 1964).

Confederate Veteran, (1921, 1923), Vols. 29, 31.

West Virginia History, Vol. 51, 1992., Vol. 24(4), July 1963,

The Upper Vandalia Historic Society Journal, (Charleston, WV: Upper Vandalia Historical Society, October 1996).

Online

https://about.usps.com/who/profile/history/postmaster-finder/postmasters-by-city.htm

Raines, Matthew J. Clio Guide to History, Village of Buffalo, Putnam County, WV. 2017. Online: https://www.theclio.com/tour.

West Virginia Sesquicentennial Online: George W. Summers: http://www.wvculture.org.

Wintz, William D. "Putnam County." Online: e-WV: The West Virginia Encyclopedia. June 2013, May 2020. https://www.wvencyclopedia.org.

Broadsides

Broadsides Collection, 1826-1944, Draft list, 1st subdistrict, Kanawha County, WV, 1863, Call No. Sc82-37 and Sc85-93. WV State Archives.

Civil War Collection, 1859-1911. Ms79-18. WV State Archives.

Stutler, Boyd B. Collection. Ms78-1, WV State Archives.

West Virginia Adjutant General Papers, Union Regiments 1861-1865, AR 383; Box 36, Broadsides and Oversized Items, No. 3. House Bill No. 5, June 1861, WV State Archives.

Maps

1850 Survey of the lower Kanawha River by C&O Railroad. 1850. Copy of original held at C&O Museum, Clifton Forge, VA. Call No. Ma3-10. WV State Archives.

1850 Map of Survey: Lower Kanawha River, showing Winfield and Red House Shoals and Winfield Road. (Chesapeake and Ohio Railway, 1850, Clifton Forge, Virginia.) WV State Archives.

Plot map of Buffalo and J. Craig lands adjoining the same. January 6, 1851. Call No. Ma29-1. WV State Archives.

Winfield plot map, 1862. Putnam County Deed Book, Vol. 1, 1848-1863, Transcribed 1921, p. 10. Putnam County Court House Archives.

Government Publications

Acts of the General Assembly of the State of Virginia passed in 1861. No. 3. Joint Resolutions inviting the other States to send Commissioners to meet Commissioners on the part of Virginia and providing for the appointment of the same. Adopted January 19, 1861. (Richmond, VA: William F. Ritchie, public printer, 1861).

Acts of the General Assembly of the State of Virginia passed in 1861. No. 1. Resolutions upon the subject of the Coercion of a State. Adopted January 8, 1861. (Richmond, VA: William F. Ritchie, public printer, 1861).

Ambler, Charles H; Atwood, Frances H; Matthews, William B. (Eds.). "A State of Convenience: The Creation of West Virginia, Chapter 13, Congressional Debate on the Admission of West Virginia, The Willey Amendment." Congressional Globe, Debates & Proceedings 1833-1873, Vol. 37, December 9-13, 1862. Online: http://memory.loc.gov/ammem/amlaw/lwcglink.html.

An Ordinance of the Convention Assembled at Wheeling, June 11, 1861. Cited in Records of Colonial Militia through World War 1. Ca. 1936. MS80-22, WV State Archives.

Biographical Directory of the United States Congress 1774-1903, House Doc. 108-142, (Washington, DC: U.S. Government Printing Office, 1903).

Cabell County West Virginia Deed Books, Vol. 4, 178-181. Cabell County Court House Records Depository, Huntington, WV.

Compiled Service Records, Record Group 95, Microfilm records of Union and Confederate regiments 1861-1865. US National Archives, Washington, DC.

Confederate Military Records, 1859-1865, Accession No. 27684, Series II, Infantry Regiments: 22nd Virginia Infantry, Boxes 52, 53, 59 & 62; 36th Virginia Infantry, Box 25; Series I, Cavalry Regiments: 8th Virginia Cavalry, Box 15; 16th Virginia Cavalry, Boxes 55-64, Library of Virginia.

Debates and Proceedings of the First Constitutional Convention of West Virginia, 1861-1863. (Huntington, WV: Gentry Brothers Printers, 1939).

Hoge, James W. House, National Register of Historic Places, West Virginia Landmarks, January 21, 2007. Record Group 79, West Virginia Landmarks, ID No. 86536037. National Archives, Washington D.C. National Park Service, National Register of Historic Places Collection, Lakewood, CO.

John Letcher, Governor, Executive Papers. Accession No. 36787, Box 30, Folder 1, Correspondence April 1861. Library of Virginia.

Naret, Benoite Henriette Last Will & Testament, August 20, 1862. Gallia County Ohio Probate Court, courtesy Gallia County Genealogical Society. www.familysearch.org/catalog.

Naret, Edward Dr. House, National Register of Historic Places Registration Form, dated June 26, 1991, "Buffalo Townsquare Historic District," Section 8, page 2. Library of Congress.

Official Roster of the State of Ohio in the War of the Rebellion 1861-1866, Vol. 1. (Akron, OH: Published by the State of Ohio. Akron OH: The Werner Company, 1893).

Rowe, Alan R. and Jim Hines. (Nov. 19, 1999) . United States Department of the Interior, National Register of Historic Places Registration Form 10-900 for Putnam County Court House, May 31, 2000, ID No. B3fea499-74ca-45c3-8fb7-f49921f279c5. National Park Service, National Register of Historic Places Collection, Lakewood, CO.

Third United States Census: 1810, National Archives Microfilm Publication M252, Mason & Kanawha County, Virginia schedules, Records of the Bureau of the Census, Record Group 29; Roll 69, National Archives, Washington, D.C.

Fourth United States Census: 1820, National Archives Microfilm Publication M33, Mason & Kanawha County, Virginia schedules, Records of the Bureau of the Census, Record Group 29; Record Group 19, Rolls 130, 142, National Archives, Washington, D.C.

Fifth United States Census: 1830, National Archives Microfilm Publication M432, Mason & Kanawha County, Virginia schedules, Records of the Bureau of the Census, Record Group19; Rolls 190, 191, National Archives, Washington, D.C.

Sixth United States Census: 1840, National Archives Microfilm Publication M432, Mason & Kanawha Counties, Virginia schedules, Records of the Bureau of the Census, Record Group 29; Rolls 566 & 568, National Archives, Washington, D.C.

Seventh United States Census: 1850; National Archives Microfilm Publication M432, Putnam County, Virginia schedules, Records of the Bureau of the Census, Record Group 29; Rolls 199A & 0992, National Archives, Washington, D.C.

Eighth United States Census: 1860; National Archives Microfilm Publications M592 & M653, Putnam County, Virginia schedules, Records of the Bureau of the Census, Record Group 29, Roll 1373, National Archives, Washington, D.C.

Ninth United States Census: 1870; National Archives Microfilm Publication M593 Putnam County, West Virginia schedules, Records of the Bureau of the Census, Record Group 29, Roll 1698, National Archives, Washington, D.C.

Sixteenth United States Census: 1940; National Archives Microfilm Publication T627, Putnam County, West Virginia schedules, Records of the Bureau of the Census, Record Group 29, Roll 4440, National Archives, Washington, D.C.

United States War Department. The War of the Rebellion: A Compilation of the Official Records of the Union and Confederate Armies. Washington, DC: [s.n.], 1894.

Weiss, C.M.; Weiss, V.W.; Collins, R.L. Revised Phase – 1 Archeological Survey of the Proposed Hurricane Bridge Park, Putnam County, WV. (December 2017). Manuscript prepared for City of Hurricane. Fairmont, WV: Allstar Ecology, LLC.

West Virginia Adjutant General Papers, Union Militia 1861-1865, AR373, 181st Regiment Virginia Militia; Union Regiments 1861-1865, AR 383; Box 36, WV State Archives.

West Virginia Marriages 1853-1970 and Death Records: www. pilot.familysearch.org; Family record of marriage contract drawn up between Edouard Naret and Benoite Henriette Pitrat was dated March 25, 1843. WV State Archives.

Whiting, William. Pension application. US Pension Files, 1861-1934, Box 33900, Microfilm T288, Roll 514, Application for Pension No. 95.545, Washington, DC: National Archives.

Wood, Andrew J. Biographies of West Virginia Statehood Leaders. 2010. Marshall University Graduate College Humanities Program, unpublished manuscript, South Charleston, West Virginia. http://www.wvculture.org/history/sesquicentennial/rossandrew.pdf.

Young, John Valley. Pension File. U.S. Department of the Interior Veteran's Pensions Claims Office. Union Soldier Pension Files, MT288 Roll 542, US National Archives.

Name Index

About the Author

Philip Hatfield, Ph.D., is a member of the Company of Military Historians, and holds a doctorate in psychology from Fielding University; a master's degree in psychology from Marshall University; and a bachelor's degree in psychology and history from the University of Charleston. Dr. Hatfield is a veteran of the U.S. Air Force and served during Operation Iraqi Freedom. He is the author of seven books and numerous scholarly articles related to the Civil War.

Other Books by Philip Hatfield, Ph.D.

Sacrifice All For the Union: The Civil War Experiences of Captain John Valley Young and his Family

The Battle of Hurricane Bridge, March 28, 1863

The Other Feud: William Anderson 'Devil Anse' Hatfield in the Civil War

The Rowan Rifle Guards: A History of Company K, 4th North Carolina State Troops 1857-1865

Treason on the Cape Fear: Roots of the Civil War in North Carolina

When Paper Collar, Bandbox Soldiers Fight: A History of the 4th West Virginia Volunteer Infantry
(Co-authored with Terry Lowry)

35th Star Publishing
Charleston, West Virginia
www.35thstar.com